INTERNET
GUIDE
TO BIRDS
AND BIRDING

INTERNET GUIDE TO BIRDS AND BIRDING

THE ULTIMATE DIRECTORY TO THE BEST SITES ONLINE

Jack Sanders

RAGGED MOUNTAIN PRESS / McGRAW-HILL

Camden, Maine • New York • San Francisco • Washington, D.C. • Auckland •
Bogotá • Caracas • Lisbon • London • Madrid • Mexico City • Milan • Montreal •
New Delhi • San Juan • Singapore • Sydney • Tokyo • Toronto

Ragged Mountain Press

A Division of The McGraw-Hill Companies

10 9 8 7 6 5 4 3 2 1

Copyright © 2000 Ragged Mountain Press

All rights reserved. The publisher takes no responsibility for the use of any of the materials or methods described in this book, nor for the products thereof. The name "Ragged Mountain Press" and the Ragged Mountain Press logo are trademarks of The McGraw-Hill Companies. Printed in the United States of America.

Library of Congress Cataloging-in-Publication Data

Sanders, Jack. 1944–

   Internet guide to birds and birding : the ultimate directory to the best sites online / Jack Sanders.

     p.   cm.

   ISBN 0-07-135324-0 (alk. paper)

     1. Bird watching—Computer network resources—Directories.

      2. Birds—Computer network resources—Directories.

      3. Internet addresses—Directories. I. Title.

QL677.5.S26 1999

025.06'598'07234—dc21   99-046836

Questions regarding the content of this book
should be addressed to
Ragged Mountain Press
P.O. Box 220
Camden, ME 04843
http://www.raggedmountainpress.com

Questions regarding the ordering of this book
should be addressed to
The McGraw-Hill Companies
Customer Service Department
P.O. Box 547
Blacklick, OH 43004
Retail customers: 1-800-262-4729
Bookstores: 1-800-722-4726

This book is printed on 40# Brightset Yellow

Printed by Quebecor Printing Co., Dubuque, IA
Design by Shannon Thomas
Project management by Janet Robbins
Page layout by Janet Robbins and Shannon Thomas
Edited by Tom McCarthy, Robert Lawson

John James Audubon (JJA) illustrations © 1999 www.arttoday.com
Dover illustrations © 1996 by Dover Publications, Inc.
All other illustrations © 1999 www.arttoday.com

Contents

VI CONTENTS

CONTENTS VII

VIII CONTENTS

CONTENTS XI

Acknowledgments

Many people helped with this book, including hundreds of Webmasters who confirmed information and contributed ideas. I especially thank the website operators who allowed me to interview them for the Meet the Masters sidebars. Thanks, too, to Tom McCarthy at Ragged Mountain Press, who offered much encouragement, and to Rob Lawson, who went over the manuscript with great care, skill, and understanding. Most of all, I thank my dear wife, Sally, who not only provided wonderful support during the months of manuscript preparation but also contributed many entries, particularly in the chapters on backyard birds, raptors, and sea birds.

Introduction

I have a friend who teases me about my wandering the Web in search of virtual birds when I could be outdoors wandering the woods in search of live ones. I tell him that there are times when it's more useful and enjoyable to be birding the Web than birding the woods. Like at night, for instance.

"Phooey," he replied. "There are plenty of owls to see at night."

The fact is, to really enjoy an avocation—especially bird-watching—you need information. You'll be a better birder if you know where to go and when to go there; if you know what to look for and how to look for it; and if you can identify what you've seen and how to record it.

Books can provide much of this knowledge, but few people could afford the library it would take to supply all the information you can uncover on the *World Wide Web*, the modern electronic library that grows by tens of thousands of pages a day. And few would have the connections for personal birding advice and the direct answers you can find on the electronic forums and e-mail groups that the Internet offers.

Whether the sources are the loftiest institutions of higher learning or the guy down the road who likes robins a lot, birding websites abound. Many people and institutions have amassed extensive collections of words, pictures, and sounds for you to enjoy and learn from. It's just a matter of finding what you're looking for.

And that's why this book was written. As anyone who has surfed the Web quickly learns, there is a lot of chaff mixed with the wheat. Birders in search of information can often waste time, employing search engines or just wandering websites, trying to find exactly what they are looking for. Worse, the process can be frustrating, so much so that many people simply throw up their hands and shut off the computer.

This book helps you find what you're looking for, quickly and easily. What's more, we introduce you to many sites new to you, with useful information to help you enjoy and appreciate birds and birding. We've researched thousands of websites in search of ones that can give you useful information, and we've organized the book so that you can efficiently select the likeliest sites.

WHAT'S HERE

A large portion of *Internet Guide to Birds and Birding* is devoted to the birds themselves, arranged in categories somewhat similar to many birding books. By far the largest species heading is devoted to backyard birds, for these are the ones we frequently see, and these are the ones that draw and inspire most of our interest and questions. Whereas quite a few of the birds in this category may not be found in the average backyard, most are possible sightings, even if rarely. The other categories are devoted to various species: raptors, such as owls and hawks, that may show up in the yard but are more likely seen in our travels; sea birds (some of whom live a thousand miles from the sea); wading birds; the swimming birds like ducks and geese; fowl-like birds; and exotics and introduced species that have adapted themselves to North America. Another category covers birds no longer here—the extinct species that, usually because of us, have disappeared.

Of the more than 900 species of birds found in North America, this book has entries for nearly 250 of the more common or especially interesting species. Although many birds are not specifically listed, sites are described where you can find information about almost any bird that sets foot on this continent. Incidentally, the Audubon Societies & Sanctuaries, Checklists, Destinations, Events, and Tours & Expeditions sections are arranged by geographical region (central, eastern, mountain, and Pacific U.S., plus international). The aim is to help you locate topics by your region of interest.

Some websites deal with habitats of birds. In the Gardening & Landscaping section, for instance, you can learn about the Backyard Wildlife Habitat Program, David Jordan Bird Habitat, Planting for Habitat, Plants that Enhance Wild Bird Habitat, Songbird Habitats in the Southeast, and Wildlife Habitat. The sites described will help you select the best plants and features for turning your yard into a bird-filled wildlife habitat.

Websites are listed that address the subject of *migration*, a phenomenon that is both mysterious and marvelous, but can sometimes be troubling. Many North American birds are *seasonal*, meaning they live in different parts of the continent—or the world—at different times of the year. Their habitual movements to and from wintering and nesting grounds have fascinated birders and ornithologists since the phenomenon was first discovered. However, environmental changes are altering migration patterns and bird populations.

Migration, as perhaps nothing else in nature, is closely linked to environments and ecosystems. Changes not just to winter and summer grounds, but to myriad stopping points along the migratory *flyways* (established airways of migratory birds) are endangering some species. Sometimes environmental changes can even lead to dangerous overpopulations of species. This book offers you not only sources to help understand these fragile relationships but also ways to help ensure that the territories used by migrating birds for nesting, wintering, and refueling are protected.

Internet Guide to Birds and Birding also tells you where you might see particular birds. One section, Destinations, lists websites describing some of the better parks and refuges in North America, as well as many of the lesser-known birding hot spots. The Tours & Expeditions section leads to descriptions of journeys to nearby and distant birding locales, accompanied by expert guides familiar with the natural history of the district.

One section, Audubon Societies & Sanctuaries, is devoted to Audubon groups, some of the best people to know on the Web when it comes to birding. Many of the websites of Audubon societies offer visual and written guides to local birding hot spots and announcements of birding expeditions, both to local and to distant places.

Of course, the most popular place to see birds is in one's own backyard. How many birds you see, however, may depend on how much effort you put into attracting them. Feeding & Watering describes sites covering different kinds of feeders and foods. Information about houses for birds can be found in Houses & Nest Boxes.

People who become interested in any avocation often want to learn more by joining organizations that cultivate that interest. For birders, Audubon societies are among the most common and popular. But the book also lists birding-related websites of societies, associations, and clubs that aren't called Audubon. Many are for sharing information and appreciation of birds specifically or wildlife generally. And many are devoted to the conservation of birds, be they all species or certain groups of species.

Hobbyists also like to read about their interests. We've included a section covering websites of print magazines and periodicals devoted to birds or birding (Magazines & Periodicals). Most of these sites provide some online samples of articles and some have useful "extra" items that supplement the print editions. This guide also includes websites that describe books that would interest birders (Books). After all, books continue to outshine computers in many ways—it's still easier to flip through the pages of a field guide than the files of a computer when you're in the woods.

The more seriously we become involved in birding, the more scientific our interests may become. *Internet Guide to Birds and Birding* includes an Ornithology section, which describes websites that are operated by professional ornithologists. Some are highly specialized and technical sites, whereas others are aimed at both rank beginners and "serious amateurs." One of the finest examples of citizens and scientists working together is Cornell's Laboratory of Ornithology website. Here, you can become more than just a bird-watcher; you can contribute information on what you've been watching to the scientific community who can use the data to track migration, bird populations, nesting habits and habitats, and species ranges. You can do this by simply reporting the birds that come to your feeder or by joining special events, such as the Christmas Bird Counts and the Great Backyard Bird Counts in February. You can report your sightings via online forms, and thanks to the speed of computers, Cornell scientists can begin using your contributions almost immediately.

We're all interested to some degree in computers— otherwise, you wouldn't be reading this introduction, and I wouldn't have written it. Aside from access to bird-related sites on the World Wide Web, various software can assist the bird-watcher tremendously—see the Software section. Nearly a dozen currently available programs can help you identify the birds you're seeing. A dozen more can help you keep records of your birding—the who, what, where, when, how, and maybe even why of each sighting. In some cases, birding software—especially the databases—can be downloaded to your computer and used immediately. A few are free (*freeware*); some are *shareware* (*see page 40*), and many others you'll have to pay for before using. The Software section also covers some of the "new media" like compact disks, and the Videos section has information about birding-related videos.

Birds appeal both to adults and children. In fact, youngsters can be among the most avid bird-watchers. Many organizations on the Web, recognizing this, offer sites or portions of their sites devoted to youngsters. Children are, after all, the future birders and potential members of their groups. We've included a Children's section on sites that should be of interest to young birders.

Both children and adults love being able to see birds close-up. *Internet Guide to Birds and Birding* provides several ways of doing that. A section on Photography lists sites that have collections of bird pictures. Some of these sites may be libraries from educational or scientific institutions whereas others may be sponsored by the photographers themselves. A lot of talented wildlife photographers have found the Web to be a gallery without the limitations of doors or business hours, an excellent way for them to exhibit their work to the whole world. Another section on avian art, Artful Birds, covers the work of artists from the past three centuries, as well as some unusual forms of bird art—such as stamps and banknotes.

Speaking of art, many of the illustrations in this book, credited "JJA," are from John James Audubon's *Birds of America*, a series of 435 prints published in England between 1826 and 1838 (we've added modern terminology in brackets to help you identify the birds). Audubon is considered the first artist or scientist to show life-sized birds in their natural surroundings. He was not only an artist but also a natural history writer, and his *Ornithological Biography*, written in the 1830s, contains many delightful descriptions of the natural history of North American birds. You can learn more about Audubon's art, writing, and life at several sites in the Artful Birds section.

Another way to see birds close-up is at zoos and aviaries, places where birds—mostly waterfowl—are raised. The Aviaries section of the book lists some of the larger zoos and also has zoo directories so you can find out if any are in your neighborhood or in the area you're traveling to. Many North American zoos participate in programs to rescue rare bird species from extinction; sites in this section tell you which zoo is assisting which birds. Besides listings for some true aviaries, there are listings for raptor centers, where you can see hawks, eagles, and owls close-up. Many of these birds are undergoing rehabilitation from accidents. Some have been nursed back to health but cannot be returned to the wild.

Birds can have problems or *be* problems. Diseases strike birds, and birds strike windows. Both are deadly to countless birds each year. But the major "unnatural" killers of birds today are domestic cats, be they pets or feral. Estimates of the number of birds killed each year by cats range from eight figures to nine figures. One midwestern state estimates that cats kill upward of 40 million birds a year within its borders alone.

Problem birds include the ones that can be pests because of their numbers or because of where they are making themselves at home. Pigeons and starlings are high on many people's lists of the most "hated" birds. The Quandaries section covers both kinds of problems, including the care of sick, injured, or baby birds by rehabilitators.

Birding doesn't require a lot of equipment. Aside from a field guide, the average birder gets by very nicely with a pair of binoculars. The Optics section covers this important aspect of birding. Selecting the right binoculars to do the job can be important. Both manufacturers and independent parties have designed websites to help you pick the right pair—at the right price. As you become more advanced—or fanatic—you may want to invest in a field scope, many of which are described online. But potential equipment purchases don't end with optics; some birders enhance their hobby with the use of special equipment bags and even boats. These, too, are mentioned, in the Gear section.

TALKING TO OTHER BIRDERS

The Internet's very name suggests interconnectivity, the fact that communication flows more than one way. In fact, the Internet started out as a place where speedy communication via the written word was possible. Like the telegram of old, words could be sent almost instantly across vast distances. The need for communication can be especially important for birders. Some sites, such as Cornell's Laboratory of Ornithology, enable bird-watchers to exchange information with scientists. Others, such as About.com, permit you to discuss birding with other birders.

One of the Internet's most popular ways of exchanging information is via Usenet newsgroups. More than 15,000 newsgroups allow people of similar interests to post messages in bulletin-board style. Your posted messages can be read by anyone visiting that group. For bird-watchers, that newsgroup is *rec.birds*, in which "rec" means the site is "recreational" in nature. Here you can ask questions, offer opinions, get migration reports, read news announcements (often including reports of new World Wide Web sites), and find advice on just about any bird-related topic. Two other Usenet newsgroups are great places to learn the ins and outs of national parks, which are great places to go birding. *Rec.outdoors.national-parks* is the more popular, and a good place to find tips on worthwhile locations for bird-watching in parks. The *gov.us.topic.nat-resources.parks* group is more official; the National Park Service posts announcements on this list. Whichever way you access newsgroups, you can choose to respond to any posted message either directly to the writer (so no one else sees it) or to the whole group (so everyone can read it).

Most *Internet Service Providers* (ISPs) include access to the Usenet; if you do not know how to set up your computer to read Usenet messages, ask your provider. Or, you can make use of Deja.com, which is a World Wide Web site that allows anyone easy access to most of world's newsgroups (*see page 153*).

Another way of communicating is via a mailing list, sometimes called a *listserve*. With lists, messages arrive at your computer as ordinary e-mail. Messages you post to the list are sent to every member. Most lists are set up to send you messages separately, which can quickly "clog" your system with hundreds of e-mail messages. Some lists, however, allow the option of receiving the day's messages strung together as a digest of one long e-mail.

You can join lists by sending a message to the listserve computer saying you want to subscribe. You'll usually get back a message welcoming you to the list, describing the mailing list rules, and explaining how to unsubscribe if you want to stop receiving list mail. Always save this message for future reference.

Still another way to communicate online is through websites that have built-in message boards. The topics are generally limited to the website's specialty, but these forums can provide useful information—and a place to get an answer.

THE DREADED "NO CONNECTION" ERROR

Few things work perfectly, as anyone who's used a computer for a while quickly learns. You're reading through this book, and you come across a website that seems to be just what you're looking for. You type in the address, and a few moments later an error message appears: "A connection with the server could not be established."

Bummer!

Well, not necessarily. Although the World Wide Web is a constantly changing phenomenon and many websites vanish each day, the connection error does not necessarily mean that the site you're seeking has disappeared. Several possible explanations may account for the error message, and you may still be able to find the site you're looking for.

Possibility 1: You goofed. This sounds obvious, but you'd be surprised how often it happens to all of us: make sure you typed in the address *exactly* as it appears in the book. The difference between having an uppercase and a lowercase letter can cause many sites to reject an address. We've double-checked all our addresses, which were literally copied and pasted electronically from browser to manuscript, and they should all be just what the server wants.

Possibility 2: It's a mystery. Although it may seem odd (that's because it *is* odd), you can get that error message and then five seconds later *not* get it. Perhaps a computer somewhere along the Internet pipeline was temporarily overloaded and couldn't handle your request. Simply try the address again and maybe even a third time. Often, I've been surprised to see a connection made after the browser has just told me it couldn't connect.

Possibility 3: The website's server is down. There might be a malfunction, the server owner may be doing maintenance or the Webmaster may be working on the site. Try again in an hour, a day, or—alas—even a week.

Possibility 4: Your Internet access provider may be having troubles. However, when this happens, usually *all* addresses don't work or connect very slowly.

Possibility 5: The Net is really busy, and your request just can't get through to the site you're seeking. Try again later.

Possibility 6: The address has changed. This is all too common, especially if the address is a complex one. After all, if you were the Webmaster of a site with a home page of <*http://www.bloppo-online.com/~jdistelfink/bigyellowbird/index.html*>, wouldn't you rather be <*http://www.bigyellowbird.com*>? Many people are switching to custom domain names or to a new website host service. Often they leave behind a page with the new address, but that doesn't always happen, especially if they also changed service providers. In creating their new address, Webmasters will often use something from the past address. For instance, in the preceding address, you could try entering either WWW.JDISTELFINK.COM or WWW. BIGYELLOWBIRD.COM. (Actually, with modern browsers, you could enter just JDISTELFINK or BIGYELLOWBIRD and the browser will search the possible .com, .org, .net, etc. addresses for you.) On many occasions I have found new addresses using this technique. Another possibility is trying the site name. For instance, if you know that the site belonged to a business called Birding Heaven, you could try typing in the address HTTP:// WWW.BIRDINGHEAVEN.COM. I've found sites doing that, too. More techniques for dealing with address changes are described in the next section on Finding Sites.

Possibility 7: The page that you're looking for is still on the site but has moved to a different address. How do you find it? Keep moving backward. Suppose you're looking for a picture of a cardinal that was at the address *<http://www.birdfeather.com/backyard/pictures/cardinal.htm>*, and the address comes back as an error. Delete the CARDINAL.HTM and see what happens. If that doesn't bring up a useful page, try deleting PICTURES/. Then BACKYARD/. Often, you'll reach a part of the site that's working, and from there, use the site's menus to find your way to that cardinal picture (which may now be at *<http://www.birdfeather.com/pictures/redbirds/cardinal.htm>*).

Possibility 8: The website has a totally new address that you can't locate using the preceding techniques. Why not try a good old search engine? Plug in the site name, such as Birding Heaven. You may find the site itself, or you may find a page on another site with a link to Birding Heaven (the link may be the old, incorrect one, but it might also be the new correct address).

FINDING SITES: READ THIS, IF NOTHING ELSE

Yes, the Web is very changeable. That's one of its beauties: pages and sites are constantly being added or updated. But change can also be a problem, and one of the unfortunate characteristics of the Web is that tendency described previously of websites moving around or changing addresses.

We have made considerable effort to have up-to-date addresses in this book and have e-mailed hundreds of Webmasters asking about their sites and their plans. However, due to the dynamic nature of the Web, address changes will always occur.

As noted earlier, a good Webmaster who is changing a home page location will leave a "forwarding address" at the old site, at least for a few months. This may be a page that has the new address in a link form—you just click on it and move seamlessly to the new location. Some Webmasters create automatic pages that appear long enough for you to read the message with the new address before sending your browser on its way to the new site.

But what if the forwarding message has expired and you get nothing but an error message saying the page you are requesting is unknown? One of the powerful features of the World Wide Web is its collection of *search engines*, websites that specialize in snooping around the Web and cataloging the pages they find. It's very likely that if the site you're looking for is still alive, one of the major search engines can find it for you.

To search, use at least two words in order to narrow down the possibilities, but three or four words are better. For instance, if you're looking for the Cool Bird Store, and you type in BIRD STORE, you'll probably wind up with hundreds of pages to wade through. But if you type COOL BIRD STORE, odds are you'll get many fewer pages, and most or all of them will refer to the site you're seeking. Even if none of the pages goes directly to the Cool Bird Store, you may find someone else's page with a link to the store. Some of these links may be old ones—with the same dead end—but others may be to the new location.

In doing the preceding search, it's important that you use whatever technique the search engine employs to do exact-phrase searches. If you searched simply for COOL BIRD STORE, every page with the words COOL, or BIRD, or STORE in it could be listed. Needless to say, we're talking hundreds of thousands of potential pages. Alta Vista's search engine, *<http://www.altavista.com>*, enables you to limit searches by surrounding the phrase you're looking for with quotation marks. Thus, a search for "COOL BIRD STORE" will locate only pages that contain those words, one after another. On most search engines, an "advanced" search feature will enable you to do this by selecting an "exact-phrase" option.

Another similar technique, but with a different wrinkle, enables you to search for pages that have all those words in them. On many search engines, putting a + sign in front of the search term means that term *must* be in the page. Thus, you could search for +cool +bird +store. Note, though, that these words don't have to be clustered together, so the chances of getting pages that aren't about the Cool Bird Store increase. (This is a handy technique when you're looking for information rather than a specific thing. For instance, if you wanted to know what kind of food to feed a cardinal, you could search for +northern +cardinal +feed.)

Sometimes employing your powers of deduction can produce the new address of an old site. For instance, in researching hawks, I ran across a link for Hawkwatch International with the address <http://www.upp.com/hawkwatch>. When I clicked it, I got the dreaded message "File Not Found: The requested URL /hawkwatch was not found on this server." Well, I knew that Hawkwatch International was no fly-by-night organization, as it were, so I thought, "bet they got rid of that long-winded address and became hawkwatch.something." The .com ending is used for commercial enterprises, which Hawkwatch isn't. Nonprofit organizations usually use .org. So I tried <http://www.hawkwatch.org>, and voilà! There it was, a picture of a hawk flying across the screen, welcoming me to Hawkwatch International's website.

In fact, I didn't need to don a Sherlock Holmes hat for that one. If I had just typed HAWKWATCH in the browser's address field, it would have found <http://www.hawkwatch.org> for me.

RIGHT ADDRESS

One final and important note about the web addresses listed here: they are exactly as they should be typed into the address field in your browser. Many people mistakenly believe that all web addresses begin with WWW. Most do. However, some don't. If we have listed an address as <http://gone.birding.com>, that's the correct address. Don't put the WWW in front, or it may not compute.

Here and in many publications, you'll see HTTP:// in front of Web addresses (*HTTP* stands for hypertext transfer protocol, the Internet system used for Web page communication). Most browsers today do not require HTTP:// in front of an address; the browsers will figure that out for you. However, we've included the HTTP:// prefix for clarity and for those readers who are firing up older systems to surf the Web.

Help!

No compilation of this kind is perfect. We probably missed some great websites out there, or new ones have shown up since the book went into production. We would appreciate your recommendations of sites you have found particularly good and useful, and think should be included here. We'd also like to hear about address changes, site closings, or major site improvements. Please e-mail them to *jacksanders@ridgefield-ct.com* or, if you like doing things the old-fashioned way, snail-mail to me at P.O. Box 502, Ridgefield, CT 06877.

Information you forward to us will be considered for future editions of this book and may be posted online on the book's updates webpage, <*http://www.acorn-online.com/hedge/birdup.htm*>. We've established this page to keep readers of *Internet Guide to Birds and Birding* abreast of the latest webpage and site address changes—and to announce new sites. Please stop by frequently to check for changes—and please feel free to contribute your reports and suggestions.

ARTFUL BIRDS

Since prehistoric man and his paintings of birds on cave walls, wild birds have been the subject of countless artists. The subject isn't easy: capturing a bird in flight or reproducing its sometimes complex colorings can challenge any artist. But it's a challenge many have successfully attempted. When one mentions birds and art, the name of John J. Audubon invariably comes to mind. Not surprisingly, the World Wide Web is rich in Audubon sources, including many pages reproducing his artwork. Also available are the majestic paintings of Mark Catesby, an English naturalist-painter who was researching and painting North American birds before Audubon. The Web offers the works of dozens of past and modern-day wildlife artists who specialize in birds. But bird art is more than paintings and drawings. Bird images grace countless postage stamps and bank notes. In fact, many birders are also *philatelists* or *numismatists*, and it's not surprising that they would develop specialty collections on birds. The Internet can help here, too. Also, a whole section, beginning on page 254, covers photographs and photography of birds, artistic and otherwise. (A note of warning: Although the images of modern paintings can be downloaded to your computer and even printed out, remember that they are almost certainly copyrighted. It is illegal to distribute or use them on a website without the owner's permission.)

FEATHERED FACTS

Underground Operator

The Burrowing Owl of the western North American plains is among the few birds on this continent that likes to live underground. It uses holes dug by mammals.

—adapted from Canadian Museum of Nature

http://www.nature.ca/notebooks/english/burrowl.htm

Cruck-will's-widow (*Antrostomus carolineses*) (JJA)

Audubon & the Art of Natural History

Kenyon Oppenheimer, a gallery in Chicago, specializes in original prints of the works of John J. Audubon and has many online to view. However, the gallery also has prints of New World birds and wildlife by other 18th- and 19th-century artists, including Mark Catesby (*see later in this section*), Alexander Wilson, and Daniel Elliot. The site also shows the work of 18th- and 19th-century artists of British birds, as well as French and German print artists.

http://www.audubonart.com

Audubon Stamps from Haiti

Douglas Cook Inc. in Las Vegas, Nevada, sells a set of 75 stamps, issued by the Republic of Haiti, honoring John J. Audubon. The stamps bear different Audubon prints and are shown on the site.

http://dci.tierranet.com/audubon.html

Audubon Watercolors of North American Birds

If you are interested in viewing only the art of John James Audubon, Nature.net has more than 50 of his bird paintings online, arranged either by common name or scientific name.

http://www.nature.net/birds/

A
B
C
D
E
F
G
H
I
J
K
L
M
N
O
P
Q
R
S
T
U
V
W
X
Y
Z

A
B
C
D
E
F
G
H
I
J
K
L
M
N
O
P
Q
R
S
T
U
V
W
X
Y
Z

Audubon's Birds of America

The Historical Museum of Southern Florida has complete sets of the first and second editions of *Birds of America* by John James Audubon (*first address*). A changing selection of prints from the *Elephant folio* (the first edition) is occasionally supplemented with prints from the Octavo edition (the second edition) in the museum's exhibition galleries, samplings of which are on the museum's website. Each is accompanied by notes, often including quotes from Audubon about the painting. Audubon was a member of the Academy of Natural Sciences in Philadelphia, joining in 1831. When he began publishing his work, the academy became a subscriber, helping support the cost. The academy is in the process of putting all 435 Audubon plates on the web as high-quality scans. No commentary or text has been included. You can see the Audubon plates by stopping by the academy's site (*second address*).

http://www.historical-museum.org/collect/audubon/
   audubon.htm

http://www.acnatsci.org/library/audubon/index.html

Audubon's Multimedia Birds of America

In 1995, Richard R. Buonanno decided the Web needed a copy of *John James Audubon's Birds of America*, and thanks to him we can view this landmark of North American natural history and art on the Web. Using material from an old, out-of-print CD, Buonanno has placed the full text, the color plates, figures, and, in many cases, bird calls on this easy-to-navigate site.

http://employeeweb.myxa.com/rrb/Audubon/

Avian Art by Chip Davenport

Chip Davenport's sometimes stylized but always accurate look at birds and nature is full of color, life, and beauty. "These images are the expression of my deep love for birds and wildlife," says Davenport. "The art is what it is, marks on paper to convey a message. In creating, I try to let nature speak *to* me rather than let it speak *for* me." Davenport, who lives in Massachusetts, shares many examples of his paintings, drawings, sketches, and published work at this site that also includes photographs of birds taken by both him and his wife, Heidi "Dee" Davenport. On the home page, look for the link to Avian Art by Chip_tg and enjoy.

http://home.sprynet.com/sprynet/chip_tg/

Avian Artisan

Anyone who has seen the *Peterson Field Guide to Hawks* has viewed the art of Brian K. Wheeler, who calls himself an "avian artisan" and whose website offers views of his work. Wheeler lives in Colorado and is both an accomplished artist and an expert photographer. He has illustrated many books and is at work on still more. You can learn about publications that carry his illustrations and sample his art and his photographs, particularly of North American raptors, at this site.

http://www.virtualbirder.com/bkwheeler/

Birds & Feathers

Birds may be the subject of much art, but they can also be literally a part of it. Native Americans have long used the feathers of birds in many of their creations, and the Birds & Feathers section of the Native Tech Native American Technology and Art website describes how this can be done. Feathers have been used in almost limitless ways, says Tara Prindle, the author of this excellently illustrated and comprehensive site. She explains how blue jay, cardinal, hawk, eagle, turkey, and other brightly colored feathers figured in jewelry, headdresses, mantles, capes, and even medicines. She gives instructions for wrapping feathers in four different styles. The site also provides a guide to feather identification—offering a little quiz for those who like a challenge. Two important site features are a summary of the laws on the taking of wild birds and links to other websites that deal with Native American uses of feathers and birds. (The Birds & Feathers section is but one part of the Native Tech site. If you are at all interested in Native American arts and crafts, explore the many other sections and even participate in the online chat service.)

http://www.nativeweb.org/NativeTech/feather/
   index.html

Birds of Nova Scotia

Most bird-watchers know Roger Tory Peterson as the artist and author of the famous Peterson bird guides. But Peterson and John A. Crosby also illustrated Robie Tufts's classic, *The Birds of Nova Scotia*. Forty full-color plates from this book are available online, thanks to the Nova Scotia Museum of Natural History. These wonderful paintings can be downloaded for free personal use and, if you are a teacher, you can use them in the classroom free of charge.

http://museum.ednet.ns.ca/mnh/nature/nsbirds/
plates.htm

Birds of the Blue Ridge by Donna Thomas

Watercolorist Donna Thomas offers individual illustrations for more than two dozen bird profiles on the site, Winging It—The Birds of the Blue Ridge. Also available are some larger paintings of grouped birds.

http://rtonline1.roanoke.com/wingingit/profiles.html

Birds of the World on Postage Stamps

Chris Gibbins has been collecting bird stamps since 1970 and has amassed more than 2,350 bird species on more than 7,500 stamps. The website (*first address*) may be by far the largest online database of birding stamps in the world. The site shows many of Gibbins' stamps, plus a map of the country from which each stamp originates. The birds are indexed by species and by nation. The main index (*second address*) is arranged by families and has more than 1,000 species listed (and often more than one stamp for each species). If you're interested in birds and stamps, Chris also has information about the Bird Stamp Society, based in England.

http://www.bird-stamps.org
http://www.bird-stamps.org/families.htm

Birds on Banknotes

Many people collect postage stamps bearing pictures of birds, but did you know that cash carries birds, too? Ruud Grootenboer of The Netherlands and Jan-Erik Malmstigen of Sweden prepared this page, based on the *Standard Catalog of World Paper Money*. It lists hundreds of banknotes bearing images of birds. When known, the species is identified by both English and Latin names, and the species is often given a brief description. Values of the bills in different conditions are provided. In many cases, scanned images of the banknotes are available online.

http://home3.swipnet.se/~w-33148/frim8.htm

Free Pictures!

One of the features that makes the Web so attractive to birders is the pictures of birds. Be they photographs, paintings, or drawings, they enliven websites and explain concepts. And virtually all of them are free and easily available for your personal use on your computer. With both Internet Explorer and Netscape on a Windows computer, right-clicking on an illustration will bring up a dialogue box that enables you to save the picture. (On a Mac, you can drag the image to your desktop.) You are offered a choice of saving the picture as a file or as wallpaper. Wallpaper is the decorative background on your desktop, and this choice will save the picture to a file called wallpaper.bmp, making the picture appear each time you turn on your computer. In the case of Save Picture As, you are offered the choice of storing the image on your hard drive as a .jpg or .bmp—JPEG or bitmap—picture. If you will use the picture in connection with the Web or wish to have as small a file as possible, select .jpg. If you plan to use the picture for an illustration in a word processor or some other program that will print out the image on paper, use a .bmp file since it is usable in more word processors and other programs than .jpg files are. Create a directory or folder called "graphics" or "pictures" and keep all of your downloaded images there. *Caution: Many pictures are copyrighted and can't be employed for anything that can be seen by others.*

NET NOTES

A Gathering Place for Your Birders

Ever wish you could have a private place on the Web where you and your birding friends could chat, exchange photos, and even transfer files? Enter eCircles.com, "a fun and simple service for small groups of friends and family members to share information and coordinate events on the Web."

eCircles is like a private bulletin board or, as many websites call them, forums. One person sets it up by becoming a member. That entails logging onto eCircles and filling out a brief form. The person can then create the "circle" and can mass-mail invitations to join the circle to everyone with similar interests. As an experiment, we set up a "circle" for four family members in about 10 minutes.

Why do this? Suppose you have a birding club in your town. You can set up an eCircle in which all the members can log in at any time and post sightings, questions, and observations. One member can comment on another's report. eCircles.com enables you to post pictures of what you saw. In fact, your club could amass a sizable album of shots taken by members.

The circle can also establish an online calendar, where members can list upcoming club jaunts or special events. Members can share files—from word processor lists of birds to software with which to keep track of them.

The cost? Nothing. eCircles is free. The company makes its money by selling relatively unobtrusive advertising on the pages you view.

http://www.ecircles.com

Diane Jacky Art Gallery

Diane Jacky, a talented oil-on-canvas artist, has been called "the world's foremost living artist of poultry and pigeon standards." You'll find plenty of pigeons, pullets, and even hummingbirds on this site. Although few of the birds are wild, they are magnificent and a lot of fun to look at. And they *are* birds.

http://home.earthlink.net/~jackynet/

John James Audubon Museum

John James Audubon spent the longest period of his adult life in the wooded hills of Henderson, Kentucky. The state-owned John J. Audubon Museum in Henderson has the largest collection found in North America of his memorabilia, including many original paintings, journals, correspondence, and personal artifacts. As a fund-raiser, the museum offers 18 by 24 inch prints, reproductions from the museum's set of the rare Double Elephant folio of *Birds of America*, published between 1827 and 1838. "Each print in this series was carefully selected as an outstanding example of the poetic beauty, spirit, and personality reflected in Audubon's work," the museum says. Each print is embossed with Audubon's personal seal. Information about ordering the print is available on this page of the museum's website.

http://www.kystateparks.com/agencies/parks/audprints.htm

American Redstart (*Setophaga ruticilla*) (JJA)

Louis Agassiz Fuertes

Louis Agassiz Fuertes is one of the early 20th century's best known bird painters and one whose works are both respected and collected today. The Chemung Valley Audubon Society in New York state (*first address*) has a collection of his works online, but they are not from art galleries or museums. The Fuertes pictures featured here are from Arm & Hammer and Cow Brand baking soda trading cards of the 1920s. Nonetheless, Fuertes is "considered by many to be one of the greatest bird painters of all time," says this Audubon chapter site. "Whatever his medium, his goal was constantly the same: to create an artistic whole by painting the living birds as accurately as possible, subjugating the environment to the bird itself." Fuertes was born in Ithaca, New York, which ironically is now the home of one of the great centers of ornithological study in North America, the Cornell University Laboratory of Ornithology. The Lab's website (*second address*) has information about Fuertes, who was also a noted ornithologist and whose collection of more than 3,000 bird "skins" is housed at Cornell. The U.S. Fish & Wildlife Service National Art Collection (*third address*) has some examples of Fuertes' work. The service owns 220 of Fuertes' paintings, which are on long-term loan to the Academy of Natural Sciences in Philadelphia.

http://www.stonecabin.com/cvas/virtual.html

http://cuvc.bio.cornell.edu/cubird/agassiz_fuertes.html

http://bluegoose.arw.r9.fws.gov/NWRSFiles/Graphics/
FWSNationalArtCollection.html

Mark Catesby

A century before Audubon was on the scene, British naturalist Mark Catesby (1682–1749) traveled to the colonies to explore its natural history. As early at 1712, he was wandering the South. Unable to afford to hire an artist to create images of the fauna and flora he saw, Catesby taught himself etching and between 1729 and 1747 produced the earliest-known, illustrated natural history of the British colonies in North America. The original watercolors for the natural history were later purchased by King George III, and they have since remained in the royal collection in the United Kingdom. Alecto Historical Editions is publishing facsimiles of all 263 original watercolors. The price for

the complete collection is very expensive—more than $50,000—but limited numbers of single lithographs are also available. Although these lithographs will not be within the budgets of many of us, we can still enjoy the many samples of Catesby's art, as well as read an extensive history of the naturalist/artist, all of which are posted in the online catalog.

http://www.catesby.com

Mr. Puzzler

Identifying birds can often be puzzling, so perhaps it's no surprise that birders might be drawn to puzzles. Mort Somer is both a birder and a puzzler, but the Webmaster of the Wasatch Audubon Society in Ogden, Utah <http://www.audubon.org/chapter/ut/wasatch/> is something more: A puzzle-maker. The society website he oversees offers many of his sophisticated word puzzles, all with a birding bent. "I'm a retiree from the Federal Government and have always been a non-professional puzzle fanatic," Mort says. "I may hold the record for most crossword puzzles solved in a lifetime." But he also creates and shares puzzles. "A couple of years ago I started up a regular Wednesday morning Breakfast-and-Birding outing," he recalls. "At one of the early breakfasts, I handed out a copy of one of the birding puzzles that I had made up, just for the fun of it. The response was most gratifying. Everybody got caught up in trying to solve the thing." So, as editor of the Mountain Chickadee, the chapter's newsletter, he decided to create puzzles regularly and share them with members. They include cryptographic puzzles, anagrams, rebuses, word squares, hidden words, and other clever concoctions. All are well-executed—and fun. All are posted on the website. And more are on their way. "I plan to keep making up these puzzles as long as I can come up with material for them," says Mort, much to the delight, no doubt, of birding puzzlers—or puzzled birders.

A
B
C
D
E
F
G
H
I
J
K
L
M
N
O
P
Q
R
S
T
U
V
W
X
Y
Z

AUDUBON SOCIETIES & SANCTUARIES

The word "Audubon" has become almost synonymous with birds, and the term "Audubon Society" with birding. That's in part because John James Audubon, the naturalist and artist who explored North America in the early 19th century, is most famous for his *Birds of America* folios (*see also Artful Birds*). Inspired by his work and concerned about the mass slaughter of so many species of North American birds, worried birders formed Audubon societies in the late 1800s and early 1900s to promote an interest in and conservation of birds. Today, hundreds of Audubon societies in the United States and a few in Canada are still aimed at conserving birds, as well as protecting wildlife and habitats in general. Many Audubon chapters have websites that are full of local information and are great places to check out if you are visiting a region. Audubon birders seem more than willing to share "insider information," and we have selected some of the most informative. However, sites that provide mostly basic chapter information, such as officers, meeting dates, bird walks, and conservation projects, have not been listed. Remember, too, that many National Audubon Society chapters exist that do not have websites; you can find a list of all chapters, whether or not they are online (*first address*). This site is also a good place to visit if a chapter has changed its Web address. You can search for the closest Audubon chapter to you by using your Zip Code (*second address*). The listings in this section also include some of the major National Audubon sanctuaries and wildlife centers that have websites. Audubon societies not affiliated with the National Audubon Society are identified as such.

http://www.audubon.org/chapter/
http://www.audubon.org/local/zipsearch/

GENERAL

Audubon International

Audubon International (not affiliated with the National Audubon Society), a nonprofit organization based in Selkirk, New York, promotes water conservation, water quality protection, and the conservation and protection of biological diversity. Through its Siena College–Audubon International Institute, the organization does research on wildlife and habitat management connected with the rapid development of our countryside. Under its Cooperative Sanctuary Program, businesses, schools, golf courses, and even private homeowners are given guidance on how to "maximize environmental quality on your property." Many other efforts—including publications—are described on this well-organized site.

http://www.audubonintl.org

Audubon News Service

The National Audubon Society has two e-mail lists for distributing late-breaking news about a variety of topics that could be of interest to birders. To subscribe to either of these, send an e-mail to *listserv@list.audubon.org* and in the body of the message specify the name of the list you want to join. Audubon-News dispatches information about the environment and about the society's various conservation campaigns and includes "action alerts" on what bills are pending in Congress that could affect the environment and how you can help. Write SUBSCRIBE AUDUBON-NEWS in the body of the message. A second e-mail list, Audubon's Endangered species campaign, can update you on current issues involving endangered species of all sorts, including birds. The list sends out alerts and news of government and other actions affecting endangered species. Write SUBSCRIBE ESA-NEWS in the body of the message. Audubon has more information about these and other lists on its site.

http://www.audubon.org/net/list/

Willow Ptarmigan (*Lagopus lagopus*) (JJA)

Hooded Merganser (Dover)

National Audubon Society

In 1886, a magazine editor became so outraged at the mass killing of North American bird species that he urged concerned citizens to form an "Audubon Society" to fight for their conservation. Nearly 40,000 people signed up, but the response was so overwhelming that editor George Bird Grinnell had to abandon his effort two years later. Continued concern prompted the formation of local groups like the Massachusetts Audubon Society in 1896. By 1899, 15 states had Audubon societies. That year, ornithologist and avid birder Frank M. Chapman of the American Museum of Natural History in New York began publishing *Bird-Lore*, a magazine that carried bird counts, as well as anecdotal observations and other items of interest that technical journals would not accept. This periodical helped to unify the Audubon movement, eventually becoming its official organ; a National Committee of Audubon Societies was formed in 1901. These are the roots of the National Audubon Society, the leading bird and wildlife conservation organization in the United States. Today, the society has more than 550,000 members, 508 chapters, 100 sanctuaries and nature centers nationwide, and some 300 full-time staff including scientists, educators, sanctuary managers, and local directors. The headquarters site has extensive information about the society and can provide local contacts and sources of birding and conservation information. The site is fact-filled, informative, and useful, including an Ask an Audubon Expert page that provides many answers to common birding questions and then gives an e-mail address for those questions not answered. The site has news, features, information about Audubon programs for children and schools, camps, workshops,

events, and information on how birders can become involved in helping ornithologists and conservationists. It also has an extensive collection of links that cover not only the society but also advocacy groups, education, endangered species, environmental groups, environmental law, international sites, John J. Audubon sites, local resources, online resources, publications, and ornithology. There's even an online gift shop. And, of course, there's information about *Audubon* magazine, the excellent bimonthly that goes to all members.

http://www.audubon.org

CENTRAL

Audubon Center of the North Woods

The Audubon Center of the North Woods, a 535-acre sanctuary on the shores of Grindstone Lake in Sandstone, Minnesota, features a wildlife rehabilitation center, classes, and a lodge that can accommodate conferences. The center provides many educational programs in the Duluth–St. Cloud region. The raptor center is particularly popular, and the site explains how you can adopt a raptor in need of rehabilitation.

http://www.audubon-center.com/audubon/Home.html

Audubon in Louisiana

The National Audubon Society chapters in Louisiana have created an umbrella site called Audubon in Louisiana that makes it easy for the surfing birder to learn about birding in the state, as well as activities of the societies. Making use of frames, the site has a well-written and well-mapped guide to where to bird in southern Louisiana. Another guide—for southwestern Louisiana—provides a collection of more than 250 pictures of birds that are on the official Louisiana Checklist, almost all of which were photographed within the state. There is news of sanctuaries, trips, rare bird sightings, conservation efforts, and lots more. The site has specific information about the Orleans Audubon Society, Baton Rouge Audubon Society, Acadiana Audubon Society, Natchitoches Audubon Society, and Central Louisiana Audubon Society. These listings mostly give local events and chapter officers.

http://www.audubon-la.org

A
B
C
D
E
F
G
H
I
J
K
L
M
N
O
P
Q
R
S
T
U
V
W
X
Y
Z

AVIAN ADVICE

The Best Food?

The most universally eaten feeder food is black-oil sunflower seeds.

—adapted from *Bird Watcher's Digest*

http://www.birdwatchersdigest.
com/faq/faq.html

Audubon Society of Central Arkansas

The Audubon Society of Central Arkansas, based in Little Rock, has a lively website that includes, in season, a nestbox webcam whose videos you can download and view, using either Real Player (*see page 150*) or Windows Media Player (which comes with newer versions of Windows). When we stopped by, a family of Carolina Chickadees was being raised in the box, and videos showed a lot of action. The site has a directory of birding hot spots in Pulaski County (around Little Rock), plus plenty of information about conservation issues, society work, activities, programs, and field trips.

http://www.aristotle.net/~asca/

Audubon Society of Missouri

The Website of the Audubon Society of Missouri offers a checklist of the state's birds, as well as some excellent tips, especially about bird identification (*see also Tips & Techniques*). The site has data on bird records in Missouri, information as to how to join the Missouri birding mailing list called *mobirds-l*, rare bird alerts, and links to sites of interest to Missouri birders.

http://mobirds.mig.missouri.edu

Audubon Society of Omaha

A readable and informative site, the Audubon Society of Omaha, Nebraska, offers something for everyone. Locals will enjoy the column, Notes from Nature, by Ruth C. Green, who reports on what's being seen in the region and what to watch for. Other interesting articles from the chapter newsletter, *A Bird's Eye View*, also are available. Particularly useful is the society's guide to places to go birding in the Omaha and Council Bluffs area. Thirty-one forests, lakes, parks, and refuges are described. If the locale has specialty birds (or other animals or plants), they are listed.

http://users.aol.com/jimmcl/ASO/aso.htm

Aullwood Audubon Center & Farm

The Aullwood Audubon Center and Farm in Dayton, Ohio, is a good resource, both in person and online. The website offers lists of species of birds, plants, mammals, trees, reptiles, and fishes that can be found in and about this facility. The center has more than 50 hands-on exhibits, including a hummingbird-butterfly garden and many walking trails.

http://www.audubon.org/local/sanctuary/aullwood/
index.html

Zenaida Dove (JJA)

Birmingham Audubon Society

The Birmingham Audubon Society has a fine directory of good birding sites not only around Birmingham but also in other parts of the state. The directory includes maps showing where the hot spots are and descriptions of each. The site further offers a chapter calendar, announcements, rare bird alerts, and links.

http://bmewww.eng.uab.edu/BAS/

Capital Area Audubon Society

The capital is Lansing, the state is Michigan, and the website of the Capital Area Audubon Society has much useful information. Besides a checklist of Michigan birds, the site offers something unusual: a list of average spring arrival dates of migrating species. The migration data were gathered from a variety of sources and are based on observations in East Lansing. The information can be applied to much of southern Michigan. Another interesting feature of the site is a collection of members' reports of their birding adventures. The accounts make fascinating reading and are quite useful for folks planning birding jaunts of their own. Trips described here range from journeys to the next state to expeditions to Brazil and Costa Rica. Also, the site's collection of Favorite Links is well worth inspecting—many are very local and useful.

http://www.msu.edu/user/mcconegh/caas/

Chicago Audubon Society

The Chicago Audubon Society's website has a very good collection of links to local birding information sources. To find it, scroll to the bottom of the home page, past all the hard-working officers and chairpersons. Even farther down are regional natural history links.

http://www.audubon.org/chapter/il/chicago/

Dayton Audubon Society

The Dayton Audubon Society website has a comprehensive guide to favorite birding spots in the Dayton, Ohio, area. For each place, the site tells the location and gives directions, a description of the habitat there, the species found at the location, and information about facilities and useful tips. It's a very nice guide that other Audubon chapters might want to emulate.

http://www.dayton.net/Audubon/

Fort Worth Audubon Society

Carl B. Haynie writes for the Fort Worth Audubon Society's website, explaining that Tarrant County in northeastern Texas "is an area blessed by a wide variety of habitats and geographical zones including the lower rolling plains, eastern and western cross-timbers, grand prairie, blackland prairie, and post oak savannah." Haynie notes that the county's 900 square miles is where "East meets West," a place where "observers have recorded over 370 species of birds . . . about 63 percent of all species documented for the state." A key feature of the site is Haynie's description of more than 25 great birding places in Tarrant County. It's one of the best-written, most comprehensive local guides on any Audubon site, and it's one of the main features of Fort Worth's website. Enjoy!

http://www.dallas.net/~birding/fwas.htm

FEATHERED FACTS

Keep Out!

To discourage predators, some species of North American nuthatches smear distasteful materials around the edges or outside of the hole to their nesting cavity in trees. Red-breasted Nuthatches are known to use sticky resin; White-breasted, crushed insects.

—adapted from Electronic Nuthatch

http://alt-www.uia.ac.be/u/matthys/nuthatch.html

A B C D E F G H I J K L M N O P Q R S T U V W X Y Z

A
B
C
D
E
F
G
H
I
J
K
L
M
N
O
P
Q
R
S
T
U
V
W
X
Y
Z

Boat-tailed Grackle (JJA)

Hawk Ridge Nature Reserve

Hawk Ridge Nature Reserve in east Duluth, Minnesota, is reported to be "one of Minnesota's premier birding locations." The site notes that Hawk Ridge "averages about 55,000 migrating raptors a year. The record number of hawks counted in any one season, however, is 148,615 birds in 1993." As many as 47,000 Broad-winged Hawks have been observed in a single day passing over the ridge, and the site has extensive statistics on all the raptor species seen there. The reserve is managed by a committee of the Duluth Audubon Society.

http://biosci.cbs.umn.edu/~mou/ridge.html

Houston Audubon Society

The Houston Audubon Society in Texas has an excellent collection of links to Texas birds and birding. To find them, scroll most of the way down the home page. For links to other pages, continue scrolling to the bottom of the page. You'll see in small type a collection of links to pages on where to go birding in not only Houston but also many locales of the region. The site has a lot of information, and anyone visiting southeastern Texas should make a stop here first.

http://www.io.com/~pdhulce/audubon.html

Hunt Hill Nature Center & Audubon Sanctuary

According to its website Hunt Hill Nature Center & Audubon Sanctuary in Washburn County, Wisconsin, offers miles of hiking trails, camping and cabin rental, lodging and "exemplary dining facilities," a floating classroom and lake lab, and canoeing. The sanctuary consists of 500 acres of "majestic forests, meadow, bogs and pristine glacial lakes." Among the wildlife are nesting osprey and loons.

http://www.audubon.org/local/sanctuary/hunthill/index.html

Jackson Audubon Society

If you're heading for Jackson, Michigan, the Jackson Audubon Society's website provides a rundown of good birding sites in Jackson County. That includes Thorn Lake, where, the site claims, "It is not uncommon to see as many as 1,100 Ring-necked Ducks, 1,000 Canvasbacks, 2,000 Canada Geese, and 200 Redheads and several Mergansers of all three species, *at the same time!*"

http://www.audubon.org/chapter/mi/jackson/

Loess Hills Audubon Society

The Loess Hills Audubon Society is a cool group. For those who run across its name for the first time and wonder what the heck "loess" is, the site's home page answers the question. What's more, it tells you how to pronounce it. Geographically speaking, the Loess Hills Audubon Society is centered on Sioux City, Iowa, a good birding area that is nicely described on the Loess Hills website. Here you can learn about the Birds of the Siouxland Area and checklists that tell you what you can expect to see and when. More than 255 species are listed. Birds that are on the Watchlist (*see Conservation, page 54*) as *troubled* are so noted. You'll also find a collection of Birding Hotspots in Woodbury, Union, and Plymouth Counties, each with nicely drawn maps.

http://www.avalon.net/~yiams/

Michigan Audubon Society

"Michigan's oldest conservation organization" has an information-packed site. Of special interest to birders is the guide to Michigan Audubon Society sanctuaries and nature centers, at least 17 of them around the state. A clickable map helps you select sanctuaries in the area you are interested in. Many of these map items offer information about birding, including local checklists. The site describes festivals, campouts, and trips, and carries the latest Rare Bird Alerts for Michigan. The chapter's newsletter, the *Jack Pine Warbler*, has an online edition; when we stopped by, Early Preparation Is Key to Establishing a Successful Martin Colony and Help Purple Martins Now were featured. The Michigan society has adopted the Purple Martin as a species of concern and hopes to increase its numbers in the state. The site describes the society's quarterly publication, *Michigan Birds and Natural History*; each issue includes information about seasonal bird summaries, the Michigan Christmas Bird Count summary, annual Michigan North American Migration Count summary, rare bird sighting accounts, features, quizzes, local artists' work, and more. There is also a lot of information on this site concerning the society's conservation efforts.

http://www.audubon.org/chapter/mi/mas/

Minnesota Audubon Council

The Minnesota Audubon Council's website is a great place to learn about the work of Audubon chapters with a linked index to all the Minnesota chapters of the National Audubon Society. The site also tells how you can be an environmental activist in Minnesota (providing access to a comprehensive database of legislators in the state). You can learn about interesting birding hikes along the northern Mississippi River (thanks to help from the Friends of the Mississippi River).

http://www.audubon.org/chapter/mn/mn/

Nebraska Audubon

Nebraska Audubon's website describes some of the better sanctuaries and wildlife viewing areas in the state and has links to Nebraska Audubon chapters where you can find out about more birding areas. Check the page on the state's natural resources, too. The site has a page of puzzles and quizzes for kids, plus news and some birding tips.

http://rip.physics.unk.edu/audubon/nebraska/

Northern Flint Hills Audubon Society

The website of the Northern Flint Hills Audubon Society, based in Manhattan, Kansas, is essentially an online version of the chapter's print newsletter, the *Prairie Falcon*. Here you'll find articles about what birds to see at different times of the year, Operation Crane Watch, and an excellent collection of links, many of them very local and offering information about good locations for birding.

http://www.ksu.edu/audubon/falcon.html

FEATHERED FACTS

Cowbird Crazy

For many years conservationists and birders feared that the Brown-headed Cowbird was decimating populations of songbirds throughout North America. But recent evidence indicates otherwise—for the most part. Cowbirds are *brood parasites*, leaving their eggs in the nests of other birds for the foster parents to raise, usually to the detriment of the parents' own chicks. Because the cowbirds' range had spread far from its original Great Plains territory and some songbird populations were declining, the theory arose that cowbirds were a main cause. However, reports the National Audubon Society, recent research indicates both that the cowbird population is declining and that they have little to do with songbird declines—except in very local situations and usually with endangered species.

—adapted from the National Audubon Society

http://www.audubon.org/bird/research/

Oktibbeha Audubon Society

The Oktibbeha Audubon Society based at Mississippi State University in Starkville, Mississippi, has a special project to protect the Red-cockaded Woodpecker, which the site says is "a relic left from a past when thousands of acres across the southeastern United States were in native pines." This species has been almost eliminated from Virginia and Kentucky and has recently disappeared from Tennessee. The site explains why the bird is endangered and what can be done to help it survive. Information is also provided about the Noxubee Refuge, a U.S. Fish & Wildlife refuge in northeast Mississippi that is home to at least 35 clusters of Red-cockaded Woodpeckers (*see also North American Birds, Backyard*).

http://www2.msstate.edu/~goodman/

River Bluffs Audubon Society

The River Bluffs Audubon Society in Jefferson City, Missouri, has a useful feature on its website. Look near the top of the site's long menu for River Bluffs Audubon Trip Reports, and you'll be taken to pages of accounts of birding expeditions in the region. These reports can be handy for planning your own trips. Many include photos, as well as lists of birds, that were spotted.

http://www.audubon.org/chapter/mo/riverbluffs/

Sabal Palm Audubon Center & Sanctuary

The Texas Audubon Society's Sabal Palm Audubon Center and Sanctuary includes 527 acres near Brownsville, Texas, that have one of the last stands of Sabal Palm, a tree that once grew profusely along the banks of the Rio Grande. The website (*first address*) has useful information about birding at Sabal Palms, noting that "the sanctuary is home to many native species of plants and animals which reach the northernmost limit of their Mexican range here and do not occur elsewhere in the United States." The site includes reports of recent sightings at the sanctuary. A special, highly graphical Sabal Palm site is available for children (*second address*). It includes a virtual tour of the center and sanctuary—interesting to adults as well as kids—and a chat area. Be forewarned, however, that

because of the site's high graphic and sound profile, downloading the home page takes much longer than for most sites.

http://www.audubon.org/local/sanctuary/sabal/
http://www.ies.net/sabalkids/index.html

St. Louis Audubon Society

The St. Louis Audubon Society in Missouri provides a good collection of information about birding in greater St. Louis. Follow the St. Louis Birding Resources link to see Birds of the St. Louis Area: When and Where to Find Them, as well as a checklist of St. Louis birds, local rare bird alerts, and reports of trips taken by chapter members.

http://www.audubon.org/chapter/mo/slas/

MEET THE MASTERS

Working the Wild Side

When it comes to birds and birding, Christine Tarski, the guide for About.com's birding site <http://birding.about.com>, does more than search with browsers and binoculars. "Last year, I along with the Gardening Guide, Deb Simpson, launched a huge project called 'Feathers & Flowers,'" she says. "We used part of my property and turned it into a habitat for birds, butterflies, and other wildlife. She covered the project from a gardening standpoint, I from the bird. We each wrote a series of articles, took photos, and actually planted the Haven in April of 1998." You can see their work at <http://birding.about.com/library/weekly/blheadq.htm>. And there will be regular updates of how the project is progressing. Meanwhile, Christine still takes time to wander the Texas countryside, looking for birds. She often carries a camera, on the prowl for the perfect photo of her favorite songbird, the meadowlark.

Tennessee Valley Audubon Society

The Tennessee Valley Audubon Society serves the Limestone, Madison, and Morgan Counties area of northern Alabama, including the cities of Huntsville, Decatur, Madison, and Athens. This artfully done site has a neat birding map—just click on the county and up comes a close-up map with hot spots for good birding, each marked with a colored coot. Click on the coot, and you'll get the details. The site also has records of recent sightings, information about sanctuaries, parks, and refuges in the region (under the menu item Sanctuaries), links, and information about the organization.

http://fly.hiwaay.net/~pgibson/tvas/index.html

Texas Audubon Society

Texas is probably home to more species of birds than any other state, so it's no surprise that it had one of America's earliest Audubon Societies (organized at Galveston, Texas, on March 4, 1899). This site explains the activities of Texas Audubon and has links to a dozen chapters within the state. You can also learn about the many Audubon sanctuaries in Texas, as well as Audubon events.

http://www.audubon.org/chapter/tx/tx/abttas.html

Texas Coastal Islands Sanctuary

The Texas Coastal Islands Sanctuary protects more than 11,000 acres on 33 natural and dredge spoil islands along the Gulf Coast. These islands are situated in most of the primary and secondary bays from Galveston Bay to Lower Laguna Madre and protect nesting and feeding habitats for wading and sea birds such as Roseate Spoonbills, Olivaceous Cormorants, many species of herons and egrets, ibis, endangered Brown Pelicans, Laughing Gulls, several species of terns, Black Skimmers, and American Oystercatchers. Access to these areas are limited, so it is recommended that you check the site for details before making a birding trip to the Gulf Coast.

http://www.audubon.org/local/sanctuary/tx-coastal/

Slate-colored Junco (*Junco hyemalis*) [Dark-eyed Junco] (JJA)

Thunder Bay Audubon Society

The Thunder Bay Audubon Society in northern Michigan has a website (*first address*) with close ties to the Northern Michigan Birding network (*second address*). Between the two of them, you can learn a lot about birding opportunities in a wide area of northern Michigan. An active message board enables you to read about the latest sightings or ask questions ("Where's a good place for a visitor to bird in Cheboygan County?"). Also available are a chat room, rare bird alerts, links, and lots of data on what has been seen locally.

http://www.northbirding.com/Thunderbay/
http://www.northbirding.com

Travis Audubon Society

Everyone interested in backyard bird feeding should visit the website of the Travis Audubon Society in Austin, Texas, one of the most helpful and all-encompassing collections of birding tips and techniques on the Web. Look for the menu item, Backyard Birding, which leads to dozens of articles by society naturalists covering landscaping, feeders, food, hummingbirds, birdhouses, and dozens of interesting observations.

http://www.onr.com/user/audubon/

A B C D E F G H I J K L M N O P Q R S T U V W X Y Z

Tracking Down Home Pages

Whether you're using this book or a search engine, you will often come upon pages of information with no links in them to send you to their home pages. For instance, you may find a page of tips on locating bluebird houses, and you might want to find out more about the source of those tips, but there's no link to the site's main page. What do you do? The answer is edit the address.

The upper left-hand corner of most browsers contains the World Wide Web address of the page you're viewing. Suppose it's **<http://www.glop.com/stuff/bluebirds/houses.htm>**. Houses.htm is the actual "document" or page that you are reading on the website. Everything before that is directories or "folders" containing all the documents, pictures, and other parts of the website.

Click into the Address window. The whole address should be highlighted in blue. Click again so that the blue disappears and your cursor is at the far right end of the address. Then, using the back space key (or whatever deletes to the left on your computer), delete the page address to the first /. Press ENTER and see what comes up. It might be an index of bluebird articles. It might be nothing or an error message. If that doesn't uncover a link to the home page, click twice back into the address field and delete the next directory name—such as "bluebirds/" in the preceding example. Press ENTER and see what happens. Keep doing it till you reach **<http://www.glop.com>**. Often you'll get a good picture of what's available on the site and maybe even discover new and useful pages.

Zumbro Valley Audubon Society

The Zumbro Valley Audubon Society in Rochester, Minnesota, has a small but useful set of local Web links to birding pages that serve mostly Rochester and Olmsted Counties. The site includes a guide to birding locations in Olmsted County.

http://www.audubon.org/chapter/mn/zumbro/

EASTERN

Audubon Center in Greenwich

The National Audubon Society considers its Greenwich, Connecticut, facility the society's "flagship sanctuary and education center." More than 900 species of ferns and flowering plants, 35 species of mammals, and 160 species of birds have been recorded there, even though the center is only about 15 miles from New York City.

http://www.audubon.org/local/sanctuary/greenwich/

Audubon Naturalist Society

"The investigation of nature is an infinite pleasure-ground where all may graze," the Audubon Naturalist Society (not affiliated with the National Audubon Society) quotes Thomas H. Huxley on its home page. The society, founded in 1897, is one of the nation's oldest regional natural history organizations and serves the "grazing" needs of thousands of people in the Washington, D.C., region. The website describes many club activities—including plenty of bird walks—and carries articles, as well as one of its columns, Focus on Birds, from the latest issues of *Audubon Naturalist News*, the organization's monthly newspaper. Information is available about events held at Woodend, the society's 40-acre sanctuary and mansion outside Washington.

http://www.audubonnaturalist.org

Audubon Society of Forsyth County

The Audubon Society of Forsyth County, based in Winston-Salem, North Carolina, does something very helpful: it devotes almost all of the site to a guide to birding and only birding in Winston-Salem. Useful both to the visiting public and newcomers to birding, the guide includes maps of each location; if you click on the map, it brings you to MapBlast!, a map site through which you can modify and print out maps. The descriptions of each birding location include insiders' tips on what to see and where you might see it.

http://www.audubon.org/chapter/nc/forsyth/

Audubon Society of Southwest Florida

The Audubon Society of Southwest Florida, based in Fort Myers, offers Vince McGrath's guide to Birding Hotspots in Lee, Charlotte, and Collier Counties. He tells how to get to each hot spot and describes unusual species you may find.

http://www.audubon.org/chapter/fl/southwest/

Audubon Society of the Everglades

Despite its name, Audubon Society of the Everglades is not really *in* the Everglades, but serves communities from Jupiter and Tequesta south to Boynton Beach, Florida, on the northeastern fringes of the Everglades. The organization runs field trips to birding hot spots throughout the area and has a concise, online guide as to where to bird in this southeastern Florida region.

http://www.flinet.com/~audubon/index.shtml

Columbia Audubon Society

If you want to learn about the birding hot spots in any part of South Carolina, connect to the website of the Columbia Audubon Society and select Table of Contents. There you'll find a comprehensive guide, arranged by regions of the state, Where to Bird in South Carolina. Compiled by Bob Wood, the guide includes helpful tips and notes on some popular species you are apt to see. The website has other interesting features and a good collection of links.

http://www.conterra.com/dsbailey/audubon/

Connecticut Audubon Society

The Connecticut Audubon Society (not affiliated with the National Audubon Society), which turned 100 in 1998, has more than 10,000 members and manages 16 sanctuaries that preserve 2,500 acres. The website's guide to the sanctuaries includes detailed instructions on how to find each. Also online are details about each of the major centers operated by Connecticut Audubon: the Birdcraft Museum in Fairfield, the headquarters in Fairfield, centers in Pomfret, Glastonbury, Hartford, Trail Wood in Hampton, Ragged Hill Woods in Brooklyn, and the Coastal Center at Milford Point. The site also offers Nature Notes (natural history features), an excellent collection of frequently asked questions (which the site calls Q&A), and much more.

http://www.ctaudubon.org

Corkscrew Swamp Sanctuary

You can take a virtual tour of National Audubon's Corkscrew Swamp Sanctuary, 11,000 acres of swamps, marshes, and pine forests near Naples, Florida, on this website. The tour notes that some of the Bald Cypress trees there are more than 500 years old and tells about some of the birds you might see, such as Wood Storks and the Barred Owl.

http://www.audubon.org/local/sanctuary/corkscrew/

Daviess County Audubon Society

The simple motto, "enjoying and protecting nature," of the Daviess County Audubon Society, based in Owensboro, Kentucky, is reflected in its website. Here you will find an Ask an Expert feature, a Where the Birds Are basic guide with contact people you can call for help, and special pages for children and for teachers. The Kids & Nature section includes bird facts and fun.

http://www.audubon.org/chapter/ky/daviess/

Prairie Chicken (Dover)

A
B
C
D
E
F
G
H
I
J
K
L
M
N
O
P
Q
R
S
T
U
V
W
X
Y
Z

Delaware Audubon Society

If there were an award for the best local Audubon chapter website, it might go to Delaware's, a model of a useful birding site. Begin with the Birding in Delaware section, which includes Maurice Barnhill's excellent Delaware Birding Locations: A Guide to Bird Finding in Delaware. Here you'll find dozens and dozens of places, lists of the specialty birds you'll be apt to see, and Barnhill's personal suggestions for seeing them. Birding in Delaware also includes a checklist of regularly occurring species—and because Delaware is on the Atlantic flyway, more than 340 species are on the list. But they are not just listed; many are linked to Barnhill's locations guide so you can find out where to see them. Talk about user friendly! For good reading, check out the interesting and sometimes humorous stories that members contribute to the Bird Tales section. The site also has information about birding trips, profiles of special birds, an Online Marketplace with bluebird boxes, environmental magazines, and lots more.

http://www.delawareaudubon.org

Florida Audubon Society

The Florida Audubon Society is one of the nation's most active societies, with some 35,000 members. That's not surprising, considering that Florida is such a fragile environment and so loaded with people. It's also one of the most bird-filled locales in North America. Florida Audubon owns more than 50 pieces of significant property in the state, and some of the largest and most important are detailed on the site. The site has a guide to Audubon nature centers and a useful, map-based directory to all the Florida chapters of the National Audubon Society. Although some of these Florida Audubon chapters appear in this section, many more are in the site's directory, including those with and without websites (those on the Web are linked). To use the directory, just click on a number in a part of the state you are interested in. Also useful is the site's FAQ page. Of course, the site has plenty of information about Florida Audubon's work, including its Birds of Prey Center. (*See also North American Birds, Raptors, Audubon Adopt-a-Bird and Florida Eagle Watch.*)

http://www.audubon.usf.edu

Four Harbors Audubon Society

Four Harbors Audubon Society covers Smithtown, Port Jefferson, Stony Brook, and surrounding communities on the north shore of Long Island, New York. Under the menu item Birding, you'll find various features that include Four Harbors Birding Sites. This guide, written by Howard Barton and arranged by season, describes birding hot spots in the region and what you can expect to see at each. Many of the locations are illustrated with aerial photographs, something not often seen on Audubon websites. The pictures give a good idea of what kind of environment to expect at each location. The site also has a nice section for kids (*see also Children*), plus features on birds, current tide tables, and weather data.

http://www.igc.apc.org/fhas/

WEB WORDS

Finding Life in Death

"Very few people ever ponder the immensity of the total amount of life, other than human, being born and dying on the earth each and every day of every month of every year, century after century. Of all the numerous carcasses lying on the ground throughout the world at any given moment, few are ever considered obnoxious by the average person, because in fact, they are seldom if ever even seen. The primary reason is that shortly after death the carcass is removed, converted to fertilizer, and spread throughout the countryside. The entity assigned by mother nature to the primary responsibility for this job is a variety of carrion eaters. Included is the family of scavenger birds which includes vultures. In much of the United States the resident agent is the Turkey Vulture."

—Bill Kohlmoos, President, Turkey Vulture Society

http://www.accutek.com/vulture/vultpurp.htm

Francis Beidler Forest

Francis Beidler Forest is the largest virgin blackwater cypress-tupelo swamp forest left in the world, reports the official website of this 11,000-acre National Audubon Society sanctuary in the heart of Four Holes Swamp in Harleyville, South Carolina, not far from Charleston. The sanctuary includes 1,800 acres of ancient trees that tower over blackwater streams, clear pools, and 300 species of wildlife. The website has a complete list of birds found at the sanctuary, including some photos and sound bites, as well as lists of other wildlife. The political and natural history of the forest can be viewed in person from a 6,500-foot boardwalk. And, of course, the site tells us who Francis Beidler was—an early hero of conservation well worth remembering.

http://www.pride-net.com/swamp/

Greater Wyoming Valley Audubon Society

The Greater Wyoming Valley Audubon Society, based in Dallas, Pennsylvania, covers the Luzerne and Wyoming Counties of northeastern Pennsylvania. The site has a guide to a half dozen birding hot spots, describing what you may see and how to get to each location. The online bird counts also give the visitor, as well as residents, an idea of what's being seen in the region.

http://www.audubon.org/chapter/pa/gwvas/

Indian River Audubon Society

The Indian River Audubon Society in Cocoa serves Brevard County, Florida, one of the top birding locales in the Southeast, thanks largely to the Merritt Island National Wildlife Refuge (*see also Destinations*) and the Canaveral National Seashore, both of which surround or border the Kennedy Space Center on central Florida's Atlantic Coast. This chapter site lists many other birding hot spots in the region, such as two of my favorites, the Ulu May Wildlife Sanctuary and the Sebastian Inlet State Recreation Area. For each, it gives directions, the best places to go, and what you might see at what time of day. The site also has information about field trips and other chapter activities.

http://www.audubon.org/chapter/fl/indianriver/

Red-headed Woodpecker (*Melanerpes erythrocephalus*) (JJA)

Kissimmee Valley Audubon Society

"Kissimmee, Florida, is best known as the home of Disney World and other attractions, but few people ever see the wild and scenic areas that surround it," notes the Kissimmee Valley Audubon Society. The great birding in the Kissimmee Valley includes some of America's rarer and most spectacular birds: Whooping Cranes, Caracara, Wood Storks, and the "highest concentration of Bald Eagles in the lower 48 states." Click on menu item Maps, and you'll get a concise guide to some of the best birding and wildlife-watching spots in the region. A valuable collection of links is also available.

http://www.phoenixat.com/audubon/

Lehigh Valley Audubon Society

The Lehigh Valley Audubon Society covers the eastern Pennsylvania counties of Lehigh and Northampton and includes the cities of Allentown, Bethlehem, and Easton. If you scroll down the home page of the chapter website, you'll find a list of Lehigh Valley birding hot spots. Unless you're a knowledgeable resident, however, you'll need a good local map to figure out where they are.

http://www.lehigh.edu/~bcm0/lvas.html

A B C D E F G H I J K L M N O P Q R S T U V W X Y Z

AVIAN ADVICE

The Friendly Pigeon

Newspapers and nature centers periodically get calls about a very friendly pigeon, wearing identification bands on both legs, showing up in someone's yard or on a porch, seemingly looking for food. Odds are, it *is* looking for food and is a homing or racing pigeon that got lost or worn out before reaching its destination. Although a nature center may be able to help you identify the owner, the Connecticut Audubon Society says most owners would just as soon not get back a bird that couldn't perform well. So what do you do? The society recommends feeding the bird for a day or so, then releasing it in a place where there are other pigeons. The bird may return home, or it may join the wild pigeons. But you don't want it to get accustomed to your place—unless you want a feathered friend for life.

—adapted from Connecticut Audubon Society

http://www.ctaudubon.org/q&a.htm

Litchfield Hills Audubon Society

Northwestern Connecticut's Litchfield Hills Audubon Society has information, including trail maps, for two good birding sanctuaries in the area. The site also describes chapter programs and carries links to local birding information.

http://www.geocities.com/RainForest/Vines/3385/

Massachusetts Audubon Society

The Massachusetts Audubon Society (not affiliated with the National Audubon Society) is one of the nation's first Audubon organizations and has one of the most high-tech, informative sites of any Audubon group. The society also says it's the largest conservation organization in New England. "We protect more than 28,000 acres of conservation land in Massachusetts [and] conduct educational programs for nearly 150,000 schoolchildren each year," the society notes, adding that it maintains 37 wildlife sanctuaries. The latter are shown on a clickable map that leads you to sanctuaries by region. Each sanctuary has a page of information that includes area and trail maps and a description of the kinds of wildlife you are apt to see. (Trail maps are available in two versions: one is viewable online and one is designed for output on a printer; both are clearly and professionally drawn.) You'll also find here a special section for children and teachers. The kids' segment provides wildlife and Audubon camp information, as well as Creatures & Creations activities. A place is provided for reporting interesting sightings—very readable—and a special feature on grassland birds gives information on such species as Savannah Sparrows, Bobolinks, Red-winged Blackbirds, Eastern Meadowlarks, Vesper Sparrows, Grasshopper Sparrows, Upland Sandpipers, and Henslow's Sparrows. Some of these birds are common, and some are very rare, but all live in environments that need special care. The well-illustrated site also has information about Audubon travel, a useful and well-organized collection of links, and much information on conservation.

http://www.massaudubon.org

Mattabeseck Audubon Society

The Mattabeseck Audubon Society covers central Connecticut. The site describes its activities, has a handsome online newsletter, WingBeat, and has links to other Connecticut societies.

http://www.audubon.org/chapter/ct/mattabeseck/

New Columbia Audubon Society

The nation's capital has no shortage of birds—perhaps it's all the hot air there. The New Columbia Audubon Society in Washington, D.C., offers Birding Around D.C., which tells you where to go and what you may find there. The scenically illustrated guide has links for more information.

http://www.audubon.org/chapter/dc/newcolumbia/

New Jersey Audubon Society

Founded in 1897, the New Jersey Audubon Society (not affiliated with the National Audubon Society) is another of the nation's oldest Audubon groups. The organization has 26 sanctuaries and eight staffed facilities throughout the state. Its website is one of the best of its kind, full of local information. One of its stars is Peter Dunne, a widely respected natural history writer, who is vice president of natural history information for New Jersey Audubon and director of the society's famous Cape May Bird Observatory (*see also Destinations*). Dunne writes a regular column, often about birds, that's on the site. Also available is a collection of reports of bird sightings from around the state; make sure you check out the latest from Cape May, an East Coast birding hot spot. One of the most useful features to visitor and New Jersian alike is the Site Guides section, a comprehensive collection of information about the best birding spots in the state, including descriptions of what you're apt to see. The guide is arranged by seasons, with different Great Spots for each season. Also visit the About Birding section, which has reviews, tips, articles, and a half dozen wildlife checklists.

http://www.nj.com/audubon/

New York City Audubon Society

Though it might surprise some people, New York City has a lot of birds. And a lot of birders. Founded in 1979 with 27 charter members, the New York City Audubon Society has grown to more than 8,000 members. The city of skyscrapers actually has many fine birding locations, including Central Park (*see also Destinations*), the grasslands of Jamaica Bay where many unusual species are seen, and uninhabited islands off the Bronx, Queens, and Staten Island. The site has information regarding a nesting bird census of Central Park, plus a complete checklist of birds regularly seen in the city.

http://www.interboro.com/nycaudubon/

North Carolina Audubon

The North Carolina Audubon Society website has a nice guide to the state's coastal waterbirds. Two dozen gulls, terns, herons, egrets, ibises, and other species are described with text and photos. The link is at the bottom of the home page.

http://www.ncaudubon.org/waterbirds_nest.html

Northern Neck Audubon Society

The Northern Neck Audubon Society covers eastern Virginia between the Potomac River south to the Rappahannock River. "Because of its proximity to the Chesapeake Bay, its large expanses of undeveloped land and wetlands, and the passion of the local community to protect and preserve its natural treasures, the four counties of the Northern Neck are a haven for over 250 species of birds," says the society's website. The site offers a list of those birds, where they are most likely to be seen, and with what frequency. The site's message board is a perfect place for a visitor to ask for information as to where to go birding or to read about what's being seen.

http://www.audubon.org/chapter/va/nn/

FEATHERED FACTS

Raspberry Finch

In 1927, the New Hampshire Federation of Women's Clubs voted on what the state bird should be. The Purple Finch won, but wasn't officially adopted for 30 more years. At the time of the vote, one supporter maintained that "Actually the Purple Finch is not purple at all. It's like a sparrow dipped in raspberry juice." He also quoted Thoreau, who said the Purple Finch "has the crimson hues of the October evenings." Because ragweed, the notorious hay fever pollen producer, is a favorite food of the Purple Finch, the New Hampshire Legislature declined to pass a law to eradicate ragweed.

—adapted from New Hampshire State Bird, Geobop

http://www.geobop.com/Eco/NH5.htm

A
B
C
D
E
F
G
H
I
J
K
L
M
N
O
P
Q
R
S
T
U
V
W
X
Y
Z

Ogeechee Audubon Society

"The coast of Georgia offers many fascinating places to bird," notes the Ogeechee Audubon Society, based in Savannah. "With many types of habitat, such as marshlands, live-oak maritime forests, and Longleaf Pine flatwoods, our area of the state is rich in diversity of not only bird life, but also other kinds of wildlife, and history. Come on down to the coast and explore!" To help those who heed the call, the society's site has a guide on Where to Bird in the Savannah Area. Nothing flashy, just good, solid information about various parks and preserves, and what might be seen there. The chapter's online newsletter, the Marshlander, is among the more interesting and newsy newsletters we've run across on Audubon sites.

http://www.audubon.org/chapter/ga/ogeechee/

Onondaga Audubon Society

The Onondaga Audubon Society, based in Oswego, central New York, has information about two top birding spots, Derby Hill Bird Observatory in Mexico, New York, and the Richard A. Noyes Sanctuary at Nine Mile Point. The descriptions of both are from a new book, nicely titled *City Cemeteries to Boreal Bogs: Where to Go Birding in Central New York*, details of which can be found on the website.

http://www.audubon.org/chapter/ny/onondaga/

Richmond Audubon Society

Richmond, the capital of Virginia, has plenty of birds within the city. The Richmond Audubon Society's website provides a long list of species, by season and frequency, that can be found in the city's James River Park.

http://www.cvco.org/science/audubon/

Saw Mill River Audubon Society

The Saw Mill River Audubon Society in Westchester County, New York, just north of New York City, describes a half dozen of its sanctuaries that are open to the public for birding (*first address*). The site also has a good collection of local birding links. However, the real treat on this site is its link to the Westchester County Birding Sites website (*second address*), which is sponsored by Saw Mill Audubon. If you live in or near New York City, or are planning to visit, check out this guide, which is probably the most comprehensive listing of Westchester parks, refuges, and other noteworthy locations where interesting birds can be found. It's broken down by region (Northern, Hudson River, Southern, and Long Island Sound) and includes a useful collection of general information about Westchester County—especially useful if you are planning a visit.

http://www.audubon.org/chapter/ny/sawmillriver/
http://www.cyburban.com/~anneswaim/

Sharon Audubon Center

The Sharon Audubon Center, in the northwestern corner of Connecticut, has more than eleven miles of scenic hiking trails and includes 758 acres of mixed forest, meadows, wetlands, ponds, and streams. The website describes the programs offered at the center, trails available, birds recently sighted, research that's under way, and more. The site includes an online trail map and handsomely illustrated descriptions of each trail.

http://www.audubon.org/local/sanctuary/sharon/

St. John's County Audubon Society

If you're headed for St. Augustine, Florida, America's oldest city, check out the St. John's County Audubon Society site to learn the best birding locations in and around this east coast county. You'll also find an excellent checklist of some 260 species that have been found in the county with information regarding their relative frequency in different seasons—and places where you are apt to spot them (for the key to the codes on the list, go to the end of the page). The site also has a gallery of birds photographed by M. C. and Amanda Morgan, who have been photographing birds in the St. Augustine area for some years. A newsy site, you can learn lots of information about local wildlife and conservation efforts.

http://members.aol.com/SJAudubon/

Theodore Roosevelt Sanctuary

The Theodore Roosevelt Sanctuary at Oyster Bay, Long Island, New York, has the distinction of being the National Audubon Society's first sanctuary, having been donated in 1923. Though only 12 acres, the sanctuary is carefully managed and rich with birds. The sanctuary has an award-winning nature center, and its programs reach more than 125,000 people a year. The site has photos and life histories of some of the raptors living in its aviary where non-releasable birds make a contribution to education.

http://www.audubon.org/affiliate/ny/trs/index.htm

Tropical Audubon Society

The Tropical Audubon Society in south Florida covers the Dade County (Miami) area and bears one of the neater names among Audubon chapters. The site also has one of the more ingenious features of any Audubon site: a Bird Finding FAQ. Compiled by Steve Mumford and Jeff Weber, the guide lists 20 sought-after species (such as Antillian Nighthawk, Canary-winged Parakeet, Crested Caracara, or Red-whiskered Bulbul). Click on the name, and you're led to a description of one or more locations where you may see the species. Clearly, the writers have been there, offering inside tips (for Monk Parakeets, for instance: "Finally, you might try in the lights at the Florida International University soccer field in North Miami, and at the University of Miami intramural practice fields on San Amaro, drive just south of Miller Road in Coral Gables"). The Tropical Audubon Society has sample articles from the current newsletter, *Tropical Audubon Bulletin*, and much information about the society.

http://www.audubon.org/chapter/fl/tropical/index.html

Archaeopteryx (Dover)

WEB WORDS

The Sweet Bird of Youth

"The thrush alone declares the immortal wealth and vigor that is in the forest. Here is a bird in whose strain the story is told. . . . Whenever a man hears it, he is young, and Nature is in her spring; whenever he hears it, it is a new world and a free country, and the gates of heaven are not shut against him."

—Henry David Thoreau, quoted by the Smithsonian Migratory Bird Center

http://www.si.edu/smbc/woth.htm

West Volusia Audubon Society

There's nothing flashy about the name, and if I offered ten dollars to everyone I met on the street who could tell me where West Volusia is (it's in Florida), I'd probably never be ten dollars poorer. However, the website of the West Volusia Audubon Society is one of the best all-purpose Audubon birding sites on the Net, clearly designed to help all kinds of people interested in birds and birding. The society is centered in DeLand, Florida (western Volusia County), and is on the east coast, north of the Kennedy Space Center. Its site provides useful information for both highly interested and casual surfers. A Guide to Volusia Birding lists the birds commonly found in the county; in many cases, short profiles of the species are provided. Birding checklists are also given for local areas and for the region. A guide to parks in the area, all good for birding, includes a clickable map to help you find where they are. Kathy Paynter, a licensed rehabilitator, provides information regarding what to do when you find a baby bird. There's much more, including an Ask an Expert e-mail link, a birding FAQ, information about outings, and lists of links. All in all, it's a well-thought-out site that's very useful to birders and people in need of bird help.

http://volusia.org/birding/wvaudubon.htm

A
B
C
D
E
F
G
H
I
J
K
L
M
N
O
P
Q
R
S
T
U
V
W
X
Y
Z

MOUNTAIN

Appleton-Whittell Research Ranch

The Appleton-Whittell Research Ranch in Arizona —a cooperative partnership among the National Audubon Society, U.S. Forest Service, Bureau of Land Management, Appleton family, and Research Ranch Foundation—is an 8,000 acre ranch-sanctuary, as well as a research and education center. Research focuses on understanding how grasslands and native wildlife function together. The sanctuary is home to such unusual species as Botteri's Sparrow, Cassin's Sparrow, Arizona Grasshopper Sparrow, Rufous-crowned Sparrow, Montezuma Quail, and Williamson's Sapsucker, all of which are discussed on the site. A complete list of birds found at the sanctuary, as well as lists of other kinds of wildlife and plants is also available. The site has a photo album of scenic vistas from the sanctuary. Public access is restricted, but information as to how to contact the ranch is provided.

http://www.audubon.org/local/sanctuary/appleton/

Central New Mexico Audubon Society

The Central New Mexico Audubon Society, headquartered in Albuquerque, New Mexico, offers information about local birding, as well as other state Audubon and birding groups. The site has a good collection of local birding links.

http://www.rt66.com/peacmyer/cnmas.htm/

Denver Audubon Society

If you're a fan of quizzes, stop by the Denver Audubon Society's website and try its Colorado Bird Quiz. Match the images with the names to see how well you know the local avifauna. The site also has interesting Backyard Birds Online columns by Hugh Kingery that focuses on news and observations about birds of Colorado. You'll also find information about *cobirds*, an e-mail list for Colorado birders and those interested in birds of the state. Information about the chapter and its activities, including birding expeditions, is also provided.

http://www.usprnet.com/denaud.html

El Paso–Trans Pecos Audubon Society

The El Paso–Trans Pecos Audubon Society calls itself "one of the largest, most influential, and most active environmental organizations in West Texas and Southern New Mexico." Its website also has a fine guide to birding locations in and around El Paso, and if you scroll down the home page, you'll find links to other useful birding sites in the region.

http://www.whc.net/cdwr/TPASHOME.HTM

Fort Collins Audubon Society

The Fort Collins Audubon Society in Fort Collins, Colorado, offers a map-based guide to what kinds of birds are found in neighboring locations. In many cases, pictures of the birds are provided and in some cases, their songs and call notes. The site has a lot of chapter news, information about its birding activities, and a good collection of birding links.

http://www.fortnet.org/Audubon/

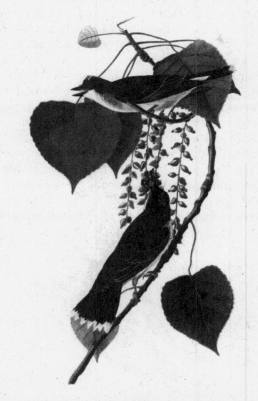

Eastern Kingbird (*Tyrannus tyrannus*) (JJA)

Golden Eagle Audubon Society

The Golden Eagle Audubon Society in Boise, Idaho, serves the southwestern part of the state. The website has a checklist of birds of the region, as well as a good collection of links to local and regional birding and outdoor information.

http://www.webpak.net/~geas/

Great Salt Lake Audubon

The website of Great Salt Lake Audubon in Salt Lake City, Utah, calls itself "Utah's online birding resource." The pleasantly designed site—rich in information about birds and birding in the state—offers a well-mapped guide to 10 top birding spots within a few hours' drive of Salt Lake City. "These sites represent the diversity of habitat northern Utah has to offer, making it a prime birding destination," the chapter says. A main map shows the general birding locations, and follow-up detailed maps (from Don McIvor's *Birding Utah*) cover each spot. Also available are descriptions of specialty birds at each location, the best times to visit, and sources for more information. The site includes a complete checklist of Utah birds— 406 species at last count—and Showcase, a special collection of stories, photos, poems, "or anything to do with birding or nature."

http://www.audubon.org/chapter/ut/gsl/

Lahontan Audubon Society

The Lahontan Audubon Society, based in Reno, Nevada, serves the northern part of the state. The website includes information about birding and nature centers, the Nevada Breeding Bird Atlas, bird alerts, and useful local links.

http://www.audubon.org/chapter/nv/lahontan/

Maricopa Audubon Society

With some 3,000 members from the Phoenix, Arizona, area, the Maricopa Audubon Society is a very active birding chapter, and its website is brimming with birding information. If you're headed for Arizona,

make sure you check out the site's Birding Guide, which has a top-notch geographical birding guide for the whole state, complete with simple, clear maps. The guide also has information about books and magazines, specialty birds, field observations, and local hot lines.

http://www.amug.org/~drowley/mas/

Northern Arizona Audubon Society

"From the Verde Valley to Flagstaff and the high country beyond, we bird the northern skies," reports the home page of the Northern Arizona Audubon Society's website. Make sure to click on the Birdy Verde icon on the home page to learn about the many birding opportunities in northern Arizona. The site reports that the Greater Pewee, Hepatic Tanager, Olive Warbler, Painted Redstart, Red-faced Warbler, and Sulphur-bellied Flycatcher all breed locally. "Common Black-Hawks are perhaps more easily and frequently seen here than any other region in North America."

http://naturesongs.com/birdyverde/NAAS.htm

Palouse Audubon Society

If you are traveling to or live in the Palouse region of north-central Idaho, the Paulouse Audubon Society website will fill you in on birding hot spots. Its online guide takes an interesting and useful approach: arranging the hot birding sites by season. Thus, you can check where to go in winter, spring, summer, or fall. And there's at least one place that's recommended all year round. The chapter is involved in several scientific studies and is always looking for volunteers.

http://www.audubon.org/chapter/id/palouse/

Sangre de Cristo Audubon Society

The Sangre de Cristo Audubon Society, based in Santa Fe, also covers Los Alamos, Española, Taos, Las Vegas, and other north central New Mexico communities. The site lists a half dozen good birding spots in the area and has links to local information.

http://www.audubon.org/chapter/nm/sdcas/

A
B
C
D
E
F
G
H
I
J
K
L
M
N
O
P
Q
R
S
T
U
V
W
X
Y
Z

Encyclopedic Knowledge

Sometimes you'd like a piece of bird-related information quickly. One of the simplest ways to find it is a good encyclopedia. Many popular encyclopedias are online and some are free of charge. Among them is the venerable Funk & Wagnalls Encyclopedia, whose free Web-based encyclopedia offers more than 25,000 articles (*first address*). We checked for the topic "heron" and Funk & Wagnalls came back with a fine 518-word essay that included an excellent photo of a Great Blue Heron, plus cross-references to related articles. Its media library includes crisp photos of more than 75 bird species. There's also a 165,000-entry dictionary and a world news searchable database.

Microsoft's Encarta, one of the best known CD-ROM encyclopedias, has an online version (*second address*). The "concise" version—on the left side of the home page—is free (a deluxe version with much longer entries and 40,000 articles costs about $50 a year or about $7 a month). The concise version had 180 words on "heron."

Encyclopaedia Britannica's online version has more than 72,000 articles and costs about $5 a month (*third address*). You can sample the encyclopedia; when we searched for heron, the result screen said there are 124 relevant articles, and we got to see the first few sentences of each.

Grolier Multimedia Encyclopedia Online (*fourth address*) is the pioneer among online encyclopedias, having started on CompuServe in the 1980s. It costs about $60 a year, plus a small registration fee, and offers 36,000 articles. Compton's Encyclopedia has 40,000 articles online and costs about $30 a year (*fifth address*).

Most fee-based encyclopedias offer free trials of a week or two.

http://www.funkandwagnalls.com

http://encarta.msn.com

http://www.eb.com

http://gme.grolier.com

http://www.comptons.com

Wood Thrush (*Hylocichla mustelina*) (JJA)

Southeastern New Mexico Audubon Society

The Southeastern New Mexico Audubon Society in Roswell is an information-packed site that includes an extensive guide to birding in the southeastern New Mexico counties of Chaves, Eddy, Lea, Lincoln, and Roosevelt. Many parks, lakes, and springs are described. There's even a guide to the average high and low temperatures for each month. The site has quite a bit of information about the Bitter Lake National Wildlife Refuge, 12 miles east of Roswell, including weekly surveys of the shorebirds, raptors, and otherwise noteworthy species seen there by refuge staff. (If you're interested in dragonflies and damselflies, the site is well endowed with information and links on that subject, too.)

http://www.rt66.com/~kjherman/4Audubon.htm

Southwest New Mexico Audubon Society

If you're interested in birding in the four counties of southwestern New Mexico, stop by the site of the Southwest New Mexico Audubon Society, based in Silver City. Using a roadrunner logo, the site covers the communities of Deming, Lordsburg, Glenwood, Cliff, and Reserve, the Mimbres Valley, and the Gila National Forest. Besides a guide to good birding spots, complete with easily printable maps, the website provides a list of chapter members who can help with directions or other information about these locations.

http://www.audubon.org/chapter/nm/swnewmexico/

Tucson Audubon Society

The home page of the Tucson Audubon Society in Arizona uses an unusual directory device: a tree full of birds that lead you to many site features. Among them are listings of programs and events, a nature shop, conservation information, links to other sites, the chapter newsletter (the *Vermilion Flycatcher*), and field trips. Look at the ground below the tree of birds for the bird that will lead you to information about Arizona Birding. This page gives sources of print information about birds and birding locales of Arizona. Also available are listings of places to stay and guides to use. Another ground bird on the home page leads to an informative Bird of the Month feature.

http://www.audubon.org/chapter/az/tucson/Index.htm

Wasatch Audubon Society

Utah is a "state with great habitat diversity," notes the Wasatch Audubon Society in Ogden, whose website offers a well-done set of profiles of the habitats and the birds you're likely to see in nearly a dozen locations around Ogden. In addition, for many locations, the site provides "trip reports"—the firsthand experiences of birders who've been to these spots fairly recently. They usually include lists of all the birds seen. The Wasatch site has many other features— don't miss Dr. Beak and the Puzzle Aerie, two of my favorite features of any Audubon site.

http://www.audubon.org/chapter/ut/wasatch/

PACIFIC

Anchorage Audubon Society

The Anchorage Audubon Society site has information about programs, meetings, newsletters, and volunteer opportunities. Menu item Birding brings up a directory of Birding Sites in Alaska, arranged by region. A nice touch is a collection of local contacts in many Alaskan towns and cities. Besides offering lists of Alaska birds, there's a guide to Useful Travel Information.

http://www.audubon.org/chapter/ak/anchorage/

FEATHERED FACTS

Flicker Picker

Some varieties of the Northern Flicker, a widespread, ground-feeding woodpecker, have been declining in recent years. Some scientists suspect it's because their nesting spots in the cavities of trees are being taken over by European Starlings. Others think it may be due to the effects of pesticides or the changing nature of maturing forests.

—adapted from Birds of North America and Cornell Laboratory of Ornithology

http://www.birdsofna.org/excerpts/flicker.html
http://birdsource2.ornith.cornell.edu/pfw/birdid/norfli/index.html

Arctic Audubon Society

Just the name can make you shiver, but as you'll discover when visiting the Arctic Audubon Society's website, a lot of interesting birds inhabit the Fairbanks, Alaska, region. Look for the link to Birding Hot Spots, which will direct you to locales that include the local dump.

http://www.ptialaska.net/~audubon/

Audubon California

Audubon California is the National Audubon Society's division in California, and its website describes its many activities and how Californians can participate. The complete list of chapters arranged by region in the state is a good place to find local Audubon information. There's also news, information about education programs, a list of sanctuaries, and a collection of useful links.

http://www.audubon-ca.org

A B C D E F G H I J K L M N O P Q R S T U V W X Y

Snowy Egret (Dover)

Audubon Canyon Ranch

Audubon Canyon Ranch in Stinson Beach, California, protects some 2,000 acres in Marin and Sonoma Counties via the Bolinas Lagoon Preserve, Cypress Grove Preserve, and the Bouverie Preserve. Established in 1962, the ranch protects one of the West Coast's largest nesting grounds for Great Blue Herons, Great Egrets, and Snowy Egrets. This illustrated site provides basic information as to when and how to visit and generally what you'll see, plus information about programs and publications.

http://www.egret.org

Audubon Society of Portland

The Let's Go Birding section of the Audubon Society of Portland's website provides a checklist of Portland, Oregon, area birds, plus a column by Harry Nehls called Field Notes that discusses birding topics and species. The column tells you what's being seen in the area and where, and gives the latest news on ornithological events and findings. An archive of past columns is available.

http://www.audubonportland.org

Black Hills Audubon Society

The Black Hills Audubon Society, based in Olympia, Washington, has a guide to the "best places for bird-watching." The well-labeled but nonclickable map shows where the sites are, and the menu next to it leads to pages that include maps, photos, birds you're apt to see, and best places to park. This site also carries recent bird sightings and has a special poetry section—a nice touch.

http://www.audubon.org/chapter/wa/bhas/

Golden Gate Audubon Society

The Golden Gate Audubon Society's website is full of readable and useful information for the San Francisco, California, area, covering San Francisco, Alameda, and Contra Costa Counties. Some material, such as information on dealing with feral cats and biographies of pioneer ornithologists, will be useful to birders anywhere in North America. You'll find conservation news alerts, reports on conservation programs such as the Save the Quail Campaign, information about classes and trips, some fascinating birding history, and articles from the *Gull*, the chapter's newsletter.

http://www.audubon.org/chapter/ca/goldengate/

Juneau Audubon Society

A big, black raven greets you on the home page of the Juneau Audubon Society. This Alaska region is known for its big birds—common ravens, eagles, and geese, for instance. The menu item Local Birding will lead you to a guide to Juneau birding that's on another site but has plenty of good information. The Audubon site also has listings for events and programs, a photo gallery, and a lot of local environmental information.

http://www.juneau.com/audubon/audubon1.htm

Kalmiopsis Audubon Society

The Kalmiopsis Audubon Society in Curry County, Oregon, has a guide to Great Birding Spots in the area (on the southwestern coast). Besides information about the Oregon Breeding Bird Atlas Project, the site also has a very extensive collection of links for children, one of the biggest we've seen.

http://www.harborside.com/cc/audubon/birds.htm

Kern River Preserve

Audubon California's Kern River Preserve protects 1,100 acres of "lush riparian forests, meadows, and wetlands" along the southern Sierra Nevada's South Fork Kern River, in Weldon, Kern County, California. According to the site, more than 330 species of birds have been sighted here. That's roughly half of California's total avifauna and includes major breeding populations of the Willow Flycatcher, Summer Tanager, and Yellow-billed Cuckoo. You learn about the birds and birding festivals associated with the preserve, its history, and much more. The site is sprinkled with some great close-ups of native birds and offers a good collection of links.

http://frontpage.lightspeed.net/KRP/

Los Angeles Audubon Society

The Los Angeles Audubon Society, one of the largest Audubon chapters in the state, has an office in West Hollywood, California, that houses a bookstore. The website includes a Los Angeles County checklist and links to birding sites covering the area, with guides to birding in the area and information regarding the Los Angeles Breeding Bird Atlas. Information is available about pelagic birds off the coast and gardening techniques that will attract birds.

http://pweb.netcom.com/~laas/index.html

Salem Audubon Society

The Salem Audubon Society has an online checklist of birds of Salem, Oregon, as well as a list of rare birds seen in the area. The site also offers a lot of information about the city of Salem.

http://www.oregonlink.com/birds/index.html

San Diego Audubon Society

The San Diego Audubon Society covers prime birding territory in southern California. A sizable library of information about the region's birds is contained in the site's San Diego County Bird Atlas, a six-year project that began in 1997 (look for the link at the bottom of the home page). This tells where to see hundreds of species of birds—and where not to see ones that have disappeared due to development and other environmental factors. A simple checklist is available, but it's not nearly as interesting as the atlas!

http://www.audubon.org/chapter/ca/sandiego/

Skagit Audubon Society

On the Skagit Audubon Society website, look for the menu items under Birding. Locations will bring up a map and capsule descriptions of a dozen good birding locations in Skagit County, Washington. Though brief, these profiles tell you what to look for at different times of the year. You'll also find checklists, bird counts, and latest sightings under Birding. The Links feature connects you to a solid collection of regional wildlife sites.

http://www.audubon.org/chapter/wa/skagit/

Veery (*Hylocichla fuscescens*) [*Catharus fuscescens*] (JJA)

FEATHERED FACTS

The Coot-Foots

The name phalarope is from the Greek for coot-foot, used as a name for this bird because of its partially webbed toes. This arrangement allows the Phalaropes to spin their bodies on water surfaces creating little whirlpools that "concentrate their aquatic prey for easy pickings."

—adapted from John Sterling, Smithsonian Migratory Bird Center

http://web2.si.edu/smbc/bom/wiph.htm

Southern California Audubon Societies

Southern California is such a hotbed of Audubon birding activity that the National Audubon Society has established a special web address to provide information about these chapters. The site covers Imperial, Kern, Los Angeles, Orange, Riverside, San Bernardino, San Diego, San Luis Obispo, Santa Barbara, and Ventura Counties. However, this is just the tip of the "icebird": Los Angeles County alone has eight different Audubon chapters, each with its own website.

http://www.audubon.org/chapter/ca/socal/

Starr Ranch Sanctuary

Starr Ranch Sanctuary, owned by National Audubon Society in Orange County, California, consists of 4,000 acres of a former cattle ranch, which adjoins another 5,000 acres owned by Orange County. The land includes "mosaics of grassland, oak woodland, riparian woodland, coastal sage scrub, and chaparral," the website notes. "All native habitat and wildlife are becoming rare in southern California and the ranch protects some especially endangered vegetation types such as coastal sage scrub and native perennial grassland, as well as species such as the Many-stemmed Dudleya (a plant) and the California Gnatcatcher (a bird)." The online checklist of birds for the ranch has nearly 150 species.

http://www.audubon.org/local/sanctuary/srs/

Vancouver Audubon Society

The Vancouver Audubon Society, which covers Clark County, Washington, has an online guide to birding the major hot spots in the area, written mostly by Wilson Cady, a local naturalist. In many cases he leads you on tours of the locations.

http://www.audubon.org/chapter/wa/vancouver/

Washington State Audubon

Anyone planning on making a birding expedition to the state of Washington—or anyone living in the state who wants to explore—should investigate the Birdwatching in Washington State link on the Washington State Audubon office's home page. The site has an encyclopedic collection of birding information, beginning with a map showing two dozen major birding spots around the state. Click on any one spot, and you'll be taken to links that describe the place, offer up-to-date sightings from the locale, and sometimes provide lists of birds found there. This site has much more, however, including a rundown of birding events in Washington; a listing (with links) of national parks, forests, and wildlife refuges in the state; a guide to state parks, public access wetlands, and other interesting places; travel information; and bird-watching tips.

http://wa.audubon.org

Whidbey Island Audubon Society

If planning a visit to Whidbey Island, off the coast of northwestern Washington, first pay a visit to the Whidbey Island Audubon Society's website for a list of 15 "great birding spots" on the island, as well as a checklist of species that have been seen there.

http://www.audubon.org/chapter/wa/whidbey/

A B C D E F G H I J K L M N O P Q R S T U V W X Y Z

AVIARIES

Not all birds are found in the wild. Some live in zoos, nature centers, raptor centers, rehabilitation centers, or educational institutions. In many cases, the captive birds have arrived as injured birds and cannot be rehabilitated enough to be returned to the wild. These are often used as demonstration birds for programs about owls and hawks, for instance. The following sites can help locate zoos and other aviaries where you and your family can view wild birds close up. *(See also North American Birds, Raptors.)*

American Zoo & Aquarium Association

As its name might suggest, the American Zoo & Aquarium Association is the ultimate authority on American zoos. The association's site has an extensive directory of its 184 member zoos, as well as aquariums, describing each, explaining which zoos care for which endangered birds, and providing a link (where available) to the zoo's website where you can get much more information. The site also describes many of the association's programs, such as the Species Survival Plan that is helping many endangered bird species around the world.

http://www.aza.org

Maryland Yellow-Throat (*Geothlypis trichas*)
[Common Yellowthroat] (JJA)

FEATHERED FACTS

Big Scales

As birds evolved from reptiles, the scales of the reptile evolved into the feathers of the bird, which the bird uses to keep warm and dry, and to help with flight.

—adapted from Environmental Education Center at Miller School, Albermarle County, Virginia

http://monticello.avenue.gen.va.us/Community/
Environ/EnvironEdCenter/Habitat/AnimalStudy/
Bird/Bird.HTML

Audubon Institute

The Audubon Institute operates the Audubon Zoo and other natural history facilities in New Orleans, Louisiana. The website introduces the zoo and explains many of its programs, including efforts to preserve endangered birds and other species. Under Attractions, you'll find information not only about the zoo but also the Louisiana Nature Center and institute's aquarium. If your browser is equipped with a Shockwave plug-in (user-friendly software that produces highly graphical, animated pages), you can tour the zoo's Interactive Swamp.

http://www.auduboninstitute.org

Busch Gardens

Busch Gardens in Tampa, Florida, one of the nation's most visited theme parks, has a sizable raptor viewing area and "bird gardens." To learn about either attraction on their website, select Attractions on the home page, and then look on the menu list for Birds of Prey or Bird Gardens. The information is minimal, but there's plenty on the site to entice you to visit Busch Gardens.

http://www.buschgardens.com

Tufted Titmouse (*Baeolophus bicolor*) [*Parus bicolor*] (JJA)

Center for Birds of Prey Aviary

Florida Audubon's Center for Birds of Prey, a leading raptor rehabilitation facility in the Southeast, has treated more than 7,000 eagles, hawks, owls, falcons, kites, and vultures since opening in 1979. "Release rate averages 39 percent of all admissions, and has totaled more than 3,000 birds of prey, including 198 Bald Eagles," according to the site. Besides the wildlife rehabilitation facilities, the center includes a lakeside exhibit aviary, which houses 20 species of nonreleasable raptors—birds that were so injured they could no longer survive in the wild. "The aviary is a favored destination of school and civic organization tours, and includes a visit to the Audubon Birding Store, a resource for novice and expert birders," the site says. The Audubon Center facilities are open to the public Tuesdays through Sundays—the site gives details, including hours, prices, and a map of its location. Also, you can learn about Audubon Eaglewatch, "a vast statewide volunteer effort to monitor bald eagle nests in Florida. With one of the nation's largest Bald Eagle populations, Florida is an important part of the recovery plan for America's national symbol." Links are available to many pages of information about Florida Audubon's activities.

http://www.audubon.usf.edu/birds.htm

Electronic Zoo

The Electronic Zoo, according to the website, was created through "the vivid imagination and late night web-surfing of Dr. Ken Boschert," a veterinarian at Washington University's Division of Comparative Medicine, in St. Louis, Missouri. The site, hosted by the university, is a large database of links to websites dealing with all sorts of creatures, including a long page of bird links. On the Electronic Zoo home page, click the image of the flying bird (or any other creature you'd like links for). The bird collection is arranged by Poultry, Pet Birds, Other Birds, and Commercial Birds. Other Birds contains many wild bird links.

http://netvet.wustl.edu/e-zoo.htm

National Zoo

The National Zoological Park in Washington, D.C., is the premier zoo in the United States, and its online presence is nothing short of grand. The National Zoo site is among the best sites on the Net for making use of much of the magic of the Web. For instance, of the thousands of websites we've visited, the National Zoo's Audio Wand Tour has the most interesting and effective use of sound. Here, the narrator tells about each of 41 different sections of the zoo as you view photos of each. It's the same kind of information you'd get if you were at the zoo. And, in a sense, you can be. The National Zoo site offers live camera views during daylight hours. The site also offers a huge library of animal photos, lets you check on the latest zoo births, and provides a clickable map for online exploration of the zoo. The Bird House, one of the site's newest exhibits, keeps you up to date on what's happening in the avian section of the zoo. You can learn about recent acquisitions, births, and the zoo's participation in the Species Survival Program (*see also American Zoo & Aquarium Association earlier in this section*). The Birds of the National Zoo section profiles some of the celebrities at the zoo, including the Double-wattled Cassowary and the Red-legged Seriema. Descriptions of the bird houses and a fine collection of FAQs about birds are also available.

http://www.si.edu/natzoo/

Northwest Waterfowl

Paul Dye began breeding waterfowl when he was 12 years old. Now retired after 32 years with Boeing, he joins his wife, Lynn, in operating the Northwest Waterfowl Farm in Everett, Washington. The farm and adjoining sanctuary consist of 22 ponds, eight acres of grainfields, about four miles of trails, a salmon stream, and five acres of aviaries. Since 1971 the collection of birds has grown from five to more than 50 species. The website offers extensive information about how to get started in *aviculture* and create your own waterfowl aviary. The site also has information about aviculture organizations and a fine collection of related links.

http://www.greatnorthern.net/~dye/

San Diego Zoo

The Zoological Society of San Diego, California, operates two of the most famous zoos in North America, the San Diego Zoo and the Wild Animal Park. Information about both is accessible from the home page. The zoo has the largest collection of birds, mammals, and reptiles in North America, numbering 4,239 specimens, representing 816 species and subspecies. The site invites you to take a look at some of the zoo's more interesting species. You can also learn about breeding programs at both the zoo and the park. And if you want to have some fun, the site lets you send postcards from a wide variety of pictures of zoo creatures.

http://www.sandiegozoo.org

Pigeon (Dover)

AVIAN ADVICE

Keep It Clean

Feeding birds carries with it some responsibilities. One is to keep your feeders clean. Otherwise, you could be spreading diseases among birds that congregate at your feeding stations. The standard protocol is to wash feeders every two weeks with a solution of a half cup of bleach in a gallon of water.

—adapted from John Kelly, Travis Audubon Society

http://www.onr.com/user/audubon/Backyard/fedhygei.htm

http://www.onr.com/user/audubon/Backyard/fedclean.htm

Top Zoos

Family Fun magazine rated the top 10 zoos and aquariums in the United States, and America's Best Online has the list, along with links to each facility's website.

http://americasbestonline.com/zoo.htm

World Center for Birds of Prey

The World Center for Birds of Prey in Boise, Idaho, established in 1984 and a project of the Peregrine Fund (*see also Conservation*), houses more than 200 birds of prey whose young are released to the wild in the United States and around the world. The center has falcons, eagles, condors, hawks, and other raptors that can be viewed by visitors. There are interactive displays, multimedia shows, and art exhibits, a gift shop, as well as a continuous guided tour.

http://www.peregrinefund.org/WCVMIntr.html

A
B
C
D
E
F
G
H
I
J
K
L
M
N
O
P
Q
R
S
T
U
V
W
X
Y
Z

A
B
C
D
E
F
G
H
I
J
K
L
M
N
O
P
Q
R
S
T
U
V
W
X
Y
Z

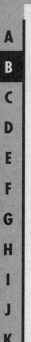

Purple finch (*Carpodacus Purpureus*) (JJA)

Zoos Unlimited

How can you find zoos in your area? Or zoos in places you plan to visit? Anywhere in the world? Stop by Zoos.com, which has an alphabetical list of zoos in many nations. Most of the zoos—more than a hundred of them—are in North America. Zoos.com also has a huge collection of wildlife links, links to animal sounds, and scores of sources of wildlife photos. An index lists animal Usenet newsgroups, to which you can jump directly from the site.

http://www.zoos.com

BOOKS

Countless books have been written about birds and birding, and many of the newer ones are represented online by websites that describe their contents, often offer sample pages and pictures, and enable you to purchase directly from the publisher. Categories include field guides, natural histories of single species or whole genera, suggestions as to where to go birding, and books on birding in general. In recent years the library of avian knowledge has expanded

to include new media such as videos, audio tapes, and compact disks that run on computers. Information and previews of many of these alternative media are also on the World Wide Web. (*See also Checklists, Magazines & Periodicals, Software, and Videos.*)

ABA Birdfinding Guides

The American Birding Association publishes a dozen regional guides to some of the best places to go bird-watching. Written by local authors and field checked by local experts, the books cover Manitoba (Churchill area), Southeast Arizona, Arkansas, Southern California, Colorado, Florida, Idaho, Eastern Massachusetts, New Hampshire, the Texas Coast, the Rio Grande Valley of Texas, Virginia, Wyoming, and the Bahamas. They include pictures, maps, and even graphs. The ABA website offers detailed descriptions of each book, and is set up for online ordering.

http://www.americanbirding.org/bfggen.htm

About Birds: A Guide for Children

Cathryn Sill, a teacher and a birder, explains to children what birds are, what they do, and how they live in this 40-page, full-color book produced by Peachtree Publishers Ltd., in Atlanta, Georgia. The beautiful illustrations are by noted wildlife illustrator John Sill, Cathryn's husband. The Sills and John's brother collaborated on three humorous bird books (*see also Sill Parodies later in this section*).

http://www.peachtree-online.com/Adults/Catalog/ aboutbirds.htm

Academic Press

Anyone seriously interested in birds will want to keep an eye on the scholarly publications of the Academic Press. Among the titles available are *Birds of the Wetlands*, *The Raptors of Europe and the Middle East*, *Birds of the Thai-Malay Peninsula*, and *Guide to the Identification and Natural History of Sparrows*. Using the site's Search function, enter BIRDS as the search word to see what's available.

http://www.academicpress.com

Attenborough on Birds

Princeton University Press is a leading publisher of books about birds. Among its titles are David Attenborough's well-known *The Life of Birds*, but Princeton has dozens of other titles, including guides and field guides to species of many parts of the world, such as Europe, Russia, Australia, India, Colombia, Kenya, New Guinea, and the West Indies. There's Nigel Wheatley's series of guides, *Where to Watch Birds*, with editions covering Africa, Asia, Australasia, and South America. Other books deal with specific genera or families of birds. PUP's website offers good descriptions of each title, plus reviews. To see a list of what's available, use the Search page and under Title, enter the word BIRDS.

http://www.pup.princeton.edu/

Audubon Online Bookstore

The National Audubon Society has an online bookstore that provides Audubon's recommendations for good nature books. The listings include books that have been featured in *Audubon* magazine, the Top 10 Nature Books for the current two months, a Kids' Corner, the society's Essential Nature Library of both field guides and multimedia guides, and Audubon calendars. You can also find a complete list of Audubon's own books. A portion of the sales goes to National Audubon Society efforts "to conserve and restore natural ecosystems."

http://www.audubon.org/bookstore

Birdfinder

Subtitled "A Birder's Guide to Planning North American Trips," *Birdfinder* is a guide to finding rare birds. Author Jerry Cooper outlines 19 birding trips and an additional Baker's Dozen of special destinations, several for each season. You can take the whole trip or select places to go within the described journeys. Along with information about what you can see and when, the book has lists of local birding guides available when you reach your destinations. The book, published by the American Birding Association in a handy wire binding, can be ordered through the ABA website.

http://www.americanbirding.org/bfgtrip.htm

Birds of North America

If you ever get seriously into birding and you have a few dollars after paying your bills each month, consider investing in *Birds of North America*, an immense undertaking that aims to publish definitive life histories of our native species in 18 volumes. To learn why these books are so special, visit the site where excerpts are posted.

http://www.birdsofna.org

Birds of the World

Dr. Charles G. Sibley's Birds of the World is one of the most ambitious and comprehensive electronic books you can find about the world of birds. If printed, Birds of the World would take up some 900 pages. As it is, the electronic book provides information and, often, pictures of more than 9,900 species, including habitats, natural history, ranges, and much more. This site provides samples of what the book is like, reviews, and information about how it can be used with Thayer Software's Birder's Diary (*see also Software*). Sibley has been one of the world's foremost experts on birds. He was professor of zoology and curator of birds at Cornell University and later at Yale University, where he was also a director of the Peabody Museum. The database comes on two 3.5-inch disks for installation on your computer's hard drive.

http://www.birding.com/sibbow.htm

Books on Birds of Prey

The Natural History Book Club in the United Kingdom has an extensive list of books about birds of prey. When we checked, more than 240 titles (a few out of print) came up, with links to basic information about each. Although you may not want to order books that must be shipped from England, the NHBC list represents a comprehensive bibliography of what's available on the subject with which you can track down a source closer to home.

http://www.nhbs.co.uk/scripts/
  sbjsrch?search=1-14-22-24.

A
B
C
D
E
F
G
H
I
J
K
L
M
N
O
P
Q
R
S
T
U
V
W
X
Y
Z

Common Birds & Their Songs

Lang Elliott and Marie Reid are the authors of *Common Birds and Their Songs*, published by Houghton Mifflin, and Elliott's website called NatureSound Studio tells you all about it. Since it's difficult to describe bird songs with words (the book does do it), *Common Birds and Their Songs* is accompanied by a CD of songs and calls recorded by Elliott. That's great, but so are the photographs by both Reid and Elliott. The site also describes other products available through Elliott's NatureSound Studio.

http://www.naturesound.com

Florida Birding Books

Florida is one of the birding centers of North America, and it's not surprising that the center of that center—the Everglades National Park—might be a good source of information about Florida birds. The park has an online wildlife bookshelf that offers about 18 publications about the Everglades, Florida, and eastern birds (plus many more titles on other kinds of creatures). Select Wildlife from the menu on the home page. Purchases help support the park.

http://www.nps.gov/ever/fnpma.htm

Handbook of the Birds of the World

"Handbook" might be misleading. This is not something you can hold in your hand, unless you're Hercules. Five volumes are in print so far, with seven more to come. So many volumes are needed simply because this is the first comprehensive work that describes and illustrates all of the more than 9,600 known species of birds in the world. *The Handbook of the Birds of the World* provides all the essential natural history, range, and identification information about each species. "The first volume was greeted with great enthusiasm by the ornithological world and received excellent reviews in almost all of the world's specialized journals," says the website of Linx Edicions in Barcelona, Spain, the publisher. "The prestige gained permitted the incorporation of renowned experts from all over the world as authors." The complete set will cover the 176 families of birds in the following volumes: 1, Ostrich to Ducks; 2, New World Vultures to Guineafowl; 3, Hoatzin to Auks; 4, Sandgrouse to Cuckoos; 5, Barn Owls to Hummingbirds; 6, Mousebirds to Woodpeckers; 7, Broadbills to Pittas; 8, New Zealand Wrens to Accentors; 9, Thrushes to Old World Warblers; 10, Old World Flycatchers to White-eyes; 11, Honeyeaters to New World Blackbirds; and 12, Finches to Crows. The aim is to produce one volume every 18 months; the first volume appeared in October 1992. The website provides a guided tour of sample pages from these clearly written and beautifully presented books. Anyone who loves birds would undoubtedly want these volumes. The publisher has a North American office in Rockville Center, New York, and can provide more information about the books, including installment plans for purchasing them—they are not inexpensive.

http://www.hbw.com

How Birds Fly

David Goodnow is a naturalist, licensed bird-bander, and wildlife photographer from Connecticut. His photos have appeared in *National Geographic*, *Outdoor Life*, *Field & Stream*, *Sports Illustrated*, Time-Life Books, and other leading publications. *How Birds Fly*, published by Periwinkle Books, explains bird flight using his spectacular photographs. Samples of pictures from the book are online; many shots are of birds the author raised himself.

http://www.us.net/birds/welcome.html

Kea, Bird of Paradox

Some consider the Kea, a New Zealand parrot, to be a playful comic. Others consider it a vicious killer. Judy Diamond and Alan B. Bond have spent years studying this odd bird and have written *Kea, Bird of Paradox: The Evolution and Behavior of a New Zealand Parrot*. "This fascinating new book offers a comprehensive account of the Kea's contradictory nature, casting new light on the origins of behavioral flexibility and the problem of species survival in human environments everywhere," says an advertisement for the book. You can read more about the book and order directly from the publisher, the University of California Press, at this page.

http://www.ucpress.edu/books/pages/8149.html

Kingbird Highway

In the 1970s, when he was 16 years old and student council president at his local high school, Kenn Kaufman quit school and hit the road—not to find himself, romance, or Jack Keruoac, but to see birds. His goal was to spot the most North American species able to be seen in one year. "But along the way he began to realize that at this breakneck pace, he was only looking, not seeing," says Houghton Mifflin, publisher of *Kingbird Highway*. "What had been a game became a quest for a deeper understanding of the natural world." *Kingbird Highway*, subtitled *The Story of a Natural Obsession That Got a Little Out of Hand*, is Kaufman's autobiographical tale of coming of age. Today, he is one of the leading writers about birds (cited several times in this guide), and this book may interest anyone who loves birds, nature, and adventure. Many excerpts, in chapter order, can be read online to tempt you into buying the book.

http://www.petersononline.com/birds/kingbird/

Natural History Book Service

The British are noted for their great interest in natural history, and England is home to one of the world's largest purveyors of natural history books, the Natural History Book Service. NHBS reports it has more than 50,000 natural history titles available. The publisher's site will bring up more than 1,000 titles related to birds, arranged by topics and geographical areas.

http://www.nhbs.co.uk/booknet/su14.html

Natural History of the Waterfowl

Frank S. Todd's *Natural History of the Waterfowl* details more than 160 members of the ducks, geese, swans, and screamers of the world. The 500-page book covers in 18 chapters and over 750 photos every aspect of waterfowl biology, including habitat, distribution, plumage, migration, feeding, courtship, predators, and mortality. The site offers sample chapters and examples of the magnificent pictures. Todd has also written the *Handbook of Waterfowl Identification*, a field guide to 160 species of the world. Both, produced by Ibis Publishing Company, are well described on Ibis's website.

http://www.virtualbirder.com/ibis/

New World Blackbirds

Alvaro Jaramillo, a California naturalist, and Peter Burke, a wildlife artist, have written *New World Blackbirds*, one of the Helm series of guides. The site gives a preview of the 432-page book, plus offers birding natural history and photos from Jaramillo who is also a birding tour guide.

http://www.sirius.com/~alvaro/

Create Your Own Birding Database

Birders love to keep lists of their birds. They may maintain life lists, backyard lists, town lists, or even "seen from the car while driving to work" lists. Many programs described in the section on software can provide sophisticated databases of information about what you saw. But if you are a do-it-yourselfer, or believe in simplicity, you may want to create your own database.

- The easiest is a simple list, created in your favorite word processor. Since even the simplest word processors or editors have a "search" function, it's relatively easy and quick to look up a bird, even in a long list.

- Many computers come equipped with software packages. They may include a spreadsheet program like Excel or the spreadsheets in Microsoft Works or Claris Works. If you are familiar with the workings of spreadsheets, these can be used to create databases with many fields (cells) of information. If you don't have a spreadsheet program, download As-Easy-As, a neat spreadsheet that's shareware (*see page 40*).

- Some computers even come with database programs that allow you to construct a highly customized record-keeping system. However, databases can also be found among the shareware offerings.

A
B
C
D
E
F
G
H
I
J
K
L
M
N
O
P
Q
R
S
T
U
V
W
X
Y
Z

Sill Parodies

In collaboration with her artist husband John and her brother-in-law, Ben Sill, teacher and birder Cathryn Sill has written a series of light-hearted books that will be enjoyed by anyone who loves birds and birding and has a bit of a mischievous sense of humor. In the spirit of their work, one is tempted to call their series "Sill-y Parodies." *A Field Guide to Little-Known and Seldom-Seen Birds of North America* is a parody of field guides (*first address*). Its sequel is *Another Field Guide to Little-Known and Seldom-Seen Birds of North America* (*second address*). Both are entertaining looks at such species as the Dowry Duck (*Bridal seductorii*) and the Grey-green Lichen Mimic (*Petriflorus imitatus*). If that isn't enough, the three Sills take on birding magazines in a parody called Beyond Bird Watching (*third address*). All three books are published by Peachtree Publishers Ltd. in Atlanta, Georgia.

http://www.peachtree-online.com/Adults/Catalog/ fieldguide1.htm

http://www.peachtree-online.com/Adults/Catalog/ anotherguide.htm

http://www.peachtree-online.com/Adults/Catalog/ beyondbirdwatching.htm

Eastern Phoebe (*Sayornis phoebe*) (JJA)

Smithsonian Suggested Publications on Birds

The Smithsonian Institution's National Museum of Natural History gets many requests for information about birds. This page provides a sampling of bird book literature, including field guides, encyclopedias, species accounts, checklists, monographs, texts on biology and behavior, and references on birds threatened with extinction. A list of Bird Clubs is also available. This site is an electronic bibliography, not a collection of links, so if a book arouses your interest, you will have to use a book dealer—new or used— or a local library to track down the volume.

http://web2.si.edu/resource/faq/nmnh/birds.htm

Songbirds: Celebrating Nature's Voices

Dr. Ronald Orenstein is a wildlife conservationist who lives in Canada and has written a half dozen books about the world around us. One is *Songbirds: Celebrating Nature's Voices*, published in Canada by Key Porter Books and in the United States by Sierra Club Books. *Songbirds* includes more than 100 photos and paintings illustrating our largest order of birds, along with Orenstein's observations about them. You can learn more about the book—and Orenstein— at either of these addresses.

http://members.home.net/ornstn/bookpage.html

http://members.home.net/ornstn/videobirding.html

Stokes Guides

Don and Lillian Stokes are probably the most popular birding writers today. Authors of more than a dozen nature guides—most of them dealing with birds and birding—they have a wide following and have even starred in a PBS (Public Broadcasting System) series, *Bird Watch with Don and Lillian Stokes*. This website describes all of the Stokes books.

http://www.stokesbooks.com

Storey Books

Great-sounding name, but tall tales aren't exactly the fare at Storey Books. This Pownal, Vermont, publisher specializes in "how-to books for country living" and produces some of the nicest volumes on birding you'll find. In the recently reorganized and revamped website, you'll find such interesting titles as *The Backyard Birdhouse Book, The Backyard Bird-Lovers Guide, Everything You Never Learned about Birds, Birdhouses: 20 Unique Woodworking Projects for Houses and Feeders*, and *Birdfeeders, Shelters and Baths: Over 25 Complete Step-by-Step Projects for the Weekend Woodworker*. Another intriguing title is *Gifts for Bird Lovers*. All the Storey books I've seen—and I own a half dozen—use handsome color pictures or drawings to illustrate species or projects; they are volumes that are beautifully designed, as well as nicely written and—best of all—useful.

http://www.storeybooks.com

University of Texas Press

Texas has more kinds of birds dwelling in and visiting within its borders than any other state. So it's not surprising that the University of Texas Press might turn out a few books on the subject. In fact, when we stopped by, the University of Texas Press had more than a dozen volumes on birding and ornithology, including such titles as *The American Robin, The Wood Warblers: An Introductory Guide, The Birds of the Trans-Pecos, The Ruby-throated Hummingbird*, and *Chasing Warblers*. What's more, many of the birds they cover extend far beyond Texas and will be of interest to birders throughout North America. The site has a search engine on its home page (*first address*), but you can also go directly to the list of books on birds and ornithology (*second address*). Each title is fully de-scribed online.

http://www.utexas.edu/utpress/
http://www.utexas.edu/utpress/subjects/bird.html

Free E-mail Wherever You Go

Many birders head off on bird-watching journeys around the country—or around the world—but like to remain in touch. If you're traveling and don't have access to your own computer or your own Internet access provider, but you do have access to someone else's computer or account, you can still check your e-mail. Many websites now offer free e-mail addresses. You can use one of these as your chief address or as an address to which your mail is forwarded from your normal address. Because you reach it through a website, not directly from your access provider, you can check your mail anywhere there's an online computer—a friend's house, a cyber café, or a public library, for instance. Each member of your family can have a separate address, too. Some systems allow you to retrieve mail from your regular e-mail service, too.

Why are these services free? Because the providers sell advertising space on their sites, and you are exposed to some ads when you log on. But that's just like a newspaper or magazine—only this is free. (Some sites also offer free website space and the facilities to create a site.)

Here are some of the free services.

AmExMail	http://www.amexmail.com
Hotmail	http://www.hotmail.com
Mailandnews.com	
	http://www.mailandnews.com
MailExcite	http://www.mailexcite.com
Net@ddress	http://www.netaddress.com
RocketMail	http://www.rocketmail.com
Switchboard	http://www.switchboard.com

For the latest list of free services, check
http://www.emailaddresses.com

For e-mail that is free, but not Web-based (you need special software), there is Juno.
http://www.juno.com

A
B
C
D
E
F
G
H
I
J
K
L
M
N
O
P
Q
R
S
T
U
V
W
X
Y
Z

Used Books

Ninety-nine percent of the books in the world are out of print, including thousands of volumes about birds or birding. However, many old titles can be found on the several online used-book "malls." Search with keywords and discover titles you didn't know existed. I typed WARBLERS in the Title field of Bibliofind (*first address*) and got a list of more than 100 books for sale with that word in the title (some, of course, were not birding related, but most were). You can search by author, keyword, and book type. Or just browse. Bibliofind recently reported that it had more than nine million books online from thousands of booksellers. On Alibris (*second address*), WARBLERS produced more than 40 volumes for sale. Alibris has better descriptions of books than Bibliofind, but neither site will give you much content detail. (However, on Bibliofind, you can e-mail the dealer directly to ask about a book.) Alibris says it has thousands of dealers and millions of books online. It even lists how many books were added in the past week (178,000 one time we visited). Bookfinder.com (*third address*) is a search engine that scans many bookseller database sites to find used, rare, out-of-print, and even new books. The search allows such limiting factors as the type of binding, the price range, and whether it's a first edition or a signed copy. The search for WARBLERS brought back more than 100 books, most of them available from used book dealers.

http://bibliofind.com

http://www.alibris.com

http://www.bookfinder.com

Moving?

Do you have a birding website that's changing its address? If so, please let us know at <http://www.acorn-online.com/hedge/birdup.htm>. We'll post it and print it in future editions of this guide.

Brown Thrasher (*Toxostoma rufum*) (JJA)

Wild Bird Guides

Stackpole Books in Mechanicsburg, Pennsylvania, has undertaken a worthy project: a series of books profiling popular North American species. The lavishly illustrated paperbacks already includes the Northern Cardinal, Tufted Titmouse, Black-capped Chickadee, American Goldfinch, Ruby-throated Hummingbird, and Downy Woodpecker. Written by experts in both ornithology and the subject species, the books run from 96 to 128 pages and have up to 165 color photos. Some text excerpts and photos are available at Stackpole's website.

http://www.stackpolebooks.com

Willow Creek Press

Willow Creek Press publishes a half dozen bird and birding-related books including *Backyard Bird Watching for Kids, Birds Do It, Too, Build a Better Birdhouse (or Feeder), Garden Birds of America, The Backyard Bird Watcher, Birds of the Backyard: Winter into Spring*, and *Spring and Summer Songbirds*. Many are described online; look under the menu items for nature, or use the search engine with the keyword, BIRDS.

http://www.willowcreekpress.com/

CHECKLISTS

Birders tend to like lists. In fact, birders who are enthusiastic keepers of lists of all the species they've seen during their lives are sometimes called *listers*. Whereas keeping a record of your sightings can be fun, it can also be valuable as a resource, especially if you maintain lists by geographical areas and/or seasons, and include information about environments. You can even put your list on the Web to share your findings with others (*see Net Notes on page 206 for how to create a website and page 158 for tips on what to put on it*). To find out more about lists, check out Diane Porter's essay, What Good Is a Life List? (*see also Tips & Techniques*). Not surprisingly, the Web is loaded with checklists that you can use to determine what species might be found in your region. Checklists are also valuable if you are traveling to unknown territory and want to know what to expect. Most checklists are compiled by state or province, but some are also local, regional, national, or continental. Some are by type of bird or by season. The better ones list not only the species but also the season or seasons in which the birds can be seen, and whether they are common, uncommon, occasional, or rare. The following entries describe list websites related to some of the hottest birding locales. If you can't find your state listed in this section, go to the Bird Checklists of the U.S. site, sponsored by the Northern Prairie Wildlife Research Center. It has the most comprehensive collection of state lists—and links to more lists—found online. The sites that follow are arranged geographically, beginning with those that cover North America, then the four major regions of the United States (Central, Eastern, and Mountain and Pacific), and finally, international sites. (*See also Audubon Societies & Sanctuaries.*)

GENERAL

Bird Checklists of the United States

If you want to know what birds might be living in your area, the Northern Prairie Wildlife Research Center of the U.S. Geological Survey has links to state-by-state checklists of birds—and you don't have to live on the northern prairies to have your state included. The directory opens with a clickable map, with a list of states below it, and an explanation of how the lists were compiled. The center notes that bird checklists are ever-changing but revisions are relatively easy to make on the Web (you don't have to send your updates to the printer every six months). What's more you can sign up to be notified whenever changes in your favorite checklists are posted. A form is available for reporting rare bird sightings. The name of the person who maintains the list is at the top of each checklist. Usually an e-mail link is also posted in case you want to ask a question or submit a new find. This is without a doubt the best collection of state checklists on the Web. Sorry the address is so long!

http://www.npwrc.usgs.gov/resource/othrdata/
   chekbird/chekbird.htm

BirdLinks

Willem-Pier Vellinga in the Netherlands and Jack Siler at the University of Pennsylvania jointly maintain BirdLinks, a huge collection of links to bird-related sites around the world. The biggest collection is for North America. Sites are arranged by topic and by location—including states and provinces. There are also collections of links to specific birds and families of birds, to birding books, software, travel and trip reports, and institutions.

http://www-stat.wharton.upenn.edu/~siler/
   birdlinks.html

Bobolink (*Dolichonyx oryzivorus*) (JJA)

A
B
C
D
E
F
G
H
I
J
K
L
M
N
O
P
Q
R
S
T
U
V
W
X
Y
Z

NET NOTES

Freeware & Shareware

One of the great adventures—and treats—of the Internet is the easy access to freeware and shareware, software you can transfer or download to your computer at no charge. Many programs can aid the birder, and some are written just for bird-watchers.

Freeware is software that's absolutely free of charge. Some are stripped-down versions of more powerful software, but they still work fine. Some are fully functional programs that are provided by companies as commercials for their products or as goodwill for their brand names. Still others are simply gifts; their authors had fun creating the programs and aren't interested in cashing in on them. Shareware is software that the author shares with you and others in the hope that you will like it well enough to pay him or her for it and become a "registered user." The best shareware is fully functional with all or virtually all of the features that a registered user gets. However, such programs usually have some sort of pop-up message that "nags" the user, reminding the user that this is shareware and should be paid for.

Why register? Because it supports programs and their authors, allowing them to work on improvements (often provided free to registered users). The shareware system works only if people support it. And usually, the price of registration is a fraction of what commercial, shrink-wrapped software costs; some shareware programs sell for only $5 although the average is between $25 and $50.

Shareware and freeware obtained from reliable sources is as safe as off-the-shelf software. The website managers carefully scan the software they carry to make sure it's free of viruses. Reliable sites include

Dave Central   http://www.davecentral.com
Download.com   http://www.download.com
Five Star Shareware
     http://www.5star-shareware.com
NoNags.com   http://www.nonags.com
Shareware.com   http://www.shareware.com
Winfiles.com   http://www.winfiles.com
ZD Net   http://www.hotfiles.com

Birds in All States

Here's an interesting concept: what birds can be found in all 49 continental North American states, as well as across Canada? Believe it or not, at least 122 species have been spotted in every state (except Hawaii). You'll find the list here.

http://www2.fwi.com/~moellering/aba-wide_list.html

Breeding Bird Species Map

This seemingly simple page, consisting of a map of North America, is a fantastic and powerful resource. If you click on any spot, you get a list of the birds that breed in that region and how abundant they are. What's more, each bird is linked to other pages that give its life history, identification tips, distribution maps, a photo, and usually a sound clip of its song. The U.S. Geological Survey's Patuxent Wildlife Research Center developed the clever system.

http://www.mbr.nbs.gov/geotech/bbsmaps3.html

Checklists in Print

The American Birding Association publishes regional checklists of birds so you can tell what you might see and keep track of what you have seen. The North American ones, covering the U.S. and Canada, can be purchased individually; the complete set of 10 is about $5.

http://www.americanbirding.org/bfgchkl.htm

Names of North American Birds

The National Audubon Society's official list of North American birds includes 1,975 species occurring in North America, Mexico, and Hawaii, with both English and Latin names. The page also gives grammatical tips on how to write bird names.

http://www.audubon.org/bird/na-bird.html

North American Checklists

By 1998, some 914 species of birds had been recorded in North America north of Mexico. If you'd like the challenge of chasing down all 914 of them, you can easily find lists of their names on the Web. Finding the birds will be a bit harder. The American Ornithologists Union offers a hyperlinked list of all known North American birds (*first address*). The Baltimore Bird Club provides an up-to-date list of species north of Mexico in a single page (*second address*). On the other hand, if you want to know in what states or provinces a certain bird may be found in breeding season, check out the North American breeding maps (*third address*). Bird-watching.com has checklists of the birds found in North America north of Mexico and the 2,009 species found in North and Central America plus Hawaii (the list includes the Caribbean, except for Trinidad and Tobago) (*fourth address*). The Warp Zone site in Finland gives the scientific and common names of hundreds of birds around the world (*fifth address*).

http://pica.wru.umt.edu/AOU/birdlist.HTML

http://www.bcpl.lib.md.us/~tross/nabirds.html

http://www.npwrc.usgs.gov/resource/distr/birds/
   breedrng/breedrng.htm

http://www.birdwatching.com/software.html

http://www.funet.fi/pub/sci/bio/life/warp/
   birds-index-a.html

Printed Checklists

Although this chapter proves that you can find many checklists on the World Wide Web, many bird-watchers like to have nicely printed lists. The American Birding Association publishes printed versions of 10 regional checklists of birds. The North American ones, covering the U.S. and Canada, are inexpensive; the complete set of 10 is about $5. The lists and the states and provinces they cover are: *Atlantic Canada:* Quebec, Newfoundland, Nova Scotia, Prince Edward Island, New Brunswick, and St. Pierre et Miquelon; *Central Canada:* Ontario, Manitoba, Saskatchewan, Alberta, and the Northwest Territories; *Western Canada and Alaska:* British Columbia, the Yukon Territory, and Alaska; *Pacific Coast:* Washington, Oregon, and California; *Rocky Mountain and Great Basin States:* Idaho, Montana, Colorado, Wyoming, Nevada, and Utah; *Southwestern United States:* Arizona and New Mexico; *South-central*

United States: Texas, Oklahoma, Louisiana, Arkansas, and Kansas; *Southeastern United States:* Virginia, North Carolina, South Carolina, Georgia, Florida, Alabama, Mississippi, Tennessee, and Kentucky; *Northeastern United States:* Maine, New Hampshire, Vermont, Massachusetts, Rhode Island, Connecticut, Delaware, New York, Pennsylvania, New Jersey, District of Columbia, Maryland, and West Virginia; *North-central United States:* North Dakota, South Dakota, Nebraska, Minnesota, Iowa, Missouri, Wisconsin, Illinois, Michigan, Indiana, and Ohio. The ABA also has checklists for some foreign countries and regions, such as the Caribbean. All can be ordered online.

http://www.americanbirding.org/bfgchkl.htm

Been Framed?

Some websites use a system called *frames*, which enables you to stay on their site while exploring other sites. About.com is one example. The framed site may have links set up within a frame so that, when you click on one and go to a new site, you are doing it through the first site, and you're still connected to the first site. Usually, you will see at least a little of the first site in the form of a frame around the new site's pages.

For some, this can get confusing or even annoying, especially if you move on to other links from the new site. Sometimes a home page on the new site will provide a clickable link that that lets you "break out" of the referring site's frame.

If not, you could try determining the address of the new site you want to explore and putting that directly into the address field of your browser. Some Webmasters put their home page addresses on the home page. In Internet Explorer, right-clicking on any page brings up a menu that includes "Properties," under which you can find the exact page address. You can copy and paste this address into your browser address field.

Or you can just ignore the fact that you've been framed, and continue onward. Often it's handy, especially if you want to return quickly to the original site to check other links there.

A B C D E F G H I J K L M N O P Q R S T U V W X Y Z

A B C D E F G H I J K L M N O P Q R S T U V W X Y Z

MEET THE MASTERS

Hard at Work

Christine Tarski, the guide for About.com's birding site <http://birding.about.com>, puts a lot of effort into her site. "Currently, I have over 5,000 links in over 50 categories, plus I am constantly adding links to the best birding information I have been able to find on the Internet," she says. "I will be greatly expanding the 'Birding Sites—U.S.' section. I've got detailed links to 100 foreign countries plus all the Canadian provinces. I've just started the U.S. states and hope to complete them this year." She also plans to further develop the kids' section, offering "many more original articles and lots of fun links, getting children interested in birds." Christine also writes—and gets writers for—special features on the Birding home page. "I have new feature articles every two weeks," she says.

State & Provincial Birds

What's your state bird? If you don't know, here's the place to not only find out but also view John James Audubon prints and text—and often songs—for each (*first address*). Not all state birds were covered by Audubon—the state birds of Hawaii, Arizona, and New Mexico were not known to him when his original works were published. South Dakota, Delaware, and Rhode Island have state birds that are not wild birds native to North America. However, the database provides non-Audubon pictures and calls for each of these six states. GeoBop (*second address*) has a nice rundown of what each of the state and provincial birds are, plus interesting essays and usually photos about each. (Although not all of the birds on this index have links attached to their names, if you click the state link, it leads to a page where you'll find a Bird link full of information.)

http://employeeweb.myxa.com/rrb/Audubon/
VolStateBirds/index.html
http://www.geobop.com/Symbols/Animals/Birds

CENTRAL

Backyard Birding in Indiana

This site is devoted to the birds of Indiana, especially those who visit the backyard, and includes many photos and sound clips. The site also has free, downloadable Windows "theme" setups using various birds and bird sounds.

http://www.slivoski.com/birding/

Colorado Birds

The Colorado Field Ornithologists are the keepers of the official list of birds known in that state. At last look there were 460 species. The website has the official list available online or a fancier version available for download as an Adobe Acrobat .PDF file (*see page 237 for information about the free Adobe Acrobat reader*).

http://www.frii.com/~hopko/birdlist.html

Snow Bunting (*Plectrophenax nivalis*) (JJA)

Indiana Birds

The Chipper Woods Bird Observatory in Carmel (*first address*) has a checklist of birds seen in Indiana that includes information about how common or rare they are in each season of the year and whether they breed in the state. (Note that this list is 11 pages long and arranged in scientific order—starting with loons and ending with sparrows; move through the list by clicking the Go to New Page arrow at the bottom of each page.) A list of northeast Indiana birds, including their earliest and latest migration dates, is also available (*second address*).

http://www.wbu.com/chipperwoods/checklist.htm
http://www2.fwi.com/~moellering/earlylate.html

Louisiana Birds

A basic checklist of Louisiana birds is provided by Eyrie (*first address*). Also available is the Official Louisiana State List, compiled by Donna L. Dittmann, secretary of Louisiana Bird Records Committee (*second address*). If you're interested in northwestern Louisiana, check the list provided by Louisiana State University at Shreveport (*third address*). A huge, annotated list of the birds of southeast Louisiana contains vast amounts of information—nearly 50,000 bytes of text (*fourth address*).

http://www.eyrieusa.com/lacklst.html
http://homeport.tcs.tulane.edu/~danny/lalist.html
http://www.softdisk.com/comp/birds/cheklist.html
http://homeport.tcs.tulane.edu/~danny/sela.html

Texas Birds

Texas is a big state, and Texas birds make a big list. In fact, more than 610 species have been confirmed in the state, according to this page (*first address*) sponsored by the Texas Bird Records Committee of the Texas Ornithological Society. They're all here, including photos of many. More detail on the Texas birds can be found on the Unofficial Texas Ornithological Society Bird Checklist (*second address*), sponsored by Jim Peterson. For each species, Peterson tells where it's apt to be seen and when. For rare species, sight-

ing location and date information is provided. Peterson also maintains the Trans-Pecos Birds website (*third address*), which is full of west Texas bird lists, maps, and other information. Only Upper Texas Coast birds are covered in the checklist at the last address.

http://members.tripod.com/~tbrc/statelst.htm
http://www.esdallas.org/toschecklist/
http://www.esdallas.org/esd/pecos/index.html
http://www.io.com/~pdhulce/utclist.html

Wisconsin Breeding Bird Atlas

This isn't a checklist in the portable sense. Instead, it's what its name suggests, an atlas that shows where bird species breeding in the state can be found. Click on the Species Map, and you'll get a long list of birds covered in the atlas. Anyone birding in Wisconsin should stop by this site at the University of Wisconsin at Green Bay.

http://wso.uwgb.edu/wbba.htm

FEATHERED FACTS

Magnetic Birds

Using special chambers, Ken Able of the State University of New York at Albany has been able to demonstrate that Savannah Sparrows, and presumably many other species of migratory birds, use the Earth's magnetic field to find their way when migrating at night. Other species may use the stars to find their way, according to studies by Stephen Emlen of Cornell University.

—adapted from Eldon Greij, Birder's World

http://www2.birdersworld.com/birders

A
B
C
D
E
F
G
H
I
J
K
L
M
N
O
P
Q
R
S
T
U
V
W
X
Y
Z

Chimney Swift (*Chaetura pelagica*) (JJA)

EASTERN

Alabama Birds

Here's a printable checklist of the birds of Alabama, provided by Eyrie.

http://www.eyrieusa.com/alcklist.html

Florida Checklists

Among states and provinces, Florida probably is second only to Texas in the number of species of birds that live or visit within its boundaries—nearly 500 species are known here. The state also has some of the best birding locations in North America, such as the Everglades and the Merritt Island National Wildlife Refuge. Among the checklists available are a statewide list (*first address*), Florida Audubon's official checklist available as a .PDF file (*second address; see page 237 for .PDF information*), and an Everglades National Park checklist of nearly 350 species (*third address*). A dozen other localized Florida lists are available from the Northern Prairie Wildlife Research Center (*fourth address*).

http://www.eyrieusa.com/flcklst.html
http://www.audubon.usf.edu/pubs.htm
http://www.nps.gov/ever/eco/birds.htm
http://www.npwrc.usgs.gov/resource/othrdata/
  chekbird/r4/12.htm

Maine Checklist

The excellent Mainebirding.net website maintains a checklist of Maine birds, provided by the Maine Audubon Society (*first address*), but you get the list directly from Maine Audubon (*second address*). Take your pick of which format you like better.

http://www.mainebirding.net/checklist.html
http://www.maineaudubon.org/bche.htm

Maryland Checklist

Ripley, believe it or not, had seen 113 species of birds in her backyard when we last stopped by her site. Arlene Ripley, that is. One can't help but wonder how many more she has added to her list now. Of course, Ripley doesn't have your run-of-the-mill backyard—it's "approximately 2.5 acres of mixed deciduous and evergreen trees and shrubs with some open areas where we host several bluebird families and other nesting birds each year. We are surrounded by rich woods and a small stream borders the back of our property which is adjacent to more acres of undeveloped woods." Stop by, compare lists, and then wander her pages.

http://www.nestbox.com/bkyd.htm

Michigan Birds

More than 400 species of birds had been sighted in Michigan, according to the website of the Michigan Bird Records Committee.

http://www.umd.umich.edu/dept/rouge_river/
  Checklist.html

Minnesota Birds

The amazing thing about the Rickert family's list of 305 "regular species" in Minnesota is that almost every one is illustrated, and many include some natural history notes. You will also find lists of 37 species that are casual in Minnesota and 80 that are accidental. Another list tells which species have nested in the state.

http://www.holoweb.com/cannon/birds.htm

Mississippi Birds

Robert B. Hole Jr. has put together a Checklist of the Vertebrates of Mississippi that includes two lists of birds: loons through terns, and doves through weavers. The site also has lists of fishes, amphibians, reptiles, and mammals.

http://www.interaktv.com/MS/MSVerts.html

Missouri Birds

The Audubon Society of Missouri maintains an up-to-date checklist of 400 or so species of birds found in Missouri. The list indicates their dwelling circumstances—summer, winter, transient, etc.—and their frequency in each season of the year.

http://mobirds.mig.missouri.edu/audubon/asmhtmls/chklstmo.html

Sharp-tailed Sparrow (*Ammospiza Caudacuta*) (JJA)

FEATHERED FACTS

Tough Eggs

Eggs of birds such as the Chipping Sparrow seem to be remarkably hardy. Even though left unattended for two or three days in near-freezing temperatures, Chipping Sparrow eggs have been successfully hatched by parents who returned to the nest.

—adapted from Birds of North America

http://www.birdsofna.org/excerpts/chip_sp.html

New Jersey Birds

Because of its varied geography—including a long shore in the east and mountains in the west—New Jersey is a great place to see birds. The New Jersey Audubon Society's official checklist (*first address*) includes more than 425 species. Audubon's Cape May County checklist alone (*second address*) contains nearly 400 species, although this list reflects species sighted on the Atlantic Ocean—birds seen up to 50 miles offshore are fair game.

http://www.nj.com/audubon/genlmenu/cklist.html
http://www.nj.com/audubon/genlmenu/cmbirds.html

New York City Birds

Birds in New York City? What could there be besides pigeons and English Sparrows? You'd be surprised. New York City Audubon Society has a long list of birds that are typically seen in the city, plus a list of rare birds that have been spotted within the Big Apple's borders.

http://www.interboro.com/nycaudubon/BIRDS/birds.htm

A
B
C
D
E
F
G
H
I
J
K
L
M
N
O
P
Q
R
S
T
U
V
W
X
Y
Z

A
B
C
D
E
F
G
H
I
J
K
L
M
N
O
P
Q
R
S
T
U
V
W
X
Y
Z

Files with "Zip"

The Internet is rich with downloadable software, programs that you can transfer from a distant computer to your own and then use (*see page 40*). You will also find some long lists of birds that you can download. Among Windows-based programs and documents, many come as files that end in .ZIP. This format does two things: It squeezes large files into much smaller files, thereby saving on download time and storage space; and it can combine a lot of files—a library of them, as it were—into one file so that you don't have to deal with moving a bunch of files for a program from one place to another. These zipped collections are sometimes called archives. If a file ends in .ZIP, you need special software to extract or decompress it. One of the most popular is WinZip, an easy-to-use utility that has become pretty much a standard. Download.com, one of the many sites where you can pick up this shareware program, reported in October 1998 that WinZip was the first title ever to reach five million downloads on its site. Clearly, it's a basic tool for many people. WinZip will allow you to not only expand .ZIP files but also create your own—handy if you are sending programs or large-sized pictures over the Internet to friends. (I used an old version of ZIP to back up copies of this book each day.)

http://www.download.com

New York State Birds

The Federation of New York State Bird Clubs publishes an annotated checklist of the state's birds, which seems to be very up-to-date. It notes that 243 species are "known to breed, to have bred, or to have established breeding in New York State." The list contains many more species that pass through the state or visit occasionally.

p://birds.cornell.edu/fnysbc/nys_list.htm

MOUNTAIN & PACIFIC

Alaska Birds

Alaska, the largest state, has plenty of birds but breaks no records for numbers. When we visited the Anchorage Audubon Society's site, 445 species had been confirmed in the state, though another 35 were the subject of "unsubstantiated" reports.

http://www.audubon.org/chapter/ak/anchorage/bird.htm

California Birds

Robert B. Hole Jr. has compiled a simple checklist of birds found in California (*first address*). If you can type the second address without a typo, you'll find more than a dozen checklists of birds at different national wildlife refuges in California.

http://www.interaktv.com/BIRDS/califbirds.html

http://www.npwrc.usgs.gov/resource/othrdata/chekbird/r1/6.htm

Gray Catbird (*Dumetella carolinensis*) (JJA)

New Mexico Birds

Robert B. Hole Jr. maintains a list of New Mexico birds, based on the New Mexico Ornithological Society's official list. Note that the list is in two parts; the second section is on the second page, reached via a link near the top of the first page.

http://www.interaktv.com/NM/NMBirds.html

Oregon Birds

Here's the official checklist of Oregon birds, as compiled by the Oregon Birds Records Committee. The home page of this birding site (*second address*) is called Oregon Birding Online and has a great deal of information about birds of Oregon.

http://www.cyber-dyne.com/~lb/obrcchecklist.htm
http://www.cyber-dyne.com/~lb/obol.html

Utah Birds

Great Salt Lake Aububon in Salt Lake City posts a checklist of more than 400 species found in Utah, based on the work of the Utah Ornithological Society Bird Records Committee.

http://www.audubon.org/chapter/ut/gsl/birding/
  chklist.htm

Bluebird (Dover)

INTERNATIONAL

All Birds

Charles G. Sibley and Burt L. Monroe Jr. compiled a well-known and well-respected list of the known living birds species of the world. Rolf A. de By in the Netherlands has placed the list online (*first address*) in various downloadable forms—ranging from around 148,000 bytes in compact, .ZIP file format (*see page 46*), to more than 635,000 bytes for the pure text version. (To learn more about Sibley and his book, *Birds of the World*, *see Books*.) Jack Siler at the University of Pennsylvania has three different lists of all the birds in the world—those recognized by the American Birding Association, by the American Ornithological Union, and by Sibley and Monroe (*second address*). You can receive them as webpages in order of English or Latin names, or by taxonomic order. Or you can receive each via ZIP files. If you need a simple but complete list of the more than 9,700 bird species in the world, Rolf-Arne Barbakken in Norway has a version of the Sibley-Monroe list (*third address*).

http://www.itc.nl/~deby/SM/sm.html
http://www-stat.wharton.upenn.edu/~siler/birdlists/
http://home.idgonline.no/rolfarne/birdlist.htm

Arizona & Mexico Checklists

Borderland Tours in Tucson, Arizona, sells the following location checklists of birds: Chiricahua Mountains, Arizona (48 pages, 1997); Huachuca Mountains, Arizona (48 pages, 1995); Sonora, Mexico (23 pages, 1998); Oaxaca, Mexico (12 pages, 1991); and Chiapas, Mexico (20 pages, 1994).

http:// www.borderland-tours.com/mercantile.html

Birds of China

Kingfisher Tours in Hong Kong has what it calls a "complete list of threatened, near-threatened, endemic and near-endemic species of China, Tibet & Taiwan." The list also links to Kingfisher Tours, on whose birding expeditions you are apt to see the species.

http://kthk.com.hk/chinabirdlist.html

A B C D E F G H I J K L M N O P Q R S T U V W X Y Z

A B C D E F G H I J K L M N O P Q R S T U V W X Y Z

FEATHERED FACTS

Traveling Diet

The Wood Thrush, which travels on average some 1,300 miles between its summer home in North America and its winter home in Central America, changes its diet in preparation for the trip. Although these birds normally eat protein-rich insects, which is good for raising a family, their pretravel diet is full of energy-rich berries.

—adapted from Mary Deinlein, Smithsonian Migratory Bird Center

http://web2.si.edu/smbc/bom/woth.htm

British Columbia Birds

Birds of a Feather, a bed-and-breakfast catering to birders in Victoria, British Columbia, maintains a checklist of more than 460 birds that have been sighted in British Columbia.

http://www.victorialodging.com

Thayer's Checklists

Thayer's Birding Software produces the popular record-keeping program called Birder's Diary. The program has built-in checklists of birds for all the states and provinces (plus some 225 countries). As a service, Thayer has put the state and provincial bird database online so you can create your own lists and print them out. Click on the map of North America for the location you want, and Thayer's site will compile a list of birds, with names and taxonomic order used in the American Ornithologists' Union 7th edition. The list even includes boxes for users to check off as they spot birds.

http://www.birding.com/chklstmap.htm

CHILDREN

Most kids love birds and nature in general. The World Wide Web offers many sites that help introduce children of all ages to birds and birding, and to conservation issues related to birds. One site even tells youngsters how to keep records of what they see. (See also Migration.)

Bird Kids

Dan Kriesberg offers suggestions on how to get children interested in the joys of birding. For instance, having your kids feed birds can spark an interest in identifying and learning more about them. "Simple feeders can be built out of plastic milk jugs or milk cartons," he says. "Simply cut out the sides and hang the feeder in a tree. If a tree is not available, bird feeders can be attached to a pole in the ground, or you can simply spread wild bird food on the ground." The page includes brief reviews of books that would be ideal for children to use as they become interested in birding.

http://www.gorp.com/nyoutdoors/articles/fam_bird.htm

Summer Tanager (*Piranga rubra*) (JJA)

Bird Trivia

The Chipper Woods Bird Observatory has some bird trivia questions for kids. The answers may amaze them—and their parents.

http://www.wbu.com/chipperwoods/kids.htm

Birder

Kids will enjoy Birder, especially the Fun and Games section, accessible from the home page. After all, where else can they find a huge collection of bird jokes. ("A duck walks into a drug store and buys a Chapstick. The clerk says, 'Will that be cash or charge?' The duck says, 'Just put it on my bill!' ") Or a list of "You know your parents are fanatic birders when. . . ." Besides offering puzzles and quizzes, the site contains a large collection of useful birding information for adults, as well as younger birders, including state checklists, birding hot spots, a geographical birding guide with links to birding sites dealing with your state, a collection of links to birding organizations, and a message board. The board consists of messages from the *rec.birds* newsgroup on Usenet. You can sort messages by date, subject, or author. Although you can reply to any message's author, you cannot post messages here unless you have access to *rec.birds* through a newsreader or a newsreader website (*see page 153*).

http://www.birder.com

Books for Young Birders

The American Birding Association has an online catalog of birding books written for youngsters. Each is described and, often, the cover illustrated. Age suitability for each is also given.

http://www.americanbirding.org/abasales/catbyb.htm

Enchanted Learning

EnchantedLearning.com, an educational website for youngsters, has a lively and well-done section, All About Birds. Children (and their parents) can learn about everything from modern bird anatomy to bird navigation by following the links in the text. Sections of the site cover bird extremes, bird fossils and evolution, bird-watching, birds as symbols, birds and people, and even bird jokes. The site also has a guide to some of the most common or most famous birds, ranging from the backyard robin to the Quetzal.

http://www.enchantedlearning.com/subjects/birds/

Endangered Birds

Kimberly Cherry's students at Taylor Road Middle School in Alpharetta, Georgia, studied endangered bird species and put together a website full of information about the Ivory-billed Woodpecker, Peregrine Falcon, Galapagos Penguin, Bald Eagle, Harpy Eagle, Northern Spotted Owl, California Condor, Whooping Crane, California Crane, Philippine Eagle, Wood Stork, Brown Pelican, and the Nene. All of their natural histories include photos and most include quizzes. It's a wonderful example of how the work of the young can be shared with the world via the Web and how the young can help teach others about the importance of wildlife conservation and care for the environment.

http://www.trms.ga.net/tucker/students/birds/

FEATHERED FACTS

Fire, the Friend

Fire is not necessarily an enemy of wildlife, especially the rare Kirtland's Warbler. The right nesting conditions for this bird occur only in upper Michigan jack pines, and only for a few years after a forest fire has burned those pines. This is so important that now, conservationists have established jack pine preserves that they periodically burn in order to preserve the remaining population of about 1,200 Kirtland's Warblers.

—adapted from Canadian Museum of Nature

http://www.nature.ca/notebooks/english/kirtwarb.htm

A
B
C
D
E
F
G
H
I
J
K
L
M
N
O
P
Q
R
S
T
U
V
W
X
Y
Z

A
B
C
D
E
F
G
H
I
J
K
L
M
N
O
P
Q
R
S
T
U
V
W
X
Y
Z

FEATHERED FACTS

Dusky Sunset

In 1979 and 1980, a last-ditch effort was undertaken to save the all-but-decimated population of Dusky Seaside Sparrows on the Atlantic Coast of Central Florida. But scientists and conservationists could find only seven birds, and all seven were males. Even attempts to cross-breed the males with females of closely related species failed. The last Dusky Seaside Sparrow died in captivity in 1987, earning it the dubious distinction of being the most recent extinction of a North American species.

—adapted from Bagheera

http://www.bagheera.com/inthewild/ext_sparrow.htm

Environmental Tours

The National Wildlife Federation's Animal Tracks offers four lively environmental tours for children: Water, Wetlands, Endangered Species, and Our Public Lands. The pages for each tour involve kids in understanding their environment through use of hands-on experiments, puzzles, quizzes, great graphics, and clear text (with hyperlinked definitions for terms a kid might not understand). Children learn why conservation is important and what they can do to be a part of it through suggested projects.

http://www.nwf.org/nwf/kids/cool/index.html

Explorations

Explorations is a new magazine of "science and technology fun for the family," published by prestigious *Scientific American* magazine. Although neither the magazine nor the website is, strictly speaking, about birds or birding, both deal with nature and have some bird-related material. Of special interest is the Further Explorations directory, which lists nature and science centers in the United States and Canada suitable for children. Many of these are great in-person sources of ornithological knowledge for kids.

http://www.explorations.org

Field Journals

The National Center for Science Literacy, Education, and Technology at the American Museum of Natural History in New York has a neat section on its site for kids on how to go birding and keep a field journal of what was seen. There's even a page they can print out to use for keeping field notes. Plenty of instructions accompany the program, reached from the Online Field Journal menu by going to the Field Journals link. Journals for other kinds of animals, as well as plants, fish, rocks, tracks, and insects are there, too. The site also has diorama kits, complete with printable backgrounds and instructions; they include a wading birds rookery, a giant cactus forest, and an Olympic rain forest—all with birds. When typing the address, pay attention to the capital letters since the site's name is case-sensitive.

http://www.amnhonline.org/NationalCenter/
online_field_journal/

Orchard Oriole (*Icterus spurius*) (JJA)

Four Harbors Kids Page

Four Harbors Audubon Society on the north shore of Long Island, New York, has put together one of the better sites for children interested in birds. Stories and photos about different species are featured, and there's an archive of past profiles. Also, a list of children's books about birds, readily available from most libraries, is provided. The site's Don't Be a Kidnapper tells children what to do if they find a baby bird or animal. And there's also a fine collection of links to child-oriented sites about birds, animals, and nature. Be sure to capitalize HTM in the address.

http://www.igc.org/fhas/kidpage.HTM

Geographical Kids

National Geographic Society, the granddaddy of outdoor exploration in North America, offers NationalGeographic.com/Kids—an online arm of the society that introduces youngsters to the wide and wonderful world around them. The site has interactive tours, including Explore the Fantastic Forest, a trip through the woods where they can try to spot birds and other wildlife. (Those who explore the forest are eligible for a Fantastic Forest Explorer certificate afterward.) The site lets your child communicate with children around the world through several message boards and an international pen pal network. In the site index, under Archives, are many past wildlife features. The site also offers games and jokes, all with a geographical slant.

http://www.nationalgeographic.com/kids

Just for Kids

This Audubon Nebraska page has some quizzes and puzzles for children, including matching pictures to names (one species may surprise you) and unscrambling bird names.

http://rip.physics.unk.edu/audubon/nebraska/kids.htm

Kids' Corner Books

Ever wonder what nature books to buy for your children? The National Audubon Society's online bookstore includes Kids' Corner, which features a dozen or more recommended books for young readers, and for older children, too. A link at the bottom of the page, Essential Nature Library, takes you to more books for children. Like the previous group, many deal with birds. In all cases the reader age ranges are given. The listing of National Audubon Society First Field Guides includes one on birds. A portion of the sales from the online bookstore benefits the society's conservation efforts.

http://www.audubon.org/market/publish/kids-corner.html

Kids Stuff

One of the bigger collections of birding and natural history pages for kids is on the website of the Kalmiopsis Audubon Society in Oregon. It includes conservation and species information, as well as fun and games.

http://www.harborside.com/cc/audubon/kids.htm

FEATHERED FACTS

Long Haul

The Northern Wheatear has one of the more unusual migrations of any bird that summers in North America. Populations of wheatears that nest in the Arctic regions of northeastern Canada winter in Africa. They travel to Canada via Greenland and Europe. Wheatears that nest in Alaska and northwestern Canada migrate across the Bering Strait through Siberia, China, and eastern Asia to reach Africa.

—adapted from Peterson Online

http://www.petersononline.com/birds/month/nowh/index.html

A
B
C
D
E
F
G
H
I
J
K
L
M
N
O
P
Q
R
S
T
U
V
W
X
Y
Z

Red-throated Loon (*Gavia stellata*) (JJA)

Kids World 2000

Kids World 2000, a "guide for the young cyber-traveler," has a page full of zoos and other online sources of information about wild creatures.

http://now2000.com/kids/zoos.shtml

Risky Critters

"Are you a sagacious scientist or a laser-witted layperson?" asks the U.S. Fish & Wildlife Service. "Barrage your brain with a battery of beastly biology questions bound to bolster your blossoming knowledge!" This clever and entertaining Jeopardy-like game gives kids a chance to test their knowledge of endangered or threatened species.

http://www.fws.gov/r9endspp/kid_cor/risky.htm

Sanctuary on the Rio Grande

The Texas Junior Audubon Club has a website connected with the Sabal Palm Audubon Center and Sanctuary on the Rio Grande. The site includes information about the club, links to other sites for young people, a virtual tour of the sanctuary, and a chat area. (Warning: The home page on this site is extremely graphical, including sound and motion images, and

takes a fairly long time to download. The result, though pretty to see and hear, requires patience.)

http://www.ies.net/sabalkids/index.html

Teen BirdChat

Teen BirdChat is a listserve e-mail mailing list for young birders sponsored by the National Birding Hotline Cooperative. To subscribe, send a message with your name, age, and location to *teenbirdinfo@nbhc.com*. This page on the American Birding Association's website explains Teen BirdChat.

http://www.americanbirding.org/ygbconnect.htm

Virtual Zoo

Members of the Wild Ones, a youth education project founded by the Wildlife Preservation Trust International, share artwork of birds and other creatures that live in different habitats, such as the Brazilian rain forests, the Arctic tundra, or even the Mid-Atlantic states. Kids can contribute work about animals and their habitats to be published on this website and in the trust's print newsletter, the *Wild Times*. Instructions are provided for submitting drawings or essays to the zoo. Children in schools around the world have submitted many of the drawings, and you can read about the kids, their schools, and the environmental projects they are undertaking.

http://www.thewildones.org/vzoo.html

Wild Bird Coloring Pages

The Wild Bird Emporium, an online store in Auburn, New Hampshire, has a collection of line drawings of birds that can be printed to produce pages for children to color. For kids who are computer savvy, the pictures can be electronically colored with a computer painting program, such as Paint, which comes with Windows. Go to the site's main page and look at the bottom of the menu on the left for the link to the coloring pages. The website had 19 images online when we stopped by and said more were planned.

http://www.wbird.com

Woodsy Owl Coloring Pages

Kids can print and color pictures of Woodsy Owl, the U.S. Forest Service's environmental mascot, at this page. Each has a simple, environmental message.

http://www.fs.fed.us/spf/woodsy/coloring.html

Youth Birder Web Ring

The Young Birder Web Ring is a website where teenage—or younger—birders can get together. "We are the next generation of birders, and for birding to progress, we have to link together," says the site, which allows young birders to set up announcements describing their interests, as well as links to their own websites and e-mail addresses. The site has a message board and links.

http://udel.edu/~france/teenbirding.html

Young Birders

Wise organizations that cater to hobbyists know that the next generation of members is important to their future and the future of their specialty. The American Birding Association, the largest organization for bird-watchers in the United States, recognizes this fact and has a division for youngsters from ages 10 to 18 called Young Birders. The ABA offers special student membership rates, which run half the price of an adult membership, and entitle youngsters to all the benefits of full ABA membership plus a subscription to *A Bird's-Eye View*, a quarterly written by and for younger members of the association. Young Birders provides many special programs for youngsters, all described on the website. They include summer camps in different parts of the United States and in Costa Rica, and more than a dozen scholarships to those camps. (The website also has reports from students who've attended past camps.) Birding contests include the Young Birder of the Year Competition, sponsored with Leica, in which youngsters (whether members or not) keep records of bird sightings for one year and write two essays; thousands of dollars in prizes are offered. In another competition, called YoungQuest, individuals or teams compete over a 24-hour period to spot the greatest numbers of birds. In the process, participants raise money for conservation

efforts. The website also describes message groups, pen pal programs, books for young birders, and contains features, a report on the ABA's efforts at education, Young Birders news, and more.

http://www.americanbirding.org/ygbgen.htm

Cleaning Your Cache

When you wander the Web in search of birds—or anything else—your browser builds up a library of pages you've visited, called a *cache*. Its aim is to save you time in the future. If you connect to a site today that you visited yesterday or last week, the page—including graphics—may be "on file" in your browser's cache on your hard disk and the page should appear much faster than the first time you visited.

The problem is that caches can grow to enormous sizes; when full, they can slow down or even stop your computer. You can clear your cache, and you can set the size of future caches so that the saved pages don't hog too much space.

In Windows Internet Explorer 4, to clear your cache, go to View, Internet Options, select the General tab, and click the Delete Files button under Temporary Internet Files. (If you select the Settings button, you can adjust how much of your hard drive you want to devote to these temporary files.)

For Windows Netscape Navigator 4, go to the Edit menu, select Preferences, click Advanced, and then Cache. Click on Clear Memory Cache and Clear Disk Cache.

On a Mac, for Explorer 4, go to the Edit menu and select Preferences. Under Web Browser, click Advanced, then on Empty Now button in the Cache section.

For Mac Netscape Navigator, go to Edit, select Preferences, then Advanced, then Cache, and then Clear Disk Cache. Newer versions of these programs may have different menus for handling caches. Check your browser's help.

A B C D E F G H I J K L M N O P Q R S T U V W X Y Z

CONSERVATION

What's being done to protect wild birds—and what can we do? Hundreds of organizations around the world are concerning themselves with the plight of birds in particular and of wildlife in general. Many are on the Web, explaining problems and offering solutions—and often seeking your assistance. For some organizations, conservation or preservation of species is their full-time task. For others, it's one of their jobs. Some work directly with birds while most fight to preserve habitats. These organizations range from pure preservationists to hunting associations that want to make sure species survive so they can be hunted. All the organizations whose sites are listed here are involved in some way in helping protect birds and their habitats—even the Smithsonian's Coffee Corner site, which educates people about the importance of supporting shade-grown coffee production. Other sites provide information about threatened and endangered birds. (*See also Audubon Societies & Sanctuaries and Organizations & Associations.*)

FEATHERED FACTS

Chumming for Birds

Whereas most birds do not seem to have much, if any, sense of smell, pelagic birds that live far at sea—such as Storm Petrels and Albatrosses—are attracted by the smell of dead fish floating on the surface. Birders who go out on expeditions to spot pelagic species often "chum" for them by tossing dead fish in the water—a technique usually restricted to anglers trying to attract fish.

—adapted from Eldon Greij, *Birder's World*

http://www2.birdersworld.com/birders/amazingbirds/1998/9810_nose.html

American Bird Conservancy

The American Bird Conservancy is a nonprofit organization dedicated to the conservation of wild birds and their habitats in the Americas. "The fundamental role of ABC is to build coalitions of conservation groups, scientists, and members of the public, to tackle key bird priorities using the best resources available," the website says. The conservancy has offices in Washington, D.C., and The Plains, Virginia, and staff in Colorado, Montana, and Oregon. One of its major campaigns, "Cats Indoors!," is described in the Quandaries section. Other ABC efforts involve pesticides and birds and the study of climate changes on bird populations. The site provides much other information about the organization and how you can join.

http://www.abcbirds.org

American Birding Association Conservation Policy

The American Birding Association has a four-step plan for encouraging bird conservation. It's spelled out on this page of the ABA site.

http://www.americanbirding.org/consgen.htm

Bagheera

In Rudyard Kipling's *Jungle Book*, Bagheera was the black panther who spoke up to save the man-cub. The namesake website is a place that's speaking up for endangered species—a voice to help save creatures from extinction. Bagheera, launched in 1996 with the help of Microsoft, has profiles on "vanishing" species (including the Short-tailed Albatross, Philippine Eagle, Hyacinth Macaw, Humboldt Penguin, and Golden-cheeked Warbler), a linked database on endangered species, information about extinct species, a classroom module for teachers, animal profiles, late-breaking news, and much more. The site is oriented toward teachers and students, but anyone interested in endangered species could learn a lot here. This site is highly graphical and tends to be slow to load unless you have a high-speed connection.

http://www.bagheera.com

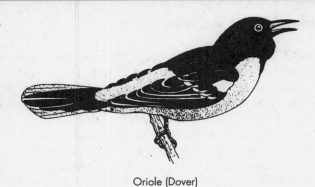

Oriole (Dover)

Camp 41

Camp 41 provides an Internet video look at the tropical rain forests and how their fragmentation and destruction affect our environment in North America, including some of our birds. The educational site has an audience in mind of students and schools, and uses research of the Smithsonian Institution to explain the importance of rain forests. To see the audio-video presentation, you will need Windows *Media Player*.

http://www.bagheera.com/Camp41/

Canadian Nature Federation

The Canadian Nature Federation, formerly the Canadian Audubon Society, started as a magazine. In 1939, Reginald Whittemore began publishing *Canadian Nature* as a memorial to his late wife Mabel Frances Whittemore, "a teacher dedicated to introducing children to the wonders of the natural world," the federation website reports. "The magazine, the cornerstone on which the Canadian Nature Federation (CNF) was built, began almost 60 years of education and action to conserve Canada's natural heritage for future generations." Among the focuses of the federation's website are what's being done to protect the more than 300 species of animals and plants that are on Canada's Species at Risk list, and what the federation is doing via its Bird Conservation Program. The site has information about the 40,000-member organization and its projects, and about *Nature Canada*, formerly *Canadian Nature*. Many features of the current issue are placed online, as are some from past issues. The site also carries late-breaking news and alerts dealing with conservation issues.

http://www.cnf.ca

CITES

CITES (Convention on International Trade in Endangered Species of Wild Fauna and Flora) is an international governmental agreement among more than 140 countries aimed at preventing unregulated trade in threatened creatures. This site (*first address*), a database of all the listed species, is useful for learning the names and ranges of creatures considered endangered around the world. You'll find the ranges of some of these species amazing. For instance, the Great White Egret (*Casmerodius albus*) is said to be found on every continent and in almost every country of the world. Nonetheless, it is in trouble. Visit the CITES home page for information about the treaty, its aims, and how it works (*second address*).

http://www.wcmc.org.uk/CITES/english/fauna.htm
http://www.wcmc.org.uk/CITES/english/index.html

Coffee Corner

What do coffee, conservation, and birds have to do with one another? Habitat. In Central and South America, coffee is one of the most important export commodities and countless square miles of rain forest have been felled to clear land for sun-grown coffee plants. These are faster-growing, high-yield, "more efficient" varieties of coffee crops. However, the original—and many feel—better-tasting coffees are from plants that grow under the canopy of the rain forest. They are called *shade-grown coffee plants*. Since the rain forests are winter habitats for many North American birds (as well as for year-round dwellers), drinking shade-grown coffee is thought to help encourage preservation of habitats for birds. Many migratory bird populations—the Baltimore Oriole, Tennessee Warbler, and the Cape May Warbler, for instance—have dropped dramatically in recent years. Some believe these and other bird species are suffering from the deforestation of Latin American rain forests. The Smithsonian Institution's site Our Coffee Corner not only describes the advantages and importance of shade-grown coffees but also tells how to create "sustainable coffee" farms—farms with "high biological diversity and low chemical inputs." It's a lesson in environmentally friendly production. (*See also Retailers.*)

http://www.si.edu/smbc/coffee.htm

A
B
C
D
E
F
G
H
I
J
K
L
M
N
O
P
Q
R
S
T
U
V
W
X
Y
Z

Ring-billed Gull (*Larus delawarensis*) (JJA)

Colorado Bird Observatory

The goal of the Colorado Bird Observatory in Brighton is to conserve birds of the Rocky Mountains and Great Plains. "The observatory's research and public education programs are designed to increase people's understanding of birds—how they interact with humans, what habitats they use, and what factors threaten their survival," the observatory says. "A better understanding of birds benefits more than bird conservation—the status of bird populations provides a measure of the health of our own environment." The site describes many bird conservation monitoring efforts, such as a Bald Eagle nest watch, grassland bird monitoring, and the Piping Plover census. And there's plenty of information about projects involving schools—and summer field ornithology camps for kids.

http://members.aol.com/CoBirdObs/

Conservation TV

Conservation TV is a website that transmits sound and video presentations about the efforts of various conservation organizations and government agencies. You can view videos about various endangered species and take zoo tours and ecotours. Although the system works with a 28.8K modem, it's better with a 56K modem and best with an ISDN (integrated services digital network) line.

http://www.bagheera.com/conservationtv/

Defenders of Wildlife

Defenders of Wildlife, the organization's website says, "is dedicated to the protection of all native wild animals and plants in their natural communities." The organization focuses on "what scientists consider two of the most serious environmental threats to the planet: the accelerating rate of extinction of species and the associated loss of biological diversity, and habitat alteration and destruction." That focus, of course, includes many species of birds and the habitats they frequent. The website has a section devoted to endangered species that includes an Endangered Species Primer, explaining how animals and plants become endangered. An essay about the importance of biodiversity and a glossary of environmental terms is also available. Sample articles from many past issues of *Defenders* magazine can be read online.

http://www.defenders.org

Earthwatch Institute

Earthwatch Institute is an international nonprofit organization that supports scientific field research worldwide by having its volunteers and scientists working together "to improve our understanding of the planet," the organization's website says. "The institute's mission is to build a sustainable world through an active partnership between scientist and citizen." Earthwatch members participate side by side with field scientists in their work in seven focused areas, including world oceans, world forests, biodiversity, and the monitoring of global change. In 1999, the organization sponsored 145 projects in 51 countries and 23 states, using volunteer teams that work from one to three weeks alongside the scientists. Among the topics of research in the 1999 catalog were Tanzania's wildlife migrations, Tanzania forest birds, saving Borneo's rain forest, Mexican forest wildlife, dancing birds of Central America, Bahamas' migrant birds, Old World songbirds (Europe), soaring birds of Eliat, Israel, loons of Maine, Whooping Cranes, Shenandoah wildlife, Andean hummingbirds, Ecuador forest birds, Bolivian savanna birds, and Brazil's rain forest wildlife. Each project is described in detail. So are the living conditions, the dates of team work, and the costs to participate.

http://www.earthwatch.org

Endangered Earth

Endangered Earth is a flashy, multimedia website with content from the Endangered Species Broadcast Network. It offers facts and features about various endangered creatures, including birds, but mostly mammals.

http://www.endangeredearth.com

Endangered Species Campaign

Thomas Jefferson once wrote, "For if one link in Nature's chain might be lost, another might be lost, until the whole of things will vanish by piecemeal." The conservation of nature's chain—all the creatures of our environment—is one of the chief missions of the National Audubon Society, so it's no surprise that the society quotes Jefferson's famous observation at the top of its Endangered Species Campaign website. Here, you can learn late-breaking news of efforts in Washington, D.C., and other capitals to help threatened species and protect their habitats. There's extensive information about the Endangered Species Act, signed into law in December 1973—visit the page Ark to the Future: 25 Years of the Endangered Species Act to learn what's been accomplished because of the act and what still needs to be done. The site also describes the act, how it works, what issues it has created, and how you can become a part of the goals of the ESA. You can read back issues of *On the Brink*, the newsletter of National Audubon's Endangered Species Campaign. The site also contains Action Alerts, information about other publications, and related links.

http://www.audubon.org/campaign/esa/

Endangered Species Information

EndangeredSpecie.com says it carries the "rarest info around." Compiled for both children and teachers (and, by extension, parents), this website provides much information and many links to help us learn more about endangered and threatened species. Among its features are a clickable map that brings up lists of endangered animals and plants in each of the 50 states. The site, which is searchable, also has information about laws protecting wildlife, sample survival plans, photos, and much more. The site offers pages just for teachers and pages designed especially for kids.

http://www.endangeredspecie.com

Endangered Species List

Birdnet, sponsored by the Ornithological Council, has an up-to-date list of species considered threatened or endangered by the U.S. Fish & Wildlife Service. The list is divided into U.S. Birds and birds of other nations.

http://www.nmnh.si.edu/BIRDNET/CHECKLISTS/Endsp.html

Endangered Species News

Endangered Species News is a website devoted to what its name suggests—or, as the site puts it, "a global news source about the earth's vanishing animals." Sponsored by ESBN, the Endangered Species Broadcast Network, the multimedia site has news and features about all sorts of species from all parts of the world—including, of course, birds—and uses text, audio, and film clips to tell their stories. The news is up-to-date. The site also has an encyclopedic array of information about endangered species.

http://www.endangeredearth.com/esnews.htm

FEATHERED FACTS

Half-Pints

Teals are the half-pints of the duck world—they're half the size of a mallard.

—adapted from Ducks Unlimited of Canada

http://vm.ducks.ca/naturenotes/blueteal.html

MEET THE MASTERS

Helping Kids

Chickadee Web <http://home.jtan.com/~jack/ckd.html> has helped many people, including youngsters, reports Jack Paul, its Webmaster. "I think the most rewarding experiences are the school-age children who write and tell me that they used my site to find information for a report about chickadees and got an 'A'!" he reports. "They are usually so excited and appreciative." For instance, one youngster wrote to ask for information. "I wrote back that part of the education process is knowing where to find information, and that the information he was asking for could be found by browsing the Chickadee Web links and reading the information about those pages. He took the time to write back that he found what he was looking for and got a very good grade. That student learned a valuable lesson not only about chickadees but also about how to use the Internet as a research tool." Jack appreciates those notes from the kids. "*That* is what makes all the hours of work worthwhile—to know that I've helped someone achieve success."

EnviroLink

EnviroLink calls itself the "online environmental community" and has many features and links related to living in an environmentally friendly way. The site has a sizable animal rights section. Presumably, that includes bird rights.

http://www.envirolink.org

Florida Scrub Page

One of the quickly disappearing environments in the United States is the scrublands of Florida. The Florida Scrub Page on Floridata's website notes that

"Florida scrub is a unique plant community that occurs in small patches scattered across the state. It is home to dozens of plant and animal species that occur nowhere else in the world." The site takes you on a visual gallery tour that lasts from 10 to 23 minutes, depending on what you want to see, and explains why scrub is so important to many bird species and why its conservation is critical. Type the address carefully, using uppercase letters where shown.

http://www.floridata.com/main_fr.cfm?state=Track& viewsrc=tracks/TrackMai.htm

Global ReLeaf

With a small donation and a click of the mouse (or a phone call), you can help American Forests plant 10 trees in a threatened forest ecosystem. The organization's Global ReLeaf program plants trees in Global ReLeaf Forest sites across the United States to restore ecosystems that have been damaged or destroyed by hurricanes, fire, disease, erosion, insects, or human abuses. If you make a contribution in memory or honor of someone, the organization will send an attractive certificate (pictured online) to the person honored or the family of the person memorialized. You can also send these certificates for birthdays, anniversaries, Christmas gifts, etc. The site describes examples of the work the group is doing.

http://www.amfor.org/programs/plant.html

Important Bird Areas in Canada

The BirdLife International partnership is working to identify and document sites "that are vital to the long term conservation of the world's birds," reports the website of the Important Bird Areas Program in Canada. These IBAs are shown on this site using regional maps. Each map notes locales that have been approved as IBAs and includes details about them. Potential IBAs are indicated but aren't described. More than 1,000 potential sites have been identified and are in the process of being evaluated. An online form enables you to nominate still more sites for consideration.

http://www.ibacanada.com

Institute for Wetland Research

The Institute for Wetland Research was set up by Ducks Unlimited in 1991 to conserve wetlands and waterfowl "by developing and sustaining a premier program of research and by educating professionals in wetland and waterfowl biology." The organization supports scientific research, especially by promising graduate students, on how to protect worldwide wetlands in the face of pressures from growing human populations and changes in the environment, which that population growth brings. This site explains many of IWWR's scientific research projects in the United States and Canada.

http://www.ducks.ca/iwwr/

Links to Endangered Species

The National Audubon Society has a page of links to websites in North America that are active in the protection of endangered species.

http://www.audubon.org/campaign/esa/Links.htm

Migratory Songbird Conservation

Each spring, more than 350 species of birds leave Mexico, the Caribbean, Central and South America, traveling thousands of miles to their summer homes in the United States and Canada. "Few of us think about what we can do to help these songbirds survive their grueling trip, and the stresses that await them—breeding and rearing their young," says the U.S. Fish & Wildlife Service, which provides an online pamphlet of information about Migratory Songbird Conservation. This basic guide for the beginner explains how to do some simple but essential things to protect songbirds. Among the suggestions: protect, create, and restore habitats (*see also Gardening & Landscaping*); eliminate poisons in your yard ("Too many popular pesticides are lethal to birds"); reduce cat predation (untold millions of songbirds are killed by pets each year) (*see also Quandaries*); address bird-window collisions (between 100 and 900 million birds are killed each year in window crashes) (*see also Quandaries*); and house sparrows and starlings (alien birds that push out natives). The page tells how you can get involved—by educating yourself and volunteering for various bird counts and surveys. The page also has an extensive collection of sources and contacts for more information (though they are not linked to websites, most are on the Web and many can be found elsewhere in this book or by using a search engine).

http://www.fws.gov/r9mbmo/pamphlet/songbrd.html

National Fish & Wildlife Foundation

Established by Congress in 1984, the National Fish & Wildlife Foundation is a conservation organization involved in education, resource management, and the protection and restoration of habitats. It does this by creating cooperative partnerships between the public and private sectors. An example of such an effort is the Neotropical Migratory Bird Conservation Initiative, or Partners in Flight, which is aimed at preventing declining bird species from ever reaching the endangered species list. "It brings public and private partners together to conserve migratory birds and the habitats on which they depend," the website says. Instead of starting a new organization, the foundation created a way that private conservation groups, federal and state agencies, and the forest products industry "could work cooperatively to seek mutually beneficial solutions." Partners in Flight has "changed the face of bird conservation in North America," the foundation says. (*See also Partners in Flight later in this section.*)

http://www.nfwf.org

Atlantic Puffin (*Fratercula arctica*) (JJA)

FEATHERED FACTS

Cold War Victim

The Ivory-billed Woodpecker, which became extinct in the late 1980s, might have been saved if efforts to conserve its last remaining territory in Cuba had begun 25 years earlier. However, the political situation made it difficult for outside scientists to work with Cuban authorities. Perhaps, says ornithologist Martjan Lammertink, the Ivory-billed Woodpecker "holds the dubious honour of being the one species that was exterminated by the Cold War."

—adapted from Neotropical Bird Club

http://www.neotropicalbirdclub.org/feature/ivory.html

National Heritage Network

Natural Heritage Programs and Conservation Data Centers are "the largest ongoing effort in the Western Hemisphere to gather standardized data on endangered plants, animals, and ecosystems," reports the Nature Conservancy, which sponsors the Natural Heritage Network site and the conservation data centers. Maps connect you with information about programs in different states, provinces, or nations; many, of course, deal with the conservation of endangered bird species. The site is fully searchable.

http://www.heritage.tnc.org

National Parks & Conservation Association

The National Parks & Conservation Association was founded in 1919 to "protect and improve the quality of our National Park System and to promote an understanding, appreciation, and sense of personal commitment to parklands." To that end the NPCA has publications—including *National Parks* magazine—

and programs to add to the appreciation and enjoyment of the park system, which provides some of the greatest birding locations in the United States. The site offers a Park of the Month feature, tells about the Ten Most Endangered Parks, describes parks tours (including ones oriented toward wildlife), has parks tips and facts, and allows you to download detailed maps of the parks.

http://www.npca.org

National Partners in Watchable Wildlife

The National Watchable Wildlife Program describes itself as an effort to combine wildlife conservation with America's growing interest in wildlife-related outdoor recreation, including birding. "The program is founded on the notion that people, given opportunities to enjoy and learn about wildlife in a natural setting, will become advocates for conservation in the future," explains the NWWP website. The program's goals include providing better opportunities for people to enjoy wildlife on public and private lands, contributing to local economic development, promoting learning about wildlife and habitat needs, and building public support for conservation of natural resources. Organizations listed as being involved in the movement include the National Park Service, the U.S. Fish & Wildlife Service, American Birding Association, Defenders of Wildlife, the Humane Society of the United States, Ducks Unlimited, and Wildlife Forever.

http://www.watchablewildlife.org

North American Lake Management Society

The mission of the North American Lake Management Society is "to forge partnerships among citizens, scientists, and professionals to foster the management and protection of lakes and reservoirs for today and tomorrow." And since lakes and reservoirs are important homes and food sources for scores of species of birds, it seems that birders would share the society's interest in healthy bodies of water. The site offers many resources, and there's a sizable section for children, with the intent of teaching them about the value of lakes.

http://www.nalms.org

Pacific Seabird Group

Pacific Seabird Group, based in North America, concerns itself with the study and conservation of Pacific seabirds and their increasingly threatened environments. The group's interest "encompasses millions of birds of over 275 species—all related by their dependence on the ocean environment, but widely divergent in their natural histories and the problems they face." The organization is concerned about such Pacific seabirds as penguins, loons, grebes, albatross, shearwaters, storm-petrels, boobies, pelicans, cormorants, frigatebirds, geese, ducks, puffins, murres, murrelets, auklets, guillemots, phalaropes, sandpipers, plovers, terns, jaegers, and tropicbirds.

http://www.nmnh.si.edu/BIRDNET/PacBirds/

Partners in Flight

Partners in Flight was started in 1990 because of growing concerns about declines in the populations of many land bird species and to emphasize the conservation of birds not covered by existing conservation efforts. "The initial focus was on species that breed in the Nearctic (North America) and winter in the Neotropics (Central and South America), but the focus has spread to include most land birds and other species requiring terrestrial habitats," PIF says. The effort involves cooperation among some 16 federal agencies, 40 private organizations, more than 60 state and provincial fish and wildlife agencies, many universities, and the forest industry. One aim of the organization is to develop bird conservation plans for every "physiogeographic area" in North America. Maps on the site show where these areas are, and other pages tell what kinds of birds in these regions are prompting special concerns. Issues of the PIF newsletter, Bird Conservation, explain many projects planned or under way and often tell when help is needed. The site posts articles from recent newsletter and says it "encourages you to download them and use them in your bird club newsletter or other outreach material." The site has plenty of bird conservation news, a calendar of events, and links.

http://www.partnersinflight.org

Peregrine Fund

The Peregrine Fund, established in 1970, works nationally and internationally to conserve nature through its focus on birds. According to the site, the Fund has been successful in "restoring species in jeopardy, conserving habitat, educating students, training conservationists, providing factual information to the public, and by accomplishing good science." Although the fund is named for the Peregrine Falcon, the organization is involved in the conservation of both raptors and songbirds. The site explains the organization's work, including its World Center for Birds of Prey in Idaho (*see North American Birds, Raptors*).

http://www.peregrinefund.org

Rare Birds

Rarebird.com "advocates and encourages public appreciation and understanding of wildlife conservation and promotes the breeding of rare and endangered bird and animal species in their pure forms." The birds here are virtually all ducks and geese—game birds—and there's a good collection of crisp, often spectacular close-up photographs of many species.

http://www.rarebird.com

Red-shouldered Hawk (*Buteo lineatus*) (JJA)

A
B
C
D
E
F
G
H
I
J
K
L
M
N
O
P
Q
R
S
T
U
V
W
X
Y
Z

Song Bird Coffee

"If you care about the survival of migratory song birds, you should know that the coffee you drink can make a difference," says the Thanksgiving Coffee Company, makers of Song Bird Coffee. This California company uses beans from coffee plants that are grown in the shade of Central American rain forests —winter habitat of many North American migratory birds. To speed up growth and production, most commercial coffees are grown in the open sun—often on lands that have been stripped of their wildlife-supporting trees. What's more, says Thanksgiving, "The coffee tree traditionally grows in the shade." The company says shade coffee also tastes better because "growing in its natural environment, it has time to mature fully with a higher sugar level, ultimately giving it a better, richer flavor. Growing in nutrient rich soil provides for more fully developed fruit, which also translates into better taste." The company also maintains that "shade grown coffee farms are second only to undisturbed rainforest as the best habitat for migrating birds. Buying shade grown coffee helps save trees for millions of birds that would otherwise have no place to live." So why doesn't everyone drink shade-grown coffee? Because it's more expensive, running $7 to $12 a pound. However, if you are a true fan of good coffee, love birds, and can afford it, you may want to give this or other shade-grown brands a try. You can buy the coffee online or at stores listed on the site. The site also sells live coffee trees, "soothing" CDs of rain forest sounds, coffee cups, and travel mugs.

http://www.songbirdcoffee.com

Species at Risk in Canada

The Canadian Museum of Nature in Ottawa, Ontario, reports that more than 270 species of all kinds of creatures and plants are "officially at risk" in Canada's 20 different ecozones (*first address*). This new and growing site explains the zones and many of the threatened species. The museum also has a set of "biographies" of more than 75 species worldwide—including many North American birds—that are endangered or extinct (*second address*).

http://www.nature.ca/english/atrisk.htm
http://www.nature.ca/notebooks/english/enexpg.htm

Threatened or Endangered Species

The U.S. Fish & Wildlife Service has a database of endangered species and where they might be seen at national wildlife refuges. You can search for the type of creature (aside from birds, there are amphibians, clams, crustaceans, fish, insects, mammals, plants, reptiles, and snails). Or if you want to know where you can find a given species, you can plug in its name and learn where it's found.

http://refuges.fws.gov/NWRSFiles/General/Query.html

Trader Joe's Coffee

Trader Joe's is a chain of specialty food stores that carries, among other environmentally friendly products, its own brand of shade-grown coffee, produced from plants that provide songbird habitats. Called Azteca Blend, the coffee comes from Equal Exchange, a worker-owned cooperative that buys from small farms. The coffee is both organically and shade grown. Trader Joe's has stores in California (where it started), Arizona, Nevada, Oregon, Washington, Massachusetts, New York, Connecticut, New Jersey, Maryland, and Virginia. This page gives precise locations for the stores.

http://traderjoes.com/tj/locations/

WatchList

More than 100 species of birds found in North America need our help, says the National Audubon Society, which sponsors WatchList. This lively site, for both youngsters and adults, identifies birds that are not yet on the official endangered species list but are in enough trouble that they have been placed on this WatchList. You can look up the birds for each state. And for each species, a page of information briefly describes the bird in words and a picture. You can learn about its ranges, the threats to its survival, and its "conservation priority score." The site suggests five ways that we can help these birds, offers interactive games and projects for children, describes how to garden for birds, lists state bird conservation priorities, and provides much other useful information.

http://www.audubon.org/bird/watch/

Wetlands Network

Until recent times, the importance of wetlands has been lost in the effort to find more land for humanity. First, early farmers drained wetlands to plant more crops. Then developers drained wetlands to plant houses. But in destroying wetlands, people are also destroying purification systems for ground water supplies, as well as habitats for countless kinds of wildlife—not the least of which are birds. The Wetlands Network, based in Canada but involving many organizations throughout North America, connects many sources of information about the world's wetlands and the efforts to preserve them. For instance, the site offers profiles of the leading organizations who are fighting to preserve wetlands. A Resources Center lists sources on why wetlands are important and has an extensive handbook on shorebirds, plus a gallery of many dozens of photos. You'll also find virtual birding tours of noteworthy wetlands, plus a shorebird quiz and archives of e-mail from mailing lists dealing with wetlands birds. This site was set up in 1996 and though some sections have not been updated since, most of its huge library of information is timeless and, we hope, will stay online for years to come.

http://www.wetlands.ca

WetNet

The Texas Wetland Information Network—WetNet for short—provides easy, online access to information about wetlands. Sponsored by the Texas General Land Office, a state agency, it has much information that is useful far beyond the borders of Texas. Especially interesting to birders is its Wetlands Species collection, accessible from the home page, which includes excellent natural histories of a couple of dozen important wetlands species, as well as links to many other sources of information.

http://red.glo.state.tx.us/wetnet/

Wildlife Management Institute

The Wildlife Management Institute is a "private, non-profit, scientific and educational organization" involved in the "conservation, enhancement and professional management of North America's wildlife and other natural resources." Established in 1911 by hunters alarmed at the declines in many kinds of wildlife, especially waterfowl, the institute "supports wise use of wildlife, including regulated recreational hunting of designated populations." It also works for the protection of endangered species. Birders who are opposed to all forms of hunting may find the institute not to their liking, but its efforts to manage populations of birds should be of interest to all.

http://www.jwdc.com/wmi/

MEET THE MASTERS

Watching His Birds

"I thought it would be neat to make a web site, and a good topic for me seemed to be birds, since bird watching is my favorite hobby," says David Jordan, age 11 when he began work on the "David Jordan Bird Habitat" website <http://members.aol.com/DJHabitat/>. "At first I spent a lot of time getting it up, and reading how to do it." The site is loaded with photos describing the creation of his backyard wildlife habitat back in 1996, with plenty of tips and links to help you with your own habitat. Now that it's set up and "functioning," the habitat "requires the feeders be filled about every other day, and the fountain needs to be cleaned out around once a month," David says. As of early 1999, he had identified 29 species of birds in the Yorba Linda, California, yard—including a Great Egret. Among his favorite visitors are the Scrub Jays. "I've had up to five of them at once in the habitat," he says on the site. "They're fun to feed because of their aggressive antics. They squawk, jump, and chase each other. I make a game out of feeding these guys. They watch me as I hide several peanuts around the yard and when they think I'm not looking, they swoop down and retrieve their reward. I once hid a peanut in the handle of the seed scoop! They don't miss a morsel!"

FEATHERED FACTS

Oologists

The study of bird eggs is known as *oology*, a word based on the Greek word for egg.

—adapted from Smithsonian Migratory Bird Center

http://web2.si.edu/smbc/bom/blsw.htm

Windstar Wildlife Institute

The theme of the Windstar Wildlife Institute, whose home page opens with a bird song, is "developing habitats for tomorrow." "The Institute was established in 1986 because of a concern for wildlife and the devastating impact commercial and residential development was having, and still is having, on wildlife habitat," says the organization, which began as an effort to save some land in Maryland. Since 1995 the institute has become nationwide in scope and focus. "The Institute's vision is to have at least one Master Wildlife Habitat Naturalist (graduate of our flagship program) in every county of the United States (3,043) within a decade." The topics that these naturalists, trained by the institute, study include challenges facing wildlife and their habitat, principles of forest and wildlife ecology and management, landscaping for wildlife, backyard biodiversity, planting native species of plants, controlling invasive exotics, how to watch and photograph wildlife, constructing water gardens, how to deal with problems in the wildlife habitat, how to create a wildflower meadow, how to create wildlife habitat and outreach plans, managing the habitat for specific wildlife species, woodworking for wildlife, feeding wildlife, and the best ways to communicate what they have learned to others. Besides an explanation of the institute's efforts, the site has a wildlife forum, poster store, and links collection.

http://www.windstar.org/wildlife/

World Conservation Monitoring Center

The World Conservation Monitoring Center in the United Kingdom "provides information services on conservation and sustainable use of the world's living resources, and helps others to develop information systems of their own." If you look under Conservation Databases and then Species Information, you'll find the Arctic Bird Library, which provides information about populations of some 125 species of waterbirds that breed in the Arctic. "The Arctic Bird Library and the Integrated Species Information database are two initiatives, illustrating WCMC's aim to provide access to integrated information on species of conservation concern," says the center. The website has a rather incredible map feature that allows you to use your mouse to select a region of the Arctic on a map and then learn what species can be found breeding there. The map is very detailed, and you can pinpoint species, even on small islands. The site also offers a great deal of information for the researcher interested in conservation efforts worldwide and has late-breaking bulletins about major environmental news, such as sizable oil spills.

http://www.wcmc.org.uk

Towhee (*Pipilo erythrophthalmus*) (JJA)

DESTINATIONS

The backyard provides the easiest venue for birding, and most of us also adventure out to community parks and refuges where more species can be seen. However, visits to more distant locales can provide access to even more birds—often exotic species or kinds seen only in limited ranges or environments. This section describes dozens of suggestions for places to expand your birding horizons, both in North America and other parts of the nearby world. Many are publicly owned parks and refuges, and some are privately owned ranches, reserves, or resorts that specialize in serving birders. We've also included a selection of directories to good birding locations so you can do your own online exploring. We've even included information on birding at the local dump! *(See also Audubon Societies & Sanctuaries, and Tours & Expeditions.)*

GENERAL

10 Best Places to Go Birdwatching in America

This article, which originally appeared in *USA Today* and is carried by the PBS *BirdWatch* website, lists Dick Hutto's 10 Best Places to Go Birdwatching in America. Hutto is the host of the PBS *BirdWatch* television series. The list includes: J. N. Ding Darling National Wildlife Refuge, Sanibel Island, Florida; Monterey Bay, California; Cape May, New Jersey; Patagonia, Arizona; Grand Teton and Yellowstone National Parks, Montana and Wyoming; Santa Ana and Laguna Atascosa National Wildlife Refuges, Texas; Central Park, New York City; Santa Monica Mountains National Recreation Area, California; the Platte River, Nebraska; and Pawnee National Grassland, Colorado. The specialties of each spot are described.

http://www.pbs.org/birdwatch/info_10best.htm

Bird Trip Reports

If you are planning to travel outside North America and are interested in birding experiences, check out this site. Urs Geiser, who lives in Illinois, has been collecting descriptions of birding trips to locales around the world. Although there are some North American birding trips here, most are in Europe, Asia, the Middle East, the Far East, Africa, Australia, and the Pacific Islands. Many of these journals are quite long and detailed in their descriptions—inveterate travelers will love it. One of the nice features of such reports is that they are written by birders who think about the kinds of things other birders will want to know—less sophisticated, perhaps, than *National Geographic*, but often more fun and practical. And usually personal—you get to know and enjoy the interests and quirks of family members.

http://www.xnet.com/~ugeiser/Birds/TripReports/TripReports.html

Down in the Dumps

"Birders go where the birds are," writes John G. Ward. "As a result, we sometimes find ourselves in places and situations that are not exactly the subject matter of the typical travel poster." In fact, landfills, parking lots, dung heaps, and jet airports can be among the hottest spots for observing birds. Ward, a Joy of Birding contributor for *Birding* magazine, offers some enlightening experiences. And he does so in an entertaining style that makes him fun—as well as informative—to read.

http://www.americanbirding.org/bdgfeat1.htm

FEATHERED FACTS

Big and Little Owls

The smallest owl weighs only two ounces whereas the largest tips the scales at some eight pounds.

—adapted from Owl Research Institute

http://www.montana.com/owl/

A
B
C
D
E
F
G
H
I
J
K
L
M
N
O
P
Q
R
S
T
U
V
W
X
Y
Z

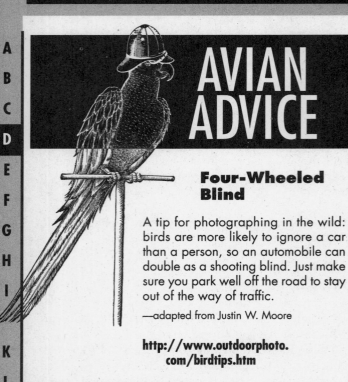

AVIAN ADVICE

Four-Wheeled Blind

A tip for photographing in the wild: birds are more likely to ignore a car than a person, so an automobile can double as a shooting blind. Just make sure you park well off the road to stay out of the way of traffic.

—adapted from Justin W. Moore

http://www.outdoorphoto.
com/birdtips.htm

Fodor's Guide to National Parks

Fodor, the company that produces the famous international guidebooks, has a wonderful online guide to the national parks of the United States. For each park Fodor's provides descriptions of facilities, as well as birds and other wildlife, the flora, and geology you can expect to see. The guide tells you the best times to visit, provides maps of the parks, and lists useful links for even more information.

http://www.fodors.com/parks/

Foundation for National Parks

The National Park Foundation, a private support group for the national parks in the United States, has an online database of information about the parks. You can search by name or state, and locate parks by special interest. The site tells about the kinds of wildlife—including birds—that a park is known for. Each park is described in detail, including geographical descriptions, addresses and contact information, travel directions, activities, fees, and other useful information. (*See also Organizations & Associations.*)

http://www.nationalparks.org

National Wildlife Refuge System

The National Wildlife Refuge System includes more than 510 refuges and 37 wetland management districts handling more than 26,000 waterfowl production areas. The U.S. Fish & Wildlife Service's sizable website (*first address*) provides much information about wildlife and wild places in the United States. In fact, the site is so huge, you can spend hours wandering it. From the home page, clicking on Wildlife and Plants brings up sections that deal with such subjects as endangered species, birds that are rare or threatened, game management, wildlife management, and other avian topics. To learn about specific wildlife refuges, you can access some powerful databases (*second address*) and zero in on specific locations by state, name, or facilities. Clicking the link to the Refuge System Information Search Page enables you to select the features you're looking for. It's best to pick a state, too; otherwise you may get hundreds of refuges (just selecting Wildlife Observation got us 265). The resulting lists have basic information about each locale, often including an e-mail address. But you'll also find links to additional information that include public uses, visitor opportunities, special programs, directions, a site description, wildlife management programs, telephone or mail sources of additional information, and Internet links to other sites that may provide even more details. Other links help with bird information, such as checklists for the United States. The second address also leads to databases on threatened and endangered species, as well as to special events.

http://refuges.fws.gov
http://refuges.fws.gov/NWRSFiles/General/Query.html

Crested Grebe (Dover)

Organization of Biological Field Stations

The Organization of Biological Field Stations is an association of more than 200 field stations and professionals concerned with field facilities for biological research and education, mostly in North and Central America. Most are situated at excellent places to go birding. The site has a clickable map that allows you to home in on field stations in your region, and then get information about the programs and facilities the stations may offer. There's information as to how much land each location has and what it's like—including whether there are trails. Often, there are links to sites operated by the stations themselves, giving much more detailed information. Although these stations are involved in the investigation of all forms of wildlife and natural history, birds are often high on the list of research projects. The site is a great way to search for interesting wildlife preserves to visit, as well as to learn about what's being studied at them.

http://www.obfs.org

Park Search

L.L. Bean's catalog site includes an excellent search engine, called Park Search, which covers state and national parks, wildlife preserves, and forests. The search device lets you select Birdwatching as what you're most interested in, so you can look for spots especially suited for this activity. Just pick Search by Location or Activity, and when that page comes up, select only Birdwatching. When we did a search recently, Park Search produced a list of 1,313 parks for bird-watching. In all, Park Search covers 782 state parks, 163 national parks, 151 national forests, 297 national wildlife refuges, and 98 Bureau of Land Management lands, and carries more than 2,000 photos of natural areas and wildlife. It's particularly strong on state parks; such a collection so well documented may not be available elsewhere on the Web.

http://www.llbean.com/parksearch/

ParkNet

The more than 370 national parks in the United States encompass some 81 million acres—and all of them are full of birds. If you are planning a trip to any of them,

ParkNet, the website of the U.S. National Park Service, is the place to start. You can find much history and background on the park service, but far more interesting are the details, maps and photos of many parks, the online tours, and the monthly special features. Each park is extensively described. The site also features Nature Net, which describes the wildlife, plants, and geology of the National Parks. You can find parks or National Historic Sites by name or by map—and you can even download free, highly detailed maps of parks.

http://www.nps.gov

Species in Parks

One of the more amazing bird databases on the World Wide Web is Species in Parks, which tells you, in several different and convenient ways, what birds are in what parks. Suppose you want to know where you can see Red-bellied Woodpeckers. Through a couple of simple steps—using either the common or scientific name—you quickly find that the Red-bellied can be seen in about 75 different parks. For each, you will be told whether the bird is present, probably present, or accidental, and if the bird nests there. You can click on each park's name to get more information about the place. But being a good database, there's more than one way to retrieve information. Suppose you're thinking of visiting a park and want to know what birds you can expect to see there. In this case you would want to use the Search the Database by Park Name option. For instance, if you pick Bryce Canyon National Park, Utah, you'll get a list of more than 150 species and their status. Operated by the Information Center of the Environment at the University of California and the National Park Service, the site points out that "the database is an evolving product, and is by no means a complete list of species residing in the National Parks." In other words, information is being added all the time. The site lists not only birds but also amphibians, fish, mammals, reptiles, and plants. But wait, there're more! If you don't like spending the few moments transferring the lists of birds or parks via the Internet, you can download the entire database of either fauna (including birds) or flora to your own computer and have it there for looking up any time you want. Is that cool or what?

http://ice.ucdavis.edu/nps/

A B C D E F G H I J K L M N O P Q R S T U V W X Y Z

MEET THE MASTERS

Sharing the Sounds

Tony Phillips, creator of the New York Bird Songs website <http://math.math.sunysb.edu/~tony/birds/index.html> enjoys sharing the sounds of nature. "I was pleased to be able to put the songs up without copyright—the birds should get the royalties! I know people are using my records on commercial pages and without attribution. That's not fair, but I don't care that much—for now."

State Parks Online

If you're interested in learning about a state's parks, State Parks Online is a wonderful source. Online since 1995, the site is still evolving. Doug Dickson says "this is the most complete list on the Web" but adds that "just like the forest, this page is growing all the time." In most cases the site links you to the state agency in charge of its state parks, where you usually find a wealth of information—often including lists of birds that may be seen in parks. Some links are to private sites. Dickson has other links, such as to regional park listings and some national park sources. A page of links to Canadian provincial parks is also available.

http://www.mindspring.com/~wxrnot/parks.html

Top 100 North American Birding Hotspots

The Joy of Birding section of Thayer Birding Software's program, Thayer's Birds of North America (*see Software*), includes a guide to the Top 100 North American Birding Hot spots. Most states and provinces are mentioned. Descriptions of locations are pithy and often humorous. Many of the listings include links to websites that provide more information.

http://www.birding.com/top100.htm

Trip Reports

One of the neat customs of various birding e-mail centers, such as *rec.birds*, is for correspondents to describe trips they have taken to interesting birding locales. Lisa Bryan, who lives in Arizona, has collected a lot of intriguing reports describing trips and arranged them by states, provinces, and countries in Central and South America. Although many of the reports may be from several years ago, what they describe is pretty much timeless. They're fun to read—and useful for tips.

http://www.azstarnet.com/~lisab/triplist.html

Oven-Bird (*Seiurus aurocapillus*) (JJA)

CENTRAL

Aransas National Wildlife Refuge

Established in 1937 to protect the wildlife of coastal Texas, the Aransas National Wildlife Refuge (*first address*) is famous for its Whooping Cranes. The refuge consists of 70,000 acres of grasslands, Live Oaks, and redbay thickets that attract nearly 400 species of birds, including the endangered crane. "One of the rarest creatures in North America, the Whooping Crane is making a comeback from a low of 15 birds in 1941," reports the U.S. Fish & Wildlife Service. "Whooping Cranes nest in Canada during the summer and winter at Aransas National Wildlife Refuge. The cranes can usually be seen from the Observation Tower from late October to mid-April." The site has full details about the park and includes a link to a checklist of birds seen there. Port Aransas, Texas, likes to say that "migrating birds know a good rest stop when they see one." The coastal town is just a short distance from the refuge, and its website (*second address*) has information about the community and birding. (*See also North American Birds, Waders.*)

http://southwest.fws.gov/refuges/texas/
  aransas.html
http://www.portaransas.org

Big Bend National Park

Big Bend National Park, Texas, has been a favorite of birders for decades: More species have been spotted here than in any other national park—over 460 species, more than the checklists of some states and provinces, including Alaska, the biggest state! One reason for the high number of bird species is that Big Bend is on the Rio Grande, bordering Mexico, and many Central America birds wander into this area. Another reason is its 810,000 acres of varied terrain. "It is . . . a place that merges natural environments, from desert to mountains," says the National Park Service. "It is a place where south meets north and east meets west, creating a great diversity of plants and animals." The official park service site (*first address*) has much information about Big Bend and how to enjoy its wonders. The park service also has a complete list of bird species found at Big Bend (*second address*), based on the Accepted Texas Species list of

the Texas Bird Records Committee of the Texas Ornithological Society. There are also special pages of information about rare bird records, endangered birds, and Big Bend's 10 Most Wanted Birds (*third address*). You can find a rather sizable list of books available on Big Bend birds here, as well. The Friends of Big Bend National Park (*fourth address*) is an organization dedicated "to the promotion and protection of this, one of the earth's last great, pristine wildernesses." The site has wonderful photos of the park. Jim Peterson's Trans-Pecos Birds website (*fifth address*) has more information about Big Bend birding and other birding locales in the area.

http://www.nps.gov/bibe/
http://www.nps.gov/bibe/birdlist.htm
http://www.nps.gov/bibe/birdpg.htm
http://www.bigbendfriends.org
http://www.esdallas.org/esd/pecos/

Searching a Page

Some Web pages, especially lists of birds or links to birding sites, can get very long. Wading through them for the subject you're looking for can be time-consuming and eye-straining. However, there's an easy way to scan the page. Almost all Web browsers have a "find" feature that lets you search the page for a word or phrase. For instance, in Internet Explorer, press Control F or go to the Edit menu, and select Find [on this page]. Enter the word or words and click Find Next. Once a reference is found, click Find Next again and repeat each time you want to proceed. You can make the search a bit more restrictive by selecting Match Case or Match Whole Word Only. (The latter enables you to avoid coming up with references to "gullet" when you're search for "gull.")

Thus, if you've found a page with a long list of birds but are interested only in Herring Gulls, try finding "herring." Or if you've found a birding book list, and you're seeking titles about nests, try whole-word searching just for the word "nest."

A
B
C
D
E
F
G
H
I
J
K
L
M
N
O
P
Q
R
S
T
U
V
W
X
Y
Z

FEATHERED FACTS

10 Benefits of Landscaping for the Birds

Landscaping to attract birds to your yard has many other benefits:

- Increased wildlife: Good landscaping can double the number of kinds of birds in a yard.

- Energy conservation: Carefully arranging conifer and hardwood trees can cut winter heating and summer cooling bills for a house.

- Soil conservation: Many plants prevent soil erosion.

- Natural beauty: Well-done landscaping increases the beauty of your property.

- Bird-watching: A properly landscaped yard draws many birds. Some people have seen nearly 200 species in a single yard.

- Wildlife photography: With all those beautiful plants attracting all those beautiful birds, you can add the hobby of wildlife photography without much extra effort.

- Insect control: Many birds drawn to your yard feed on insects and help get rid of pest species.

- Food production: Some plants that attract wildlife also attract people—to the dinner table. Cherries, chokecherries, strawberries, and crabapples are good to eat for people, too.

- Property value: A well-landscaped yard adds to the dollar value of your property.

- Educational: All that wildlife can be an outdoor classroom if you have children. With your help it can teach them much about the natural world.

—adapted from Baltimore Bird Club

http://www.bcpl.net/~tross/by/attract.html#2

Chicago Area Birding Guide

Jim Frazier of Batavia, Illinois, has created a guide to birding for anyone visiting the Chicago area. The site describes various nooks and crannies of the lakeshore —including how-to-get-there driving instructions—as well as good birding areas in the suburbs and nearby Indiana. One of our favorite asides is in the description for Miegs Field. "This is the airport that you take off from in Flight Simulator," writes Frazier. "I don't think they normally show the Snowy Owl that frequents the area in the winter." He gives insider tips as to how to get to the observation deck at the terminal, from which you can use a scope or glasses to scan for Snowy Owls in winter. One page describes some of the more interesting or unusual Chicago area species (Gray Partridge, Sandhill Crane, Upland Sandpiper, Snowy Owl, Monk Parakeet, for example) and where to find them. If you live in or are visiting the Chicago area, this is a must-see site.

http://www.gadwall.com/birding/guide/index.html

Grand Island

For six weeks each spring, the Grand Island, Nebraska, region becomes a huge way station for migrating birds. Up to 16 million ducks and geese, a half million Sandhill Cranes, endangered Whooping Cranes, plus Prairie Chickens, Bald Eagles, and other species make their appearance. The Platte River Valley is a stopping point or home for some 300 species of birds, reports the website of the Grand Island Hall County Convention and Visitors Bureau, which offers a fine website to describe the region's birding and other recreational possibilities. "Designated as the Number One place in the world for bird watchers to visit by Forbes FYI, Grand Island and Hall County are at the heart of the central flyway," the site reports. "The annual migration has been happening in the Platte Valley for thousands of years, and heralds the arrival of spring to the high plains." The website describes the territory and lists special events of interest to birders. From the home page, select Spring Migration. At the bottom of the page, you can read about Crane Watching Etiquette tips.

http://www.visitgrandisland.com

Great Texas Coastal Birding Trail

The Great Texas Coastal Birding Trail is a planned 500-mile chain of birding sites with no single connecting road more than an hour's drive. Visit the official state site describing the trail (*first address*); you can also find more details including a list of the 95 distinct sites that will be linked by the trail (*second address*).

http://www.tpwd.state.tx.us/adv/birding/btrail.htm

http://www.eyrieusa.com/texastrail.html

Harlingen

Harlingen, Texas, calls itself a "tropical birder's paradise." Located in the heart of the Rio Grande Valley, Harlingen was named one of the top 12 birding hot spots in the United States by Roger Tory Peterson. "Every year, thousands of naturalists converge upon the Rio Grande Valley in search of some of the 465 species which have been sighted in the area," says this website operated by the Harlingen Chamber of Commerce. "These species include numerous exotics and neotropicals." In its section on birding, the site describes "seven spectacular stopovers," all within an hour of Harlingen. These great birding spots include Santa Ana National Wildlife Refuge, Sabal Palm Grove Sanctuary operated by the National Audubon Society, and—believe it or not—the "famous" Browns-ville Sanitary Landfill where the Mexican Crow nests. This species, which has been declining in recent years, appeared in the United States in the late 1960s. "Opportunities for spotting the Mexican Crow are so bountiful at the city landfill, it is sometimes referred to as Mexican Crow Park." This chamber of commerce-sponsored website has plenty of information about tourism, accommodations, sightseeing, and just about anything else you'd need to learn about Harlingen and its environs.

http://www.harlingen.com

Important Bird Areas of Texas

Ted Eubanks has compiled a list of some of the most important bird areas of Texas, arranged by region of the state. Places that are homes to threatened or endangered species are noted. Only a few have links for further information, but it's easy enough to use a search engine to seek information once you've found the spot.

http://texasbirding.simplenet.com/iba/

Iowa Birds & Birding

Iowa may not seem a hotbed of cool birds, but reading the Hot Birds update on the Iowa Ornithologists' Union website tells otherwise. When we stopped by, an Arctic Tern and MacGillivray's Warbler were headlining a long list of interesting species that had been seen. The site has a thorough guide to Iowa Resources that include books (at least three just on Iowa birds) and a database of people in the state who can point you to the best birding sites when you visit any of nine regions. The e-mail address of each helper is listed. There's also a place to sign up for mailing lists on Iowa birds, information on birding clubs around the state, and a sophisticated live chat feature. The Iowa Rare Bird Alert and a state checklist are also available.

http://www.iowabirds.org

Kearney

Kearney, Nebraska, claims to have the world's largest concentration of cranes, plus millions of geese and ducks. In fact, in March and April, the viewing is "breathtaking," says the Chamber of Commerce, which sponsors this site. The whole Platte River Valley has great birding, but Kearney proudly maintains the best area for viewing is on the river. On the home page, click on the photo of the Sandhill Crane to learn more about this species, for which the region is famous. Menu items at the left lead to more information about birding in the area.

http://www.kearneycoc.org

A B C D E F G H I J K L M N O P Q R S T U V W X Y Z

A
B
C
D
E
F
G
H
I
J
K
L
M
N
O
P
Q
R
S
T
U
V
W
X
Y
Z

Kenmare

Kenmare calls itself the "birding capital of North Dakota." Within 50 miles of the town are four national wildlife refuges, where more than 300 species of birds have been seen. Perhaps the best known sanctuary is the Des Lacs National Wildlife Refuge, which consists of nearly 20,000 acres along the Des Lacs River from the Canadian border to about eight miles south of Kenmare. Famous as a place to view the spring courtship dance of the Western Grebe, one of five species of grebe that nest there, the area also has Baird's and Le Conte's Sparrows, Sharp-tailed Grouse, Ferruginous Hawks, Godwits, Piping Plovers, 16 species of duck, and American White Pelicans. This website, provided by the Kenmare Chamber of Commerce, also has information about the community. Use the Recreation link for information about Des Lacs National Wildlife Refuge.

http://tradecorridor.com/kenmare/

Wood-Pewee [Eastern Pewee, *Contopus virens*] (JJA)

King Ranch

King Ranch, Texas, is both a National Historic Landmark and a natural history treasure. Recognized as the birthplace of the American ranching industry, the ranch was founded by Captain Richard King in 1853 and today covers some 825,000 acres of South Texas—an area larger than Rhode Island. The ranch has a variety of habitats that attract more than 300 kinds of birds, including many tropical and migratory species. Among the more unusual species a visitor can expect to see are the Ferruginous Pygmy-Owl, Northern Beardless Tyrannulet, Tropical Parula, Least Grebe, Sprague's Pipit, and Audubon's Oriole. This site, operated by Texas A&M University, explains the various birding and nature tours of the ranch. There's also information about historical aspects of King Ranch.

http://furff.tamu.edu/~king/

Reagan Wells Ranch

This 200-acre guest ranch in the hill country of Texas specializes in birding and nature trails. The ranch has three blinds set up for observing birds.

http://www.reaganwells.com

Rockport-Fulton

Because of its temperate climate, varied habitat, and location in the central flyway, the Rockport-Fulton area of Texas has become popular with both birds and birders. The location is famous for its wintering Whooping Cranes at the Aransas National Wildlife Refuge (*see earlier in this section*), but one should not overlook its migrating passerines, its shorebirds, waterfowl, raptors, and other kinds of birds—a total of nearly 500 species. According to the website, sponsored by the Chamber of Commerce, one can see up to 200 species in a day in spring. The site describes both land and boat birding tours in considerable detail and also has links to other birding sites of interest. From the home page, select Birding.

http://www.rockport-fulton.org

Andean Condor (Dover)

Texas Hill Country

Texas does many things big, including, in this case, domain names: this site has 22 letters all together. Southern Texas is home to such species as the Golden-cheeked Warbler, the Black-capped Vireo, and the Curve-billed Thrasher. "More than 400 species of birds can be sighted in our region," Penny C. Reeh of the local Chamber of Commerce tells us. She adds that June Osborne, who has written a birding book for Uvalde County, conducts an Elder Hostel program at a local lodge each year. The site offers information about how to get to the Texas Hill Country and where to stay.

http://www.texhillcountryvacation.com

Upper Texas Coast

The Upper Texas Coast, one of the great birding regions in the United States, includes Galveston and the counties of Harris, Fort Bend, Brazoria, Chambers, and Jefferson. David Sarkozi's Birds of the Upper Texas Coast website includes a guide to two dozen local and state parks, nature trails, sanctuaries, and national wildlife refuges in the area with a capsule profile for each. If the locality has its own website—and many do—he provides a link. Often additional information is available about specific birds or checklists of birds found at the locales.

http://texasbirding.simplenet.com/location.htm

West Texas

This page on Jim Peterson's Trans-Pecos Birds website includes maps of West Texas and links to information about the best birding areas in the region—and some say, in the United States. Among the famous birding locales here are Big Bend National Park and Big Bend Ranch State Park along the Rio Grande.

http://www.esdallas.org/esd/pecos/

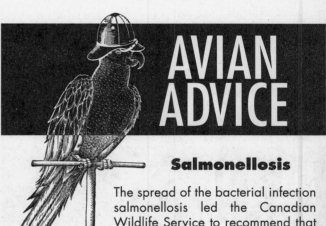

AVIAN ADVICE

Salmonellosis

The spread of the bacterial infection salmonellosis led the Canadian Wildlife Service to recommend that bird feeders in affected areas be taken down for at least a month in the winter of 1998. Smaller birds like finches, redpolls, goldfinches, and siskins were most affected by the disease, which is spread through direct contact with sick birds, bird droppings, or exposure to contaminated food or water. Keeping birds from gathering in large groups was the goal of taking down the feeders, when an area had numerous reports of dead and dying small birds. Feeders should be cleaned thoroughly with soap and water and then disinfected in a solution of one part bleach and nine parts water.

—adapted from Nova Scotia Bird Society

http://www.chebucto.ns.ca/Recreation/NS-BirdSoc/salmonella.html

A B C **D** E F G H I J K L M N O P Q R S T U V W X Y Z

EASTERN

Birding from the North Coast

Birding from the North Coast actually refers to the south coast of Lake Erie, but it's the coast northeasterly of Cleveland, Ohio, which locals call the *North Coast*. Just in case you were wondering. Dick and Jean Hoffman of Cleveland Heights have put together a website to aid birders in that region and for those planning a visit. Check out Dick's Cleveland Area Birding Site Guide, which has descriptions of lakefront, as well as inland parks and reserves that are noted for good birdwatching. Jean has a special report, one whose title might surprise you: The Breeding Birds of Lake View Cemetery. Since 1971, she has been birding this 285-acre tract, nearly a quarter of which is still "undeveloped," and has found more than 75 species breeding there. The website has the latest reports about interesting sightings in the area and an excellent guide to shorebirds (*see also North American Birds, Sea & Shore, Swimmers, and Waders*). This is an altogether readable, enjoyable, and valuable website that folks near to and far from Cleveland can learn from.

http://pw1.netcom.com/~djhoff/home.html

MEET THE MASTERS

To Hear a Nightingale

"I'd been a birder since childhood and interested in songs for quite a while," says Tony Phillips, creator of the New York Bird Songs website <http://math.math.sunysb.edu/~tony/birds/index.html>. "I wanted my website to encourage other people to make their own, so I could hear what birds around the world sounded like. For example, I had never heard a nightingale, although, of course, I'd heard a lot about nightingales, and I hoped someone would put one up for me to hear." Since then it's happened; you can hear the legendary nightingale on your computer. Try <http://www.springer.de/newmedia/lifesci/eti/by/nighting.htm>.

Belted Kingfisher (*Megaceryle alcyon*) (JJA)

Birding in New England

Don't be too put off by the fact that Chuck Seggelin's Birding in New England page has dates from 1995 and 1996. Although Chuck hasn't added much lately to his site, he still supports it, and the birding trips he describes are as interesting and useful today as they were when written. Most locales are in eastern Massachusetts, Rhode Island, and southern New Hampshire, and the birds seen at each are listed.

http://www.tiac.net/users/pdragon/birdtrip.html

Birding New Jersey

Birding New Jersey is a site "dedicated to providing current and accurate information to inform, entertain, and educate the average birder on the aspects of Birding New Jersey." Webmaster "Owen" includes a list of birds you are apt to see in New Jersey, as well as suggestions on Hot Spots at which to see them. The site also lists festivals, publishes New Jersey Rare Bird Alerts, and has a lot more information.

http://www.birdnj.com

Cape May Bird Observatory

Cape May at the south end of New Jersey is a leading birding location on the East Coast. The New Jersey Audubon Society's website offers a list of the nearly 400 species of birds that have been positively sighted in or just off Cape May County (*first address*). In fact, birds are so important that the community of West Cape May recently passed an ordinance that regulates the cutting of trees—for instance, fell one for a new house, and you have to plant another in its place. Depending on zoning, between 35 and 45 percent of a lot must have plant coverage, preferably native plants that provide food. This law is aimed at retaining places for migratory birds to stop, rest, and feed. Countless seabirds and land birds can be seen here, and the area is so important to birds that in 1975, the New Jersey Audubon Society established its now-famous Cape May Bird Observatory. The observatory "is a leader in research, environmental education, bird conservation, and recreational birding activities," the organization's site reports. "Our mission: to understand and instill appreciation of the needs of resident and migrating birds so that human ambitions do not undermine them." The observatory draws tens of thousands of visitors, and its staff has some of the top naturalists in the country, including Pete Dunne, the director, who is widely known for his writings on birds. The observatory has both spring and fall festivals that coincide with migrations, but schedules many events throughout the year—all described on its websites (*second and third addresses*).

http://www.nj.com/audubon/genlmenu/cmbirds.html
http://www.pressplus.com/content/birds/cmbo.html
http://www.nj.com/audubon/calmenu/calcmbo.html

Central Park Birdwatcher

Who would think that a park in the middle of one of the world's biggest and busiest cities is also one of the "14 best birdwatching sites in North America"? But indeed, New York City's Central Park can be teeming with birds, especially at migration times, and new media consultant Christopher Hayes has put together the Central Park Birdwatcher, an artful and interesting site about this world-famous urban oasis of trees and water. Follow Hayes' Next Leaf icons to take a tour of the park and its birds. Hayes tells us he has many

plans for expansion and improvement of the site—and since "new media" is his profession, one can expect the work will be beautiful, as well as informative.

http://hisoffice.com/birds

Everglades National Park

Few places in North America are as big, wild, life-filled and life-sensitive as the Everglades, a 1.5-million-acre national park in southwestern Florida. As park superintendent Richard G. Ring observed, "Everglades National Park is one of our nation's treasured lands; its significance matched only, and unfortunately, by its fragility." The Everglades—the only place in the world where alligators and crocodiles still exist side by side—is a birder's paradise. If you follow the link to the expanded website, the park service has a list of nearly 350 species of birds that live in the Everglades, with information as to when they can be seen and how common they are. (There are also checklists of other species.) The main and expanded websites are full of information, pictures, maps, and books about the Everglades that you can order online—many describe birds of the Everglades or of Florida.

http://www.nps.gov/ever/

Harlan's Hawk (*Buteo borealis*)
[Red-tailed Hawk, *Buteo jamaicensis harlans*] (JJA)

A
B
C
D
E
F
G
H
I
J
K
L
M
N
O
P
Q
R
S
T
U
V
W
X
Y
Z

J. N. Ding Darling National Wildlife Refuge

The J. N. "Ding" Darling National Wildlife Refuge is 6,300 acres of wonderful bird habitat on Sanibel Island off the southwest coast of Florida, 2,800 acres of which have been designated wilderness. Nearly 240 bird species have been identified using refuge habitats, as well as 51 species of reptiles and amphibians and 32 species of mammals. The refuge includes a five-mile automobile or bicycle tour route, and canoes or kayaks are also available to rent for wandering through the mangrove wetlands. Expect to see plenty of alligators sunning themselves alongside the edges of the water. This U.S. Fish & Wildlife Service site gives extensive information about the Ding Darling refuge.

http://www.fws.gov/r4eao/wildlife/nwrjnd.html

John James Audubon State Park

John James Audubon, considered the first artist or ornithologist to depict life-size birds and animals in their natural surroundings, lived in Henderson, Kentucky, for several years. The commonwealth of Kentucky has established the John James Audubon State Park, Museum, & Nature Center to commemorate the famous personage. Here you'll find not only birds but also the world's largest collection of Audubon memorabilia and "one of the most extensive collections of his work." Four galleries cover Audubon, his life, his work, and his legacy. The collection includes many original drawings. The nature center has a binocular-equipped observatory and an interactive discovery center, especially great for kids. The 692-acre state park, situated on the Mississippi flyway, has more than five miles of trails. In the spring, you are apt to see up to 20 species of warblers here. The first site is sponsored by the Henderson County Tourism Commission, whereas the second is the official Kentucky Department of Parks address. Even more information about Audubon State Park can be found at the Friends of Audubon site (*third address*).

http://www.go-henderson.com/audubon.htm
http://www.state.ky.us/agencies/parks/audubon2.htm
http://www.dynasty.net/users/rawham/FOA.HTM

Little St. Simons Island

Accessible only by boat, Little St. Simons Island, Georgia, is a 10,000-acre barrier island off the coast, containing a fine, old hunting lodge built in 1917. The virtually undeveloped island is also a birder's paradise, nicely situated on the Atlantic flyway and offering both nesting and migrating species. In fact, more than 220 kinds of birds have been spotted here. Either of these addresses provides plenty of information about the island lodge and the wildlife around it, but the first is the newer one.

http://www.LittleStSimonsIsland.com
http://www.pactel.com.au/lssi/

Golden Eagle (*Aquila chrysaetos*) (JJA)

Maine Birding

Mainebirding.net is a marvelous website for any birder who lives in Maine, plans to visit Maine, or would just like to know more about the birds and birding of the northeasternmost state. "The State of Maine offers some of the best birding in the continental United States," says Paul Garrity, creator and Webmaster of this comprehensive site. "That may sound like a biased comment (and it is!) but I have lived and birded in Maine for over 40 years and I have yet to find a wider variety of birding habitats available within a fairly short distance." He adds that Maine offers the only Atlantic or Common Puffin nesting colonies in the United States (*see also North American Birds, Sea & Shore*). The website has suggestions for where to go birding in the state and offers many links to other Maine and Maine-oriented sites, as well as to sites with general information about the state. A message board is provided for Maine birding, where lots of ideas and helpful suggestions are exchanged.

http://www.mainebirding.net

Merritt Island National Wildlife Refuge

Although most people think of the Everglades when Florida wildlife is mentioned, Merritt Island is one of the best wildlife viewing areas in the entire Southeast. The 220-square-mile reserve has more than 330 bird species, including 10 federally listed endangered or threatened species, as residents or visitors. Situated on a barrier island and surrounding John F. Kennedy Space Center, the refuge is part of the Atlantic flyway. "November brings large numbers of waterfowl, including Northern Shoveler, American Wigeon, Northern Pintail, Green-winged Teal, Blue-winged Teal, Lesser Scaup, Ruddy Duck, and Ring-necked Duck," says the Florida Fish & Game Commission site (*first address*). "November also begins nesting season for Bald Eagles. . . . Wading birds court and nest in spring, and crowd the flats to fish year-round. Roseate Spoonbills and Black-necked Stilts are summer residents. Look for Scrub Jays on their perches along Highway 3." The seven-mile Black Point Wildlife Drive can be traversed by car, bicycle, or foot, and will expose you to dozens of species of often exotic birds. There is also an observation tower and a photo blind. Admission is free. The National Wildlife Service has more information (*second address*).

Professor Gerry Rising, who writes for the *Buffalo News*, tells of a trip to Merritt Island (*third address*). Adjacent to the Merritt Island refuge is the Canaveral National Seashore, operated by the National Park Service. "The park offers sanctuary for over 1,000 species of plants, 300 species of birds, including 14 threatened or endangered species," says its website (*fourth address*).

http://fcn.state.fl.us/gfc/viewing/sites/site33.html

http://www.fws.gov/r4eao/wildlife/nwrmrt.html

http://www.acsu.buffalo.edu/~insrisg/nature/nw98/merritt.html

http://www.nps.gov/cana/

Mohonk Preserve

If you live in the Northeast, consider a visit to the Mohonk Preserve, part of the northern Shawangunk (pronounced *SHON-gum*) Mountains in Ulster County, New York. The 38-square mile natural area, "a natural environment for diverse species, such as hawks, ravens, beaver, and turtles," includes almost 25,000 acres of semi-wilderness used by hikers, birdwatchers, climbers, cross-country skiers, bicyclists, and other outdoor enthusiasts. "Only 90 miles north of Manhattan," according to the site, the preserve is "a world of Hudson Valley and Catskill vistas, sheer white cliffs, and stately hemlock forests."

http://mohonkpreserve.org

North Hero House

Each spring, North Hero House, a Vermont inn on Lake Champlain, hosts with the Green Mountain Audubon Society several birding events in the Champlain Islands, which are located on an important northern corridor of the Atlantic flyway. "Each year hundreds of species make their way through the Islands on their way to their summer nesting sites," says the inn, whose owner, Walt Blasberg, adds some notes of his own regarding the spring and fall migrations. Full details about the programs and the inn, as well as the North Hero area, are available on the inn's site.

http://www.northherohouse.com/birds.html

A B C D E F G H I J K L M N O P Q R S T U V W X Y Z

A
B
C
D
E
F
G
H
I
J
K
L
M
N
O
P
Q
R
S
T
U
V
W
X
Y
Z

MEET THE MASTERS

The Real vs. the Virtual

"Fortunately, nature never becomes outdated—that was why I thought it would still be interesting to some folks to read articles from 25 years ago, or more," says Sandra Bray, Webmaster of the Utah Natural History Society's website <**http://www.softcom. net/users/naturenotes**>. Sandra has placed online more than 150 articles from the society's print publication, *Nature News Notes*, some of which date back a quarter century or more, and many of which relate to birds. "Putting these articles on the Web can make them available to more people," she notes. Sandra admits that "it is a little bit incongruous to use the Web for nature study —we should be encouraging people to spend more time outside with their hands in the dirt and their eyes and minds on the real world rather than on the virtual world of their computers." However, she adds, "computers have become a great way to preserve information and to communicate it to others." And thus, the wonderful archive of the Utah naturalists.

MOUNTAIN

Alta Meadow Ranch

Alta Meadow Ranch in Alta, Montana, promotes itself as a comfortable place to go birding in the northern Rockies year-round. "Alta Meadow, several hundred acres of grassland, marshes, forests and ponds, surrounded by hundreds of miles of Montana and Idaho wilderness, is prime habitat for raptors, shore birds, waterfowl, forest dwellers and migratory birds on their way over the Bitterroot Mountains," the website reports in its Activities section. The site is full of information about the natural history—and human history (Lewis and Clark went through, and so did the Nez Perce)—of the wilderness that surrounds the ranch.

http://www.altameadow.com

Casa de San Pedro

Casa de San Pedro is a bed-and-breakfast on the edge of the San Pedro Riparian National Conservation Area at Hereford, Arizona. Hosts Chuck and Judy Wetzel report that their neighborhood is ideal for bird-watching. In fact, they list 47 resident species that are unique to that area and that you would be apt to find. If you click on the website's season of the year, you get a list of the birds likely to be sighted then. There's also information about area ecotourism programs.

http://www.naturesinn.com

Colorado Birding Spots

The Colorado Birding Society has a listing of dozens of top birding spots in the state, with very precise directions to each spot, sometimes noting which special birds you might see at certain places.

http://home.att.net/~birdertoo/albirdingspots.htm

New Mexico Birding

Robert Hole Jr.'s New Mexico Birding website has information on close to a dozen top birding spots in the state where the Greater Roadrunner is the official bird. Robert has links to national parks, national forests, state parks, historic sites, and other good birding locations. There are also links to interesting birding places in adjacent states.

http://www.interaktv.com/NM/NMBirding.html

Roadrunner (Dover)

Stillwater National Wildlife Refuge

For thousands of years, the wetlands of Stillwater National Wildlife Refuge 60 miles east of Reno, Nevada, were visited by uncountable migrating ducks, Tundra Swans, Dowitchers, and other birds. It was also home to the Paiute Indians. In the last century, the work of humans has reduced these wetlands as the waters that fed them were diverted for agricultural uses. By 1992, what had once been 150,000 acres of wetlands was but 2,000. However, recently, measures have been taken to preserve the land, as well as the water that makes it so important. Federal legislation in 1990 allows the refuge to purchase water rights. The article (*first address*) from the *Refuge Reporter* details the fight to save Stillwater and why it's so important. Preserving bird habitats is one of the most important reasons given, and the article tells much about the birds that visit and live there. Birds are so important, in fact, that Stillwater has a Spring Wings Bird Festival each May to celebrate the migrants. The area is home to nesting Black Terns, Forster's Tern, American Bitterns, Black-necked Stilts, phalaropes, White-faced Ibises, Great Blue Herons, Redheads, California Gulls, and many kinds of grebes. The page includes a map of the refuge. For more on Stillwater National Wildlife Refuge, the Nevada Wildlife Federation has a page (*second address*) explaining its history, its wetlands, its many wild creatures, and the fight to preserve this nationally famous resource. The WetNet (*third address*) provides a summary of land use, management, and environmental threat information.

http://www.gorp.com/gorp/resource/us_nwr/ nv_still.htm

http://www.nvwf.org/nevada/places/pl_still.htm

http://www.wetlands.ca/wi-a/whsrn/stilwatr.html

Teller Wildlife Refuge

The Teller Wildlife Refuge consists of 1,300 acres in Montana's Bitterroot Valley. The refuge, which has its own lodgings, reports that more than 230 kinds of birds frequent the place, including four species of owls. The website notes that the "Teller Wildlife Refuge is one of a growing number of private conservation initiatives in Montana intended to counter the trend of subdividing agricultural land into real estate

developments, and it is one of the first privately owned and managed wildlife refuges in the state." Mary Stone, the guest manager, adds that "one of our favorite things to do is spoil our guests rotten." Detailed descriptions and plenty of photos are available on the site.

http://www.bitterroot.net/teller/lodging.html

Tucson Planner

Tucson, Arizona, reports that it's in one of the five best bird-watching areas of the United States. More than 450 species can be found in and around the city, including Gambel's Quail, the Greater Roadrunner, Black-chinned Hummingbird, Costa's Hummingbird, Inca Dove, Gilded Flicker, Gila Woodpecker, Curve-billed Thrasher, Cactus Wren, Verdin, Pyrrhuloxia, and Black-throated Sparrow. This page (*first address*) gives a rundown on birding around Tucson, including great birding spots and other sources of information. For more on Tucson, you can fill out a form (*second address*) to a request for a free Tucson Vacation Planner that includes information about birding adventures, maps, birding tips, and—of course—about Tucson.

http://www.visittucson.org/vacationplanner/ birdwatching/index.html

http://www.visittucson.org/

FEATHERED FACTS

Lot of Food

"Backyard bird feeding is a convenient way to enjoy wildlife. According to a recent Census Report, over 65 million Americans, young and old, have given it a try."

—Baltimore Bird Club

http://www.bcpl.net/~tross/by/feed.html

Duck Hawk (*Falco peregrinus*) [Peregrine Falcon] (JJA)

PACIFIC

Arcata Birding

"For a wide variety of birding habitats—and several hundred species of birds—all within a relatively small area, come to Arcata on northern California's Redwood Coast," urges the City of Arcata website. Many birding hot spots in the area are described, including a map showing the local wastewater treatment plant—which draws a lot of species! The site tells you how to get a booklet called *A Guide to Birding in and around Arcata* and has a fine collection of local birding links, including many parks and refuges in the region.

http://www.tidepool.com/arcatacy/birding.html

Birding the Denali Highway

The Denali Highway is 130 miles of gravel road, one of the few east-west routes in Alaska, that joins Paxton to Cantwell and is on the eastern edge of the Denali National Park. The road is open from May 1 to Oct. 1. Tina and Duncan MacDonald spent three days in June 1998 exploring the road and offer at this site a log of their findings. "Birders looking for high tundra breeding birds can spend many enjoyable days" on the Denali Road, says Tina (who operates Birding Hotspots Around the World (*see also Destinations, International*). She kept a mile-by-mile log of the birds she and her husband, Duncan, saw, and shares that with you along with many tips for your own trip along the Denali.

http://www.camacdonald.com/birding/Hotspots/Denali1.htm

Fairbanks

Fairbanks, the most inland of Alaska's cities, is only a hundred or so miles south of the Arctic Circle. The area is home to more than 200 interesting bird species, most of them migrants, and the Arctic Audubon Society has put together this guide (*first address*) to Birding Hot Spots around Fairbanks. The Alaska Bird Observatory in Fairbanks also has a page (*second address*) of suggested birding places.

http://www.ptialaska.net/~audubon/birding.html
http://www.alaskabird.org/ABOBirdingInFbx.html

Kilauea Lodge

Kilauea Lodge is a country inn located in Volcano Village, on the island of Hawaii. The lodge caters to birders, noting that it's but a mile away from Hawaii Volcanoes National Park. "The park, home of Hawaii's active volcano Kilauea, offers miles of scenic overlook and trails," the inn's website says. "Endangered birds—the Nene, I'iwi and Amakihi—make their home in and near the park."

http://www.kilauea-lodge.com

FEATHERED FACTS

Quail in the City?

A relative of the myna bird, the European Starling is almost as good a mimic as its cousin, frequently imitating the calls of many other species of birds. If you hear a Bobwhite Quail or a meadowlark in the middle of a city, look up at the wires and trees for a starling.

—adapted from William J. Kern Jr., University of Florida

http://hammock.ifas.ufl.edu/txt/fairs/uw118

Lake Clark National Park

Silver Salmon Creek Lodge (*first address*) is situated in Lake Clark National Park, Alaska, which is an excellent place to see coastal pelagic birds, including Horned and Tufted Puffins, kittiwakes, eiders, murres, Bald Eagles, and Trumpeter Swans. There are many more exotic and common species, according to the lodge's website, which has full information—including photos—about the facilities. For more details regarding Lake Clark National Park, visit the second address.

http://www.alaskan.com/silversalmon/

http://www.nps.gov/lacl/

Malheur National Wildlife Refuge

Professors Del Blackburn and Donna Loper at Clark College in Washington have put together a website devoted to the wildlife of the Malheur National Wildlife Refuge, a huge wetland in southeastern Oregon. This site has a great checklist of interesting birds, including photos and field notes, and a 29-stop tour of the area. Malheur Lake has one of the largest freshwater marshes in North America, covering up to 60,000 acres and rich in birdlife.

http://www.clark.edu/Academics/AppliedTech/EP/
   BioWeb/bioweb.html

Nome

"There's no place like Nome," says the Nome Convention and Visitors Bureau. That's right, this remote northwestern Alaska outpost has a convention and visitors bureau. And if you're a birder in search of the exotic, Nome may be right up your alley. "Nome is a little known treasure for birders," the bureau says. "Once the ice begins to break up, migration begins. Virtually the entire area of the Seward Peninsula that is accessible by road from Nome is comprised of extremely valuable nesting areas for many bird species including most North American waterfowl." Interesting species around Nome include Emperor Geese; Steller's Eiders; Harlequin Ducks; Oldsquaws; Arctic, Pacific and, Yellow-billed Loons; Tufted and Horned Puffins; Crested Auklets; Pelagic Cormorants; Gyrfalcons; Golden Eagles; Peregrine Falcons; Wheatears; Bluethroats; Wandering Tattlers; Bristle-

thighed Curlews; and Arctic Warblers. At least 10 services offer Nome tours. This page provides information about birding and links to the Nome home page which has plenty of information for would-be visitors. Oh, and in case you thought Nome is some kind of eternal icebox, when we stopped by the site in late winter, the high temperature in Nome was 29°F. That was warmer than the high temperature at our home in southern Connecticut the day before.

http://www.alaska.net/~nome/birds.htm

Oregon Birding Maps

This site's collection of maps would be useful for anyone planning more than casual bird-watching in Oregon. They include a map that shows where all the national wildlife refuges are, as well as detailed maps of several of the refuges, plus maps of other birding spots.

http://www.spacerad.com/birding/oregon.html

Common Nighthawk (*Chordeiles minor*) (JJA)

A B C D E F G H I J K L M N O P Q R S T U V W X Y Z

FEATHERED FACTS

Lumpers and Splitters

In the field of taxonomy, a lumper is a scientist who tends to emphasize the similarities among species and group them together in the same genus wherever possible. A splitter tends to go the opposite way, emphasizing differences between species and increasing the number of genera. In modern taxonomy lumpers appear to outnumber splitters and many formerly separate genera are no longer considered separate.

—adapted from the Bird Dictionary

http://birdcare.com/birdon/birdindex/

Wrangell

"Stop!" warns the home page of the Wrangell, Alaska, Chamber of Commerce. "Before you explore any further throughout this web site, make sure you really want to be here. We are not like other larger Alaska cities you may be more familiar with. We don't have stop lights. You won't find a McDonald's, or a shopping mall." But what you will find are eagles and more than a hundred other birds that migrate to this southeastern Alaska community on the Stikine River. If you select Things to See & Do, then Birding, you'll learn that in mid-April, more than 14,000 Snow Geese, 10,000 Sandhill Cranes, and nearly 2,000 Bald Eagles begin arriving on the delta. "The concentration of eagles is the largest reported springtime concentration in North America," the chamber says. "The eagles arrive to feast on the hooligan (smelt) migrating up the Stikine River to spawn." The area offers other treats, including dozens of shorebird species, plus Short-Eared Owls and Northern Harriers.

http://www.wrangell.com

INTERNATIONAL

Birding Hotspots around the World

"The success of this site has literally overwhelmed me!" said Tina MacDonald of Edmonton, Alberta, Webmaster of Birding Hotspots around the World. "Birders obviously have wanted a 'one-stop-shopping' kind of site regarding birding travel." Tina has created the best site of its kind we've seen. She draws on hundreds of state, provincial, and national sources to give detailed descriptions of countless great birding locations. It's a great site for exploring, especially if you are planning a trip. Tina also provides space for exhibits of wild bird photography, has an index of photographers from around the world, and displays scores of their photos online. The site offers much more—and has become one of the most popular and praised on the Web. Make sure you bookmark it. From the home page you can select birding locations by world region.

http://www.camacdonald.com/birding/birding.htm

Birding in British Columbia

Every province and state should be so fortunate as to have someone like Kevin Slagboom, the Webmaster of Birding in British Columbia. This is a textbook example of compiling an up-to-date library of information about regional birding—from the latest Rare Bird Alerts and provincial species list to places to go. The site features articles about birding techniques—some via links and some via the expert pen of Slagboom himself. This is an excellent site to learn about where to go birding in British Columbia and how to do it well when you get there.

http://birding.bc.ca

Canada Goose (Dover)

Birds of a Feather

Birds of a Feather is a bed-and-breakfast inn that caters to birders. Located on the water in Victoria, British Columbia, the establishment borders the 120-acre Esquimalt Lagoon Migratory Bird Sanctuary. More than 70 species of shorebirds and waterbirds have been found in this area. From the main home page, click the link to WebSite, then look at the frame menu at the left for Local Birding; here, you'll find information about local birds and birding guides, a British Columbia checklist, and even a live webcam view of the shore at Esquimalt Lagoon Wildlife Migratory Bird Sanctuary. By the way, lest you think Victoria is in some icy region of Canada, they have flowers there in February.

http://www.victorialodging.com

Canadian Birding Hotspots

Gord Gallant's Birding in Canada site has a growing collection of links to Canadian Birding Hotspots. Some link to articles on birding locations, whereas others bring you to birding websites.

http://www.interlog.com/~gallantg/canada/sites.html

Bald Eagle (*Haliaeetus leucocephalus*) (JJA)

Chan Chich Lodge

Imagine an inn sitting in 250,000 acres of a private tropical jungle preserve full of exotic birds. That's what the owners of Chan Chich Lodge, Belize, want you to dream of as they show you views of the lodge. And if that's not enough of a birder's dream, consider that the lodge is also located on the lower plaza of an ancient Mayan archaeological site (with the government's blessings, by the way), so you can explore not only nature but history. Chan Chich, incidentally, is Mayan for "little bird," and since the preserve has the highest Christmas bird count in Belize and the fifth highest of any place in Central America, one can assume there are a lot of little birds around. Even if you're not traveling to Chan Chich, the site and its fine photos are fun to explore.

http://www.chanchich.com

Ellis Bird Farm

The Ellis Bird Farm in Lacombe, central Alberta, is one of the more unusual places in North America. For decades, it has been a refuge for Mountain Bluebirds, thanks to the Ellis family, which set up hundreds of bluebird boxes and established a program of bluebird preservation and research. Today, the farm is owned by Union Carbide and operated by a conservation association, which opens it to the public in summer.

http://www.wep.ab.ca/ellisbirdfarm/

Hotel Punta Leona

The Hotel Punta Leona at Carara on the Pacific Coast of Costa Rica calls itself the "new birding hotspot." The website explains why. "There is a variety of habitats in our primary and secondary forests that attract hundreds of species of birds," the site says. "Additionally on our trails, we have two hummingbird feeding stations and several feeders that attract birds and mammals." In fact, the site has a list of 336 local birds seen on the hotel property or nearby. That "nearby" includes the Carara Biological Reserve. However, the hotel is on a 750-acre reserve, and each day a staff naturalist leads walks through the property.

http://www.hotelpuntaleona.com

A B C D E F G H I J K L M N O P Q R S T U V W X Y Z

A
B
C
D
E
F
G
H
I
K
L
M
N
O
P
Q
R
S
T
U
V
W
X
Y
Z

AVIAN ADVICE

Birds & Windows

Birds may strike windows because they don't see the glass or, in nesting season, because they see their reflection in the glass and want to drive off the intruder. Hanging sheer cloth or netting in front of the window breaks the reflection and the open-flight-path appearance. Taping crinkled plastic wrap onto the glass can have the same effect. Some people hang cloth or aluminum foil strips in front of the window, or plant shrubs. Others put hawk or owl silhouettes in the window to frighten birds, but this reportedly has limited effectiveness.

—adapted from Ron J. Johnson, Extension Wildlife Specialist, University of Nebraska

http://www.ianr.unl.edu/pubs/wildlife/g1332.htm#dwnw

Laguna del Lagarto Lodge

Laguna del Lagarto Lodge is situated on 1,250 acres of tropical rain forest in northern Costa Rica, and, according to its website, more than 350 different species of birds have been identified here, among them the rare Great Green Macaw. The website even has a detailed list of species in the area, including notes on their abundance and whether they are permanent or seasonal residents. The nicely designed site has information about the lodge, including a gallery of tempting photos.

http://www.adventure-costarica.com/laguna-del-lagarto/

Las Ventanas De Osa

According to its website, Las Ventanas De Osa is a 90-acre private wildlife sanctuary and preserve with a lodge "in the midst of one of the few remaining stands of virgin rain forest on the Pacific Ocean side of Costa Rica." The sanctuary's lodge, says the site, "was built to be enjoyed by people in touch with nature!" More than 350 species of birds have been identified on or near the property, which overlooks the Pacific. If you click on Birds on the home page, you'll find a page with a huge list of species that can be seen at Las Ventanas De Osa—and an e-mail address from which you can get even more up-to-date information.

http://www.lasventanasdeosa.com

Nova Scotia Birds

Anyone who lives and birds in Nova Scotia is probably familiar with Robie Tufts's *Birds of Nova Scotia*, first published in 1961. The most recent edition came out in 1986, four years after his death, and the Nova Scotia Museum of Nature History has placed the text online in an electronic version that you can read by topic or literally page through. "Not only is it an excellent resource for anyone wanting to know about the birds that visit Nova Scotia, it is a pleasure to read, full of interesting observations, amusing anecdotes and beautiful illustrations," the museum website says. What's more, the museum hopes that putting the book online will generate more data and dialogue that will result in an updated and revised version of the book. Meanwhile, if you're planning to visit Nova Scotia and enjoy its many species of birds, this site is a must-see. Usually, Tufts will tip you off to locations where he's seen the species.

http://museum.ednet.ns.ca/mnh/nature/nsbirds/bons.htm

Bald Eagle (*Haliaeetus leucocephalus*) (JJA)

Parks Canada

Canada has 38 national parks and national park reserves, situated in every province and territory, and most are summer nesting grounds for many species of birds. Canadian national parks range from a tiny 8.7 square kilometers in size to more than 44,000 square kilometers. Currently, the national parks system totals about 224,466 square kilometers or about 2 percent of Canada's land territory. When the system is complete, it is expected to cover just over 3 percent. The Parks Canada website has extensive information about all the parks, including guided tours with photos and inviting descriptions. There are maps, directions, weather, history, natural history, recreation, and other details for each park.

http://parkscanada.pch.gc.ca

Rancho Naturalista

Rancho Naturalista, Costa Rica, is another of those Central America hostelries where serious birders go to see the exotic and add to their life lists. And there's apparently plenty to see. "We invite those in love with nature to revel in one of the richest concentrations of birds, butterflies and plant species to be found in nature's realm," says Rancho Naturalista's website. To make its point, the operators of the 125-acre rancho include a list of 407 species of birds that have been sighted on the property.

http://www.ranchonaturalista.com/rancho.htm

Redberry Lake

Redberry Lake, near Saskatoon, Saskatchewan, is home to a colony of White Pelicans (among other migratory bird species). The Redberry Pelican Project was formed in 1989 to protect the habitat and en-courage "environmentally sound ecotourism of the area." The site describes this natural resource and lists the 189 species of birds that have been spotted at the lake.

http://www.redbay.com/redpel/pelicans.htm

Trinidad & Tobago

Trinidad and Tobago Islands in the Caribbean (off the coast of Venezuela) are home or stopping places for some 434 species of birds, including some of the world's rarest, such as the White-tailed Sabrewing Hummingbird. The tourism website (*first address*) includes plenty of tourism and nature information, but look especially for the well-written feature article Jewels of Nature by Harold Olaf Cecil (*second address*). Cecil will take you into an island forest preserve and describe in detail seeking the likes of the Purple Honey Creeper, Green Honey Creeper, Tufted Coquette Hummingbird, Copper-rumped Hummingbird, Blue-crowned Motmot, Bearded Bellbird, Blue-Gray Tanager, Silver-beaked Tanager, Boat-billed Flycatcher, Golden-headed Mannequin, and Black-tailed Tityra. The site offers ecotourism maps and descriptions of the islands' many preserves. Incidentally, if birds aren't the only winged creatures that interest you, these two islands are also home to some 600 species of butterflies. (On the first address, follow the links What to Do Here, then EcoTourism, then Trinidad and Tobago Eco Guide, which brings up a list of articles related to nature.)

http://www.visittnt.com
http://www.visittnt.com/ToDo/Eco/guide/jewels.htm

FEATHERED FACTS

Gluttons

Although the Cedar Waxwing is famous for consuming huge amounts of berries, these peripatetic birds can also eat massive numbers of insects. For instance, one flock of 30 birds was estimated to have consumed 90,000 canker worms in a single month.

—adapted from Robert Rice, Smithsonian Migratory Bird Center

http://web2.si.edu/smbc/bom/cewa.htm

A
B
C
D
E
F
G
H
I
J
K
L
M
N
O
P
Q
R
S
T
U
V
W
X
Y
Z

A
B
C
D
E
F
G
H
I
J
K
L
M
N
O
P
Q
R
S
T
U
V
W
X
Y
Z

EVENTS

Everyone loves a get-together, and bird-watchers are no exception. In the past decade or two, special events for birders have proliferated. Across North America, dozens of birding festivals and symposiums have sprung up, many drawing thousands of visitors. Some events may be far away, others as near as your "backyard" (or your computer). Festivals usually include speakers, seminars, guided bird walks, art or nature shows, and vendors. Often, they are keyed to some special natural phenomenon, such as the arrival of a species or group of birds on a seasonal migration. Divided geographically to facilitate your search, this section also includes ornithological events, the Christmas bird counts and the Great Backyard Bird Count chief among them. Remember that many annual festivals and special events may not post information or forewarn you about their next event until a few months before the occasion. Consequently, you may find the previous year's at these addresses. But the sites will usually give you a good sense of what the event is about and a contact link so you can e-mail the sponsors. This section even has a site with information about how to start your own birding event. And there are some directories of birding festivals, many of which do not have websites but do have e-mail or at least snailmail addresses. (See also Audubon Societies & Sanctuaries.)

GENERAL

ABA Big Day

Each spring, the American Birding Association sponsors the "Big Day," in which teams of birders identify as many birds as possible. "A Big Day Count is a single-team effort in which the primary objectives are to identify as many bird species as possible during a single calendar day and to strive to have all team members identify all species recorded," say the official rules, which are posted on the ABA website, along with results of recent competitions. The site is also set up so your team can submit its findings electronically. How many birds might a team see? Well, in 1997, two men in New Mexico saw 200 species in less than 24 hours.

http://www.americanbirding.org/ababdyrep.htm

Bird Activity Calendar

Although most of this section is devoted to special events for humans, we thought it appropriate to include what birds are doing at different times of the year. This Bird Activity Calendar, found on the Nutty Birdwatcher's site, is written for folks in the eastern half of the United States and southern Canada.

http://nuthatch.birdnature.com/birdactivity.html

Birdathons

Some Audubon chapters have been running fundraisers called Birdathons for more than 40 years. Usually held in May, these events raise money for local chapters and conservation organizations. Teams of birders find sponsors to support their efforts to scour the countryside in search of as many species as possible in a 24-hour period. Anyone is welcome to join the efforts or to sponsor birders. To learn whether your area has a Birdathon, check the Audubon chapter index page for a chapter or chapters near you.

http://www.audubon.org/chapter/

FEATHERED FACTS

Seizers

Hawks, falcons, owls, eagles, ospreys, and kites are all called *raptors*, which is Latin for "one who seizes." Whereas many birds "seize" insects and other small critters such as worms, frogs, and minnows, the raptors grab bigger things—mostly mammals and other birds, but also sizable fish. They are, as Diane Porter puts it, "birds of grander bearing."

—adapted from Raptor Rapture

http://www.birdwatching.com/stories/hawks.html

Birder's World Calendar of Events

Birder's World, a popular magazine for bird-watchers, has a website that includes an excellent calendar of birding events, arranged by state and province. Check here for information about happenings in your area or in places you are planning to visit.

http://www.2.birdersworld.com/birders/Meetings/ Meetings.html

Birding Festivals

Here's a comprehensive catalog of birding festivals around the United States (*first address*). If website links are known, they are included. The collection is compiled by Magnolia Software, which make O'See, a birding database (*see also Software*). Another good guide to birding festivals in the United States is provided by the U.S. Fish & Wildlife Service. However, your fingers may cramp up trying to type the address (*second address; use capital letters where shown*).

http://magnoliasoftware.com/festival.htm

http://bluegoose.arw.r9.fws.gov/NWRSFiles/ PublicUseMgmt/birdingfestivals.html

Christmas Bird Counts

Probably the best-known annual birding event is the Christmas Bird Count, sponsored by the National Audubon Society. That's probably because it's been happening annually since December 1900. Everyone—from beginning bird-watchers to veteran ornithologists—may participate in the December event (it's not really on Christmas Day; different groups schedule their counts for different days, but all around the Christmas holiday). Observers head into the field in an established 15-mile circle and count every bird they see. Around 50,000 people participate each year across North America, and their findings are used by scientists at Audubon, at the Cornell Laboratory of Ornithology, and elsewhere to study such phenomenon as migration, weather effects on birds, and changing populations and ranges of species. The Cornell Lab site (*first address*) tells you about the Christmas Bird Count and how to participate. You can even find a database of a century's

worth of sightings—if your neighborhood had a count in 1924, you can view what they saw. This kind of long-range information is useful even to amateur birders who want to know more about what has been and can be seen in their communities. For one person's experiences as a participant in four Christmas Bird Counts, read Professor Gerry Rising's column from the *Buffalo News* (*second address*).

http://birdsource.cornell.edu/cbc/

http://www.acsu.buffalo.edu/~insrisg/nature/nw98/ cbc97.html

Hudsonian Chickadee (*Penthestes hudsonicus*) [Boreal Chickadee, *Parus hudsonicus*] (JJA)

A
B
C
D
E
F
G
H
I
J
K
L
M
N
O
P
Q
R
S
T
U
V
W
X
Y
Z

Eskimo Curlew (*Phaelopus borealis*) [*Numenius borealis*] (JJA)

Great Backyard Bird Count

Each February, scientists and ordinary bird-watchers join in one of the great citizen-science efforts, the Great Backyard Bird Count. Cosponsored by the National Audubon Society and Cornell's Laboratory of Ornithology, the event runs Friday through Monday. You count the birds you see in your yard (or park or other location) and report them on Cornell's BirdSource website each day via an easy-to-use form. You can see up-to-date totals of how many species in your state or province have been spotted, and their numbers. "Bird-watching is the fastest-growing pastime in the country, which 54 million people enjoy each year," said Frank Gill, senior vice president of science for National Audubon. "When we combine this interest with the Internet technology of BirdSource, we can immediately begin to assess the status of North American wintering birds." In 1998, the count's first year, 14,000 people reported more than a half million birds, resulting in important finds about the effects of El Niño on populations. Counts in subsequent years are helping scientists evaluate the effects of post–El Niño numbers and species distributions. John Fitzpatrick, director of the Cornell Lab, says that "the more information we have, the better we'll be able to help ensure our common birds will remain common, and take measures to protect species already in decline. This is why it's so important to get as many people as possible to tell us what they're seeing." While visiting the site, you can also fill out a "favorite bird survey" and tell the Lab about yourself and your degree of interest in birds.

http://birdsource.cornell.edu/gbbc/index.html

Start Your Own Birding Festival

Ever thought of having your own birding festival—or at least, a bird day? A local birding festival can be as simple as a few dozen people showing up for a lecture or a hawk watch, but it can be a lot more. "Most often they involve a series of lectures, guided tours, art shows, trade shows, and other events to celebrate nature in a local community," says Mary Anne Young of the Division of Refuges at the U.S. Fish & Wildlife Service. "Every community has something special to offer—Hinckley, Ohio, annually celebrates the return of the vultures!" This page provides many tips to help you decide whether you might want to set up a festival, how to do it, what its advantages are, and where you can find help. It's a very nice service of a government agency that wants the public to appreciate the wildlife in the United States—and the habitats in which they live.

http://bluegoose.arw.r9.fws.gov/NWRSFiles/
PublicUseMgmt/BirdfestHP.html

WEB WORDS

Avalanche of Birds

"We saw a flock of 500 or more, and when they arose it seemed that a hole had been rent in the earth. Two miles farther along we came to Ed Ward's. Such a sight I have never seen before nor since. Chickens were flushing everywhere, and droves of fifty to a hundred would take down the corn rows, sounding like a moving avalanche. As we thrashed back and forth across the grain field, the chickens arose in flocks of 50 to 500. Mr. Ward and I estimated that there were from 3,500 to 4,000 chickens in this one field, a sight never to be forgotten."

—Walter Colvin, describing the now-endangered Lesser Prairie Chicken, *Outing* magazine, February 1914

CENTRAL

Big Stone Bird Festival

East meets west in the Big Stone Lake region of Minnesota, on the South Dakota line. And that includes species of birds according to the Chamber of Commerce for the sister cities of Ortonville, Minnesota, and Big Stone City, South Dakota. The chamber sponsors the Big Stone Bird Festival in early May, offering field trips led by the top birders in Minnesota and South Dakota, and centering on the Big Stone National Wildlife Refuge, located in prairie pothole country. "The spring shorebird migration can be spectacular," says the chamber. "Upland prairie birds will be arriving to nest. The focus is birds of the mudflats and upland grasslands." For details, check the Festivals and Events link on the chamber's home page.

http://www.bigstonelake.com

Bluebird Festival

Each March for more than 15 years, the Dahlem Environmental Education Center of Jackson Community College, Michigan, hosts the Bluebird Festival, a Saturday and Sunday event that includes two-dozen birding and other natural history lectures, walks, an art show, environmental and conservation displays, and more. The site provides a full rundown and links to more information about the area.

http://www.jackson.cc.mi.us/DahlemCenter

Least Bittern (*Ixobryclius exilis*) (JJA)

FEATHERED FACTS

A Murder of Crows

A group of crows is called a murder of crows, "based on the persistent but fallacious folk tale that crows form tribunals to judge and punish the bad behavior of a member of the flock. If the verdict goes against the defendant, that bird is killed (murdered) by the flock." This belief is probably based on the fact that sometimes crows will kill a dying crow who doesn't belong in their territory or because they sometimes feed on carcasses of dead crows. "Also, both crows and ravens are associated with battlefields, medieval hospitals, execution sites and cemeteries (because they scavenged on human remains). In England, a tombstone is sometimes called a ravenstone."

—adapted from American Society of Crows and Ravens

http://www.azstarnet.com/~serres/crowfaq.html

Detroit Lakes Festival of Birds

Detroit Lakes is in northwestern Minnesota, east of Fargo, North Dakota, "a place where the tallgrass prairie, with its gently rolling plains and potholes, meets the edge of both northern hardwood and boreal forest ecosystems. The diversity of bird and animal life here is unique. In a small geographic area, birders can find a tremendous variety of species. Mid-May, which is usually peak songbird migration here, can be spectacular!" At least 25 kinds of warblers have been spotted here, and the website includes a list of birds along with information about the annual festival that consists of speakers, field trips, and a banquet that takes place around the third week in May. If you go to the Chamber of Commerce link, you'll learn much travel and sightseeing information about Detroit Lakes and Becker County.

http://www.detroitlakes.com/chamber/bird/bird.html

A
B
C
D
E
F
G
H
I
J
K
L
M
N
O
P
Q
R
S
T
U
V
W
X
Y
Z

FOR THE BIRDS

Help!

Did you run across a Web address that doesn't seem to work? If so, check out our connection tips, starting on page xx. If it still doesn't work, check the list of addresses on our updates Web page <http://www.acorn-online.com/hedge/birdup.htm> to see if your site is among them. If it isn't, please leave a message. We'll try to track down a new address and post it on the page.

Great Texas Birding Classic

They do things big in Texas. And that includes the Great Texas Birding Classic, called "the biggest, longest and wildest birdwatching tournament in the United States." In late April, during the height of the spring migration, birders from all over the world descend on the southern part of the state. They form teams of bird-watchers who spend three official "big days" visiting various locations, counting, and observing birds that flock to the Texas coast. While it's fun, it also benefits bird conservation. Teams vie for prizes of $25,000, $15,000, and $10,000, which are awarded to avian conservation projects of the winning teams' choices. In 1998, 352 species were spotted during the weeklong event. According to the website, "there are opportunities to test your bird identification skills, participate in local community birding activities, attend the Classic-sanctioned events. . . . Birders of all ages and skill levels are invited to join us for one day or all week of the Classic." More than a dozen Texas coastal communities put on special events and festivals of their own during the classic, so there's no shortage of places to go and things to do. Start counting, Pard! You can find the GTBC page on the Texas Parks & Wildlife site (*first address*) by selecting Nature, then Birding. There, you'll find not just this festival, but others in the state. You can also go directly to the GTBC site (*second address*).

http://www.tpwd.state.tx.us

http://www.tpwd.state.tx.us/nature/birding/bclass/index.htm

Kirtland's Warbler Festival

Kirtland's Warbler is one of North America's least common nesting birds and in recent years has been threatened with extinction by changing environmental conditions (*see North American Birds, Backyard*). Each year, Kirtland Community College in Roscommon, Michigan, honors efforts to bring back Kirtland's populations and celebrates nature in general with its Kirtland's Warbler Festival. The event takes place on one Saturday in late May and includes presentations by nature artists and others. In 1998, some 2,500 people attended the festival from as far away as England, California, and South Carolina. "Birders are curious folks and for those who have not seen the rare Kirtland's Warbler, there is certainly an attraction here," Jerry Werle, on the staff of Kirtland Community College, tells us. This page offers full details as the plans for each year's program develop.

http://www.kirtland.cc.mi.us/~warbler/

Rio Grande Valley Birding Festival

Each November, birders from throughout North America converge on Harlington, Texas, where the Chamber of Commerce sponsors the annual Rio Grande Valley Birding Festival, a chance to see many of the 465 species that have been sighted in the region. The festival includes birding trips to many famous refuges and parks, seminars by leading birders and ornithologists, a trade show, an art show, and more. Full details may be found on this page, sponsored by the Harlington Chamber of Commerce. (*See also Destinations.*)

http://www.harlingen.com/birdfest.html

Razor-billed Auk (*Alga torda*) (JJA)

Northern Phalarope (*Lobipes lobatus*) (JJA)

Texas Tropics Nature Festival

McAllen, in the southernmost tip of Texas, is good
birding territory, where some 450 different species of
birds (and 260 kinds of butterflies) have been spotted.
Early each April, the McAllen Chamber of Commerce
sponsors the Texas Tropics Nature Festival, which
focuses primarily on the rich variety of birds in this
region of the lower Rio Grande. The event includes
speakers, seminars, and field trips, and the website
describes them all as soon as the year's schedule is
known. But even if you're not planning to go to the
festival, this site has plenty of information about
McAllen to tempt you into visiting any time of the
year for some top-notch "tropical" birding.

http://www.mcallen.com

Wings over the Platte Festival

The Wings over the Platte Festival and the accompanying website are sponsored by the Grand Island Hall
County Convention and Visitors Bureau. This festival
celebrates the arrival of millions of migrating birds on
this major stop on the central flyway in Nebraska.
Scheduled for three days in mid-March, the celebration includes guided tours of top bird-watching locations, seminars by experts, and a banquet with a major
speaker. Full details and a registration form can be
found (when plans have been set) on this site by
selecting Spring Migration from the sidebar menu.

http://www.visitgrandisland.com

EASTERN

Birding Festivals in Pennsylvania

The Pennsylvania Audubon Society maintains a page
that describes upcoming birding festivals in the state,
such as the Spring Birding Festival of Western Pennsylvania and the Annual Hawkfest at Tamarack
Wildlife Rehabilitation & Education Center in
Saegertown.

http://pa.audubon.org/festivals.html

Cape May Spring & Fall Weekends

Cape May, New Jersey, is one of the great birding
spots on the East Coast, especially in migration seasons. The Cape May Bird Observatory has a variety of
special events. Among these events are its famous
Cape May Spring Weekend in mid- to late May and
the Cape May Autumn Weekend in early November.
The observatory also has many birding workshops.
The page from the New Jersey Audubon Society (*first
address*) lists the observatory's many events; you can
also find general information about the observatory
and the Cape May area—including places to stay
(*second address*).

http://www.njo.com/audubon/calmenu/
    calcmbo.html

http://www.nj.com/audubon/abtnjas/cmbo.html

Lake Champlain Birding Festival

The Lake Champlain Birding Festival had its debut
in late May 1999 at the Basin Harbor Club on the
lakeshore in Vergennes, Vermont. The publishers and
editor of *Bird Watcher's Digest* were among the many
scheduled speakers, as was magazine artist Julie Zickefoose. The four-day event included daily field trips, a
sunset dinner cruise, and up to 30 vendors in the retail
marketplace, including optics, publications, birding
gear, books, and more. To learn about the next scheduled festival, stop by the website of the Addison
County Chamber of Commerce, one of the sponsors of
the event.

http://www.midvermont.com

A
B
C
D
E
F
G
H
I
J
K
L
M
N
O
P
Q
R
S
T
U
V
W
X
Y
Z

Virginia Rail (*Rallus limicola*) (JJA)

Lake Ontario Bird Festival

Countless songbirds and raptors pass by or stop at Mexico Point State Park on New York's shore of Lake Ontario each spring. And early each May, various organizations in Oswego County and vicinity sponsor the Lake Ontario Bird Festival at Mexico, New York. The weekend event includes many birding seminars, field trips, hikes, wildlife art, live bird demonstrations, wildlife rehabilitation and conservation programs, arts, and crafts, all described on the website as the event nears. (For information, go to the Oswego County tourism page and look for the link to Festivals & Attractions. From there, take the link to the Lake Ontario Bird Festival.)

http://www.co.oswego.ny.us/tourism/

Midwest Birding Symposium

The Midwest Birding Symposium, one of the largest birding gatherings in North America, takes place each September on the Ohio shores of Lake Erie, and runs Thursday through Sunday. A modest fee gets you into four days of seminars, exhibits, an art gallery, and a vendor hall. There are plenty of birding field trips—more than 220 species were sighted during one recent year's symposium. Around 1,000 people attend this well-known and well-liked event in Ohio, arranged by *Bird Watcher's Digest*.

http://birdwatchersdigest.com/bird_symposium.html

Space Coast Flyway Birding Festival

The Space Coast Flyway Birding Festival, Titusville, Florida, features birding competition, seminars, and field trips with nationally recognized speakers, kayaking, and Kids' Day activities with live animal exhibits and hands-on arts and crafts demonstrations. The event takes place in November in and about this east-coast Florida town (about halfway between Jacksonville and Miami, and next to Merritt Island National Wildlife Refuge, which is right next to Cape Canaveral, from which all the space rockets are launched—the really big birds).

http://www.nbbd.com/fly/

Wings over Water Festival

The Wings over Water Festival styles itself as a "celebration of wildlife and wildlands in eastern North Carolina." The early November festival takes place on the Outer Banks and includes more than 100 workshops, field trips, and seminars. The festival website reports that "participants, enjoyed such varied experiences as venturing into areas with combined bird lists of nearly 400 species" and "visiting North Pond on the Pea Island National Wildlife Refuge on Hatteras Island, the hottest spot for fall birding in North Carolina."

http://www.northeast-nc.com/wings/

World Series of Birding

How many birds can you see in a day in New Jersey? That's the goal of the World Series of Birding, sponsored each May by the New Jersey Audubon Society. At midnight, teams from all over North America take off in a 24-hour marathon of birding, trying to spot as many species as possible. In 1999, the team sponsored by Nikon came in first with 223 species. In all, more than 50 teams saw 262 species (one year, 270 were spotted). The event is more than a challenge; it's a fund-raiser that brings in more than $600,000 for various conservation causes. Complete details are online.

http://www.nj.com/audubon/calmenu/wsb.html

MOUNTAIN & PACIFIC

Coeur d'Alene Eagle Watch Week

The annual Coeur d'Alene Eagle Watch Week, sponsored by the U.S. Bureau of Land Management, takes place in late December near Coeur d'Alene, Idaho. Volunteers, wildlife biologists, and the general public gather at the Lake Coeur d'Alene–Wolf Lodge Bay wildlife viewing area to observe between 30 and 50 bald eagles feeding on the lake's spawned Kokanee Salmon. The week includes staff presentations, eagle exhibits, and observation of hundreds of waterfowl on the lake.

http://www.id.blm.gov/upcolumbia/eagle.html

Copper River Delta Shorebird Festival

The Alaskan scene is spectacular: "The world's largest concentration of migrating shorebirds" is viewed as they arrive in the Copper River Delta region of Alaska. We're talking as many as 14 million shorebirds—including nearly all of the West Coast's Dunlins, some five million of them. For more than 10 years, the people of Cordova, Alaska, have been running the Copper River Delta Shorebird Festival in early May to celebrate this event. Aside from the amazing number of birds to see, there are field trips, speakers, and educational workshops. To learn more about the festival, visit this Cordova Chamber of Commerce's site.

http://www.ptialaska.net/~midtown/

Festival of the Cranes

Bosque del Apache National Wildlife Refuge in central New Mexico is the winter home of as many as 17,000 Sandhill Cranes, 45,000 Snow Geese, endangered Whooping Cranes, Bald and Golden Eagles, and many species of ducks, hawks, and other birds. In mid-November each year, the refuge, the U.S. Fish & Wildlife Service, and the city of Socorro cosponsor the Festival of the Cranes to celebrate this wonderful place. The website has details of the tours, speakers, workshops, silent auction, crafts fair, photography contest, and other programs during the four-day event. You can also find links to information on the refuge itself and on Socorro.

http://www.nmt.edu/mainpage/festival/

Grays Harbor Shorebird Festival

"Which is more exciting—studying the features of sandpipers feeding among the mudflats but so close you can't focus your binoculars, or watching a Peregrine Falcon hunt through a huge flock of darting shorebirds?" So asks the Grays Harbor Audubon Society's website. Toward the end of April, the society joins the U.S. Fish & Wildlife Service to sponsor a shorebird festival in Hoquiam, Washington. It's timed to match the annual migration of thousands of shorebirds as they pause at the Grays Harbor estuary to feed and rest before departing for their nesting grounds in the Arctic. Perhaps the most spectacular of these is the Western Sandpiper. Literally hundreds of thousands of these wading birds may gather on the shores of Grays Harbor at this time of year (*see also North American Birds, Waders*). The festival has field trips (usually including an all-day pelagic trip), lectures, a competitive bird race, and exhibits. The Grays Harbor Audubon Society website is the place to find the latest details.

http://www.audubon.org/chapter/wa/ghas/index.html

Monterey Bay Birding Festival

The Monterey Bay Birding Festival takes place the first weekend of October in Moss Landing, California. The Monterey Bay area offers "an amazing variety of birding opportunities, from the quiet mudflats of Elkhorn Slough to the pounding surf of the Monterey Peninsula, from the dry uplands of coastal hills to the freshwater wetlands of the Pajaro Valley," the festival website notes. "This array of habitats attracts birds throughout the year, but fall brings thousands of shorebirds and waterfowl south in their annual migration along the Pacific flyway." The event has birding walks, field trips (including kayaking), workshops, booths, music, exhibits, live bird demonstrations, and more. To find out the coming year's schedule, go to the home page of the Elkhorn Slough Foundation and look for the link to the festival pages.

http://www.elkhornslough.org

A B C D E F G H I J K L M N O P Q R S T U V W X Y Z

A
B
C
D
E
F
G
H
I
J
K
L
M
N
O
P
Q
R
S
T
U
V
W
X
Y
Z

Morro Bay Winter Bird Festival

Most bird festivals are in the spring or fall, timed to migration peaks, but in Morro Bay, California, the celebration is in mid-January. That's when the birds are returning to this national estuary, so designated by the Federal Environmental Protection Agency. The area, halfway between Los Angeles and San Francisco, has more than 230 species (209 were tallied just in the 1998 Christmas Bird Count!), reports this well-endowed website. The site includes descriptions of the Morro Bay Bird Festival events (tours, talks, exhibits, and more), as well as photos of species you're apt to see, bird counts, links, and local tourist information.

http://www.morro-bay.net/birds/index.htm

Point Reyes Bird Observatory

Established in 1965, the Point Reyes Bird Observatory at Stinson Beach, California, aims "to conserve birds and the environment using science to understand and find solutions to problems threatening wildlife populations and ecosystems." The observatory has many public programs, and at its Palomarin Field Station on the Point Reyes National Seashore, visitors can hike trails and view self-guided visitor center exhibits 365 days a year. You can also participate in banding demonstrations. "We welcome school field trips, private groups and individuals, especially during the spring and summer months, when visitors are treated to the activity of the breeding season," the observatory says. The website has bird news, details of its annual Birdathon (mid-September), reports of planned bird walks, descriptions of the observatory's research, online newsletters, and links to related sites.

http://www.prbo.org

Salton Sea International Bird Festival

The Imperial Valley of California is in the state's southeastern corner, bordered to the north by the Salton Sea, the east by the Colorado River and Arizona, the south by Baja California, Mexico, and the west by the Anza Borrego Desert State Park. It is a bird-rich region, a fact that's celebrated each February with the Salton Sea International Bird Festival (*first address*). This site has full details as the event ap-

proaches, including who will be speaking, the seminars, tours, exhibitors, and such. Eldon R. Caldwell at Imperial Valley College has a wonderful page (*second address*) that describes many of the birds of Imperial County and the Salton Sea region, and a whole lot more. The site has many, many bird photos.

http://www.imperialcounty.com/birdfest/
http://www.imperial.cc.ca.us/birds/

Vulture Festival

The Kern Valley Turkey Vulture Festival takes place in September in Weldon, California, and features workshops, field trips, and bird spotting. Although the festival celebrates the fall migration of the Turkey Vulture, events cover all kinds of birds and birding. During the 1998 festival, for instance, 13 species of raptors were seen, and there's a complete list of 140 birds you're apt to spot.

http://frontpage.lightspeed.net/KRP/tvfest.htm

MEET THE MASTERS

Geometrical Origins

Tony Phillips is a mathematician and the creator of the New York Bird Songs website <http://math.math.sunysb.edu/~tony/birds/index.html>, one of the better places on the Net to hear the birds and one of the first to carry sounds. The site, he told us, may owe its origins to geometry. "In 1995 I was working at the Geometry Center in Minneapolis and learned how to make a Web page and how to put sound files on it," he says. "The next spring it suddenly occurred to me that I might be able to record bird songs (using the equipment I had on hand for recording mathematicians warbling about their theorems), digitize them, and put them on the Web." He tried it out on a robin in his own backyard. "It worked just fine," he notes.

INTERNATIONAL

Brant Wildlife Festival

The countless thousands of Brant that visit the Parksville–Qualicum Beach area of British Columbia have inspired the Brant Wildlife Festival. The three-day festival in April includes the Big Day Birding Competition in which individuals or teams scour the area for birds. In 1998, the winning team spotted 109 species out of 137 species seen by all participants. The festival includes many natural history programs for both adults and children and an art show. The website, sponsored by the local tourism association, has plenty of information about the festival, as well as accommodations.

http://www.island.net/~bfest/

Creston Valley Osprey Festival

The Creston Valley Osprey Festival at Creston, British Columbia, celebrates the Osprey and promotes the Creston Valley Wildlife Management Area as a "vital Osprey nesting and nursery habitat." The three-day event in late April includes Osprey viewing, an art show, a banquet, birdathon, walks, films, equipment demonstrations, van tours, and more. In the past, festival organizers even provided breakfasts. To get the details on the next festival, visit the Creston Valley Wildlife Management Area home page and look for a link about the festival. While there, check out some of the birding information they have online.

http://www.cwildlife.bc.ca

International Migratory Bird Day

International Migratory Bird Day in early May draws attention to the importance of our migratory birds, the contributions they make, and the habitats they need. The American Birding Association provides information about the day and activities that are appropriate for it. To help with programs marking the event, the website has a catalog of products, such as neat posters, T-shirts, banners, art, and various kits of educational materials. The site lists some of the sponsoring partners in International Migratory Bird Day.

http://americanbirding.org/imbdgen.htm

Ground Dove (*Columbigallina passerina*)
[Common Ground-Dove, *Columbina passerina*] (JJA)

Wings over the Rockies

Wings over the Rockies is a weeklong bird and nature festival that takes place in the Columbia Valley of British Columbia. The Valley "contains North America's longest continuous series of wetlands," the festival's website reports. "One hundred and eighty kilometers of Columbia River wetlands, flanked by grasslands, forests and alpine tundra, lure in more than 250 species of birds, including Lewis' Woodpecker, Blue Grouse, Great Blue Heron, Osprey, Golden Eagle, and American Dipper." The festival takes place at the height of migration season and includes presentations, interpretive walks, floats on the Columbia River, workshops, art displays, a children's festival, and live music. The well-illustrated website has much additional information, such as profiles of many of the popular species found in the area and stories about birds—often funny—which can be contributed by anyone via the site's LiveUpdate. Plans are to add a slide show of the area, plus student art work, poetry, and stories about birds. It's a very readable site, whether or not you're heading for the Columbia Valley.

http://www.adventurevalley.com/wings/

A
B
C
D
E
F
G
H
I
J
K
L
M
N
O
P
Q
R
S
T
U
V
W
X
Y
Z

FEEDING & WATERING

Feeding the birds is perhaps the single greatest pastime in North America. Although people who feed birds are often lumped with birders, many people just enjoy feeding and watching the birds that their feeders attract and wouldn't think of going on a birding expedition. They are more challenged by keeping the squirrels away than by catching a glimpse of an elusive warbler. This section covers websites that tell about feeding the birds and what birds eat. Many sites are provided by companies that manufacture bird feeders and feeds of all kinds. Other sites will tell you how to make your own feeders. You'll also find information about birdbaths, bird ponds, water heaters, and other devices in this section. (*See also Houses & Nest Boxes, Optics, and Retailers.*)

Backyard Bird Feeding

Selecting the right feeder for your yard should be more involved than walking into a store and looking for the prettiest model. Selecting a feeder includes deciding where it should be placed, how durable it is, whether it can keep seeds dry, how easy it is to clean, and what species can and will use it. One of the best guides to selecting a feeder is the Backyard Bird Feeding page on the Baltimore Bird Club website. Here, you'll also find information about what kinds of foods to use to attract different species and how to fend off squirrels, commonly asked questions about feeding, and more.

http://www.bcpl.net/~tross/by/feed.html

Bird Feeders for People

Aspects makes bird feeders and says they are "the first birdfeeders designed for people." That means that, whereas birds can enjoy them, people will find them convenient. These include hummingbird feeders, seed tube and thistle feeders, and window feeders. The company, located in Warren, Rhode Island, also makes outdoor thermometers decorated with bird images. The site has an illustrated product catalog, as well as a nice collection of birding links.

http://www.aspectsinc.com

Bring Nature Home

Opus, whose motto is "bringing nature home," is an international manufacturer of bird feeders and accessories based in Wayland, Massachusetts. Its very graphical website offers information about its many feeders, as well as its Sunswept Ceramics line of terra cotta feeders and hanging birdbaths. The site offers suggestions for finding the right bird feeder, and does so by asking you to evaluate yourself as to whether you are a casual, enthusiastic, or—the most serious level—hobbyist feeder of birds. The site also has an excellent collection of FAQs (called Ask the Experts), a section of Fun Facts about hummingbirds, orioles, and songbirds, and an online songbird identification chart that covers the most commonly found backyard feeder birds.

http://www.opususa.com

Fork-tailed Flycatcher (*Muscivora tyrannus*) (JJA)

Building Feeders

The Northern Prairie Wildlife Research Center carries Chris Grondahl's and John Dockter's guide to Building Nest Structures, Feeders, and Photo Blinds for North Dakota Wildlife. Despite the geographical name, the feeder plans are good for birds that live far beyond the bounds of North Dakota and include a two-liter plastic soda bottle bird feeder, milk carton feeder, large self-feeder, Linda tray feeder, hardware cloth suet feeder, and dowel suet feeder, as well as the barrel feeder for wildlife. Plans are very clear, specify supplies and tools needed, and can easily be printed out from the site.

http://www.npwrc.usgs.gov/resource/tools/ndblinds/ ndblinds.htm

Did You Clean the Feeder?

Havegard Farm Inc., established in 1974 by the Sheehy family in Green Bay, Wisconsin, produces a wide-ranging line of bird feeding products. Aside from sunflower, black niger, safflower, and other seeds, mixtures, and caked suet, Havegard makes some unusual products. One is Best Nest Builder, a package of natural nesting material for goldfinches. Also for goldfinches is the Thistle Pouch. "This amazing feeder comes pre-filled with niger thistle seed and is ready to hang and enjoy," the Havegard site says. "Goldfinches love the natural feel of feeding from the Thistle Pouch. Refill this feeder again and again for hours of enjoyment." The company also sells Feeder Fresh, a cleaner for birdfeeders and birdbaths. Havegard says that, although it contains bleach, Feeder Fresh does not use dyes or "harsh chemicals found in many household cleaners."

http://www.birdfeed.com

Feeder Challenges

Birds can get caught in feeders. Squirrels attack them. Pairs of squirrels can even learn how to circumvent sophisticated feeders. These are some of the topics Lauren Hansen of the Delaware Audubon Society touches on in her light-hearted essay, "Feeder Challenges." You'll learn something, as well as enjoy yourself reading this.

http://pages.prodigy.com/delaud/bt2.htm

Feeder Devices

Although the name seems a bit odd for a bird feeder manufacturer, Perky-Pet, in Denver Colorado, is a major producer of feeders, and its site describes its seed, nectar and suet feeders, as well as devices for hanging the feeders and foiling squirrels and ants. In addition, the site has general information about feeding birds and enjoying bird-watching.

http://www.perky-pet.com

Feeders & Tips

Duncraft, founded in 1952 in Concord, New Hampshire, is a popular manufacturer of bird feeders. The company's website (*first address*) includes a catalog, as well as an excellent collection of backyard bird feeding tips. Duncraft offers a free monthly newsletter, called Wing Tips, that comes via e-mail and provides many seasonal bird feeding suggestions. Sign up at the site. Duncraft sells official National Audubon Society feeders and accessories (*second address*). This page will tell you about that relationship, as well as lead you to Duncraft and to other sources of Audubon-approved products.

http://www.duncraft.com

http://www.audubon.org/market/licensed/birdfeeders/ index.htm

Feeding Birds

"Bird feeding is a popular and convenient way to observe birds up close, and it augments the primary habitat formed by backyard and neighborhood plantings," says Ron J. Johnson, an extension wildlife specialist with the University of Nebraska. In this illustrated page, Johnson tells when and where to feed birds, describes the kinds of feeders and foods you can put in them, offers tips for managing your feeder, and even explains the value of grit.

http://www.ianr.unl.edu/pubs/Wildlife/g669.htm

A
B
C
D
E
F
G
H
I
J
K
L
M
N
O
P
Q
R
S
T
U
V
W
X
Y
Z

A
B
C
D
E
F
G
H
I
J
K
L
M
N
O
P
Q
R
S
T
U
V
W
X
Y
Z

Feeding Wild Birds

"Do not feed seed mixes," emphasizes Calvor Palmateer in this essay that describes many kinds of bird foods—and candidly tells which to avoid and which suits what kinds of birds. Palmateer operates a birders and gardeners shop in Victoria, British Columbia, and he warns that many mixes contain large amounts of inexpensive seeds that are eaten by few birds. Red millet is an example. His lists of more than a dozen kinds of seeds include some we might not realize are available as bird feeds—rapeseed, sorghum, and hemp, for instance. He also discusses suet as a food.

http://birding.bc.ca/articles/birdseed.htm

Handmade Bird Feeders

Apex Bird Feeders in Apex, North Carolina, specializes in handmade, cedar feeders that are easy to clean. "Our feeder is one-of-a-kind with a pull-out drawer boasting a perforated aluminum screen bottom," says Apex. "It is so easy to brush or hose clean that we are thrilled . . . and so are the birds!" The nicely illustrated site not only shows feeders, but offers tips about feeding. You can order online.

http://www.apexbirdfeeders.com

Is Your Feeder Safe?

"Poorly maintained feeding stations may contribute to the occurrence of infectious diseases and even death," note Janet M. Ruth and Milton Friend on the Travis Audubon Society's website (Texas). Five diseases can strike birds who use feeders: Salmonellosis, Trichomoniasis, Aspergillosis, Avian Pox, and Mycoplasmosis. Ruth and Friend describe techniques for keeping your feeder birds healthy, including using more than one feeder, cleaning up wastes, making sure the feeders themselves are safe, keeping the feeders clean, using good food, preventing the food from becoming contaminated, and letting others know about these measures. "Encourage your neighbors who feed birds to take these precautions as well," they say. "Remember that birds normally move among feeders and can spread diseases as they go."

http://www.onr.com/user/audubon/News/a-safebf.htm

WEB WORDS

The Evil Eagle

"The Bald Eagle . . . is a bird of bad moral character; he does not get his living honestly; you may have seen him perched on some dead tree, where, too lazy to fish for himself, he watches the labor of the fishing-hawk; and, when that diligent bird has at length taken a fish, and is bearing it to his nest for the support of his mate and young ones, the Bald Eagle pursues him, and takes it from him."

—Benjamin Franklin

http://www.acsu.buffalo.edu/~insrisg/nature/nw98/franklinturkey.html

Live Food

Want your bird food wiggly? Many retailers, both online and traditional, have seeds for sale. Not a lot have worms. Mealworms, that is. Or fly larvae. Even crickets. "For years, nutrition experts have emphasized the importance of a balanced diet among humans," says Nature's Way. "It stands to reason that a balanced diet is also important for birds . . . as well." If you want to feed your backyard birds live food—the food most desired by many species—as well as seeds, Nature's Way is an online dealer in live foods. Insects are prime sources of protein and may attract bird species you've never seen before at your feeders. This website is an online catalog, with full descriptions of the products, but to place the order, you must telephone Nature's Way, which is in Hamilton, Ohio. And keep in mind when you're weighing whether or not to buy that fly larvae that, according to Nature's Way, it's "yummy—at least to them (but then, they'd probably choke at the thought of eating a hamburger or pizza, so we're even)."

http://www.herp.com/nature/

Making a Birdfeeder a Safe & Healthy Place

One of the problems with having a lot of birds gather at a backyard feeder is the same kind of problem kids have in a classroom: it's easy for diseases to spread. However, notes Dr. Astrid Kasper, a veterinarian, "by setting up more than one feeder, you will avoid crowding and reduce the stress levels of your birds, thereby contributing to their health." Kasper has many other observations and recommendations regarding bird feeder hygiene on this page. She also tells how to recognize a sick bird and describes some of the common diseases birds can get.

http://www.birdware.com/astrid.htm

Milk Carton Birdfeeders

"If you ever need a well-behaved, automatic seed dispenser, tailored to your specific . . . requirements, you may find the materials sufficient to build one right in your own kitchen," says Tor Ivar Bjønness of Norway. "You can recycle two, old one-liter (quart) milk or juice (usually of more robust quality) cartons into one effective new birdfeeder!" And Bjønness shows you how with lavish and detailed drawings (clearly, he is an artist, as well as a bird lover). So feed your birds, save your money, and recycle your trash all at once!

http://home.sol.no/~tibjonn/seedbox.htm

National Bird-Feeding Society

Since it's estimated that more than 60 million people regularly feed birds, it's no surprise that there's an organization just for the bird-feeding public. The National Bird-Feeding Society, the "club for backyard bird lovers," has a website whose main feature is its questions and answers column and its collection of Web resources about bird feeding and feeders. Of course, the site also has information about the society, its bimonthly newsletter, *Bird's-Eye reView*, and how to join.

http://www.birdfeeding.org

Swamp Sparrow (*Melospiza georgiana*) (JJA)

Natural Bird Food

Ever wonder just what birds really eat when they're not at your feeder? Kelly Jensen, a wildlife rehabilitator, has put together a database of the foods that birds eat in the wild. Click on the name of the bird on the index page to get the diet details. Whereas the aim is to help rehabilitators, it's also interesting information for anyone who likes birds. And if you ever want to feed your local White-breasted Nuthatch some "natural" food, you'll know it loves weevils, ants, and spiders among other live treats.

http://www.snowcrest.net/kellyj/wildbirdcare/

Plastic Bird Feeders

Sure, we all know Rubbermaid products: food canisters, plastic bins, trash cans. But did you know Rubbermaid makes a sizable selection of bird feeders? Visit this page and look for the link to Wild Bird & Pet supplies. There you'll find window-style feeders, bottle- and disk-style hummingbird feeders, small bird feeders, lantern/barn-style bird feeders, and large capacity feeders. If you've got a lot of birds in your yard, one "gazebo feeder" can hold 10 pounds of seeds!

http://www.rubbermaid.com/hpd/index.htm

B
C
D
E
F
G
H
I
J
K
L
M
N
O
P
Q
R
S
T
U
V
W
X
Y
Z

Sidebar index: A B C D E F G H I J K L M N O P Q R S T U V W X Y Z

FEATHERED FACTS

Two Travel Coats

Franklin's Gull is unique among gulls in having two molts of feathers each year. That's because of the colossal distances these birds must travel migrating between the prairies of the United States and Canada, and their wintering grounds in northern Chile and southern Peru—5,000 miles each way.

—adapted from John Sterling, Smithsonian Migratory Bird Center

http://web2.si.edu/smbc/bom/frgu.htm

Porcelain Feeders

You've seen plastic feeders. You've seen metal, wood, and even glass ones. But how about porcelain? The Big Island Bird Feeder Company in Monroe, Washington, has feeders of high-temperature-fired porcelain. "Each feeder is made individually by hand and is marked and numbered by Big Island artist Thomas Roberts," the Big Island website says. "No two feeders are exactly the same." Two models—hanging and standing—are available, and can be ordered from the site. Big Island also makes porcelain birdbaths and birdhouses. The site has good illustrations of all the products. All are reasonably priced, too, especially considering they are hand-made and long-lasting.

http://www.hawaiibirdfeeder.com

Project FeederWatch

Thousands of young and old people put their hobby to work each winter by participating in Project FeederWatch. Participants count the birds at their feeders and periodically enter their counts through the Project FeederWatch Data Entry form, available on Cornell University Laboratory of Ornithology's website. The information helps ornithologists track changes in the abundance and distribution of numerous bird species, including the sometimes mysterious irruptions or sudden increases in the populations of birds. Project FeederWatch, an ideal way in which children as well as adults can assist in real scientific study, is sponsored by the Cornell University Laboratory of Ornithology, the National Audubon Society, the Canadian Nature Federation, and Bird Studies Canada. The site has maps that show you the findings of watchers—useful for the public, as well as participants; to reach the site, click the menu item PFW Birds at the top of the page. Some of the maps have very late-breaking information, with data as recent as a week before. For example, when we checked in Project FeederWatch was monitoring the irruptions of Pine Siskins, and you could see a map of where Siskins were being spotted in heavy concentrations in the Pacific Northwest and in the Rockies.

http://birdsource.cornell.edu/pfw/

Seeds for the Birds

Pennington produces many kinds of seeds, and among them are seeds for birds. If you select Bird Feeding on the menu, the site provides tips for attracting and feeding birds, describes types of feeds available, and leads to a backyard bird identification chart that lists the kinds of food each of more than two dozen species eats.

http://www.penningtonseed.com

Selecting the Right Feed

Kaytee, a leading producer of seeds for wild birds (as well as for pet birds), estimates that between 40 and 50 percent of the homes in North America feed the birds. And although the company produces many kinds of packaged foods, the site is mostly devoted to information about feeding birds. There are tips on attracting specific kinds of birds, advice on finding the right foods, and even a list that tells—species by species—what types of foods will attract which types of birds. The site also lists stores where you can find Kaytee products.

http://www.kaytee.com

Shrubs as Food Sources

Many kinds of decorative shrubs not only enhance the beauty of your yard but also feed the birds. Here are Horticulturist Pat Thompson's suggestions for shrubs, along with the kinds of birds each feeds. (*See Trees Used Primarily for Food later in this section.*)

http://www.birdware.com/NHS/shrubs.htm

Squirrel-X

"Feed the birds, not the squirrels!" says Five Islands Products of Scarborough, Maine. Five Islands invented, produces, and sells the Squirrel Beater, a guaranteed squirrel-proof bird feeder. "You can hang it up and relax, knowing that the squirrels will not be able to empty it or chew through it," says Thomas F. Ewing, president of Five Islands. "Sit back and enjoy their antics as they try to outsmart it." The site shows the feeder, explains how it works, and tells you how to order one.

http://www.squirrelproof.com

Subscription Seeds

The Wild Bird Emporium in Auburn, New Hampshire, offers something different: "subscriptions" to bird seeds. You can automatically receive shipments of what you want, when you want it, and in the amount you want (*see also Retailers*).

http://www.wbird.com

Hermit (Dover)

Suet Suggestions

"Render therefore unto suet the thing that was beef fat!" Who says birders don't have a sense of humor? That "old adage" leads an informative page sponsored by the Baltimore Bird Club (*first address*) on the benefits and use of suet, which is raw beef or mutton fat that is among the most popular foods for birds. According to the club, suet is "the best food to attract woodpeckers, and among the other birds fond of suet are wrens, chickadees, nuthatches, kinglets, thrashers, creepers, cardinals, and starlings. Mixtures of suet and peanut butter may attract woodpeckers, goldfinches, juncos, cardinals, thrushes, jays, kinglets, bluebirds, wrens, and starlings." The page explains the differences between raw and rendered (cooked) suet, why it's best to use the latter when temperatures rise above 70, and how to make suet cakes and other tasty, fatty concoctions. Among the online recipes are ones for making bird treats that include peanut butter, cornmeal, and other goodies along with the suet. Birds, after all, don't have to worry about cholesterol counts —as far as we know. More recipes for creating suet for birds are available on the Northern Michigan Birding website where members contribute their own tried-and-tested concoctions (*second address*).

http://www.bcpl.net/~tross/by/suet.html
http://www.northbirding.com/suet/

Thirsty Birds

Birds get thirsty, too, and Happy Bird Corporation in Weston, Massachusetts, specializes in making products that help quench the thirst of wild birds. One particularly interesting device is called a Solar Sipper, which holds a quart of water—even in winter—but does not use electricity to keep it from freezing. Its patented solar top safely generates enough heat in winter sun to prevent the water in the container from freezing at air temperatures of 20°F, even lower, depending on sun and wind conditions, Happy Bird says on its website. You can order the Solar Sipper online or find out the names of dealers who carry it. (The company also makes versions of the Solar Sipper for dogs and for cats.) Happy Bird manufactures a window-mount bird bath that is not "solar" in design but good for wetting the whistles of birds in warmer weather.

http://petsforum.com/happybird/

A
B
C
D
E
F
G
H
I
J
K
L
M
N
O
P
Q
R
S
T
U
V
W
X
Y
Z

A
B
C
D
E
F
G
H
I
J
K
L
M
N
O
P
Q
R
S
T
U
V
W
X
Y
Z

Black-throated Mango (*Anthracothorax nigricollis*) (JJA)

To Feed a Hummingbird

The natural diet of hummingbirds is flower nectar, tree sap, and small insects and spiders that are often captured in or near flowers, note Ron J. Johnson, an extension wildlife specialist, and Donald H. Steinegger, an extension horticulturist, at the University of Nebraska. They list what to plant in your yard to attract and feed hummingbirds, including wildflowers, cultivated flowers, and shrubs. They also offer suggestions for feeders, noting that you should not use honey in mixtures, nor should you use red dye to make the sugar water the color that attracts hummingbirds. "If your feeder doesn't have red, you can add a red plastic flower, red ribbon, red tape, or even red nail polish on the surface of feeding ports."

http://www.ianr.unl.edu/pubs/wildlife/g1331.HTM

Trees Used Primarily for Food

Here's a list of landscape trees that produce fruits that various kinds of wild birds enjoy. Horticulturist Pat Thompson also lists the kinds of birds that eat each. (*See Shrubs as Food Sources earlier in this section.*)

http://www.birdware.com/NHS/trees.htm

Tubular Feeders

In 1969, artist, engineer, inventor, and birder Peter Kilham created a tubular bird feeder that led, as the site says, "to a new and exciting approach to bird feeding." That model, called the A-6, is still sold and is still popular. But the Droll Yankees, the company that sprang from Kilham's feeder, now has many other models to choose from—all described on this website.

http://www.drollyankees.com

Watering the Birds

Like the rest of us, birds need water. And that's the realm of Patio Garden Ponds of Oklahoma City, Oklahoma, which reports that it's the largest supplier of water garden products in the United States. Whereas most of its products are meant for water gardeners—plants, food, and pumps, for instance—the site also offers many items of special interest to birders, including birdbaths, heaters, bird ponds, misters, and drippers. And, of course, if you want to go the full pond route, it's all there. To see the company's Birdponds U.S.A. equipment, look for that link on the home page.

http://www.patio-garden-ponds.com

FEATHERED FACTS

All Food, Large and Small

The Great Blue Heron, which stands at up to 4½ feet tall, is North America's largest heron. And whereas it typically uses its huge beak to feed on fairly sizable creatures, such as frogs, eels, mice, snakes, and rats, this heron is not averse to catching lowly insects and is adept at doing so.

http://www.nature.ca/notebooks/english/grtbluh.htm

FEATHERED FACTS

The Horse Bird

One reason for the rapid spread of the House Sparrow after its importation from Europe in the 1850s has all but disappeared in many places. These birds were fond of the grains that were fed to horses and would also eat the undigested grain in horse droppings. Thus, they survived well in cities, as well as in the country on farms. With the rapid decline in the number of horses after the invention of the car, as well as the gradual decline in the number of farms in parts of the country, the numbers of House Sparrows has also dropped.

—adapted from Robie Tufts, *Birds of Nova Scotia*

http://museum.ednet.ns.ca/mnh/nature/nsbirds/
bns0411.htm

Wild Bird Feeding Preferences

Just what do birds *really* like to eat at feeders? Dr. Aelred D. Geis of the U.S. Fish & Wildlife Service's Patuxent Wildlife Research Center in Laurel, Maryland, studied the relative attractiveness of various foods, and to do it, put out feeders in California, Ohio, Maine, Missouri, and Maryland. The study also looked at the most efficient locations and types of feeders. The result is a 5,000 word essay on the effectiveness of various feeds. Dr. Geis evaluated buckwheat, canary seed, cracked corn, flax, German millet, red proso millet, white proso millet, oats, peanuts, rapeseed, rice, safflower seed, milo or sorghum, black striped sunflower seeds, eller, large black striped sunflower seeds, gray striped sunflower seeds, sunflower kernels, oil-type sunflower seeds, niger, and wheat. Some were clearly unattractive to most birds whereas others were very attractive—particularly certain sunflower seeds. If you want the official, scientific word on birdseed, here it is.

http://www.birdware.com/fpref.htm

Wild Bird Food

The Consumer section of Lyric Wild Bird Food's website offers Lyric Notes, with tips on feeding birds, plus the opportunity to subscribe to the Lyric Bird Club. The site contains a catalog of feeds—many specially geared at certain kinds of birds, such as finches, cardinals, chickadees, and woodpeckers. The site also shows different Lyric feeders and has a search engine that lists stores selling Lyric products.

http://www.lebsea.com/lyric/

Wooden Feeders

Wildwood Farms in Fulton, Illinois, manufactures and sells a line of more than 150 bird feeders and feeds, as well as some bird houses. All feeders and houses are made of wood. Wildwood Farms also sells food for wild game and wild game calls. And though it may seem anathema to backyard birders, Wildwood sells not only squirrel feeders, but squirrel feed—and even a squirrel call!

http://www.wildwoodfarms.com

Cedar Waxwing (*Bombycilla cedrorum*) (JJA)

A
B
C
D
E
F
G
H
I
J
K
L
M
N
O
P
Q
R
S
T
U
V
W
X
Y
Z

GARDENING & LANDSCAPING

The natural way to draw birds to your yard doesn't require manufactured feeders, though they certainly help. Instead, the bird-friendly backyard offers herbaceous plants, shrubs, and trees that provide food, shelter, and nesting areas. The more thought you give to your plantings, the more kinds of birds—and other wildlife—you can draw to your yard. The Web provides plenty of information about bird-attracting plants, as well as such techniques as having pools or brooks for birds to drink or bathe in, and specialized flowers for hummingbirds. Some sites will show you what people have done, and others will provide sources of plantings. (See also Feeding & Watering.)

Audubon Cooperative Sanctuary System

The Audubon Cooperative Sanctuary System (ACSS) is an effort by Audubon International to encourage businesses, schools, and private homeowners to use and manage their land in ways that will benefit wildlife, including birds. Audubon International supplies information so that "cooperators have an opportunity to learn about and become involved in landscaping for wildlife, using native plants and naturalizing areas of their property, monitoring water quality, planting special gardens for hummingbirds or butterflies, and many other wildlife enhancement and conservation activities that are designed for their property." The site explains how we can become "environmentally friendly," in not only our landscaping and yard design but also our lifestyles. If you join the formal program (about $35 a year for backyard sanctuaries), you'll receive a bimonthly newsletter, called Field Notes, plus educational materials, a survey, a wildlife art print, and the availability of telephone help with your own sanctuary. Your property can even become a Certified Audubon Cooperative Sanctuary.

http://www.audubonintl.org/acss/index.htm

Backyard Birding

Martha Renfroe has written a series of articles for the Travis Audubon Society in Austin, Texas, that offers suggestions for building a bird-friendly backyard habitat. Among the many topics she covers are creating a backyard pond for birds, introducing wildscaping, designing your landscape, establishing plants that provide shelter for birds, selecting hummingbird plants, developing habitat with a container garden, reducing pesticide use, and going native with a shady garden.

http://www.onr.com/user/audubon/Backyard/bkydintr.htm

Backyard Wildlife Habitat Program

For a quarter of a century, the National Wildlife Federation has been sponsoring the Backyard Wildlife Habitat Program that encourages people to make their properties more attractive to wildlife. It's especially written for the average homeowner, but can also apply to schools, industries, and apartment dwellers. The idea is to create a good environment for wildlife, particularly birds. This entails providing four basic elements: food, water, cover, and places to raise young. Plants can supply three of the four needs. Something as simple as a birdbath can take care of the fourth. The NWF site has full details on the program, tips for creating your backyard habitat, and an online application to have your place designated an Official Backyard Wildlife Habitat.

http://www.nwf.org/habitats/

Painted Bunting (Passerina ciris) (JJA)

Bird-Friendly Golf Courses

The Colorado Bird Observatory (*first address*) and the United States Golf Association (*second address*) have joined forces to create "bird-friendly" golf courses. Financed by the USGA, the observatory has written a manual for golf course architects and superintendents, explaining how to design and manage golf courses to benefit birds. "The manual should also prove useful to a wider audience," the observatory says. "Birds can find homes in areas altered by humans, provided some natural areas are retained and managed properly. City parks, open space areas, privately owned acreage, industrial and municipal complexes, and cemeteries can all make significant contributions to bird conservation *if* they are designed and managed properly. This manual provides the necessary information." At the website, you can find details on obtaining a copy (*first address*). The United States Golf Association has also been working with the National Audubon Society on the Audubon Cooperative Sanctuary Program for Golf Courses (*second address*). According to the USGA, "this program promotes ecologically sound land management and the conservation of natural resources. Its positive impact extends beyond the boundaries of the golf course and helps benefit the community beyond." The USGA page also has a list of certified Audubon sanctuary courses around the United States and Canada. The Golf Course Superintendents Association of America (*third address*) has more information about golf courses and wildlife. The site describes golf courses as refuges and reserves, and by searching for Birds on the site's home page, you can find other articles of interest (and a lot about dealing with Canada geese!).

http://www.cbobirds.org/projects/golf.html

http://www.usga.com/green/environment/
audubon_program.html

http://www.gcsaa.org/

David Jordan Bird Habitat

David Jordan was 13 years old when we visited his site, which describes a textbook example on how anyone of almost any age can turn a small backyard into a special place for birds. "The David Jordan Bird Habitat is a member of the network of registered habitats organized by the National Wildlife Federation," says David, who lives in Yorba Linda, California. "Anyone can turn their backyard into a habitat—all it takes is some time," he writes. "If you have food for them to eat, water for them to drink, shelter, and places to raise their young (a tree counts), you have a habitat." In well-organized fashion, David tells how he created his habitat—which includes no fewer than 12 bird feeders! He even offers tips on how to create your own simple equivalent of moving water for birds—a hanging bucket with tiny holes and a piece of cloth to regulate the flow. The site shows what the yard looked like in 1995 before David and his dad began working on the habitat and offers pictures of him working at building the habitat, and later renovating it. David's site has a lot more, including a link to the National Wildlife Federation's pages on backyard habitats, and is a splendid example of how anyone—young or old—can use the Internet to share valuable information.

http://members.aol.com/DJHabitat/

MEET THE MASTERS

Fun of Feedback

David Jordan, 13, Webmaster of "David Jordan Bird Habitat" website <http://members.aol.com/ DJHabitat/>, likes working on both his backyard wildlife habitat and his website about it. "One of the most enjoyable aspects of web authoring in my opinion is feedback from users—it gives you an even greater appreciation of the Internet as a whole," he says. "My most exciting experiences come from international visitors, including Sweden, Canada, and the Netherlands." Although he's not certain yet what career he will pursue, he's sure what it will include. "I hope to have a job concerning computers, maybe a computer engineer or something like that—even just a job that uses computers frequently." Meanwhile, if you are thinking of setting up a backyard wildlife habitat, check out David's site. You'll find not only practical information, but also a lot of infectious enthusiasm.

A B C D E F G H I J K L M N O P Q R S T U V W X Y Z

MEET THE MASTERS

Labor of Love

Jack Paul's wife and two children support his efforts at creating his website devoted to chickadees, Chickadee Web <http://home.jtan.com/~jack/ckd.html>. "They think it's cool, but I'm basically the birding nut in the house. They like watching the birds at the feeders, but aren't serious about birding. I'm still an amateur, but I'm learning, thanks to the Internet, birding friends and our local nature center." He continues to work on improvements for the Chickadee Web. "Maybe someday there will be video clips, a chickadee chat room, a chickadee that flies around the page," he says. "Chickadee Mania!" But all the work is worth it, says Jack Paul. "The site truly is a labor of love—a love of computing, technology, nature and the little bird that brought all those things together in my life."

Hummingbird Flower Seeds

Vital Video in Vassar, Michigan, offers hummingbird flower seeds. Although the seeds themselves are free, there's a postage and handling charge for the first packet, and another, lesser, charge for each additional packet. This is probably a good deal compared to what you would pay if you mail-ordered from a seed catalog. Available seeds are morning glories, sweet peas, and a "hummingbird butterfly mix" that includes 22 species of wildflowers. Planting tips for each are provided online.

http://www.cyberforest.net/freeseeds.htm/

Landscaping to Attract Birds

"Among the fondest and most memorable moments of childhood are the discoveries of songbirds nesting in the back yard," says this page, based on a U.S. Fish & Wildlife Service pamphlet (*first address*). "The distinctive, mud-lined nests of robins and their beautiful blue eggs captivate people of all ages. Likewise, the nesting activities of house wrens, cardinals, chickadees, and other common birds can stimulate a lifelong interest in nature." Baltimore Bird Club's Terry Ross has turned the pamphlet into an online guide that covers the benefits of landscaping for birds, the basics of doing the job, the kinds of plants wild birds like, tips on how to get started, and a list of books that cover the subject in more detail. You can also find the government's original version of the pamphlet (*second address*).

http://www.bcpl.net/~tross/by/attract.html
http://www.fws.gov/r9mbmo/pamphlet/attract.html

Must-Have Backyard Plants

Arrowwood Viburnum, Elderberry, Little Bluestem. Karen Williams of the New Jersey Audubon Society describes a dozen "must-have" backyard plants in this essay. "Plants are part of an interwoven web of soil, water, plants and space called habitat," she writes. "Wildlife must gather all it needs to survive from its habitat. Food for young, shelter from the storm, raw materials for nests, and more, all must come from the habitat. Plants provide many of these needs." Her recommendations include important trees and shrubs, grasses, and wildflowers that help make up a habitat for not just birds but butterflies. Williams also suggests novel ways to arrange your plantings in either a Weed Patch or Meadow or a Clipped Meadow.

http://www.nj.com/audubon/genlmenu/dozen.html

Nest Box

Arlene Ripley's southern Maryland home is situated on 2½ acres of trees, shrubs, open areas, ponds, and a small stream. This habitat attracts many kinds of resident and migrant birds, 120 species so far, Ripley reports on her website, the Nest Box. Plantings and a series small ponds were added to attract wildlife. "This little pond system is fascinating to watch throughout the seasons," Arlene says. "Less common birds like the Louisiana Waterthrush and Prothonotary Warbler have been lured up from the stream in the ravine to drink and forage around the ponds." The site also tells what plants attract bluebirds and which draw hummingbirds, and offers useful links to landscaping for wildlife.

http://www.nestbox.com/plants.htm

Planting for Habitat

Both songbirds and other wildlife will benefit from the planting suggestions in this University of Nebraska guide that includes valuable tips for selecting effective plants. The authors note, for instance, that a "back-yard with a variety of different plants generally attracts more wildlife species, and is often more attractive in appearance, as well. A variety of plants also offers a greater choice of food and cover."

http://www.ianr.unl.edu/pubs/wildlife/g671.HTM

Plants that Enhance Wild Bird Habitat

Horticulturist Pat Thompson offers suggestions for trees, shrubs, annuals, perennials, and grasses that are used as foods by various wild birds—both bird and plant species are specified. A special page identifies flowering plants that attract hummingbirds is also available.

http://www.birdware.com/NHS/NHS.htm

Songbird Habitats in the Southeast

The University of North Carolina has a concise guide to the kinds of habitats that birds in the southeastern United States favor.

http://www.ces.ncsu.edu/nreos/forest/steward/www4.html

Black-billed Cuckoo (*Coccyzus erythropthalmus*) (JJA)

AVIAN ADVICE

Starling Stumpers

If you're inundated with starlings that want to munch the seeds you leave out for native songbirds, try using a tube feeder and limit your food offerings to black-oil sunflower seeds.

—adapted from *Bird Watcher's Digest*

http://www.birdwatchersdigest.com/faq/faq.html

GEAR

The well-equipped birder heads off into the field with two essentials: a field guide and binoculars or a scope. But the *really* well-equipped birder may want a few more pieces of equipment, most of them to help hold the essentials. Here are some sites with the "extras." *(See also Feeding & Watering, Houses & Nest Boxes, Optics, and Photography.)*

Birders' Buddy

"This is definitely a cottage industry," says Betsy McKellar. Birders' Buddy is just "me and my sewing machine." What's a Birders' Buddy? A vest for birders, designed and made by McKellar. It has plenty of pockets just the right size to hold field guides, binoculars, glasses, notes, pencils, and more, and is adjustable for both summer and winter use. The site describes the vest and even shows McKellar at her sewing machine, making them. There are also plenty of testimonials to convince you that this could be the ideal apparel for your next expedition to the local park or a Central American rain forest.

http://members.aol.com/birdvest/vest.html

A B C D E F G H I J K L M N O P Q R S T U V W X Y Z

White-crowned Pigeon (*Columba leucocephala*) (JJA)

Fieldfare Field Guide Covers

Fieldfare, named for a European robin-like bird, is a Rhode Island company that makes field guide "cover/carriers." These waterproof, heavy fabric covers hold all standard-sized field guides and, depending on model, can be attached to a belt or slung over the shoulder. The fancier of the two versions includes a pad and pen holder for taking field notes, and has a pocket for a checklist or map. It also has a "wide, covered elastic hand strap that allows the birder to hold the open guide in one hand as he/she holds the binoculars in the other." Both cases are described and illustrated in detail on the site, which also includes useful birding tips and links.

http://www.fieldfare.com

Kopi Corporation

Kopi Corporation makes specialty birding equipment, such as a "hands-free front pack" that holds your binoculars and field guide, and special protective clothing for feet and body. One of its more interesting products is a set of "overwhites," clothing that covers you virtually from head to foot and "made of a superior fabric, wind resistant and fully breathable, allowing its wearer to remain warm and dry even in the coldest and most humid weather conditions." That's gear for the serious birder.

http://www.kopico.com

L.L. Bean

L.L. Bean is undoubtedly the most famous mail-order supplier of outdoor equipment and clothing—many items ideal for the wandering birder. However, the website also has some free features of interest to birders, including its excellent parks guide (*see also Destinations*) and an online gallery of the nature photography of Ansel Adams—pictures you can send as electronic postcards. Bean produces nearly a dozen general and specialty catalogs, all of which you can order online for free.

http://www.llbean.com

Poke Boat

Some of the best birding is up a slow creek or in a lazy swamp. But many of these locales are virtually inaccessible by foot. You could use a canoe or kayak, but according to a Berea, Kentucky, company, you might be more interested in a Poke Boat. "The Poke Boat is the boat for people who are afraid of kayaks and feel even a canoe is on the tippy side," says Phoenix Poke Boats. "Low profile, quiet and 22 pounds of accessibility are all reasons why many birdwatchers and outdoor photographers are using the Poke Boat." The website describes the various Poke Boat models, which range from a Micro Poke Boat that's less than eight feet long to a Maxi Poke Boat at nearly 12 feet and a Maxi II at nearly 19 feet. The site includes an article from the December 1994 issue of *Birding* magazine, called "The Poke Boat & the Place Out of Reach," in which expert birder Pete Dunne, director of the Cape May Bird Observatory, describes his experiences using the boat.

http://www.pokeboat.com

REI

Whereas REI, which stands for Recreational Equipment Incorporated, has a huge online catalog, the site also has a lot of information for anyone who loves the outdoors. Birders will be interested in the hiking and camping section (on the home page, under Get Out There, select Community, then Climbing/Hiking). You will find descriptions of favorite trips, tips, equipment, and more. Under Community, you'll also find guides on how to select equipment and links to other outdoor sites. REI carries an extensive line of outdoor equipment and clothing. Products include binoculars, compasses, boots, vests, and other gear that more adventurous birders would find useful.

http://www.rei.com

W. Waller & Son

Some birders head into the woods and fields with little more than a small pair of binoculars and a field guide. Others need more, and carry cameras, scopes, tripods, tape recorders, and other equipment to capture the beauty of birds. W. Waller and Son in Grantham, New Hampshire, is a family-owned business that produces fine bags to hold all that equipment—and maybe even some lunch. The site has full descriptions of such products as the Original Waller Range Bag and the Original Waller Field Bag, as well as information about ordering.

http://www.wallerandson.com

Yellow-billed Cuckoo (*Coccyzus americanus*) (JJA)

Find a Great Site We Don't List?

If you discover a new birding website or an old one that we overlooked, please pass on the address. E-mail us at jacksanders@ridgefield-ct.com or visit our updates page, <http://www.acorn-online.com/hedge/birdup.htm>.

GENERAL

Many websites are devoted simply to birding or, relatedly, to natural history, and this section includes many of these sites that are great for browsing and for learning about birds and bird-watching. Many of these sites cover a wide range of topics—from species profiles to bird-friendly landscaping; they are like electronic magazines. This section is also a catch-all, for here you'll also find specialized sites such as the birding dictionary or the Puzzle Aerie that don't fall into the subjects of other sections in the book.

American Museum of Natural History

The American Museum of Natural History in New York City has one of the fancier, graphically loaded sites on the Web, and it has useful information about birds. Use its Search option and look for the topic: we found 235 pages with references to "birds" when we searched. Among them were bird-related scientific activities for children, tips on how to look for identifying features of birds, and information about habitat variety and bird abundance. (You'll also find an article about Roland T. Bird, a museum paleontologist who enjoyed traveling the West on his Harley Davidson motorcycle, searching for dinosaur fossils.) Use the Site Map to learn about the ancestors of birds— find the Fossil Halls and wander through them, inspecting the timelines on the way. (*See also Children.*)

http://www.amnh.org

A
B
C
D
E
F
G
H
I
J
K
L
M
N
O
P
Q
R
S
T
U
V
W
X
Y
Z

A
B
C
D
E
F
G
H
I
J
K
L
M
N
O
P
Q
R
S
T
U
V
W
X
Y
Z

Are You a Birder?

Do you criticize TV programs and commercials that depict a Bald Eagle but play a Red-tailed Hawk call? Are your kids named Buteo and Accipiter? Do people stop and stare when you "pish" at the shrubbery at the local mall? These are a few of the characteristics that might qualify you as being a birder. This light-hearted piece is offered by the Greater Wyoming Valley Audubon Society in Pennsylvania.

http://www.audubon.org/chapter/pa/gwvas/
MiscellaneousFolder/birderquiz.html

Ask Dr. Beak

For anyone who's ever wondered if birds and birders can be funny, there's Ask Dr. Beak, a tongue-in-cheek, question-and-answer column that opens: "Someone ruffling your tail feathers? Something stuck in your craw? Got a situation that's left you with egg on your face?" The column, brought to us by the folks at Wasatch Audubon Society in Ogden, Utah, alleges to offer "bird-based advice to the fowlorn," written by one Dr. Beak (also known as Jay Hudson), who studied at the "Hudson Institute of Social Ornithology." It's downright funny and well worth visiting regularly to keep up with the latest avian advice (Dr. Beak tells us that he's at least two years ahead on his columns, so expect him to be around for quite a while).

http://www.audubon.org/chapter/ut/wasatch/
dr_beak.htm

Backyard Birding in Baltimore

"If you need to know how and what to feed the birds, or how large to make the entry hole on a bluebird box, or which shrubs and flowers to plant in order to attract birds, you've come to the right place," says the Baltimore Bird Club. This straightforward, information-packed site has tips provided by the club and lots of links to other useful sites. It is often cited as one of the most useful and frequently visited birding sites on the Web.

http://www.bcpl.net/~tross/by/backyard.html

Backyard Birding in Indiana

Although dedicated to the birds of Indiana, John and Janet Slivosky's Backyard Birding website contains information useful to birders east of the Rockies and north of the Gulf Coast. The site is strong on pictures and sounds of several dozen species of both common and not-so-common birds.

http://www.slivoski.com/birding/

Bird Chat

Birdchat is a national mailing list of birding-related messages. Jack Siler's site, Birding on the Web, enables you to read the chatter, as it were. Discussion covers virtually any bird-related topic but is clearly for the more serious birder. You'll find scientists, as well as amateurs and backyard birders here, and you can't help but learn. Siler also maintains archives of recent messages. This is an easy way to sample the *birdchat* mailing list to see if it's something you'd like to join (*see Mailing Lists Online later in this section*). When we last checked, more than 2,400 people subscribed to *birdchat*.

http://enkidu.wharton.upenn.edu/~siler/chat.html

FEATHERED FACTS

Illegal Pets

Of all wild birds that have been kept as pets, crows are the most common, probably because they are so smart. However, because crows are migratory birds, under federal law, they are illegal to keep without a difficult-to-obtain permit.

—adapted from American Society of Crows & Ravens

http://www.azstarnet.com/~serres/crowfaq.html

Bird Dictionary

Need to know what *caudal* means? Do you know why a fault bar is sometimes called a *starvation mark* or a *hunger trace*? Or maybe you'd like to know what goes on in a lek. These and hundreds of other terms, simple and sophisticated, common and rare are contained in the Bird Dictionary, an online version of *The Birdwatcher's Dictionary* by Peter Weaver.

http://birdcare.com/birdon/birdindex/

Bird Extremes

What is the largest bird? The smallest? What species can fly the highest? Fastest? Longest? These are some of the questions that are answered on this page on the Enchanted Learning.com website. Although written for children, the information is of interest to anyone who enjoys birds—and records!

http://www.enchantedlearning.com/subjects/birds/
Birdextremes.shtml

Bird Guide Forums

Bird Guide, a website serving birders in the Pacific Northwest, has a set of forums with long but effective titles, such as Help Me Identify This Bird I Saw or I'm Going to Be in (some Pacific Northwest Location). Where's a Good Birding Location Nearby? There are forums on directions to recent rare bird sightings, on binoculars, scopes, cameras, and other equipment, on bird feeding, on where to find specific species, and on pelagic trips. You do not need to register to read or post messages, and the system is easy to use. You can also easily e-mail people who've posted messages without having to post one online.

http://www.teleport.com/~guide/forum.htm

Bird Identification Starter

Twenty of the more common, popular, or unusual backyard feeder birds are described on Project FeederWatch's A Bird Identification Starter site at the Cornell University Laboratory of Ornithology. Using the top-notch illustrations of Larry McQueen, plus

sounds from Cornell's extensive collection, the guide provides short life histories and extensive identification information, including tips on telling races apart. For certain species, range maps are provided—some of them animated with data from bird counts over the past century. The birds covered here are the Red-bellied Woodpecker, Downy Woodpecker, Hairy Woodpecker, Northern Flicker, Black-capped Chickadee, Carolina Chickadee, Mountain Chickadee, Boreal Chickadee, Chestnut-backed Chickadee, Tufted Titmouse, Red-breasted Nuthatch, White-breasted Nuthatch, Carolina Wren, American Tree Sparrow, Dark-eyed Junco, Purple Finch, Common Redpoll, Pine Siskin, American Goldfinch, and Evening Grosbeak.

http://birdsource.cornell.edu/pfw/birdid/
birdid.htm

Birding at About.com

About.com, which used to be the Mining Co., is one of the best places on the Internet where people are introduced to scores of activities. It's like a search engine, except that someone else has done the searching for you, has come up with lots of information about your favorite subjects, and presents it in bulletin board or website fashion. One of the site's best boards is Christine Tarski's Birding board: it's great for beginners, offering features that introduce you to many aspects of birding. There are also links to dozens of useful resources, including backyard birds, bird behavior, bird cams, bird checklists, bird identification, birding sites on all of the continents, birdhouse building, feeder building, fun sites, kids' area, mailing lists, optics, photography, software and CDs, sounds and songs, things to buy, types of birds, and videos. About.com's birding message board is not as active as the Usenet newsgroup, *rec.birds*, but it keeps messages online and readily available much longer (up to a year). You must register to post messages, but you don't need to register just to read them—click Guest Access. (Even unregistered users can reply directly to people who post messages.) About.com also has live chat, which is set up so you can surf the Web while you're chatting so you can share your findings with others in the group. Chat is accessed from the same home page and does not require formal registration.

http://birding.about.com

A B C D E F G H I J K L M N O P Q R S T U V W X Y Z

A B C D E F G H I J K L M N O P Q R S T U V W X Y Z

FEATHERED FACTS

Eggs-travagant!

The Great Tit, a European songbird, is probably the world's champion egg-layer. This bird produces eggs that represent 10 percent of her body weight. Although that's a big enough task, the Great Tit averages 11 eggs per clutch—a total more than her own weight!

—adapted from National Zoo

http://www.si.edu/natzoo/zooview/exhibits/birdhs/
birdfaq.htm#largestbird

Birding in Canada

Gord Gallant's Birding in Canada is a rich source of information about the birds and birding places of Canada. The site includes pages of checklists for most provinces and for many parts of the world, bird books, publications, events, bird counts, birding hot spots, observatories, societies, publications, links, and more. "My objective is to make this website as informative as possible with respect to Canadian birding," Gallant says. A neat feature of this site is the Birders with E-mail page, arranged geographically, so that you can contact bird-watchers in areas that interest you. This is particularly handy if you're planning a trip to some part of Canada and want tips on which birds to see or the places to see them.

http://www.interlog.com/~gallantg/canada/

Birding in the Pacific Northwest

The Bird Guide, one of the earliest websites serving birders, is aimed at birding in the Pacific Northwest. The site has lists of birds in the region, profiles of species, and migration timing information. It's especially strong on information about upcoming festivals in the region, listing information many months in advance so you can plan. There are also forums, as well as notices of coming birding trips, particularly pelagic voyages.

http://www.teleport.com/~guide/

Birding on the Web

One doesn't think of the World Wide Web in historical terms. However, Webmaster Jack Siler tells us, Birding on the Web "was the first birding site on the web." It's still one of the best for finding information. Based at the University of Pennsylvania in Philadelphia, this site is a sizable but simply organized library of links, messages, photos, and other Web sources. If you can't find it here, it's probably not on the Web yet.

http://www-stat.wharton.upenn.edu/~siler/birding.html

Birds of the Upper Texas Coast

Anyone who lives near or plans to visit the upper Texas coast—in the greater Houston area—will appreciate David Sarkozi's comprehensive Birds of the Upper Texas Coast website. The region is an important gateway for migrating birds entering and leaving North America, and Sarkozi devotes a lot of his site to migration information, timetables, and even animated radar graphics showing flocks of migrants. Profiles of several dozen "specialties" of the upper Texas coast are provided, along with photos and sometimes sounds. One of the nicest regional sites on the Web, with scores of links to other worthwhile sites, the site offers information about where to go birding in the region and what you might see.

http://texasbirding.simplenet.com

BirdWatch on PBS

BirdWatch is a PBS television series about birds and birding, carried by Public Broadcast System stations. The site describes the shows, tells where they might be seen on the air, introduces the hosts, and also offers videos about birds and birding. The site has links for more information.

http://www.pbs.org/birdwatch/index.html

Fox Sparrow (*Passerella iliaca*) (JJA)

Bird-Watching

"Birdwatching," says Birdwatching.com, is "your life-time ticket to the theater of nature." The nicely organized commercial site has some feature articles, including interviews with authors and naturalists. An excellent FAQ collection, tips, bird stories, and catalogs of birding books, videos, and software are available.

http://www.birdwatching.com

Bird-Watching Myths

Don't throw rice at a wedding—birds will eat it, and the grains will swell and kill them. Take down your feeders in the fall because your backyard birds won't migrate, and they'll freeze to death. Purple Martins eat 2,000 mosquitoes a day. These and other myths that circulate among bird-watchers are debunked by Eirik A. T. Blom, one of the star writers at *Bird Watcher's Digest*. It makes very entertaining—and informative—reading.

http://www.petersononline.com/birds/bwd/
   features/0697-myths.html

Breeding Bird Atlases

Many states and regions maintain online atlases of the birds that breed in their localities. The University of Wisconsin at Green Bay offers links to around 20 atlases (some outside North America), including those covering Arabia, Georgia, Illinois, Iowa, Kansas, Los Angeles County, Maryland–District of Columbia, Missouri, Nevada, New Jersey, Oklahoma, Orange County (Cali-

fornia), Oregon, San Diego County (California), South Africa, South Dakota, and Washington State.

http://wso.uwgb.edu/websites.htm

Breeding Bird Survey

The Breeding Bird Survey is a huge effort undertaken by the U.S. government to estimate population changes for songbirds. "It is a roadside survey, primarily covering the continental United States and southern Canada, although survey routes have recently been initiated in Alaska and northern Mexico," the National Bureau of Standards website notes. "The BBS was started in 1966, and the over 3,500 routes are surveyed in June by experienced birders." The massive quantity of data here is available to anyone interested in what's happening with North American bird populations. For instance, I could quickly determine that the population of Canada Geese in Connecticut has tripled since 1966 while the numbers of American Woodcocks in New York have been declining since 1967. You can search for trend estimates of most North American species and view very up-to-date distribution maps based on densities. For example, the breeding and winter distribution maps for the Black Vulture, a formerly "southern" bird that has been moving into the Northeast, were much more realistic than ones found in some field guides published as late as 1997. The site also offers an extensive collection of links to other useful birding and ornithological sites. Any serious birder should bookmark this site.

http://www.mbr.nbs.gov/bbs/bbs.html

Moving?

Do you have a birding website that's changing its address? If so, please let us know at <http://www.acorn-online.com/hedge/birdup.htm>. We'll post it and print it in future editions of this guide.

MEET THE MASTERS

A Sooty Cardinal

Born and raised in the Pittsburgh, Pennsylvania, area, Julia Pahountis, Webmaster of the Nutty Birdwatcher <http://www. birdnature.com>, is a senior computer technologist for a manufacturing firm, and her well-designed website shows her computer savvy. But she's also a veteran and curious birder. "I have been watching birds for approximately 20 years," she says. "I was hooked in the early-to-mid-1970's when I saw my first cardinal—I can remember being excited about spotting that first cardinal because of the pollution and smog from the steel mills." Although she has never officially studied ornithology, Julia is well read in the subject of birds. "When I look at my 'bird library,'" she said, "I think I have every bird book that has been published!"

Canadian Bird Trends

The Canadian Bird Trends Database has useful information about North American bird species in Canada including: population trends, range distribution, and national conservation designations. Population trends come from the Canadian Breeding Bird Survey (BBS) data and are updated annually. Maps tell where the species breed.

http://www1.ec.gc.ca/~cws/

Canadian Museum of Nature

The Canadian Museum of Nature in Ottawa, Ontario, has an excellent collection of brief essays and drawings of about four dozen species of birds. Most are North American, but all the presentations demonstrate different features or aspects of birds, or highlight threatened species.

http://www.nature.ca/notebooks/english/birdpg.htm

Code of Birding Ethics

"Everyone who enjoys birds and birding must always respect wildlife, its environment, and the rights of others," says the American Birding Association. "In any conflict of interest between birds and birders, the welfare of the birds and their environment comes first." That said, the ABA in its Code of Birding Ethics details how good birders should conduct themselves. Everyone should read and follow its recommendations.

http://www.birdware.com/abaethic.htm

Dan Victor's Website

If you live in the Pacific Northwest, Dan Victor's website—it doesn't seem to have a name—is probably the richest source of birding information. In fact, Victor's site is full of links that can be valuable to birders throughout the world. The site is particularly strong on information about birding in Washington State and in British Columbia, and includes good birding locations, books, and links to websites belonging to local Audubon societies. There is nothing flashy about this site—it's just a straightforward collection of useful sources.

http://www.scn.org/earth/tweeters/

Grasshopper Sparrow (*Ammodramus savannarum*) (JJA)

East Coast Birds

"East Coast," in this case, is the east coast of Canada. This site, sponsored by the Nova Scotia Museum of Natural History, offers the online magazine, East Coast Birds, with features about species of interest to eastern Canada birders. The site also provides an online version of Robie Tufts's book, *Birds of Nova Scotia*, the authoritative source on birds of this province. You can also find links to Nova Scotia birding sites.

http://museum.ednet.ns.ca/mnh/nature/nsbirds/

Economic Value of Birders

Bet you didn't think of birding as a boost to the economy, but according to the American Birding Association, "birders who travel to see birds are a significant economic asset to those communities that live close to good bird habitats" (*first address*). In fact, the ABA has studied the economics of birding and reports its findings extensively on its website. You'll also find statistical profiles of members of the ABA, the largest birding organization in the United States, including their spending habits, background, ages, interests, and much more. The ABA is so interested in promoting the economics of birding that it has prepared a list of nearly three dozens suggestions for how communities in birding regions can be more birder friendly (*second address*).

http://americanbirding.org/consecon.htm
http://americanbirding.org/conseconbfc.htm

Eyrie

The Eyrie, the Webmasters say, "was created for the birding enthusiast—from the backyard birdwatcher to the active birder. Our goal is to make finding birding information on the Internet a little easier and even more fun!" The site has three main sections: the Bird's the Word includes information about hot lines, rare bird alerts, checklists, birding festivals, and state birding information; Goods and Services has lists of sources for literature, equipment, and tours; and Classified Ads, which are free. The Eyrie also has interesting featured sites-of-the-month.

http://www.eyrieusa.com

Key West Quail-Dove (*Oreopeleia chrysia*)
[*Geotrygon Chrysid*] (JJA)

Field Guide to Birds on the Web

This huge library, arranged by either systematic index or name index, by Ruud Grootenboer, a birding enthusiast in the Netherlands, has links to literally thousands of photos of birds on the Web, as well as to many hundreds of websites that cover specific species. The links collection may not be the most up-to-date, but most worked when we stopped by.

http://www.geocities.com/RainForest/Vines/7576/

Fugleskue

Fugleskue is Norwegian for *BirdBase*. Although Tor Ivar Bjønness is Norwegian and the site is in Norway, there is plenty of information, sources, suggestions, and links on this site that would be of interest to any birder anywhere. Also, if you're planning to travel, check out this website's links to other international birding sites.

http://home.sol.no/~tibjonn/

Geographical Birding Guide

This page presents a clickable map of North America north of Mexico and enables you to choose a state or province to home in on birding information for that area.

http://www.birder.com/birding/gbg/

A B C D E F G H I J K L M N O P Q R S T U V W X Y Z

Harlan's Hawk (*Buteo Borealis*)
[Red-tailed Hawk, *Buteo jamaicensis harlans*] (JJA)

Hinterland Who's Who

Baffled by the bufflehead? Loony over loons? The Canadian Wildlife Service (CWS) sponsors an in-depth look at many kinds of birds (and mammals) found in Canada. The appearance, life history, and habits of each of dozens of species are described, accompanied by excellent photos, distribution maps, and sources for further reading. Although not every species is here, the ones that are covered are done so comprehensively that you'll want to bookmark this site for regular reference. And the CWS is always adding new species. The site also covers environmental issues related to birds, such as lead poisoning of waterbirds and the effects of oil pollution on birds.

http://www.ec.gc.ca/cws-scf/hww-fap/eng_ind.html

Mailing List Archives

You can join at least a half dozen lists that exchange e-mail on the topic of birding. The headquarters for the most popular is at the University of Arizona. There, you'll find not only information about joining lists and how many people currently belong to each but also archives of past messages—saved in a way that you can read them, as well as e-mail the authors directly yourself; thus, you can join in a conversation without actually joining a list. The mailing lists col-

lected at this site include *birdband* (a bird banders forum), *birdchat* (the National Birding Hotline Cooperative, where noteworthy sightings are reported—this is by far the most popular birding list), *birdcntr* (a central states forum), *birdeast* (an eastern states forum), *birdhawk* (for hawk watchers), *birdtrip* (for reports of birding expeditions—this one is grand fun to read as you follow birders on expeditions to great sites), *birdwest* (western states forum), and *bird_rba* (rare bird alerts from around the country). These libraries are easy to roam around and read, and they provide the ability to search through all the messages in archived lists for a specific topic. The system even includes the ability to change the type of viewing fonts that are displayed—proportional fonts are easier to read when the message is on the long-winded side. The URL also indexes many e-mail lists that have nothing to do with birding.

http://listserv.arizona.edu/lsv/www/index.html

Mailing Lists Online

If you would like to read current messages from the various birding mailing lists, Birding on the Web has a page full of links to 40 different lists involving birding. Many larger states—such as California, Michigan, Massachusetts, New York, Texas, and Michigan—have their own lists, whereas others—like the Carolinas—are regional. Some are very local; San Diego, California, has its own. Lists from several foreign countries are online. There are specialty lists for those interested in seabirds, as well as Rare Bird Alerts.

http://www-stat.wharton.upenn.edu/~siler/birdmail.html

Microsoft Network Chat

You can chat live with other birding enthusiasts on the Birding Forum, sponsored by the Microsoft Network (MSN) and the Outdoors Network. The forum is also building an online bird identification guide slated to have not only photos but also birdcalls and songs. Besides features about birds, the forum also offers a link to MSN's birding discussion newsgroup. (You don't need to belong to MSN to use this forum.)

http://forums.msn.com/OUTDOORS/birding

Names of North American Birds

If you need a list of the official English and scientific names of the approximately 1,975 species of birds occurring in North America, Mexico, and Hawaii, visit this page on the National Audubon Society's site. You'll get 200,000 bytes worth of names, as well as information about how to write the names properly, right down to where to put the capital letters (for example, *Red-Throated Loon* is wrong; *Red-throated Loon* is right). And you'll learn why it's done that way.

http://www.audubon.org/bird/na-bird.html

National Birder's Forum on Yahoo! Clubs

The National Birder's Forum on Yahoo! Clubs offers both a message base and a chat room on the subject of birding. The messages on the bulletin board can be read by anyone, but you have to be a Yahoo! Clubs member to post. Joining is simple and free, and enables you to use other Yahoo! special services. The chat area also requires membership as does the forum's library of photos. This feature can be used any time, although a weekly group chat is scheduled—see the home page for day and time. The forum also has a collection of links that is open to the public.

http://clubs.yahoo.com/clubs/nationalbirdersforum

FEATHERED FACTS

Rapid Rail

The secretive Virginia Rail is adept at two ways of fleeing enemies, neither of which is flying. The bird is fleet of foot, able to escape by running; it also can dive and swim, using its wings as fins.

—adapted from Birds of North America

http://www.birdsofna.org/excerpts/varail.html

Blue-Gray Gnatcatcher (*Polioptila caerulea*) (JJA)

National Museum of Natural History

The Division of Birds of the National Museum of Natural History, which is a part of the Smithsonian Institution in Washington, D.C., has the third largest bird collection in the world, with more than 600,000 specimens—all dead, of course. This represents about 80 percent of the 9,600 known species of birds in the world. The website isn't going to show you all these specimens—or any of them, for that matter. Instead, it explains the museum and its collection. It offers searchable databases of nearly 4,000 type species—ones that help define a species—in its collection, and details on where they were collected. There's visitor information, policies, selected photos of birds by staff members, and other information that is mostly of interest to the scientific community. You'll also find links to other ornithological websites.

http://www.nmnh.si.edu/vert/birds/birds.html

Natural History Museums

One of the best places to learn about birds—and anything natural—is a natural history museum. The University of California's Museum of Paleontology at Berkeley's website has a huge collection of links to natural history museums in the United States, Canada, and the world. You could spend weeks exploring these sites. They are also useful if you are planning a trip to a region served by one of the museums. The list is purely alphabetical, though, and you may have to use your browser's page search function to find locations you're looking for.

http://www.ucmp.berkeley.edu/subway/nathistmus.html

A
B
C
D
E
F
G
H
I
J
K
L
M
N
O
P
Q
R
S
T
U
V
W
X
Y
Z

FEATHERED FACTS

Two-Story Housing

The Black Tern, found in wet areas in the upper Midwest and Canada, sometimes nests on top of muskrat homes.

—adapted from Northern Prairie Wildlife Research Center

http://www.npwrc.usgs.gov/resource/othrdata/
marshbrd/blktern.htm

Nature Net

Nature.Net has public, online message forums for Bird-Watching, Bluebirding, Hummingbirds, Optics, and Wildlife Gardening. The messages are easy to reach, read, and reply to, and it's not unusual to see 20 replies to one question or observation.

http://www.nature.net/forums/

Nature Watch

Nature Watch, a column that has appeared each Monday since the early 1990s in the *Buffalo* (New York) *News*, is written by Gerry Rising, professor emeritus of the State University of New York. In an engaging style, he offers observations and information about some aspect of natural history. Many of the columns posted online deal with birds, and the website index breaks these out into a separate list (as it does with other natural history topics). Some bird columns deal with individual species whereas others cover subjects that would interest any birder: how and why to start an annual birding list, diseases that affect birds, hazards faced by migrants, visits to interesting birding locales, and recent ornithological discoveries. All are informative, thoroughly readable, and enjoyable.

http://www.acsu.buffalo.edu/~insrisg/nature/

Neornithes

Neornithes is the name used by scientists to classify creatures considered "modern birds." These sites give a picture of how scientists break down the classifications of different kinds of birds. The first site is more graphically pleasing than the second and includes many pictures that show the relationship between ancient birds and modern, but pages take a little longer to load. (However, its address is not as finger-twistingly long as the second.)

http://dinosaur.umbc.edu/taxa/neornith.htm

http://ag.arizona.edu/tree/eukaryotes/animals/
chordata/dinosauria/aves/neornithes.html

Northern Prairie Wildlife Research Center

You'll find references to pages on the vast website of the Northern Prairie Wildlife Research Center scattered throughout this book. That's because the site is such a trove of information. And although it is especially written for the Great Plains, most of the wildlife and the issues it covers extend far beyond the Plains. The center, operated by the U.S. Geological Survey, has many resources dealing with birds, not the least of which are its state-by-state species checklists, its hundreds of pages of information about birds of the Plains, countless feature articles, maps, and much more (check especially the link to Biological Resources, then look for the links to Waterfowl and to Non-Waterfowl Birds). You can look up birds (and other creatures) by geographical area, too. This site is fun to explore—it's like opening a huge encyclopedia of North American nature.

http://www.npwrc.usgs.gov

Sandpiper (Dover)

Nutty Birdwatcher

The Nutty Birdwatcher offers information about bird-watching, eastern U.S. birds, backyard bird feeding, bird migration, the dos and don'ts of building nest boxes, guides to identifying birds, habitats of birds, galleries and profiles of birds, and "everything relating to birds," according to its creator. Far from nutty herself, Webmaster Julia Pahountis has created a site that fills in the gaps in services offered by most birding websites. For example, one of the Nutty Bird-watcher's features is a bird identification guide that helps you find a species by its color: blue, black and white, brown, red and orange, and yellow birds are listed. Pahountis is also creating a sizable collection of online natural histories of eastern species. (*See also Meet the Masters sidebars to learn more about Julia Pahountis and her work.*)

http://www.birdnature.com

Obsolete English Names

Nicasio Wren, Mountain Mockingbird, Desert Sparrow—what are they talking about? In fact, these are among the many names you might find in the older North American ornithological or birding literature but not in recent field guides or checklists, says Dr. Richard C. Banks in his introduction to Obsolete English Names of North American Birds and Their Modern Equivalents. Banks, a noted zoologist who was, from 1994 to 1996, president of the American Ornithologists' Union, works at the Patuxent Wildlife Research Center, which has posted his exhaustive compilation of old and new names. The collection appears on this site in both list and searchable database form. Wandering through the pages, you find many entertaining names—for example, that the American Woodcock was once called a Bogsucker and the Sage Grouse, a Cock of the Plains. A Dabchick was a grebe, a Dunk-a-Doo was an American Bittern, and a Hell-Diver was a Horned Grebe. Click the link at the top of the home page for the search engine. The search page icon—not very clear when we visited the site—is the one with the magnifying glass over the page.

http://www.pwrc.nbs.gov/research/pubs/banks/ obsall.htm

ONElist

ONElist is a huge, central clearinghouse of mailing lists devoted to thousands of different topics, including a dozen or more related to birding. "Mailing lists are communities of people formed around a topic of common interest, and have been around since the beginning of the Internet," notes ONElist. "Instead of e-mailing everyone on the list, subscribers of a mailing list can send their e-mail to one address, which will then automatically send the message to everyone else." With ONElist, the address that you send e-mails to is *listname@onelist.com*, in which *listname* is the name of the list. ONElist enables you to receive messages individually and immediately, or in digest form, that is, as a bunch of messages strung together in one message, sent nightly. Try searching on the ONElist home page for BIRDS, BIRDING, or BIRDWATCHING (note that BIRDS will include many groups of pet owners). Or search for the names of species you're interested in. Each list includes a description, age level it's suitable for, and whether the list is moderated by someone who makes certain people stay on topic and who deals with people who behave badly. You can read archives of recent messages in each list to get a better idea of its content. And if there's nothing quite like what you're interested in, start a mailing list of your own! The Help Center gives plenty of advice on how to do it, including how to promote the list. The site is free; ONElist makes its money by selling ads by placing ads in the e-mails it sends out.

http://www.onelist.com

House Wren (*Troglodytes aedon*) (JJA)

NET NOTES

Searching in Style

SearchIQ is a sort of world headquarters for all search engines, great and small. This site not only lists, but also rates hundreds of search engines that work the Web. You can learn about some of the latest and most sophisticated searching sites and try them out. Displaying a frame at the left side of the home page, SearchIQ lists, describes, and rates search engines that you can make appear in the main page frame. Thus, you can easily move from engine to engine in your quest for information. This is a great site for just wandering the possibilities of the Web, but it's also a wonderful way to track down elusive information about that bird you're researching.

http://www.searchiq.com

Ornithology Online

The Ornithology Website has a good collection of online articles covering such subjects as how to attract hummingbirds, cleaning birdhouses, hawk watches, creating backyard bird habitats, and using care when mowing or pruning trees in the spring and early summer. The site has some fine photos of birds by Gregg Pasterick.

http://mgfx.com/bird/

Patuxent Bird Identification InfoCenter

Looking for an online guide to bird identification? The Patuxent Wildlife Research Center in Maryland offers photographs, songs, identification tips, maps, and life history information for North American birds, and it provides a forum for commentary and discussion regarding bird identification (*first or second address*). Patuxent is one of the most useful sites on the Web for learning about North American birds. For each species, you can find identification tips, life histories, range and breeding maps (often including an animated range map), songs, calls, and pictures of the bird—and its egg. What's more, Patuxent likes feedback. For each species, a comment form is provided. "We encourage you to comment on any component of the identification tips, life history or other information," the site says. "Your comments will be reviewed for content and edited for style, and placed in the forum for each species." The forums are species-specific. Not all kinds of birds may have forums since no one may have commented on a given species—feel free to get one going with your own observations. This wonderful index seems to have two addresses; just in case one disappears, we've included both here. From the main page of the Patuxent Wildlife Research Center (*third address*), you can learn vast amounts of information about the center's wildly ranging wildlife work.

http://www.mbr.nbs.gov/id/framlst/framlst.html
http://www.mbr-pwrc.usgs.gov/id/framlst/framlst.html
http://www.pwrc.nbs.gov/

Peterson Online

Peterson Online, the Web arm of the famous Roger Tory Peterson publications, has a beautiful collection of bird profiles that include both common and uncommon species from all parts of North America. Illustrated with the work of Roger Tory Peterson, each page includes identification techniques, a range map, explanations of feeding and breeding habits, its conservation status, and more. To help you distinguish one bird from others like it, the site often offers plates of illustrations showing similar birds—just like a Peterson field guide; in fact, the plates come from the Peterson guides. The site is designed to demonstrate the *Peterson Multimedia Guides to North American Birds*, published by Houghton Mifflin, and provides full information about those products. The site is also fun to peruse. The species described are, Canvasback, Sandhill Crane, Northern Flicker, Northern Gannet, Eared Grebe, Blue Grosbeak, Broad-winged Hawk, Ruby-throated Hummingbird, White Ibis, Great Kiskadee, Horned Lark, Limpkin, Oldsquaw, Barn Owl, Great Horned Owl, Brown Pelican, Gray Partridge, Red Phalarope, Western Sandpiper, Buller's Shearwater, Tufted Titmouse, Elegant Trogon, Wild Turkey, Turkey Vulture, Kirtland's Warbler, Red-faced Warbler, Northern Wheatear, and Red-headed Woodpecker.

http://www.petersononline.com/birds/month/index.html

Pioneers of Birding

Who was Nuttall of Nuttall's Woodpecker? Or the Cassin of five different California birds' names? Who got their names attached to birds because of their friendship with John James Audubon? Harry Fuller of the Golden Gate Audubon Society in California has written fascinating, readable biographical sketches of some of the pioneers of birding and ornithology in America, a few with a slant toward California, but most of general interest. Among the people covered are: Dr. Thomas Mayo Brewer, John Cassin, Meriwether Lewis, Charles Allen, Thomas Say, Thomas Nuttall, Joseph Mailliard, Dr. Adolphus Heermann, and George Wilhelm Steller.

http://www.audubon.org/chapter/ca/goldengate/
ggasearlybirds.htm#Early Birds

Orange-crowned Warbler (*Vermivora celata*) (JJA)

Puzzle Aerie

If you enjoy word puzzles, as well as watching birds, stop by the Puzzle Aerie, a feature of the Ogden, Utah, Wasatch Audubon Society's website. You'll find sophisticated puzzles like Crypto-Birds, in which each letter in a bird's name has been replaced by another; Bird Anagrams, in which terms like *rob lawn* or *oink blob* can be arranged into bird names; and Two-Part Birds, in which one set of terms, such as *royal personage; allow*, can define a bird name—in this case, *kinglet*. You can also solve bird rebuses, bird puzzle squares, bird word ladders, birds hiding in sentences, and a name-that-bird quiz from crossword-like clues. These all originally appeared in the *Mountain Chickadee*, the newsletter of the Wasatch Audubon Society and were created by the multitalented Mort Somer, who is Webmaster of the site and editor of the newsletter.

http://www.audubon.org/chapter/ut/wasatch/
puzzle_aerie.htm

Queer Birds

Naturalist and author Christopher Majka offers an entertaining essay online called Queer Birds: Marsupial Avians, Compost Heaters, and Obligate Parasites. Here you will learn why certain birds—and it's not just cowbirds and cuckoos, but species that may surprise you—lay their eggs in the nests of other birds. This article originally appear in the *New Brunswick Naturalist* newsletter.

http://www.chebucto.ns.ca/Environment/NHR/
queer.html

Ranges of North American Breeding Birds

The Northern Prairie Wildlife Research Center of the U.S. Geological Survey has maps that show how the populations of many bird species have changed between 1970 and 1989. To compare effectively the data shown on these maps, you must either open more than one browser on your screen and arrange them side by side or you must print the maps.

http://www.npwrc.usgs.gov/RESOURCE/DISTR/BIRDS/
BREEDRNG/BREEDRNG.HTM

A
B
C
D
E
F
G
H
I
J
K
L
M
N
O
P
Q
R
S
T
U
V
W
X
Y
Z

Dead Link?

Web addresses that don't work are annoying. Nonetheless, we ask readers of *Internet Guide to Birds and Birding* to tell us about them so we can find a new address—or maybe an alternative site. Stop by <http://www.acorn-online.com/hedge/birdup.htm> and check to see if the dead link has already been reported and a new one posted. If not, please pass on your report, using the e-mail link on the page.

Rare Bird Alert Readers

Real Birds (*first address*), a service of the Virtual Birder e-zine, an online magazine, opens with a map of the states and provinces; click on a location and up comes complete Rare Bird Alert information, including the last few alerts, the names of compilers and transcribers, and much more. The Wild Bird Center of Walnut Creek, California, maintains a page (*second address*) that enables you to read the latest Rare Bird Alerts for all the states and provinces that have them. Links to other birding sites within each state are also available. Jack Siler's Birding on the Web has a Hot Birds reader (*third address*) that enables you to view the "most recently received hotline mail." *Winging It!* (*fourth address*), the monthly newsletter of the American Birding Association, has concise, online summaries of Rare Bird Alerts for the past year. These summaries provide a quick look at interesting sightings around North America based on RBA reports. The University of Arizona, which distributes eight birding lists including Rare Bird Alerts, has an online archive for current and past messages (*fifth address*).

http://www.virtualbirder.com/vbirder/realbirds/
   RealBirdsMid.html

http://www.birdware.com/lists/rba.htm

http://enkidu.wharton.upenn.edu/~siler/birdmail.html

http://www.americanbirding.org/wggen.htm

http://listserv.arizona.edu/lsv/www/index.html

Rare Bird Alert Telephone Numbers

Rare Bird Alerts start out as taped messages on a telephone line, designed so people can call any time of the day or night and listen to the latest news. If you are more comfortable with audio than with visual technology—or just like to hear the sound of the human voice, here is a complete listing of telephone Rare Bird Alerts, arranged by state. This is especially handy if you're traveling and want to know what kinds of rare birds are being seen in the region of your destination. The list is taken from *Winging It!*, the monthly newsletter of the American Birding Association.

http://americanbirding.org/wgrbaadd.htm

Rare Bird Alerts

One of the important services that the Internet has added to the enjoyment of birding is the North American Rare Bird Alerts (RBAs), sponsored by the National Birding Hotline Cooperative. These, typically, weekly notifications of sightings of rare or at least interesting bird species in an area often include directions on how to get to the location of the sighting. These notices may be obtained in a number of different ways: via direct messages sent through a listserve, from a website, from messages posted on services like CompuServe, and from messages sent to newsgroups. And, if you're old-fashioned, you can also pick them up by telephone. Listserve RBA messages are done by region: eastern, midwestern, and western. Each region will have bunches of messages from states or areas within states. To subscribe to these, send a message to *listserv@listserv.arizona.edu*. In the body of the message type SUBSCRIBE BIRDEAST for eastern region RBAs, SUBSCRIBE BIRDCNTR for central, and SUBSCRIBE BIRDWEST for western. Almost immediately you'll get a message confirming your subscription, with instructions on how to stop service, should you ever want to. Save the message for later reference.

http://www.virtualbirder.com/vbirder/realbirds/NBHC/
   NBHCRBAInfo.html

Rare Record Documentation Form

Hey, that's a Many-spangled Flagwaver at the feeder! Wow! What do I do now? If you are fortunate enough to spot a really rare bird in your neighborhood, there's an official form for reporting it to the people who care. The form on the Northern Prairie Wildlife Research Center site asks a lot of questions—all aimed at pinning down and helping confirm the sighting. A good birder who wants to know what to look for in a sighting—rare or otherwise—would do well to look over this form to see the kinds of information that firm up or confirm a sighting. You might even want to print one out for your records. The first address is the actual form; the second is the page from which you can find the state authorities to which to send the form. Select the state and then look for the link to the person who maintains the list. Often, an e-mail link is included. Also, don't forget to tip off your Rare Bird Alert correspondent, which you can find at the third address.

http://www.npwrc.usgs.gov/resource/othrdata/ chekbird/form.htm

http://www.npwrc.usgs.gov/resource/othrdata/ chekbird/chekbird.htm

http://www.virtualbirder.com/vbirder/realbirds/ RealBirdsMid.html

Tree Swallow (*Iridoprocne bicolor*)
[*Tachycineta bicolor*] (JJA)

NET NOTES

Searching for a Bird

If you are looking for websites that deal with a specific kind of bird, make sure you do the most effective scan with your favorite search engine. For instance, if you want sites that tell about the feeding habits of the robin, don't search for "robin" or you'll wind up with thousands of pages, only a fraction of which may deal with birds (you'll get every website that mentions actor Robin Williams or anyone else named Robin for that matter). Instead, be like a scientist and use the scientific name, *Turdus migratorius*. Just as an example, we searched for "robin" on Alta Vista which reported 1,250,682 pages mentioning that word (the first page on the list was a Spanish website dealing with "Robin y Batman"). However, when we searched for "Turdus migratorius," a respectable 644 pages were found, and you can bet they all had something to do with our friend, Robin Redbreast.

Recreational Birding Guide

GORP, also known as the Great Outdoor Recreation Pages, has a sizable site devoted to bird-watching. You'll find features on the hobby—including excerpts from books, the GORP Recreational Birding Guide on where to go birding across North America and around the world, descriptions of species, birding adventures, photo galleries, travel, books, refuges, and a birding forum.

http://www.gorp.com/gorp/activity/birding.htm

Riddles

The Yakima, Washington, Audubon Society has a set of 10 bird riddles—higgledy-piggledy style—to challenge your wit and possibly your wisdom. Good luck!

http://www.audubon.org/chapter/wa/yakima/ riddle.htm

A B C D E F G H I J K L M N O P Q R S T U V W X Y Z

A
B
C
D
E
F
G
H
I
J
K
L
M
N
O
P
Q
R
S
T
U
V
W
X
Y
Z

Loggerhead Shrike (*Lanius ludovicianus*) (JJA)

Southern California Birds

The Biology Department of Loyola Marymount University in Los Angeles has an online field guide called Southern California Natural History that includes a guide to the birds of the region. For each species, crisp, close-up photos are provided (click on the thumbnail to get a bigger version), as well as brief descriptions of characteristics, links to similar species, and range information. In many cases, especially when it's most interesting, the species page will include a recording of the bird's song or call. Although short on words, the site has such a huge collection of birds and the basics about each, plus excellent photos, that it is among the best of its kind on the Web for finding regional data.

http://eco.bio.lmu.edu/socal_nat_hist/birds/birds.htm

Tautonyms, Tautonyms

When a species' first and last scientific names are the same, its name is a *tautonym*, and this website lists 25

North American birds whose Latin names are the same coming or going. One of the most appealing birds, with a less-than-appealing-sounding name, is the Winter Wren, or *Troglodytes troglodytes*. Or try this one, *Perdix perdix*, which sounds like a great name for the Gray Partridge. The Red-footed Booby is the *Sula sula*, whereas the common crane is *Grus grus*. Check out the others at Birdwatching.com.

http://www.birdwatching.com/tips/tautonyms_aba.html

Tweeters

Tweeters is a Pacific Northwest birders e-mail mailing list serving Washington State, British Columbia, and parts of Oregon and Idaho. "Tweeters started around the end of 1992 with three people sharing messages about bird sightings," reports Dan Victor, who runs the site and belongs to the Washington Ornithological Society. The list serves universities, as well as a "diverse mix: some are expert birders, some like myself are of the intermediate variety, some beginners, and others have just expressed an interest," Victor says. To subscribe, send the following message text to *listproc@u.washington.edu*: SUB TWEETERS JOHN DOE in which you replace John Doe with your name. More information about Tweeters is at this website.

http://www.scn.org/earth/tweeters/

Unofficial List of Current Rarities

A Jackdaw shows up at St. Johns, Newfoundland. A Brambling is spotted in Portland, Oregon. Someone sees a White-collared Seedeater in Zapata, Texas. If you're a bird-chasing fanatic or just like to know what odd and interesting birds are being seen, here's the place for you. Greg Miller scans Rare Bird Alerts for truly interesting sightings around North America and posts them on this simple page. Links are designed to lead you to where you can read the actual RBAs to get the details on the sightings. Incidentally, we like Greg's disclaimer: "This list is totally unofficial, unconfirmed, travel at your own risk, blah-blah-blah. In other words, you're on your own. If you don't see rarity listed, it's because I hastily overlooked it. If something's listed here that shouldn't be, I'm sorry."

http://www.erols.com/gregorym/rarities.html

Utah Nature Study Society

"I spent the summer traveling," wrote Louis Agassiz, a well-known 19th-century scientist, naturalist, and educator. "I got halfway across my backyard." With these wonderful words, the Utah Nature Study Society opens its home page and invites visitor to wander through more than 150 articles on nature—many of which deal with birds. The website is straightforward and beautiful, despite the fact that it has little of the glitz of the most modern-looking sites. It offers many insights, tips, and entertaining reports about nature and natural history trips. People who like to read will particularly enjoy this site, which has an archive of well-written essays dating back more than 25 years. You don't have to be a member to enjoy and learn from this site, nor do you have to be from Utah. However, if your focus is Utah, links will lead you to other sites in the state and the region that have birding and nature information.

http://www.softcom.net/users/naturenotes/

Not Birds Only

"Natural history has been an avocation and not a vocation for me," says Professor Gerry Rising, whose Nature Watch website <http://www.acsu.buffalo.edu/~insrisg/nature/> is rich with his essays—mostly from his newspaper columns—on many aspects of nature, but is especially strong on birds. "I spent my professional life as a mathematics teacher and have returned to a lifelong hobby of bird watching in my dotage," Professor Rising says. In the early 1990s, he heard that a new writer for the *Buffalo* (New York) *News'* "Nature Watch" column was needed. He asked Editor Murray Light if he could do the column but stick to writing about birds. "His answer was straightforward: 'No,'" Rising recalls. So he took over the column, but expanded his natural history horizons, thanks to Editor Light. "I have come to thank him for that response as it has forced me to extend my interests in many directions."

Cerulean Warbler (*Dendroica cerulea*) (JJA)

Virtual Birder

The Virtual Birder comes as close as you can to a genuine e-zine (online magazine) for birders. Because its content is so useful and its design so well executed, the Virtual Birder has also become one of the most popular birding sites on the World Wide Web. "Our goal is to regularly bring compelling content to birders via the Web," said editor and Webmaster Don Crockett. "This content should inform, educate, and entertain birders with a variety of experience, from someone just getting into birding to someone who has birded their entire life." The Virtual Birder manages to take full advantage of the Web. Practice Your Shorebird Identification is an electronic tour of different hot birding spots around North America with not just photos and maps but also calls of birds you're apt to see along the shore (*see also Tips & Techniques*). An April issue of the Virtual Birder offered Birding by Ear—Spring Tune-Up, which used both words and sounds to help birders sharpen their skills at identifying species by their songs. The Virtual Birder is full of photographs and features about birds, and also maintains an up-to-date collection of national Rare Bird Alerts (carried in its Real Birds section). You can find loads of links to sites for local birding information. The Media section has scores of books, videos, CDs, and tapes, with reviews of many of them. And since Webmaster and editor Crockett is skilled at both Web design and birding, you're apt to find many new features—and ways of using the Web for presenting them.

http://www.virtualbirder.com/vbirder/

A B C D E F G H I J K L M N O P Q R S T U V W X Y Z

Song Sparrow (*Melospiza melodia*) (JJA)

WebDirectory

This address leads to the WebDirectory's collection of links to birding sites of all sorts from all parts of the world. You will also find folders about Audubon societies, products and services, bird-related companies, publications, and waterfowl.

http://www.webdirectory.com/Wildlife/Birds/

WetNet Birds & Waterfowl

WetNet, a project of Texas Wetland Information Network, has a collection of profiles and good photos of about two dozen species of water-oriented birds that are found in Texas and beyond. Some species described here are hard to find elsewhere, so if you're looking for shorebirds or wetland birds that winter in the South, check this out. The page also indexes profiles of aquatic and land animals and plants.

http://red.glo.state.tx.us/wetnet/species.html#Birds

Winging It: Birds of the Blue Ridge

This website is a collection of profiles of some of the most familiar backyard birds (mostly Eastern) with entertaining text by Jeff Crooke and illustrated with watercolors by Donna Thomas. Crooke answers e-mail and exhibits a great sense of humor, judging by his essays and his answers to questions. The site includes a Squirrel Warroom and a mailbag. Other useful information includes a piece on identifying an unusual visiting hummingbird, complete with extensive photographs, marked to facilitate understanding of the points under discussion.

http://rtonline1.roanoke.com/wingingit/profiles.html

Don't Throw Out Your Web Work!

Webmasters: before you pull the plug on a useful website, consider donating your efforts to others.

In researching literally thousands of sites, I've run across more than a dozen that provided excellent and otherwise hard-to-find information—and then disappeared. Some were top-notch regional birding guides and others were extensive indexes of places to see birds or information on birding. For whatever reason—a different job, a new interest, exhaustion—the Webmaster decided to give up the site and shut it down.

Although you might have a good reason for shutting down, it's hard to justify throwing out all your hard and useful work. Why not donate it to others? For instance, if you have a regional birding guide, offer it to a National Audubon Society chapter in your area that has a website. Your pages might help boost the chapter's content and depth. Another option is to look for a site with similar interests but lacking either the detail or depth of work you've done. That Webmaster might appreciate the opportunity to rework your pages into his or her site. Still another option is to post a message on the Usenet newsgroup, *rec.birds*, offering to give away your website.

Few of us would throw away a good book when we're finished with it. Why throw out a good website?

AVIAN ADVICE

Getting the Kids Involved

Classroom BirdWatch was developed by the Cornell Laboratory of Ornithology to get youngsters involved in scientific pursuits, specifically learning the observation and recording techniques in preparation of an annual feeder-bird survey conducted by Cornell ornithologists. Sign-up information is available on the site.

http://birdsource.cornell.edu/cfw/watiscfw.htm

HOUSES & NEST BOXES

Feeding the birds is fun, but watching them raise a family can be even more fun. In the case of some species—such as owls, Wood Ducks, and bluebirds—you'll be helping to preserve and expand populations that have run into trouble, mostly because of changes in the environment wrought by human development. In this section you can find websites that will show you how to build or buy various houses or nesting platforms for bluebirds, ducks, Purple Martins, Osprey, and many other species. And you'll also learn what any realtor will tell you: location, location, location. For the target species to use the houses you provide, you'll have to place them properly. You'll also learn how to maintain them off-season. (*See also Feeding & Watering and Retailers.*)

All about Nest Boxes

"Supplying a nest box/birdhouse will attract birds into the yard and will encourage the winter birds to stay and it even helps the species that are struggling to find a suitable nesting site," observes Julia Pahountis, Web-

master of the Nutty Birdwatcher. She offers a list of do's and don'ts for establishing nest boxes, describes how to keep records about them, and offers dimensions for nest boxes for the following species: American Kestrel, American Robin, Ash-throated Flycatcher, Barn Owl, Barn Swallow, Bewick's Wren, Brown-headed Nuthatch, Carolina Wren, chickadees, Common Goldeneye, Common Merganser, Downy Woodpecker, Eastern Bluebird, Great-crested Flycatcher, Hairy Woodpecker, House Finch, House Wren, Mountain Bluebird, Northern Flicker, Osprey, Phoebe, Pileated Woodpecker, Prothonotary Warbler, Purple Martin, Pygmy Nuthatch, Red-bellied Woodpecker, Red-breasted Nuthatch, Red-tailed Hawk, Saw-whet Owl, Screech Owl, Song Sparrow, starling, titmice, Tree Swallow, Violet-Green Swallow, Winter Wren, Wood Duck, and Yellow-bellied Sapsucker. Illustrated instructions for building the basic "enclosed nestbox" are also provided.

http://nuthatch.birdnature.com/nestintro.html

Big Brother for the Birds

Ever wonder what goes in inside that birdhouse you have hanging from the garage? If you aren't worried about being a Big Brother (in the Orwellian sense) in the bird world, check out TV Bird. This Ohio company sells birdhouses whose interiors are equipped with miniature TV cameras. Connect it to your television with the cable provided, and you'll be able to watch the occupants raise a family. TV Bird sells video-equipped birdhouses, as well as kits for you to equip an existing birdhouse. The systems range from black-and-white, without sound, to color cameras and color with sound. TV Bird also sells camera-equipped feeders so you can snoop on your birds' dining habits. The website has many sample photos as well as action videos (requiring RealPlayer to view, see page 150).

http://www.tvbird.com

Birdhouse Dimensions

This handy table, devised by the U.S. Fish & Wildlife Service, gives the dimensions for both birdhouses and nesting platforms for dozens of species, from tiny chickadees to huge owls.

http://www.bcpl.net/~tross/by/dimen.html

A
B
C
D
E
F
G
H
I
J
K
L
M
N
O
P
Q
R
S
T
U
V
W
X
Y
Z

A
B
C
D
E
F
G
H
I
J
K
L
M
N
O
P
Q
R
S
T
U
V
W
X
Y
Z

American Robin (Dover)

Bluebird Boxes

Perhaps no kind of North American bird has been the subject of more extensive home-building efforts than the several species of bluebirds, particularly the Eastern Bluebird. One retired fellow who lived near me erected literally thousands of bluebird boxes during the 1970s and 1980s. The effort has been fueled largely by the fact that bluebirds have been in decline, partly because of loss of habitat and partly because of competition from introduced species of European birds. You can learn more about bluebirds in the section on backyard birds (*see North American Birds, Backyard*), but the following are all pages dealing with how to make a bluebird box—a very simple, easy-to-do project that can involve the whole family. A dozen design variations can be found at one website (*first address*). The Ellis Bird Farm in Alberta describes its housing techniques for the Mountain Bluebird (*second address*). The North American Bluebird Society offers one book designed for the Eastern or Western Bluebird and another for the Mountain Bluebird (*third address*). The New York State Bluebird Society, which has sponsored nest box design studies, offers it favorite (*fourth address*).

http://hometown.aol.com/jimmcl/bbbox/nestbox/
nestbox.htm

http://www.wep.ab.ca/ellisbirdfarm/programs.
htm#boxes

http://www.nabluebirdsociety.org/plans.htm

http://www.geocities.com/RainForest/2414/nysbsbox.
htm

Building Nest Boxes & Birdhouses

"It's easy to build your own birdhouses," says the Texas Parks & Wildlife Department. "Most cavity-nesting birds, such as bluebirds, chickadees, wrens, and even owls will use a birdhouse, *if* you build it to the right dimensions." On this page, the agency provides the dimensions for housing many backyard and woodland species. A 90-second audio clip (*see page 150*) tells of the importance of bluebird boxes.

http://www.tpwd.state.tx.us/adv/birding/birdhous/
birdhous.htm

Building Nest Structures & Photo Blinds

Chris Grondahl and John Dockter of the North Dakota State Fish & Game Department have put together a guide called *Building Nest Structures, Feeders, and Photo Blinds for North Dakota Wildlife*, which is posted on the Web by the Northern Prairie Wildlife Research Center. The good news is that most of the wildlife of North Dakota is widespread, and you'll find plans and advice for building nest boxes for the House Wren, Black-capped Chickadee, White-breasted Nuthatch, Tree Swallow, Eastern Bluebird, American Robin, Barn Swallow, Purple Martin, Northern Flicker, American Kestrel, Wood Duck, Common and Hooded Mergansers, and Eastern Screech-Owl, as well as open boxes for American Robins and Barn Swallows, nest tunnels for Burrowing Owls, nest tubs for Canada Geese, nest baskets for Mourning Doves, and platforms for Great Blue Herons.

http://www.npwrc.usgs.gov/resource/tools/ndblinds/
ndblinds.htm

Building Songbird Boxes

Building songbird boxes is a simple, inexpensive way to attract songbirds to your property, notes the University of North Carolina, which offers this fact sheet describing how to build, install, and maintain nest boxes successfully. Plans for the boxes include predator guards.

http://www.ces.ncsu.edu/nreos/forest/steward/
www16.html

Duck Boxes

Four species of North American ducks—Wood Duck, Hooded Merganser, Common Goldeneye, and Bufflehead—are cavity nesters and can be drawn to nesting boxes that are properly constructed and located. If you live near a wetland, you can try inviting these ducks to your neighborhood. The Northern Prairie Wildlife Research Center of the U.S. Geological Survey has detailed plans and instructions on how to make and place duck boxes (*first address*). The site is well illustrated, and you can download the entire package as a .ZIP file for use with your browser at any time. Wood Ducks are among the most handsome of the ducks and are also a game species. However, loss of habitat severely cut the Wood Duck populations in the first half of the 20th century. Consequently, various measures, including the erection of many thousands of human-made nesting boxes, are bringing these birds back. One of the major organizations involved in promoting the building of these boxes is Ducks Unlimited, a conservation group supported especially by duck hunters. Ducks Unlimited has online nesting box plans and a printable diagram—plus plenty of information about these birds (*second address*). The University of North Carolina tells about the natural history of Wood Ducks and offers plans for wood duck houses—including a metal predator guide (*third address*).

http://www.npwrc.usgs.gov/resource/tools/nestbox/
nestbox.htm

http://www.ducks.org/info/woodduck_box.asp

http://www.ces.ncsu.edu/nreos/forest/steward/
www6.html

American Pipit (*Anthus spinoletta*) (JJA)

FEATHERED FACTS

Billions of Birds!

Though hunters had driven the Passenger Pigeon to extinction in the wild by 1900, it was once the most populous bird in North America. In 1813 John James Audubon took a trip from his home on the Ohio River to Louisville, Kentucky, when a flock of passenger pigeons passed overhead. There were so many birds, they shut out the sunlight from noon until sundown. More flocks followed in the next three days. Audubon calculated that every three hours, more than one billion birds flew by!

—adapted from Steve's Book of the Not-So-Grateful Dead and Audubon's *Birds of America*

http://www.aristotle.net/~swarmack/pigeon.html

http://gopher.science.wayne.edu/animals/bird/pigeon/
index.html

Flicker Box

The Northern Flicker is one of our most handsome woodpeckers. Cavity nesters, they can sometimes be attracted to nesting boxes. Alan Bower has created a design for a homemade box that has worked successfully around his home in Michigan.

http://users.aol.com/jimmcl/bbbox/nestbox/flicker.gif

Hollow Log Birdhouses

Calvin Grimes of Nebo, Illinois, makes bluebird and wren houses out of logs—hollow logs. Among other things, they are very natural looking and, because they are fashioned from osage orange, they will "last a lifetime," says Grimes, who can supply houses—both hanging and post-mounted—in other woods as well.

http://www.geocities.com/Heartland/Lane/9917/

A B C D E F G H I J K L M N O P Q R S T U V W X Y Z

A
B
C
D
E
F
G
H
I
J
K
L
M
N
O
P
Q
R
S
T
U
V
W
X
Y
Z

FEATHERED FACTS

A Million Landlords

In the eastern half of the United States, Purple Martins will not nest and breed unless humans supply the nesting houses (in the West, they'll breed in the wild). It is estimated that at least one million Americans are Purple Martin landlords.

—adapted from Robert Rice, Smithsonian Migratory Bird Center

http://web2.si.edu/smbc/bom/puma.htm

Homes for Birds

Terry Ross of the Baltimore Bird Club has revised a U.S. Fish & Wildlife Service pamphlet into one of the most comprehensive online guides to birdhouse building that you'll find. Terry has information online about houses for bluebirds, robins, chickadees, nuthatches, titmice, Brown Creepers, Prothonotary Warblers, wrens, swallows, Purple Martins, flycatchers, woodpeckers, and owls. The site tells how to select a house, what materials and designs to use (including such factors as ventilation and drainage), placement, and protection from predators such as mammals, snakes, insects, and other birds. Also, information about how to make nesting platforms for various large species, such as Red-tailed Hawks and Great Horned Owls, is available.

http://www.bcpl.net/~tross/by/house.html

Owlboxes

"The urge to build an owl house finally overcame me during that dreaded period between New Year's Day and the Superbowl," writes the author of the Owlbox website. "While numerous 'experts' had advised me that it was a long shot, the thought of watching flightless barred owlets from the comfort of my home made it seem worth a try." Not only was the experiment a success, but the nest box builder installed a video camera to capture some spectacular photos of Northern Barred Owls, their eggs, and their babes, along with many wonderful sound recordings. The site tells how to build your own box and has plenty of tips and diary-style information that could tempt any of us into becoming owl house developers. It's a great site and a lot of fun.

http://members.aol.com/owlbox/owlhome.htm

Purple Martin Houses

East of the Rockies, Purple Martins rely on humans to provide them with nesting facilities. Yet they were once wild, nesting in old woodpecker holes. What changed their nesting habits? On this page (*first address*) the Purple Martin Conservation Association explains the remarkable adaptation of Purple Martins to the newly arrived aborigines. For more on martins and the kinds of houses they inhabit in yards, visit the home page of the Purple Martin Conservation Association (*second address*).

http://www.purplemartin.org/history.html
http://www.purplemartin.org

Swallow-tailed Kite (*Elanoides forficatus*) (JJA)

INTERNATIONAL

Although this book is devoted mostly to North American birds and birding, there are at least three reasons why you might want to wander websites that deal with birds in other parts of the world: curiosity, travel, and "accidentals." Many people who are interested in backyard birds become interested in birds in general and don't let geographic boundaries limit that interest. Only about 10 percent of the world's species are found in North America, so that means more than 8,000 kinds live elsewhere. Of course, if you're traveling to any of that "elsewhere," you will find the Web a handy source of information about the birds of the region you'll be visiting. Finally, being creatures of the air that can often travel long distances, birds can get off course and show up in territories they don't normally live in. These are called *accidentals*. If you live in northeastern North America, you may come across an accidental from Europe. Asian species sometimes show up in the northwest, and along the southern borders and shores of the United States, odd tropical birds from Central America and the Caribbean often appear. These sites can also be good sources for asking questions, especially if you are planning a visit to a distant destination or come upon an unusual exotic. *(See also Destinations and Tours & Expeditions.)*

FEATHERED FACTS

Well, It's a Cute Name . . .

The Yellow-rumped Warbler has a yellow rear end, which has earned it the nickname among birders of "Butter Butt."

—adapted from Garrett Lowe and Russ Greenberg, Smithsonian Migratory Bird Center

http://web2.si.edu/smbc/bom/yrwa.htm

Pigeon Hawk (*Falco columbarius*) (JJA)

African Bird Club

Barely a quarter of the world's birds exist on and about the African continent, and the African Bird Club, based in the United Kingdom, is for those seriously interested in the birds of Africa. The club promotes conservation of African birds, works with regional African ornithological societies, publishes a bulletin, and encourages observers to "visit lesser-known areas of the region, and search actively for globally threatened and near-threatened species." The website carries news of developments in bird research and allows exchange of information about African birds. The club also sells some wild T-shirts!

http://www.africanbirdclub.org

Atlas of Southern African Birds

If you're planning a trip to southern Africa, the Avian Demography Unit Department of Statistical Sciences at the University of Cape Town has information about this two-volume set of books, published by BirdLife South Africa.

http://www.uct.ac.za/depts/stats/adu/p_atlas.htm

Australian Birding Links

Australia has some of the earth's most incredible birds, well worth investigating if you are planning a trip down under. Frank O'Connor maintains a collection of some of his nation's best birding websites.

http://www.iinet.net.au/~foconnor/links.htm

A B C D E F G H I J K L M N O P Q R S T U V W X Y Z

FEATHERED FACTS

Avian Lifespans

Although the average songbird probably lives around two years, most can live much longer if they avoid predators, disease, starvation, or human-made problems like tall-building windows. Wild cardinals have lived at least 13 years, Black-capped Chickadees 10 years, and American Goldfinches, seven years. At least one Red-bellied Woodpecker lived more than 20 years. In captivity, some waterfowl have survived for 30 years, and some gulls up to 40 years.

—adapted from *Bird Watcher's Digest*

http://www.birdwatchersdigest.com/faq/faq.html

Biodiversity, Taxonomy, & Conservation in Australia

The Biodiversity, Taxonomy, & Conservation site at Charles Sturt University in Australia has sizable databases on fauna and flora of Australia. For birds, the complete list is about 100,000 bytes long, providing names and where the birds generally are found. The site has much ornithological information about Australian birds and wildlife.

http://www.csu.edu.au/biodiversity.html

Bird Links to the World

When we last visited Denis Lepage's mammoth collection of birding links, he had 2,327 of them. He organizes them by geographical regions, by specific species, images and sounds, museums, scientific links, newsgroups, publications, optics, software, books, travels and tours, and conservation. He also has a collection that he calls the Best Bird Web Sites. Explore away!

http://www.ntic.qc.ca/~nellus/links.html

Bird Web of the United Kingdom

The Bird Web has been serving the bird-watching population of Scotland since 1990. For visitors from elsewhere the site is invaluable, offering clickable-map guides with very extensive descriptions of where to go birding in Scotland. The site, created by Paul Doyle, also has a huge, illustrated database of birds of the United Kingdom and Europe, with many photos (click them to view larger versions). At the bottom of the home page, follow the graphic link to the UK Birding Web Ring, where you'll find many more websites of interest. This site works best if you have a frames-capable browser.

http://www.abdn.ac.uk/~nhi019/intro.html

Golden Eagle (*Aquila chrysaetos*) (JJA)

BirdLife International, Americas Division

BirdLife International works to protect birds and their habitats throughout the world. "BirdLife is a global alliance of non-governmental conservation organizations with a focus on birds who, together, are the leading authority on the status of birds, their habitats and the issues and problems affecting bird life," Adrian Long of BirdLife's communications department at the headquarters in England told us. "Overall our mission strives to conserve birds, their habitats and global biodiversity working with people towards sustainability in the use of natural resources." As this book was going into print, BirdLife International was still planning a headquarters website (links to which you may find on the sites below). However, many of its regional offices have well-established sites. The Americas Division (*first address*), based in Quito, Ecuador, focuses on the conservation of birds in most countries of South and Central America. The page is hosted by the Latin American Alliance, a related environmental organization, about which you can learn more by following the link at the bottom of the page. Indonesia is home to 104 threatened species of birds, and BirdLife International's office in Bogor has a complete online list by region (*second address*). Conservation programs and a new book on Indonesian birding are also described, and there's a useful page of links to international bird sites. BirdLife forms partnerships with local conservation organizations, and the Important Bird Areas website of the Canadian Nature Federation has a page of links to such groups around the world (*third address*). Many of these sites can provide information on local birds, though usually they're the rare or threatened varieties. Another source of worldwide BirdLife International links is the group's site in Japan (*fourth address*).

http://www.latinsynergy.org/birdlife.html
http://www.kt.rim.or.jp/~birdinfo/indonesia/
http://www.ibacanada.com/partner.htm
http://www.wnn.or.jp/wnn-n/w-bird/bli/bli_e.html

Birds Australia

Birds Australia is the home of the Royal Australasian Ornithologists Union, one of Australia's oldest conservation organizations. The site has information about birding down under, including a complete list of Australian birds (more than 700 species). The site has a guide to beginning birding, useful no matter where you live, and a sampling of the calls of some of the more interesting Australian birds. If you look under the menu entry, Birding, you will find a link called Migration—though it may sound like a place to learn about bird movements, it's actually Birds Australia's way of saying "links." And there's a fine international collection of them. For anyone planning a trip to Australia or who just wants to learn more about the fascinating variety of birds there—from gorgeous honeyeaters to huge cassowarys that can kill a human—this site is well worth a visit. And if you are of a scholarly bent, you'll find abstracts from *Emu*, the union's journal. Check out, too, the section on the *Atlas of Australian Birds* project; the union is soliciting the help of both professionals and bird-knowledgeable visitors in compiling the newest version of this important document.

http://home.vicnet.net.au/~birdsaus/

Birds of the Amazon

Marine Expeditions, which offers cruises to the Amazon and other remote regions of the world, has a sizable page of information about birds found in the Amazon. Although not illustrated, the page has many tips about birding in the region and what you can expect to find.

http://www.marineex.com/amazonbirds.html

FEATHERED FACTS

Snakeskin Liners?

The nests of Blue Grosbeaks often contain shed snake skins and nearly always have a piece of paper or paper-like material woven into the open cup-style construction.

—adapted from Jennifer D. White, California Partners in Flight

http://www.prbo.org/

A B C D E F G H I J K L M N O P Q R S T U V W X Y Z

British Ornithologists Union

The British Ornithologists Union publishes a line of books, which it calls *checklists* but which are more like field guides, complete with color photos and maps. If you are heading to any of these destinations, check out the BOU books that can help you figure out what you may be seeing: St. Helena, St. Lucia, Togo, Cape Verde Islands, Nigeria, Cyprus, The Gambia, The Philippines, Sicily, Sumatra, South Bahamas, Ghana, and Wallacea. Guides to Corsica, Angola, Cayman Islands, Gulf of Guinea, and Morocco are on the way.

http://www.bou.org.uk/index.html

EuroBirdNet

EuroBirdNet is a mailing list for persons interested in reports of rare bird sightings and migrations in Europe. "It's also open for discussions on identification, systematics, requests for hotspots, accommodations, travel reports, etc.," says Erling V. Jirle of the Department of Ecology at Lund University, Sweden. This page explains the list—a good thing to join if you're planning on some serious European birding—and also has information about and links to other sources of European and world birding.

http://www.pheromone.ekol.lu.se/EuroBirdnet.html

Find a European Bird

Need a description or even a picture of a European bird? This site in England, Find a Bird Sketch Book, covers most species and often provides pictures or paintings.

http://www.birdcare.com/bin/searchsketches

Internet Flyway

The Internet Flyway, sponsored by the Oriental Bird Club in the United Kingdom, is a collection of links described as "where to find birds—and birders—on the 'Net." The page is arranged by regions of the world and by topics.

http://www.orientalbirdclub.org/flyway/

Neotropical Bird Club

Central and South America, including the Caribbean Islands, have the world's richest biodiversity and nearly 3,000 species of birds, reports the Neotropical Bird Club's website. The organization, based in England, fosters an exchange of information about birds of this region, supports conservation efforts, and tries to "mobilize the increasing number of enthusiastic birdwatchers active in the region to contribute to the conservation of Neotropical birds." The site contains news and announcements about Neotropical birds and regional organizations, as well as information about the club and its publications.

http://www.neotropicalbirdclub.org

Middle Eastern Promise

Middle Eastern Promise, a page provided by the Ornithological Society of the Middle East, provides links to birding and natural history websites, and feature articles about Armenia, Bahrain, Cyprus, Israel, Lebanon, Lesbos, Oman, Saudi Arabia, Turkey, United Arab Emirates, Yemen, and elsewhere.

http://www.osme.org/osmeweb/promise.html

Oriental Bird Club

The Oriental Bird Club, also based in the United Kingdom, supports "ornithologists throughout the world, both amateur and professional, who share a common interest in the region's birds and wish to assist in their conservation." That region consists of the Indus River, Pakistan, in the west through India and southeast Asia to the Wallacea line, East Indonesia in the east, and from the Yangtze basin, China, in the north to the Lesser Sundas and Christmas Island in the south. "This vast area embraces tropical and temperate forests, outstanding wetlands and grasslands providing habitat for over 2,000 bird species, many of them little known," the club says. The site is especially interesting for its library of well-researched and illustrated profiles of Asian species. Some spectacular birds to see and read about are on this site.

http://www.orientalbirdclub.org

Ornithological Society of the Middle East

The Ornithological Society of the Middle East, formed in 1978, was originally the Ornithological Society of Turkey. Today, it collects, collates, and publishes ornithological data about birds of the Middle East and encourages an interest in and conservation of birds of this region. One of the best features of the site is its sizable collection of trip reports to places like Egypt, Israel, Turkey, the United Arab Emirates, and Yemen —be sure to check them out if you are planning a trip to the Middle East. The website carries many articles from the current issue of the *Sandgrouse*, the society's bulletin, as well as recent bird and conservation news from the Middle East, and round-ups of interesting bird sightings. The site includes a useful search function and information about joining the organization, which is headquartered in the United Kingdom.

http://www.osme.org

Sparrow Hawk (*Falco sparverius*)
[American Kestrel] (JAA)

FEATHERED FACTS

Branch-Breaking Birds

The Passenger Pigeon, hunted to extinction, was once the most numerous bird species in the world. A single flock of them could have two billion birds and their nesting colonies in the northeastern forests could stretch for 20 miles and contain so many birds per tree that branches broke under their weight.

—adapted from Bagheera

http://www.bagheera.com/inthewild/ext_pigeon.htm

Parrot Mailing List

An e-mail discussion group providing a forum for those involved in the scientific study and conservation of wild parrots has been formed to encourage the exchange of information and advance the scientific study and conservation of parrots. It is called *apc-list* and is sponsored by the Association for Parrot Conservation, hosted by the University of Maryland. To join, send an e-mail message to *listserv@umdd.umd.edu*, leaving the subject line blank and writing in the message body SUB APC-LIST FIRSTNAME LASTNAME (substitute your first and last names). There may be a slight delay while your subscription is approved.

Rarest Birds in the World

Some of the rarest birds in the world live on Mauritius, the island off Africa that was once home of the infamous and long extinct Dodo (*see also North American Birds, Extinct*). On this site, sponsored by Mauritius Island Online, you can learn about the Mauritius Kestrel, once the world's rarest bird; the Pink Pigeon, still the world's rarest pigeon; and the Echo Parakeet, the world's rarest parrot.

http://www.maurinet.com/wildlife.html

A B C D E F G H I J K L M N O P Q R S T U V W X Y Z

A
B
C
D
E
F
G
H
I
J
K
L
M
N
O
P
Q
R
S
T
U
V
W
X
Y
Z

Society of Caribbean Ornithology

The Society of Caribbean Ornithology, based in the Dominican Republic, is devoted to the scientific study of birds of the Caribbean islands. If you're interested in the birds of this region, the site provides e-mail links, as well as some news of the conservation efforts of the SCO.

http://www.nmnh.si.edu/BIRDNET/SCO/

WorldTwitch

WorldTwitch is a no-frills, information-packed site where you find late-breaking information about noteworthy bird observations around the world. When possible the site provides directions to the places where rare birds have been observed. The site often has bird lists, maps, and illustrations to go with sightings. Here, you can find feature articles about rare species and accounts of birding expeditions to exotic locales like the Amazon, Southeast Asia, or Central America. One specialty is the Thailand Bird Reports from Phil Round, who lives in Thailand and sends information regularly. "As a consequence, there is more information about recent bird observations in Thailand on the Web than about sightings in any other tropical country," Webmaster John W. Wall tells us. You can also pick up news of the discovery of new species. The site also has a fine collection of links to sites outside North America.

http://www.geocities.com/RainForest/Vines/9684/

Gyrfalcon (*Falco rusticolus*) (JJA)

FEATHERED FACTS

Disease Jumps Species

The winter of 1993–94 was a harsh one on the East Coast. Songbirds of all sorts had difficulty finding food. Scientists speculate that House Finches, somewhere in Maryland or Virginia, began eating food put out for poultry. Those chickens were infected with a common poultry disease, *Mycoplasma gallisepticum*—or simply MG. This form of conjunctivitis was picked up by the finches and, transferred by contact with other birds, often at feeders, the disease spread throughout the East and by late 1997 had infected countless finches in more than 30 states. Many died as a result.

—adapted from James Cook, House Finch Conjunctivitis

http://members.aol.com/FinchMG/IntroBac.htm

MAGAZINES & PERIODICALS

The Internet provides access to many thousands of newspapers, magazines, and newsletters on an almost limitless variety of subjects—including birds. In some cases, a good deal of content is online, whereas in most cases, enough to tempt you into subscribing to the print version of the publication is there, along with instructions on how to subscribe. And that's handy, for the Web enables you to sample many specialized periodicals that you might not otherwise run across, even at huge magazine stores. However, there are also e-zines—periodicals that appear only electronically on the Web or via e-mail. This section is devoted mostly to print periodicals with an online presence. *(See also Audubon Societies & Sanctuaries, Books, Conservation, and Organizations & Associations.)*

Audubon Magazine

Audubon is probably the premier natural history periodical in North America. It is also the oldest popular magazine of its kind, having been established in 1898. Although not strictly a "birding magazine," much of its content deals with birds or their environments, and the preservation and enjoyment of both. Each issue has features, columns, profiles, book reviews, and news—all usually accompanied by magnificent photography. Advertising is the kind that would appeal to birders, especially those interested in travel. *Audubon* is published six times a year by the National Audubon Society and comes with membership (reasonably priced). The organization's website carries sample features and columns from the magazine.

http://magazine.audubon.org

Backyard Bird News

Backyard Bird News, published by *Bird Watcher's Digest*, is a 12-page, bimonthly publication that "delivers a vast amount of information about backyard birds. If you love watching and feeding the birds in your backyard, you need to read *Backyard Bird News*," says the newsletter's website, which adds that the publication can help you attract more birds to your yard. "It delivers more information in 12 pages than most publications provide in 100 pages." You can sample some of the newsletter's features online, such as species profiles.

http://www.birdwatchersdigest.com/bbn/
  bbn_index.html

Bird Watcher's Digest

Bird Watcher's Digest is an excellent magazine for the casual amateur, as well as the serious bird-watcher. The family-owned bimonthly contains features on birds, bird-watching, and equipment, as well as book reviews, questions and answers, interviews with birding and ornithology experts, and, of course, advertising for all sorts of birding-related products and services. *BWD* is a top-notch, all-around magazine, the kind people save for reference (its "digest"

size makes that easy, too). Its website (*first address*) has features from past issues, as well as Backyard Birdwatcher's columns by Dr. David M. Bird (his real name!) and Bird Watchers Question Box, with answers to reader questions. You'll also find a large collection of answers to frequently asked questions—there's information here not readily available elsewhere. Bill Thompson III, the magazine's editor, says that a big advantage for visitors is that "our site offers one-stop shopping for address changes, letters to the editor, subscriptions, renewals, questions for us or for our columnists, and info on our other publications (*Backyard Bird News* and *The Skimmer*), and products (booklets, prints, gear, etc.)." *BWD* also has a presence on Peterson Online (*second address*). Here you'll find some features and profiles that may not be on the magazine's main site. However, Thompson reports that many of these articles will eventually be on the *BWD* site, where a new "greatest hits" section will feature such topics as the top 20 birding controversies and cats versus birds.

http://birdwatchersdigest.com
http://www.petersononline.com/birds/bwd/

FEATHERED FACTS

Grim Reaper

The Eastern Meadowlark shared the wide open spaces with the bison and survives today in the cow and cattle pastures, as well as in the fields of grain that have replaced the bison territory. It's a ground-nesting bird, which is a tough way to raise a family since so many predators scour the ground. However, it is not nature but machine that is the meadowlark's biggest threat: the blades of the mower or reaper destroy many nests.

—adapted from Birdwatching.com

http://www.birdwatching.com/stories/
  storymeadowlark.html

A
B
C
D
E
F
G
H
I
J
K
L
M
N
O
P
Q
R
S
T
U
V
W
X
Y
Z

A
B
C
D
E
F
G
H
I
J
K
L
M
N
O
P
Q
R
S
T
U
V
W
X
Y
Z

Birder's World

Birder's World is a bimonthly produced by Kalmbach, a leading publisher of hobbyist magazines. *Birder's World* carries some of the best avian photography in the world; in wandering the magazine's website, you can see some samples of published pictures, although not nearly as spectacular or as numerous as those found in the print magazine. The website offers an informative collection of feature articles covering many topics you may not find elsewhere, such as how birds migrate, groom their feathers, and hold onto branches. The site also has an excellent calendar of birding events, broken down by state; a collection of links to other birding sites; information about birding tours; and, of course, information about subscribing to or contacting *Birder's World*. Recently expanded, the site also has a useful Ask Birder's World Q&A column, online classified ads, and a Birding Hotspots section.

http://www.birdersworld.com

Birding

Birding, the bimonthly magazine of the American Birding Association, carries major field-identification articles (and photo quizzes), book, media, and equipment reviews, and guides for top birding locations, not just in North America but throughout the world. This magazine is for intermediate and advanced field birders. Several features (Gleanings from the Technical Literature, A Birding Perspective, and Letters to the Editor) provide an on-going, active forum in print for bird identification, taxonomy, and birdfinding ethics. The accuracy of its numerous maps and color photographs of birds is commendable. The website has indexes of what has appeared in each issue for the previous year or so, and has a few samples of feature articles from the magazine.

http://www.americanbirding.org/bdggen.htm

Birdwatch

British birders or Anglophiles anywhere can learn more about birds and birdwatching in the United Kingdom via *Birdwatch* magazine, whose website offers a taste of each issue of the monthly print publication. But perhaps more useful to the wider, online community is its buyers guide to binoculars and scopes. Since most of what's sold in England is also sold in North America, the guide is helpful on both sides of the pond. It offers tables of specifications on many models, allowing you to compare their features without paging through verbiage. Avid birders will also enjoy the sightings described in the Rarities Report. Also entertaining are the online Guest Sightings, which, when we stopped by, included a report of a catbird harassing a cat in Atlanta, Georgia. However, most reports are from places like the Cotswolds and East Anglia of such un-American species as Yellow Wagtails and Rough-legged Buzzards.

http://www.birdwatch.co.uk

Chip Notes

Chip Notes is the feature-filled newsletter of the Baltimore Bird Club, one of the more active birding groups in the country. The newsletter has articles and reports with useful information for nonmembers, including ideas for good places to go birding. Back issues to April 1996 are online. The newsletter's listing appears a short way down the club's home page, under the heading Baltimore Bird Club Information.

http://www.bcpl.net/~tross/baltbird.html

FEATHERED FACTS

Too Trusting

One reason you'll rarely find a Spruce Grouse around civilization is that they are too trusting. They have so little fear of humans that it's said that hunters don't need to waste a shot on them—they can just walk up to the birds and hit them on the head with a stick.

—adapted from Birdwatching.com

http://www.birdwatching.com/stories/sprucegrouse.html

FEATHERED FACTS

Carnivorous Chickadees

Did you know that the Black-capped Chickadee is a more-than-occasional carnivore? Studies indicate that 70 percent of a chickadee's diet comes from nonvegetable sources, such as insects and spiders, and they have been observed feeding on the fat of dead deer or skunk and on fish. Thus, suet makes a good chickadee food.

—adapted from Mullen's Home Page of Western Maryland, Wildlife, Parks & Forests

http://www.fred.net/mullen/chicad.html

Condor

The *Condor* is "an international journal of avian biology." Although not the stuff of the average backyard bird-watcher, the *Condor* would be of interest to amateur ornithologists and serious birders. The quarterly publishes articles about research in the biology of wild birds and comes with membership in the Cooper Ornithological Society (*see also Organizations & Associations*).

http://www.cooper.org/Pubs.html

Dick E. Bird News

"*The Dick E. Bird News* is the world's greatest newspaper ever," says its modest editor, one Mr. Bird. "It includes everything you ever wanted to know about birdfeeding, squirrelly neighbors, senior citizens, humor, poetry, puns, and the environment, but were afraid to ask." This offbeat monthly tabloid is for birders with a sense of humor and who love to read. Each issue is crammed with articles, notes, jokes, puzzles, and more—all more or less related to birds or their arch-competitor, Hairy Houdini, the squirrel. The web-site gives a good sampling of the kind of material you'll find in the Dick E. Bird News. You can also subscribe to a free mailing list of Mr. Bird's notes. And don't miss the Squirrelly Neighbors—Breed 'Em & Feed 'Em page, which warns: "Your parents must be at least 21 and have 12 birdfeeders to view this site. It contains squirrelly material like you have never seen before."

http://www.traverse.com/media/dbnews/home.html

Field Notes & North American Birds

North American Birds (formerly *Field Notes*), a quarterly publication of the American Birding Association and the National Audubon Society, offers reports from "North America's largest, widest and best-established networks of field birders." According to the site, "you'll find a comprehensive summary of an entire season in each issue, and so discover whether migration was early or late, and for which species the nesting season was successful. Which irruptive species invaded, and where? Which species expanded their ranges and which were in decline?" *North American Birds* can help traveling birders determine where the rarest birds are being seen so they can plan their next birding expedition. Though the online edition contains only indexes, some photos, and each issue's editorial, the site will tempt the serious birder into subscribing.

http://www.americanbirding.org/fldngen.htm

Journal of Field Ornithology

If you get really serious about birds and birding, you may want to investigate joining the Association of Field Ornithologists and reading its *Journal of Field Ornithology*. This quarterly contains articles describing techniques, conservation, life histories, and assessments of published studies or issues. Online, you can read the *abstracts*—summary versions—of scores of articles with titles like "Chick Behavior, Habitat Use, and Reproductive Success of Piping Plovers at Goosewing Beach, Rhode Island" or "Observations of Hummingbirds Ingesting Mineral-Rich Compounds"—it's the stuff of serious birders. The abstracts are fully searchable, a handy tool.

http://www.afonet.org/journal.html

A B C D E F G H I J K L **M** N O P Q R S T U V W X Y Z

FEATHERED FACTS

200 Birds in a Day

How many different kinds of birds can be seen in one day? That's one of the aims of the American Birding Association's Big Day competition. And good birders can see a lot. In the 1997 competition, the winner was a team of two men in New Mexico, who traveled 593 miles by car and two miles by foot to spot a total of 200 different species in 23½ hours. Obviously, they knew just where to go and when to go there.

—adapted from American Birding Association

http://www.americanbirding.org/ababdyrep.htm

Living Bird

Living Bird, the quarterly magazine you get when you join the Cornell Lab of Ornithology (*see also Ornithology*), contains stunning color photographs of birds, articles by top experts in birding and ornithology, reviews of the latest books, binoculars and other equipment, and advice on how to improve your birding skills. The lab puts a sampling of each issue online, including at least one feature article and some of the columns, such as Greetings from Sapsucker Woods. The site provides information about joining the lab and receiving the print magazine.

http://birds.cornell.edu/Publications/livingbird/

Online Birding Newsletter

Duncraft, a birdfeeder manufacturer, will send you a free, monthly newsletter called Wing tips via e-mail, carrying backyard birding tips, news, questions and answers, and seasonal advice. For instance, a September newsletter suggested: "Fall clean-up is around the corner. Remember that trimmings from your trees and shrubs can be made into an excellent brush pile (in a far corner of your yard or property) for wintering ground birds. Juncos, sparrows and many others seek protective brush for roosting shelter as fall and winter storms approach." To sign up, visit the Duncraft website and look for the menu link, Free Newsletter.

http://www.duncraft.com

Ornithological Literature

Where can you find an index of articles about topics such as "Food Habits of Bald Eagles Breeding in the Arizona Desert," "Sanderlings Exploit Beached Animal Carcasses As a Source of Fly Larvae," or "Diets of Northern Pygmy-Owls and Northern Saw-whet Owls in West-Central Montana"? At the Recent Ornithological Literature Online website, of course. This site, sponsored by BirdNet and the Ornithological Council, has a huge library of citations and abstracts from the worldwide scientific community relating to birds and the science of ornithology. You can read the compilations online, or you can download them in several word processing formats. Remember that these are indexes, not the actual articles; you must go to a good, old-fashioned library for those.

http://www.nmnh.si.edu/BIRDNET/ROL/

Refuge Reporter

The *Refuge Reporter* is an independent quarterly journal with a mission to increase the recognition and support of the National Wildlife Refuge System. "Each issue provides visitor information, in-depth commentaries by refuge officials and observers, exciting stories of successful programs, as well as critical issues affecting the system's welfare, and more," reports editor Jim Clark. Birders will enjoy the website's library of well-written feature articles on an expanding list of the best refuges in the United States, almost all of them great places to go birding. The site also explains how the National Wildlife Refuge System got its start and has a wonderful photo gallery, featuring many shots of birds.

http://www.gorp.com/refrep/

FEATHERED FACTS

Three-Route Bird

Purple Martins, the earliest of the swallows to return to their North American breeding grounds each year, use a number of different routes from their wintering grounds in South America. This includes three different paths that cross the Gulf of Mexico. Some Purple Martins arrive via Florida as early as late January. Another group comes into Louisiana and a third, Texas. Western Purple Martins tend to stay over land through Central America and Mexico.

—adapted from Robert Rice, Smithsonian Migratory Bird Center

http://web2.si.edu/smbc/bom/puma.htm

Skimmer

The *Skimmer* contains "serious bird news for the serious birder," reports this page on the website of *Bird Watcher's Digest*, which publishes the bimonthly newsletter. Eirik A. T. Blom, one of North America's leading authors on birds, writes the *Skimmer*. According to the site, he "possesses an encyclopedic knowledge of the subject. He reads all of the scientific and popular ornithological literature, combs many bird club newsletters, and talks to all of the insiders (and outsiders!) in the field. Blom's passion for learning is the source of this witty, irreverent, informed newsletter." Sample it online.

http://www.birdwatchersdigest.com/skimmer/ skimmer.html

WildBird

WildBird is a glossy, monthly magazine that carries the work of some of the leading writers and photogra-

phers in birding. The website offers brief samples of articles from current issues, as well as a table of contents, and has subscription information.

http://www.animalnetwork.com/wildbird/

Winging It!

Winging It! is a monthly newsletter that comes with membership in the American Birding Association. The website offers a sampling of the features from publication and also has an interesting feature: concise summaries of Rare Bird Alerts from around the country, providing an idea of what hot species have been sighted recently.

http://www.americanbirding.org/wggen.htm

Indigo Bunting (*Passerina cyanea*) (JJA)

A B C D E F G H I J K L **M** N O P Q R S T U V W X Y Z

A
B
C
D
E
F
G
H
I
J
K
L
M
N
O
P
Q
R
S
T
U
V
W
X
Y
Z

MIGRATION

Migration is one of the most fascinating aspects of birds and one that brings us a tremendous variety of species, even if only temporarily. Birds migrate primarily to take advantage of food availability and good breeding grounds. In our part of the world, they generally head north as the weather gets warmer and supplies of insects or nectar appear and increase. Migration provides nesting places, often in areas where there are less competition and crowding, or fewer predators, such as the Canadian and Alaskan Arctic. Some birds move from one part of North America to another in the spring. Others come from Central America and the Caribbean, whereas still others fly in from South America—from as far as the southern reaches of Argentina. Although most may not nest in the area in which we live, many can be spotted as they stop to rest, eat, and gather strength to continue northward in spring or southward in fall. The progress of some species, such as hummingbirds, has so fascinated birders that whole websites are devoted to it. Many migrants face problems, and quite a few are threatened. The current reduction of habitat through loss or fractionalization of rainforests in Central and South America is destroying winter homes. For some species, that's also happening in their northern nesting grounds. Even places that they traditionally stop at along the way are important; loss of these can mean that the birds won't have food to continue their journey. Environmental changes throughout their range can affect many dozens of migrating birds, and that's why many websites devote pages of information about the importance of habitat. (*See also Events and Quandaries.*)

White Pelican (Dover)

FEATHERED FACTS

Almost Gone

Habitat disturbance, over-hunting, and draining of wetlands almost killed off all of North America's Whooping Cranes by 1941, when only 21 were known to exist. Thanks to efforts to bring them back, more than 300 can be found today, but the species is still considered endangered in the United States and Canada.

—adapted from Canadian Museum of Nature

http://www.nature.ca/notebooks/english/whocrane.htm

Bird Migration Tables

The Nutty Birdwatcher (*first address*) offers a great site on migration that includes a "spring and fall migration table" for states east of the Mississippi. It gives approximate spring arrival and fall departure dates of many migratory species and does it by counties or regions of the state. It includes birds of northern states that leave in the spring to go farther north and return in the fall—folks in New England, New York, Michigan, and Wisconsin may not think of their regions as a winter migratory destination, but for many cold-tolerating species, they are. The data appear to be based on thousands of reports, and the Webmaster welcomes your own sightings to add to the database. If you live along the Gulf Coast, particularly in the Houston area, you should stop by David Sarkozi's Spring Migration Windows on the Upper Texas Coast page (*second address*), which is based on the eighth edition of *A Birder's Checklist of the Upper Texas Coast* by the Houston Outdoor Nature Club Ornithology Group. Using graphical devices to indicate the expected numbers in March, April, May, and June, the table covers the arrivals of several dozen important migrants.

http://nuthatch.birdnature.com/migration.html
http://texasbirding.simplenet.com/migration/spring.htm

Birding Spectacles

No, they're not special glasses for watching the birds. Instead, *birding spectacles* are special natural events usually associated with migration. "A birding spectacle can be defined as a concentration of birds large enough to capture the imagination of even non-birders," says Peterson Online. "They are gatherings of birds in one location at one time so spectacular that anyone would be struck by the majesty of the natural world." This neat calendar describes major spectacles in North America, arranged by season and then by locations. The well-done descriptions are fun to read and may inspire you to journey to "spectacle spots" around the continent. For instance, you may want to head for Grays Harbor, Washington, in late April to see as many as a half million Western Sandpipers massing, and partake in the Grays Harbor Shorebird Festival. Or you might wish to journey to Chase Lake National Wildlife Refuge, North Dakota, where in June you can see up to 12,000 nesting White Pelicans. Or perhaps you'll head for the southeastern New England coast, where hundreds of thousands of tree swallows visit the bayberry bushes in early autumn—as many as 300,000 have been seen in one area in late September.

http://www.petersononline.com/birds/calendar/
  spectacles.html

FEATHERED FACTS

Underground Operator

The Burrowing Owl of the western North American plains is among the few birds on this continent that likes to live underground. It uses holes dug by mammals.

—adapted from Canadian Museum of Nature

http://www.nature.ca/notebooks/english/burrowl.htm

California Quail (Dover)

Birds on Radar

On his Birds of the North Texas Coast website, David Sarkozi offers some radar animations of activity around Houston. Most show flocks of birds migrating or just moving around. Working with an expert from NOAA (National Oceanic & Atmospheric Administration), he analyzes the images, finding that, in at least one case, the image was not of the birds he was looking for.

http://texasbirding.simplenet.com/nexrad/

Fall Bird Banding

One of the techniques that ornithologists use to track bird movements, especially migrations, is banding. Birds are captured and labeled with small, harmless bands, which are attached to a leg. Depending on the locale, banding is often done in the spring and fall to mark passing-through migrants or in the summer to catch nesting birds. Professor Gerry Rising notes in this nature column that first appeared in the *Buffalo (New York) News* that banders can have special problems in the fall (*first address*). Rising heads out with veteran bander Jerry Farrell on a fall banding expedition. In another column (*second address*) he visits the banding station at the Braddock Bay Bird Observatory outside Rochester, New York, one of the premier banding sites in North America, and describes what he sees.

http://www.acsu.buffalo.edu/~insrisg/nature/nw98/
  farrell.html

http://www.acsu.buffalo.edu/~insrisg/nature/nw97/
  band.html

A
B
C
D
E
F
G
H
I
J
K
L
M
N
O
P
Q
R
S
T
U
V
W
X
Y
Z

A
B
C
D
E
F
G
H
I
J
K
L
M
N
O
P
Q
R
S
T
U
V
W
X
Y
Z

First Migration

"When young songbirds are ready for their first migration, they would seem to have a problem," writes Eldon Greij. "Their parents have already migrated, and they're on their own. How will they know where to go?" This is one of the great marvels and mysteries of migration, and Greij, a veteran ornithological writer for *Birder's World*, tells about some of the latest thinking on how birds know when and where to travel to their wintering grounds (*first address*). The recent discoveries indicate that birds are amazing navigators, whether they are using stars or subtle magnetic fields. Greij focuses on star navigation in a second article for the magazine (*second address*).

http://www2.birdersworld.com/birders/amazingbirds/
1998/9808_migration.html

http://www2.birdersworld.com/birders/amazingbirds/
1998/9804_star.html

How & Why They Do It

Why do many birds, living in the seeming lap of tropical luxury, bother to migrate thousands of miles north each spring to raise a family? Food. Heading north provides them with plenty of insects, fresh fruits and nectar, probably with less competition than in their winter grounds. But there are other, more subtle advantages, notes Don Richardson in his excellent About.com essay on the whys and hows of migration. "Northern summers have very long days that provide many hours for gathering food," Richardson writes. "Tropical days are only 12 hours long. Days in the north may reach 16 hours or more. It takes a great effort and a lot of time to gather enough food to feed three or four youngsters that will increase to 50 times their hatching weight in just 13 days." Richardson's Birds and Migration, Why and How Do They Do It covers the historic beliefs about migration, its advantages, and the stimuli, times, and patterns for migration. You may think that all birds migrate in straight lines—"as the crow flies," says Richardson—but the fact is some do loops, others dog-legs, leap-frogs, and vertical trips (up and down mountains), whereas others are just plain vagrants. There are even "explosions." The page includes links to other sites dealing with migration.

http://birding.about.com/library/weekly/aa011599.htm

Hummingbird Migration Map

One of the questions we ask ourselves each year is when should we put out the hummingbird feeder. The answer is at this website. Each spring hummingbird fans await the arrival of these amazing birds that weigh a fraction of an ounce and yet can fly more than 1,000 to 2,000 miles from Central America to their breeding spots as far north as southern Canada. You can track them as they move north, and birders report them to this site. Add your own reports, too. Until the new spring is under way, the previous spring's map is posted online to give you an idea of when to expect your hummers to arrive. Although all species of North American hummingbirds are covered, the most commonly reported is the Ruby-throated, which is the East's only regular species.

http://www.birdwatchers.com/hmap.html

Journey North

One of the beauties of the Internet is its ability to enable us to communicate quickly, conveniently, and effectively. This is particularly useful in collaborative observations. Whole families—as well as whole classrooms and schools—can participate in efforts to track the migration of the various birds and the monarch butterfly via Journey North. This website, devoted to tracking the signs of spring's return to North America, is a great place to find information about migratory birds' progress north. It's also a great place for the winter-weary to find hope! Members of the public are encouraged to submit observations. Journey North is an educational effort financed by a grant from the Annenberg/CPB Math & Science Project, and more than 4,000 schools involving 200,000 students participated in the spring of 1999. Students keep records on what they see and when, and exchange it with other students across the continent. Among the species covered are Bald Eagles, hummingbirds, orioles, and robins (not to mention earthworms and frogs, which, although not migrants, are signs of spring). The site lets you search for information about past years' migrations. In the fall, information about the Journey South is sought. The site includes a teacher's guide—which, of course, can also be a parents' guide—with information about how to record information properly.

http://www.learner.org/jnorth/

Saw-whet Owl (*Cryptoglaux acadia*)
[*Aegolius acadicus*] (JJA)

Migratory Max

Migratory Max is a Golden Plover, a bird that lives in the Arctic in the summer and in the pampas of southern South America in the winter. To do this, Max and his fellow golden plovers, who weigh only about a half pound, must fly more than 20,000 miles a year, reaching speeds of up to 100 mph. And, interestingly enough, the northern journey is not over the same route as the southern one. What's more, in one portion of their journey, plovers must traverse the Atlantic from eastern Canada to northern South America—some 3,000 miles nonstop. To learn about Max's Grand Adventure, stop by the Wilderness Society's marvelous Earth Day site. You can also learn about other migratory Arctic birds, such as the Tundra Swan, and find links to related sites.

http://www.wilderness.org/migmax/index.htm

Project Flight Plan

More than 250 species of waterfowl, raptors, and songbirds migrate from Mexico and Central and South America to breed in the United States and Canada. But life is perilous, particularly for migratory songbirds, and it has been estimated that 60 percent of those that hatch each year never make it to their first birthday. Aside from natural hazards such as storms, starvation, and disease, migrant birds of all kinds increasingly face human hazards. "Collision with cars and buildings, pesticide poisoning, cat predation, shooting, and loss of

key resting and feeding habitats are among the threats birds may encounter," says Audubon International, which has begun Project Flight Plan in an effort to lend a hand. This site tells how corporations, organizations, and individuals can help migratory birds.

http://www.audubonintl.org/flightplan/index.htm

Shorebird Migration Pages

The Shorebird Migration Pages at the University of Tennessee at Martin provide valuable information about sandpiper and plover migrations and ranges in the lower 48 states. Maps for more than four dozen migrating species show states in which they maintain winter homes, summer nesting areas, or live year-round. For the birds that just pass through, maps are color-coded to indicate whether there have been recent or "not-so-recent" reports of the species. The authors says their pages contain "semi-current" information, but when we stopped by, it looked quite up-to-date. The data are especially interesting to anyone wanting to know where shorebird species can be found and whether sightings in their region might be unusual. The site, maintained by Paul Hertzel of the university's Department of Mathematics, also carries links to other shorebird sites so you can find more information about the subject and species.

http://www.utm.edu/~phertzel/migration.htm

FEATHERED FACTS

Tree Duck

The Black-bellied Whistling Duck was once called the Black-bellied Tree Duck because it often nests in tree cavities.

http://www.wildtexas.com/wildguides/whistlingduck.htm

A
B
C
D
E
F
G
H
I
J
K
L
M
N
O
P
Q
R
S
T
U
V
W
X
Y
Z

Smithsonian Migratory Bird Center

The Smithsonian Migratory Bird Center (*first address*) is a magnificent site devoted to telling us about the many song- and seabirds that head north each spring and south each fall. For starters, lists are given of birds that winter in Central and South America that breed in North America—click on any of the countries shown on the maps and up pops a list of species that winter there. The Bird of the Month section (*second address*) offers natural histories of several dozen migrant species, including photos; you will find that these are some of the most interesting, best written, and authoritative essays on individual species that you'll find on the Web. Fact Sheets cover such subjects as Why Migratory Birds Are Crazy for Coffee and Have Wings, Will Travel: Avian Adaptations for Migration. These features and profiles are written by experts in the field in language that's clear and lively—not dull and "scientific." The site also offers a collection of publications about migratory birds, tells all about how buying shade-grown coffee helps migratory birds, and offers rather scientific abstracts of a conference on the conservation of neotropical birds.

http://web2.si.edu/smbc/
http://web2.si.edu/smbc/bom.htm

What's Up with Migratory Birds

In the United States, a total of 836 species of birds are officially recognized as migratory by the U.S. Fish & Wildlife Service, which, because they travel across many states, is responsible for their general "management." In contrast, resident species that don't migrate, such as wild turkeys, quail, and pheasant, are managed by state agencies. Of the 836 migrants, 59 species are considered game birds, including ducks, geese, swan, various species of doves, woodcock, snipe, rails, certain pigeons, and gallinules. The 777 of the remaining migrants that are nongame birds (93 percent of the total) include marsh and wading birds (6 percent), birds of prey such as hawks, owls, and eagles (9 percent), shorebirds (10 percent), seabirds (16 percent), and perching birds (59 percent). This last group, notes Richard Coon on this Fish & Wildlife Service page, makes up the "song birds that come to our feeders, and the neotropical migratory

birds that usually do not (because they are insect eaters and not seed eaters)."

http://www.fws.gov/r4eao/wildlife/migbrd.html

Winter Finches Irrupt!

In certain winters, bird-watchers in southern Canada and the United States enjoy superflights of winter birds, mostly finches, that are normally eating seeds well to the north. For instance, Red-breasted Nuthatch, Red Crossbill, White-winged Crossbill, Pine Grosbeak, Common Redpoll, and Hoary Redpoll crossed the border in large numbers in the winter of 1997–98, delighting backyard birders whose feeders were invaded for periods of days or weeks by the usually uncommon or rare species. The BirdSource North American Winter Finch Survey, sponsored by Cornell's Laboratory of Ornithology, keeps track of these irruptions and invites participation from anyone who observes these northern guests. There are pages devoted to each species with photographs, sounds, and maps showing each bird's recent incidences.

http://birds.cornell.edu/winfin/WFsuperflight.htm

FEATHERED FACTS

The Sex of Crows

Although it's easy to tell the sex of many bird species by their plumage coloration or size, male and female crows look so much alike that DNA testing of blood is often needed to tell them apart. Only close study of their daily life, especially during nesting season, can provides clues as to sex, and few people can get close to nesting crows.

—adapted from For the Love of Crows

http://www.zeebyrd.com/corvi29/

NORTH AMERICAN BIRDS

BACKYARD

"Backyard birds" isn't any kind of scientific category of birds. For the purposes of this book, the term pretty much encompasses what are called the *perching* and the *clinging birds*—mostly songbirds or "passerines." To see some of them, your backyard would have to have quite a varied habitat: wooded, open, wet, dry, remote, and mountainous. But for the most part, these species are possible in suburban and rural—and often even urban—neighborhoods, depending on the part of the continent you live in. The perchers include the flycatchers, swallows, wrens, thrushes, warblers, crows, jays, and finches. The clingers are mostly the woodpeckers. But we have also included humming-birds, swifts, doves, and the kingfisher in the back-yard category. This is a huge and very visible collection of bird groups, and we won't pretend to try to direct you to websites or pages for every species. Instead, we offer sites on many of the most popular, interesting, and sometimes endangered species among the "backyard birds." However, you will also find

FEATHERED FACTS

Robins in Winter

Although the first robin in the yard is one of the most famous harbingers of spring, many people in northern states and southern Canada are surprised to learn that many American Robins spend all winter in their commu-nities. They are facultative migrants, meaning they move only as far as they need to when winter comes. And in many places—despite snow and cold—they remain all winter, eating berries instead of the worms and insects they consume in summer.

—adapted from Bird Watcher's Digest

http://www.birdwatchersdigest.com/faq/faq.html

directories and databases that should quickly lead you to the bird you're looking for; the biggest is the Patux-ent Wildlife Research Center in Maryland, whose index of bird identification guides is found at *<http://www.mbr-pwrc.usgs.gov/id/framlst/framlst.html>*. It's a page that every birder should bookmark. *(See also Feeding & Watering, Gardening & Landscaping, Organi-zations & Associations, and Songs & Sounds.)*

Backyard Wildlife Questions & Answers

The Windstar Wildlife Institute in Jefferson, Maryland, has a message forum which enables you to ask ques-tions about backyard wildlife. Most of the chatter seems to be about birds.

http://www.windstar.org/wildlife/hps.htm

Blackbird, Red-winged

Undoubtedly the most popular and probably the most common blackbird is the Red-winged Blackbird (*Age-laius phoeniceus*), which is often noted in the North as one of the sure signs that spring is arriving. Red-wings usually move into their breeding range in early spring or late winter and are among the easier black-birds to identify, both by their song and by the distinc-tive bright red patch on the male's wings. A yellow border trims the red, though it may be missing in some races. The females are brown and white with some yellow tinge to the face and throat, but certain races are very much darker. Patuxent (*first address*) provides details for identification of these birds, and the Birds of North America site (*second address*) has detailed descriptions of the behavior of the red-wings. Some fine photos of the bird, both male and female, plus a sound clip of its song, are available on the Back-yard Birding website (*third address*).

http://www.mbr.nbs.gov/id/mlist/h4980.html
http://www.birdsofna.org/excerpts/rwblbird.html
http://www.slivoski.com/birding/blkbird.htm

A B C D E F G H I J K L M **N** O P Q R S T U V W X Y Z

A
B
C
D
E
F
G
H
I
J
K
L
M
N
O
P
Q
R
S
T
U
V
W
X
Y
Z

Blackbirds

Blackbirds tend to travel with their relatives: It's always fun to see a flock of them and then try to figure out who's directly related to whom. Peter Burke and Alvaro Jaramillo are the authors of *New World Black-birds: The Icterids* and at their website have detailed discussions of the various species and their identifications. No one should ever be confused again by the Rusty Blackbird (*Euphagus carolinus*) and Brewer's Blackbird (*Euphagus cyanocephalus*) after reading the treatment of the two birds' similarities and differences in all seasons.

http://www.sirius.com/~alvaro/bbirds_identification. html

Bluebird Box

The Bluebird Box is a huge collection of links and pages of excellent information about all aspects of bluebirds, put together by Jim McLochlin, with help from Bluebird Recovery Project, and Bluebirds Across Nebraska. Jim's FAQ page is a concise, yet complete guide to the basics of bluebirds and bluebird boxes. You can find at least four different designs for blue-bird boxes on the site, as well as information about how to keep proper track of your bluebird sightings. The site has many articles about the natural history of bluebirds. Bluebird "enemies" are described and there are plenty of photos and even sounds.

http://hometown.aol.com/jimmcl/bbbox/

Bluebird Mailing List

If you're a serious bluebird fan, you might want to join an e-mail network for persons interested in blue-birds and other North American cavity nesters. You can compare your bluebird experiences with others, exchange suggestions, and ask questions. To sub-scribe, send a message to *listproc@cornell.edu* with the text (leave the subject line blank) SUBSCRIBE BLUE-BIRD-L YOUR NAME (substitute with your name).

Bluebird, Mountain

Henry David Thoreau said the bluebirds "carry the sky on their back." One of the best loved birds on the continent—they rank high in the popularity survey for the Great Backyard Bird Count—bluebirds have long symbolized peace and hope. Since they'll readily accept nesting boxes built by humans, they've become the focus of one of the most widespread and success-ful conservation efforts in North America. The Ellis Bird Farm in Lacombe, Alberta, is one of the more unusual places in North America. For decades, it has been a refuge for Mountain Bluebirds (*Sialia corru-coidis*), thanks to the Ellis family, which set up hun-dreds of bluebird boxes and established a program of bluebird preservation and research. Today, the farm is still doing all that and more under the ownership of Union Carbide Corporation. The Ellis Bird Farm site explains this unusual cooperation between industry and naturalists—and tells you a great deal about Mountain Bluebirds. The farm is open to the public during the summer. *(See also Destinations.)*

http://www.wep.ab.ca/ellisbirdfarm/

Eastern Bluebird (*Sialia sialis*) (JJA)

Bluebirds

Few birds have endeared themselves to humans as the bluebirds. I once edited a diary of a mid-19th-century farmer who, each February, would note the date of arrival of the first bluebird. Over two years, he never mentioned any other kind of wildlife. Bluebirds are great insect-eaters and, as such, help keep pests under control. They're also beautiful birds. But bluebirds have been declining in many areas as fields, their habitat, become subdivisions or revert to forest. Also, alien birds have been pushing them out of traditional nesting places. Widespread efforts to install bluebird boxes have helped bring back bluebirds. Wild Birds Forever, which is happily situated in Blue Jay, California, gives a good rundown on what bluebirds need to make them happy and keep them around (*first address*). Habitat, food preferences, types of feeders, and nesting requirements are all detailed. Range maps are provided for the similar Eastern Bluebird (*Sialia sialis*) and Western Bluebird (*Sialia mexicana*), as well as the bluer Mountain Bluebird (*Sialia corrucoidis*). The Nest Box (*second address*), a website in southern Maryland, has much information about bluebirds, including a comprehensive FAQ page (called the Question Box). The site also shares nesting data, banding information, and a lot of useful links. As might be expected, the North American Bluebird Society is another good place to learn about bluebirds (*third address*). So is the New York State Bluebird Society, which has a fairly elaborate site with a lot of information (*fourth address*).

http://www.birdsforever.com/bluebird.html
http://www.nestbox.com/bluebird.htm
http://www.nabluebirdsociety.org/
http://www.geocities.com/RainForest/2414/nysbs.htm

Bobolinks

Bobolinks (*Dolichonyx orzivorus*) are among our longest-migrating songbirds, spending the summers in the northern United States and southern Canada, and the winters in southern Brazil, Paraguay, and northern Argentina. Bobolinks are closely related to meadowlarks, and so it's not surprising that they are famous songsters. According to Mary Deinlein of the Smithsonian Migratory Bird Center in Washington, D.C. (*first address*), the Bobolink's song has been

described as "a bubbling delirium of ecstatic music that flows from the gifted throat of the bird like sparkling champagne," "a mad, reckless song-fantasia, and outbreak of pent-up, irrepressible glee," and "a tinkle of fairy music, like the strains of an old Greek harp." If that makes you want to hear one, Patuxent Wildlife Research Center's vast collection of birdsongs has an excellent recording as a .WAV file (*second address*). Meanwhile, make sure you read Deinlein's fascinating "biography" of this much persecuted and often-eaten songbird. For a tight profile of the Bobolink, check Peggy Jahn's report (*third address*) for the Delaware Audubon Society. She notes that the "early mowing of hay fields and the development of open meadows have caused a decline of the birds."

http://web2.si.edu/smbc/bom/bobo.htm
http://www.mbr.nbs.gov/id/htmwav2/h4940so.wav
http://pages.prodigy.com/delaud/bob.htm

Bobolink (*Dolichonyx oryzivorus*) (JJA)

Bunting, Indigo

For most people, the Indigo Bunting (*Passerina cyanea*) is just a spectacularly colorful bird. But for scientists, however, the Indigo Bunting has led to discoveries about avian navigation. "This stellar migrant has enabled us to advance our limited understanding of the mind-boggling capabilities of migratory birds, and allowed us enhance our view into the curious world of avian social life," says Mary Deinlein at the National Zoo in Washington, D.C., who wrote this fascinating piece about the brilliantly hued Indigo Bunting. She describes how a scientist in the 1960s used trickery to determine that these buntings—and other birds—use star patterns to fly at night on their migratory journeys north and south.

http://web2.si.edu/smbc/bom/inbu.htm

A
B
C
D
E
F
G
H
I
J
K
L
M
N
O
P
Q
R
S
T
U
V
W
X
Y
Z

Bunting, Snow

The Snow Bunting (*Plectrophenax nivalis*) heads south for the winter. But unlike many birds that migrate to warmer territories when the cold comes, "south" for the Snow Bunting means southern Canada or the northern United States—where there's usually snow all season. In summer, the Snow Bunting heads for the real north, far above the Arctic Circle, where it raises its family of up to seven fledglings, reports the Canadian Museum of Nature.

http://www.nature.ca/notebooks/english/snowbunt.htm

Buntings

Among the most colorful of birds, the buntings are a treat for the eyes, whether it's the Indigo (*Passerina cyanea*), the Lazuli (*Passerina amoena*), or the Painted Bunting (*Passerina ciris*) one chances to see. This site has links to photographs of these beautiful birds, as well as information about ranges and songs and connections to sites for bunting species around the world.

http://birding.about.com/msub1-buntings.htm

RealPlayer

Many bird-related websites carry songs and calls that you can listen to with a program called RealPlayer. This free program enables you to do much more than listen to birds—it has become an unofficial Web standard for receiving continuous (streaming) audio. With it, you can listen to live radio broadcasts from around the world. In fact, you can even listen to Jack Benny from 50 years ago. It's an invaluable addition to your browser, and easily downloaded and installed.

http://www.real.com

Cardinal, Northern

Everyone loves to have a pair of Northern Cardinals (*Cardinalis cardinalis*) as steady visitors to the backyard feeder. Not only is the male's brilliant red plumage eye-catching on the grayest day, but the *cheer-cheer-cheer* and *purty-purty-purty* calls of the cardinal are day-brighteners all on their own. Christine Tarski's site at About.com (*first address*) has some good information about the birds' habits (they mate for life; the father cardinal takes charge of the young birds once they can fly, while mother cardinal hatches a second brood), and links to cardinal pages. Chipper Woods Bird Observatory in Carmel, Indiana (*second address*), has handsome close-up photographs of both male and female, and a juvenile, as well as photos of flight feathers. John and Janet Slivoski's Backyard Birding website, designed to cover birds of Indiana, has a page on Northern Cardinals—the Indiana state bird—that includes not only an audio clip but a video that shows cardinals in various situations—at the feeder, in a tree, on snowy ground (*third address*). Also on the site are ordinary photos, plus a concise biography of the bird. You can download a "cardinal desktop theme" for use on Windows 95 or 98. Patuxent Wildlife Research Center (*fourth address*) has range maps and other information about the Northern Cardinal. (*See Quandaries, Bald Birds.*)

http://birding.about.com/library/weekly/aa121397.htm
http://www.wbu.com/chipperwoods/photos/ncard.htm
http://slivoski.com/birding/cardinl.htm
http://www.mbr-pwrc.usgs.gov/id/framlst/
i5930id.html

Cardinal (*Richmondena cardinalis*)
[Northern Cardinal, *Cardinalis cardinalis*] (JJA)

Catbird, Gray

Though its name fails to reflect it, the Gray Catbird (*Dumetella carolinensis*) is one of our finest backyard singers. Some—like me—think it ranks right up with its cousin, the mockingbird. One of the mimic thrushes, the catbird can roll off a huge collection of beautiful songs—and even imitations of sounds it hears, such as squeaky doors or telephones ringing. Bill Snyder describes the catbird (and many other creatures, winged and otherwise) on the Wildlife Neighbors page (*first address*). "Like all other thrushes, the gray catbird is very fond of bathing and rolls itself in the dust or sand of the roadsides or fields," notes the Nutty Birdwatcher, whose site (*second address*) provides a nice summary of catbird facts. "Several are frequently seen together on the borders of small ponds, splashing the water all over themselves and then going to the nearest bush or tree." On the Patuxent Wildlife Research Center's catbird page (*third address*), you can read about and see the bird, as well as hear some good samples—albeit brief—of its wonderful songs. There are distribution maps and plenty of facts about the bird. For more sounds of the catbird, visit Lang Elliott's NatureSound Studio (*fourth address*). Elliott has an excellent recording and photo, plus he passes along the famous observation of Oliver Wendell Holmes: "I hear the whispering voice of spring, the thrush's trill, the catbird's cry."

http://www.baylink.org/wpc/catbird.html

http://nuthatch.birdnature.com/catbird.html

http://www.mbr.nbs.gov/id/framlst/account/
  h7040id.html

http://www.naturesound.com/birds/pages/catbird.html

Chickadee, Black-capped

"The North wind is cold, as cold as can be, but I'm not afraid, said the chickadee. The chickadee stays to see the snow and loves to hear the North wind blow." So says a late-19th-century ditty. Among the friendliest of birds, Black-capped Chickadees (*Parus atricapillus*) are at home in the northern two-thirds of the United States and much of southern Canada. They're eager feeders at most stations and with a little encouragement will eat from a host's hand. The Chickadee Web (*first address*), created by the Paul family of (where else?) Chickadee Lane, Berks County, Pennsylvania,

has a wealth of chickadee lore, art, poems and stories, as well as links to scores of more sites for the chickadee-smitten. Notes the site's creator, chickadees "have the most complex social structures of any feeder bird and one of the largest vocabularies of calls, more than 15 different ones." Audio clips provide samples of some calls; others are scattered throughout the home page. There's a special section of Chickadee Stuff Just for Kids and information about the many other varieties of chickadees around the world. The Chickadee Web provides links to many other sites. For an animated map of the Black-capped Chickadee's range, visit this Patuxent page (*second address*), which has other information, as well. John and Janet Slivoski's Backyard Birding site offers a profile of the bird—and free chickadee-theme desktop art for Windows computers (*third address*). Cornell Laboratory of Ornithology has both a write-up and a sample of the famous song of the Black-capped Chicakdee (*fourth address*). Finally, read what John J. Audubon said about what he called the "Black-cap Titmouse, or Chickadee" (*fifth address*).

http://home.jtan.com/~jack/ckd.html

http://www.mbr-pwrc.usgs.gov/bbs/anim/h7350.html

http://www.slivoski.com/birding/themes/chickdee.html

http://www.tc.cornell.edu/Birds/black.capped.
  chickadee.html

http://www.50states.com/bird/chickade.htm

Black-capped Chickadee (*Penthestes atricapillus*)
[*Parus atricapillus*] (JJA)

A
B
C
D
E
F
G
H
I
J
K
L
M
N
O
P
Q
R
S
T
U
V
W
X
Y
Z

Chickadee, Boreal

As its name suggests, the Boreal Chickadee (*Parus hudsonicus*), a year-round resident of the far north, can be found across Canada and Alaska, but only in the very northern reaches of a few border states in the Lower 48. This page from the Birds of North America site (*first address*) gives great detail on the eating habits of the bird. There is also much information about the bird's many vocalizations. The Cornell Laboratory of Ornithology provides pictures, a range map, and a sound bite, along with identification information, on its page (*second address*).

http://www.birdsofna.org/excerpts/bchickadee.html

http://birdsource2.ornith.cornell.edu/pfw/birdid/borchi/index.html

Chickadee, Carolina

The Carolina Chickadee (*Parus carolinensis*), one of the seven chickadee species in North America, is found in the southeastern United States. This page, provided by the Chipper Woods Bird Observatory, has wonderful close-up photos plus natural history notes.

http://www.wbu.com/chipperwoods/photos/chickadee.htm

Chickadee, Chestnut-backed

We often hear about how the ranges of some species of birds are decreasing because of changing habitat. The beautiful Chestnut-backed Chickadee (*Parus rufescens*) is a different story. This species is expanding its range in the Pacific Northwest reports the Cornell Laboratory of Ornithology, which tells you a couple of reasons why this is happening. Cornell also provides drawings, a photo, a sound bite, and a range map on this page to help you identify the species.

http://birdsource2.ornith.cornell.edu/pfw/birdid/chbchi/index.html

Chickadee, Mountain

The Mountain Chickadee (*Parus gambeli*) is found in the mountains of western North America, from Alaska to Mexico. Although they typically live at high elevations, they sometimes irrupt into lower territory, reports the Cornell Laboratory of Ornithology. This is not directly due to harsh weather, but to food shortages that may be caused by other factors. This page illustrates the bird and provides identification information, a sound bite, and a range map.

http://birdsource2.ornith.cornell.edu/pfw/birdid/mouchi/index.html

Cowbird, Brown-headed

The Brown-headed Cowbird (*Molothrus ater*) is an irony. This handsome, native species once had a way of life that limited its territory. Today, however, humans have changed the face of North America, and as a result the very adaptable cowbird has changed the way it lives. Cowbirds are called cowbirds because they used to follow the cows—well, the herds of buffalo that once roamed most of the continent. They fed on the insects that the animals carried or that were flushed from the grass. Because they followed the herds, they didn't have time to build nests and raise young. So they learned to sneak their eggs into the nests of other species, whose parents usually dutifully raised the birds—often at the price of losing their own children. That was part of the balance of nature centuries ago, but Europeans arrived in North America, cut down forests, and eliminated wild herds—opening much more territory to the cowbird and its parasitic eggs. Today, cowbirds are a problem, contributing to the reduction in numbers of certain sensitive migratory species. Lisa Petit of the Smithsonian Institution describes the problem and what might be done about it. (*See also Quandaries.*)

http://web2.si.edu/smbc/fxshts/fxsht3.htm

Cowbird (*Molothrus ater*) [Brown-headed Cowbird] (JJA)

NET NOTES

Newsgroups for Anyone

Usenet newsgroups are like electronic bulletin boards, where people around the world can post and read messages. They can ask questions, seek opinions, or offer advice. On AOL or CompuServe, your software can connect you to these newsgroups. Many Internet service providers give you software for connecting to the Usenet newsgroups directly, but some connections are not very reliable. An easy way for anyone with Web access to use newsgroups—more than 15,000 of which were online by 1999—is a website called Deja.com.

Using Deja.com is a little slower than accessing the Usenet directly, but in many ways it's less complicated and more powerful, since you can quickly search thousands of newsgroups for topics that interest you. Suppose you want to read suggestions on locating bird feeders. Type the word BIRDFEEDER (try BIRD FEEDER, too) into Deja.com's search window, and up will pop dozens, perhaps hundreds of messages culled from all available newsgroups, but probably mostly from the *rec.birds*.

With Deja.com, you can also quickly set up a personalized "newsreader" that will access only the subjects that you wish to follow. And if all that isn't enough, Deja.com's online message editor includes spellchecking!

http://www.deja.com

Another place to read newsgroups easily and for free is MailandNews.com, which has a friendly yet powerful interface.

http://www.mailandnews.com

Crossbill, Red

"Crossbills are seed-eating finches of mountains and conifer forests, known for their unique lifestyle," says Jeff Groth of the American Museum of Natural History in New York City. "They are nomads, and search over broad areas for ripened conifer cones. Their unusual, crossed bill allows them to rip and tear between cone scales to extract seeds." There's a problem with crossbills, however: several distinctive varieties of them have been grouped together under one species, Red Crossbill (*Loxia curvirostra*). Recent studies have indicated these Red Crossbill forms should be separate species. Although it's difficult to tell these forms apart by appearance, vocalizations among them differ enough so that even the amateur birder can tell them apart. If your browser has sound capabilities, you can join Groth in an exploration of crossbills, their sounds, and their natural history. It's an excellent glimpse into the work of the professional ornithologist, one that even the amateur can appreciate and enjoy. Scores of sound samples from seven types of crossbills, along with sonograms, are online for you to compare. There's information about the natural history of each and there are pictures—though not a lot. The Birds of North America site has an extensive report on the variations and subspecies—and cites the work of Groth (*second address*).

http://research.amnh.org/ornithology/crossbills/
http://www.birdsofna.org/excerpts/crossbill.html

Crossbill, White-winged

If you live in the States and are ever lucky enough to spot a male White-winged Crossbill (*Loxia leucoptera*), you won't soon forget its rich carmine-crimson color. However, this bird of the Canadian Arctic rarely dips down into the United States—and then usually only because of severe cold. It prefers the coniferous Canadian woods, reports the Nutty Birdwatcher, where it eats seeds in winter and insects in summer.

http://nuthatch.birdnature.com/whtwngcrbl.html

Crow Message Board

Crows have an amazing following. Many, of course, consider them the smartest and most personable birds. And well they might be. If you like crows and enjoy talking to others about crows, the message board at this website is the place to go. The board is easy to read and use, and requires no special passwords or applications—just good taste. And if you're a *corvidophile* (crow-lover), you must have that!

http://www.corvus.org/wwwboard/

A
B
C
D
E
F
G
H
I
J
K
L
M
N
O
P
Q
R
S
T
U
V
W
X
Y
Z

A
B
C
D
E
F
G
H
I
J
K
L
M
N
O
P
Q
R
S
T
U
V
W
X
Y
Z

Crows & Corvids

Crows and ravens belong to the Corvidae or Crow family of birds, notes the Aviary, a site that specializes in the Corvids (*first address*). "This family is comprised of more than just crows, though. It also includes magpies, blue jays, jackdaws, rooks, nutcrackers, and several others." The Aviary has natural history, folklore, illustrations, photos, and sounds for many species, plus links to lead you to more sources of information. Corvus.org (*second address*) says it's a "website devoted to information, issues, and blatant admiration of the American crow." The site sets about answering the question: "What makes the crow any more interesting than any other bird?" It offers natural history, a crow FAQ, and a crow message board, as well as crow links, sounds, pictures, quotes, and bibliography. Another good source of natural history, photos, and general crowabilia is For the Love of Crows (*third address*), where you'll also find a page of crow humor. No exploration of crows would be complete without a visit to the website of ASCAR, the American Society of Crows and Ravens (*fourth address*). Among the many features of this site is information about crows as pets (see the FAQ). For an excellent profile of crows, read A Hearty Bird to Crow About, written by Milan Bull, director of the Connecticut Audubon Center in Fairfield (*fifth address*).

http://www.shades-of-night.com/aviary/
http://www.corvus.org
http://www.zeebyrd.com/corvi29/
http://www.azstarnet.com/~serres/
http://www.ctaudubon.org/Nature/crow.htm

Doves, Mourning

Mourning Doves (*Zenaida macroura*), familiar to backyard birders as ground feeders, are also a target in some states where they are hunted seasonally as game birds. Ohio, for one, has allowed Mourning Dove hunting for several years, despite attempts by friends of these handsome, soft-spoken birds to rescind the law (a vote to ban hunting failed in a 1998 statewide referendum). As many as 400,000 of these birds were killed in Ohio in one recent season. The Mourning Dove is found throughout the United States, Mexico, and Cuba, one of the most common species of wild

Mourning Dove (*Zenaidura macroura*) (JJA)

birds. Although they prefer open fields and lawns with trees and shrubs, they can also be found abundantly in farmlands and even in deserts. They nest as far north as Alaska and New Brunswick, and winter as far north as the northern United States. A gray and sandy colored bird with black wing spots, the Mourning Dove feeds on seeds, while its young, after an early diet of "pigeon milk" regurgitated by their parents, eat insects and when mature go on to the seed diet. The birds mate for life and share nest time: reportedly, the male takes the day shift while the female stays on the eggs through the night. The following three sites offer a good look at this popular bird.

http://www.lcanimal.org/dove.htm
http://www.siu.edu/departments/rso/siuctws/
  critters/mourningdove.html
http://www.sbceo.k12.ca.us/~mcssb/sbpanda/
  mourningdove.html

Finch, House

The House Finch is both a native and an introduced species in North America, depending on where you live. (*See North American Birds, Exotics.*)

Finch, Purple

Similar to the House Finch (and they're sometimes found in each other's company), the Purple Finch (*Carpodacus purpureus*) is more raspberry red in appearance and lacks the streaks on breast and belly that its relative shows. Jeff Crooke, on his Winging It site, says the Purple Finch is more of a country bird, whereas the House Finch prefers city life (*first address*). For a comparison of the males and females, see the Patuxent page (*second address*) and also check out the photos and art at the Cornell site (*third address*) where the Cassin's Finch is also included in the discussion. Purple Finches breed in the northern tier of states and in Canada, usually in conifers, and they feed on seeds, buds, blossoms, and fruit. They have declined in number, it's thought, because of the competition with the interloping House Sparrows and House Finches. The bright little bird is also noted for his song, as recounted by Robie Tufts at the Birds of Nova Scotia site (*fourth address*): "His song in its fullness is a rich, rapidly enunciated, loud ecstatic warble, sometimes poured out in a torrent of melody as he hovers on outspread trembling wings."

http://rtonline1.roanoke.com/wingingit/pfinch.html

http://www.mbr.nbs.gov/id/framlst/account/
h5170id.html

http://birdsource.cornell.edu/gbbc/birdid/purfin/
index.html

http://142.227.51.1/educ/museum/mnh/nature/
nsbirds/bns0402.htm

Flicker, Northern

The Northern Flicker (*Colaptes auratus*) is unusual among North American woodpeckers because it often forages on the ground, whereas other woodpeckers tend to hunt in trees. Found throughout North America and adapting well to fairly urban environments, the flicker has five subspecies, according to this sample page from the book, *The Birds of North America*, which provides information primarily on its ranges and migration (*first address*). For identification information, including pictures, a sound bite, and a range map, visit the Cornell Laboratory of Ornithology (*second address*). Peterson Online has excellent illustrations of the flicker on its site, along with plenty of general information about the species (*third address*).

Flicker (*Colaptes auratus*) [Northern Flicker] (JJA)

http://www.birdsofna.org/excerpts/flicker.html

http://birdsource2.ornith.cornell.edu/pfw/birdid/norfli/
index.html

http://www.petersononline.com/birds/month/
nofl/index.html

Flycatcher, Gray

The Gray Flycatcher (*Empidonax wrightii*) went through a long period of having an identity crisis, reports John Sterling of the Smithsonian Migratory Bird Center, who details its confusion with the Dusky Flycatcher. But the much greater part of this essay tells of the life and habits of this Great Plains species. He also explains the best technique for telling the Gray from the look-alike Dusky Flycatcher.

http://web2.si.edu/smbc/bom/grfl.htm

NET NOTES

The Wonders of the Rings

Imagine a place on the Web where you can look for a subject of interest and immediately find a dozen, or maybe a hundred, websites that reflect that interest. WebRing (*first address*), a center of Web neighborhoods, was inspired by a high school student in 1995 who devised the system for interlinking websites of similar subjects. A ring "allows anyone to create their own little community," Sage Weil of Ashland, Oregon, told the *New York Times* in January 1999. Sage was then a college student in computer science, but still involved in WebRing.org, probably the largest operation of its type. More than 60,000 WebRing communities connect more than a million sites. Visit the site and search RingWorld, the WebRing directory, for the word "birds." You'll find more than 140 rings, each involving from three to more than 800 sites (some will be pet bird rings, but most will involve wild birds). Select a ring and start wandering through the sites, looking down at the bottom of each home page for the WebRing linking logo. Quality will range from rank amateur to sharp professional, but usually, you will find information of interest. And it's always fun to see what other birders are up to. (Remember, you can always start your own website—free of charge—and then join a ring yourself; *see page 158*.)

Two other rings are worth checking out. Looplink (*second address*) and The Rail (*third address*) have fewer sites but are still good sources. The Rail uses a train metaphor; look under the Animals train for birds.

http://www.webring.org
http://www.looplink.com
http://www.therail.com

Goldfinch, American

From its swooping, flitting flight, to its rapid, high-pitched twittering, the American Goldfinch (*Carduelis tristis*) shows a certain lightness of being. Males of the species are a brilliant yellow with black wings (white bars) and a jaunty black cap, and both male and female lift observers' spirits with their aerobatic joie de vivre. Put out a thistle feeder, and they should come. In winter the birds are much more subdued, the males and females both a similar buff-gold hue. But as spring approaches, the males begin showing the yellow feathers that led to one of their nicknames, "wild canary." Chipper Woods has good close-ups of their varied plumage (*first address*). Look there, too, for the great picture of a female showing the brood patch, the breast area that loses feathers when she's is on the nest, to allow better heat transfer to the eggs. The Darien (Connecticut) Audubon Society's page (*second address*) shows two beautiful shots of male goldfinches in breeding plumage, one posed on pokeweed and the other with a thistle seed in its bill, perched on a thistle plant. For one observer's essay on the appeal of these birds, visit the third address. The Cornell Laboratory of Ornithology page on the goldfinch (*fourth address*) notes that it's the most common finch reported by Project FeederWatch participants; this page also carries a link to a goldfinch recording.

http://www.wbu.com/chipperwoods/photos/goldfinch.htm

http://www.darien.lib.ct.us/audubon/birdpgs/gldfinch.htm

http://www.audubon.org/chapter/wa/rainier/wing/a-goldfinch.htm

http://birdsource2.ornith.cornell.edu/pfw/birdid/amgo/index.html

Goldfinch (*Spinus tristus*) [American Goldfinch, *Carduelis tristis*] (JJA)

Grosbeak, Blue

The Blue Grosbeak (*Guiraca caerulea*) is described as being a dull blue with tan wingbars; a big finch, up to seven and a half inches long, as compared with the Indigo Bunting, which is usually about five and a half inches. Interestingly, it's when the Blue Grosbeak's feathers are old and tattered before a molt that it's more brilliantly blue (*first address*). Immature birds are a mix of brown and blue and the female is a warm brown, showing some blue shading on the rump. The Blue Grosbeak has been extending its range northward and breeds as far north as New Jersey, with sightings further yet, in Nova Scotia (*second address*). Peterson Online has an excellent page, detailing the life and identification techniques for the Blue Grosbeak and including fine illustrations and a range map (*third address*).

http://www.imperial.cc.ca.us/birds/bluegros.htm

http://museum.ednet.ns.ca/mnh/nature/nsbirds/bns0354.htm

http://www.petersononline.com/birds/month/blgr/index.html

FEATHERED FACTS

Killer Cats

Americans have an estimated 60 million pet cats. If each cat killed only one bird a year, that's more than 60 million dead birds, which is more than any oil tanker spill has killed. However, studies show that each year, cats kill a lot more than that—probably hundreds of millions of migratory songbirds. In 1990 researchers estimated that "outdoor" house cats and feral cats killed some 78 million small mammals and birds in the United Kingdom each year.

—adapted from U.S. Fish & Wildlife Service

http://www.fws.gov/r9mbmo/pamphlet/songbrd.html

Grosbeak, Evening

Like a gang, they fly into a town, noisy and full of themselves. They devour whatever food is available and move on, leaving behind people impressed by their boldness and their beauty. Until the 20th century, they were not known east of the Great Lakes. Evening Grosbeaks (*Coccothraustes vespertinus*) are described by the Cornell site's writer (*first address*) as "large, gregarious, nomadic finches that travel in raucous flocks." The yellow, brown, white, and black coloration of the males is distinctive. The females and immature grosbeaks are dusky, with white wing patches and show the distinctive short, forked tail and heavy finch beak. They look, some say, like overgrown goldfinches. Although Evening Grosbeaks can be seen in nearly every state during their winter travels for food, they head north in summer to raise their families in the evergreen forests they prefer. For details, visit the Patuxent Center pages (*second address*), which include range maps, as well as identification tips.

http://birdsource.cornell.edu/gbbc/birdid/evgr/index.html

http://www.mbr-pwrc.usgs.gov/id/framlst/account/h5140id.html

Grosbeak, Rose-breasted

The male of the species has been described as a gentleman in evening dress with a bright red scarf at his throat. With his big finch bill and bold color, the Rose-breasted Grosbeak (*Pheucticus ludovicianus*) is unmistakable. The female has black and white brow stripes and a dark brown upper body, with streaks on white below. The male has red wing linings, the female yellow. Immature Evening Grosbeaks are similar, with the young males showing some red on the breast. For good descriptions and photos, visit the Patuxent Center page (*first address*). For a fine photo and a sample of its song, visit the Nature Sound Studio page (*second address*).

http://www.mbr-pwrc.usgs.gov/id/framlst/account/i5950id.html

http://www.clarityconnect.com/webpages2/naturesound/birds/birds.html

A B C D E F G H I J K L M **N** O P Q R S T U V W X Y Z

A
B
C
D
E
F
G
H
I
J
K
L
M
N
O
P
Q
R
S
T
U
W
X
Y
Z

Hummingbird, Anna's

Imagine having a tiny hummingbird living with your family. It snuggles in dad's beard while he's watching TV, comes to Mom when she calls it, landing on her outstretched finger, and sleeps on a coat hanger next

Free & Easy Personal Websites

You can share your knowledge of birds—or your group's or club's knowledge—by setting up a simple website. And you can do it for free.

Many Internet Service Providers—from America Online to your neighborhood access company—give you website space on their computers as part of your membership. In most cases you have to learn a bit about creating webpages, using your own software or something supplied by your provider. But even easier—and totally free—alternatives exist, as long as you can get online. And even getting online can be free if you connect to the Internet from your local library or a friend's house.

Several companies provide free website space in exchange for your allowing them to stick advertising on your site. With some free-space providers, the advertising is unobtrusive. With others, it stands out almost like a sore thumb. Check out providers and decide which you like best.

What's really nice about most of these site providers is that they make it incredibly easy to set up a website. They may ask you to fill in the blanks, or they may supply you with a simple program that remains on your computer only for your site-creation session. Some of these programs, such as that used by Deja.com, produce some amazingly sophisticated sites without your having to know a jot of HTML coding, the programming language that makes webpages work.

Free site providers include

Deja.com	http://www.dejanews.com
Tripod	http://www.tripod.com
Yahoo	http://www.yahoo.com
Geocities	http://www.geocities.yahoo.com/home/

to daughter's bed. Sound like a fairy tale? Hardly. It's the true story of Henrietta Hummer, an Anna's Hummingbird (*Calypte anna*) adopted by a California family. You can find out about Henrietta, as well as about her species on this About.com page.

http://birding.about.com/library/weekly/aa090697.htm

Hummingbird, Ruby-throated

The Ruby-throated Hummingbird (*Archilochus colubris*) is probably the most widespread and popular hummingbird in North America; it's also the only one whose range is most of the continent. The Birds of North America site offers a top-notch, scientific look at its eating and breeding habits. More on these and other species of hummingbirds can be found at this website. (*See also Migration.*)

http://www.birdsofna.org/excerpts/rth.html

Hummingbirds

The Hummingbird Website (*first address*) offers information about feeding and attracting hummingbirds through special gardening techniques. Photos by a growing collection of online photographers are featured, and you can also buy hummingbird supplies, such as feeders. The site carries conservation alerts, provides opportunities for pen pals, lists volunteer opportunities, and has hummingbird links (as well as links to butterfly sites—both hummers and butterflies are nectar-eaters, and thus are drawn to the yard full of flowers). Hummingbirds! is an award-winning site (*second address*) that calls itself your "WWW source for information on attracting, watching, feeding, and studying North American hummingbirds." The site has a guide to hummingbird species, describes how to attract hummingbirds with gardens, provides maps and natural history information, tells about current hummingbird research, debunks myths, lists organizations, recommends when to put up and take down your feeders, offers many photos, and has much more. (*See also Organizations & Associations.*)

http://hummingbirdwebsite.com
http://www.derived.net/hummers/

Jay, Blue

Were they not so common, and loud, Blue Jays (*Cyanocitta cristata*) would no doubt be treasured backyard visitors for their beautiful plumage and large size, not to mention their intelligence. Actually, many birders from other parts of the world make a point of looking for the Blue Jay when they visit North America because they consider the bird to be one of the continent's most handsome species. For a nice essay on the jay, visit the Real Indiana Jones Page (*first address*). Although jays get bad marks for their nest-raiding activities (and just let someone get near a jay nest—aerial attack is nearly guaranteed!), they are renowned for their acorn-planting activities. The jays, of course, are merely caching a food item when it's plentiful, intending to consume it later. But in doing so, they have planted many an oak tree (*second address*). In fact, they are probably more responsible for planting oak forests than squirrels. The Blue Jay, a relative of crows, is very common in the eastern half of the United States and just about totally absent in the west (*third address*), where the Steller's Jay and Scrub Jay reign.

http://www.realindy.com/bluejays.htm

http://danr.ucop.edu/ihrmp/oak44.htm

http://www.mbr-pwrc.usgs.gov/bbs/htm96/map617/ra4770.html

Blue Jay (*Cyanocitta cristata*) (JJA)

Jay, Florida Scrub

The Florida Scrub Jay, which some name *Aphelocoma ultramarina* (though this is generally considered the Mexican Jay) and others list as *Aphelocoma coeruluscens coeruluscens*, is a threatened species because of loss of habitat in Florida. It's the only bird species confined entirely to the state of Florida. A good close-up of this friendly bird can be found at the first address, but to see how very friendly these birds are, visit the third address as well. The U.S. Fish & Wildlife Service lists the Florida Scrub Jay as having a population of only 2,000 or so in the area surrounding the Kennedy Space Center. The bird is described as a "disjunct race of Scrub Jay which is widespread in the western U.S. and Mexico." The Space Center page on the jay offers photographs and considerable scientific commentary about the bird and its prospects for survival (*second address*).

http://www.camacdonald.com/birding/DesJardin/FloridaScrubJay.htm

http://atlas.ksc.nasa.gov/threat/scrubjay.html

http://www.floridata.com/tracks/scrub/animals/aph_coer.htm

Jay, Green

The Green Jay (*Cyanocorax yncas*), with its blue head, green back, and black bib, is one of our more spectacular birds but alas, has a relatively small range. The bird's behavior is described in considerable detail in this page from the Birds of North America site.

http://www.birdsofna.org/excerpts/greenjay.html

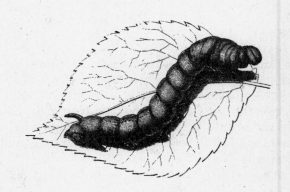

A B C D E F G H I J K L M N O P Q R S T U V W X Y Z

Jay, Scrub

The Scrub Jay (*Aphelocoma coeruluscens*) is another mischievous bird who loves acorns and in California is estimated to plant one billion a year. The jay can carry as many as six at a time in its throat and esophagus (*first address*). The western version of the Scrub Jay is known as *Aphelocoma californica*, and the coloration of this bird varies somewhat by location. Along the West Coast the bird, which has a blue head but no crest, is generally a brighter blue and has a whiter throat overall than its interior-dwelling relatives. The Mexican Jay is similar (*second address*).

http://tqd.advanced.org/2899/virtual/scrubjay.html

http://www.mbr-pwrc.usgs.gov/id/framlst/account/
  h4810id.html

Jay, Steller's

In 1987, the children of British Columbia chose the Steller's Jay (*Cyanocitta stelleri*) as their official Provincial Bird, notes the Naturepark website (*first address*). This year-round resident of the Pacific Northwest and the mountains down to Nicaragua is a popular feeder bird. Naturepark also provides a sampling of its distinctive call. So does the Royal British Columbia Museum's site, which has a fine page devoted to Steller's Jay (*second address*). Here you can learn details about its distribution, both breeding and non-breeding, plus much information about its breeding and nesting habits.

http://www.naturepark.com/stellars.htm

http://rbcm1.rbcm.gov.bc.ca/nh_papers/gracebell/
  english/st_jay.html

Juncos

The Dark-eyed Junco (*Junco hyemalis*) is the bird most likely to be found at a backyard station, according to Project FeederWatch data (*first address*). If you see a junco on the East Coast, it'll be slate gray on top and light underneath, whereas in California, the same species has a black head, brown back and sides, and white belly. The bird's white outside tail feathers flash when a flock takes flight. They are ground feeders who will dine at platform feeders, and they enjoy a wide variety of seeds, as well as finding their own insects. They are said to eat ragweed seeds, to which allergy sufferers can only say, more power to them! They come to feeders in flocks and are generally unobtrusive, medium-size birds, rarely causing a commotion. You can find the junco at edges of woodland, parks, hedges, old fields, and cedar or spruce groves. They breed from Alaska and Canada to Georgia and Arizona in the mountains, and they winter throughout the United States and northern Mexico. The female builds a cup-shaped nest of grass and small twigs; both birds tend the young, which leave the nest at two weeks. Visit the Patuxent Wildlife Research Center site (*second address*) for a detailed description of the varieties of Dark-eyed Junco that can be found in the United States, from the Slate-colored to the Pink-sided. The Yellow-eyed Junco (*Junco phaeonotus*) can be found in southeast Arizona. Finally, for an excellent profile of juncos, read Eirik A. T. Blom's feature for *Backyard Bird News* (*third address*).

http://www.tc.cornell.edu/Birds/dark.eyed.junco.html

http://www.mbr.nbs.gov/id/framlst/account/
  h5670id.html

http://www.birdwatchersdigest.com/bbn/articles/
  bbn99/winter99/winter99.html

Slate-colored Junco (*Junco hyemalis*) [Dark-eyed Junco] (JJA)

Kingbird, Eastern

The kingbirds go by the generic Latin name of *Tyrannus*, which means "tyrant." That's because of their aggressiveness in defending their territory and in generally lording over other birds. The Eastern Kingbird (*Tyrannus tyrannus*) is the most common and widespread of the clan in North America and despite its name, can be found coast-to-coast. And these kingbirds have quite a trip getting here: they winter in the Amazon River region of South America. The page from the Birds of North America site describes the Eastern Kingbird's habits and habitats.

http://www.birdsofna.org/excerpts/ekingbird.html

Kinglet, Golden-crowned

The appearance of a kinglet—be it the Golden-crowned (*Regulus satrapa*) or the Ruby-crowned (*see later in this section*)—is always a treat for backyard birders. These wiggly migrants often show up with Titmice and nuthatches, checking out the bushes and

shrubs for insects, says this profile on the Nutty Bird-watcher. Its Latin name means literally "king with a golden-crown," referring to the patch of orange atop its head. Although migrants, they pretty much stick to the continent, wintering in Florida, the Gulf Coast regions, and Central America. Their summer range extends from Alaska to the Carolinas. Thus, almost everyone gets a chance to see them, whether as residents or pass-throughs.

http://nuthatch.birdnature.com/gck.html

Kinglet, Ruby-crowned

Although the Ruby-crowned Kinglet (*Regulus calendula*) prefers coniferous forests, it will show up in gardens, reports the Nutty Birdwatcher (*first address*), which offers some fair photos but good natural history on the widespread species. They often migrate with warblers, coming north in the spring from Central America and the Gulf Coast. More natural history and pictures are available on the site of the Royal British Columbia Museum (*second address*). But for a really good photo of this kinglet showing its ruby crown, visit John Cooke's Birds of the Northern Sierra Nevada site (*third address*).

http://nuthatch.birdnature.com/rckinglet.html

http://www.rbcm.gov.bc.ca/nh_papers/gracebell/english/rc_king.html

http://www.geocities.com/RainForest/Canopy/7360/tc01021.html

FEATHERED FACTS

Warbler for Dick

Birds do a lot for humans, but a Prothonotary Warbler sighted on the banks of the Potomac River may have helped create a President. A birder named Alger Hiss was so excited by seeing this more southern species that he told a fellow birder named Whittaker Chambers. Unfortunately for Hiss, the fact that Chambers knew about the sighting became evidence that the two knew each other, and helped a virtually unknown freshman congressman in his successful efforts to have Hiss convicted as a spy. The congressman was Richard M. Nixon.

—adapted from Lisa Petit, Smithsonian Migratory Bird Center

http://web2.si.edu/smbc/bom/ptwa.htm

Lark, Horned

The Horned Lark (*Eremophila alpestris*) likes open spaces: fields, shores, even busy airports. In the summer, when many head from the United States to Canada, it likes tundra (though many Horned Larks spend the whole year in the States). According to Peterson Online, the Horned Lark does well on lousy land, such as overgrazed fields or territory that's been "abused." Consequently, the page says, its numbers have probably increased "with the advance of civilization."

http://www.petersononline.com/birds/month/hola/index.html

A
B
C
D
E
F
G
H
I
J
K
L
M
N
O
P
Q
R
S
T
U
V
W
X
Y
Z

A B C D E F G H I J K L M N O P Q R S T U V W X Y Z

Martin, Purple

Few people realize that, without the help of humans, there would be no Purple Martins (*Progne subis*) east of the Rockies. That's because over a period of many thousands of years, Native Americans and now just plain North Americans wooed them from their wild life of living in old woodpecker houses to dwelling in "artificial" houses—hollowed-out gourds at first. How this happened makes a fascinating story, which you'll find on the site of the Purple Martin Conservation Association (*first address*). You'll find lots more information here, too. One of the best profiles you'll find about the life and times of the Purple Martin is provided by Robert Rice of the Smithsonian Migratory Bird Center (*second address*). Purple Martins are one of our first seasonal migrants, hitting the shores of North America as early as January on their journey north from South America. Why is that? Rice will tell you.

http://www.purplemartin.org/history.html
http://web2.si.edu/smbc/bom/puma.htm

Purple Martin (*Progne subis*) (JJA)

Martin, Purple: Forum

The Purple Martin Forum, the Internet meeting place for martin enthusiasts, is "for all experience levels, from the novice who is just getting started with martins, to the expert on purple martin behavior and colony management techniques." The moderators emphasize that Purple Martin education and information sharing are the primary goals—"no question is too simple to post and you don't have to live where there are martins to post an article." On the forum you will find messages about Purple Martin biology and behavior, attraction tips, colony management techniques, selecting, preparing, and maintaining housing, controlling competitors and predators, troubleshooting, and much more. The easy-to-use site is divided into two frames, with message titles at the top and messages at the bottom. No special sign-ups are needed—just join in!

http://www3.vantek.net/pmh/forum/

Meadowlark, Eastern

The song of the Eastern Meadowlark (*Sturnella magna*) is almost legendary. To hear it, go to the first address at Patuxent. The bird is neither a lark, nor a "big little starling," as its scientific name suggests, says the Nutty Birdwatcher (*second address*). Instead it is a blackbird. The ground-dwelling species is widespread in North America, though locally less common than in the past because of the loss of many open fields, which have either been subdivided or allowed to return to woodland. The Birds of North America site offers many details concerning the Eastern Meadowlark's behavior (*third address*). Diane Porter provides a detailed essay on the lifestyle of the Eastern Meadowlark, noting that the best place to look for them is open fields with horses or cattle (*fourth address*). She also covers the Western Meadowlark, which has a different song.

http://www.mbr-pwrc.usgs.gov/id/htmwav2/
    h5010so.wav
http://nuthatch.birdnature.com/meadowlark.html
http://www.birdsofna.org/excerpts/meadowlark.html
http://www.birdwatching.com/stories/
    storymeadowlark.html

Mockingbird, Northern

The Northern Mockingbird is subdued in color and form, a grayish, medium-size bird with lighter underparts, but when he sings, no one could call him plain! His Latin name tells the story—*Mimus polyglottos*—a mime of many voices. The mockingbird can imitate more than three dozen bird species' songs and even more calls, not to mention barking dogs and squeaking door hinges. The singer prefers to perform from the uppermost branch of a tree or the top of a pole or TV antenna, so when you hear what sounds like a flock of different species all giving voice from the same location—usually repeating each sound twice, look up for a jaunty gray bird. One of the greatest treats a mockingbird occasionally delivers is to burst into song in the middle of a summer night; it's an odd yet joyful experience to wake to the mockingbird's song and realize that it's not announcing dawn, but rather just getting in some more riffs when the spirit, apparently, has moved it. Mockingbirds can be found throughout the United States; their range has extended northward in recent years. They feed mainly on fruit and insects. The Texas Parks & Wildlife's site devotes a page to mockingbirds. To hear samples of how well the mockingbird can mimic, visit Tony Phillips' site (*second address*). He has cuts of the mocker doing Blue Jays, Wood Thrush, Carolina Wren, and Common Flicker, with the actual voices of the species that were imitated. You can even hear an imitation of a digital alarm clock (or a peeping frog).

http://bb35.tpwd.state.tx.us/nature/wild/birds/mockbird.htm

http://math.math.sunysb.edu/~tony/birds/mimics.html

Nighthawk, Common

The Common Nighthawk (*Chordeiles minor*) is neither a hawk nor, in some parts of its former range, particularly common. This bird, a member of the goatsucker family, hunts insects at night and lays its eggs on the ground, notes the Canadian Museum of Nature. But since development has reduced the amount of safe ground, the numbers of nighthawks have declined—though some are adapting to cities and suburbs by laying eggs atop flat-roofed shopping centers, factories, and schools.

http://www.nature.ca/notebooks/english/night.htm

Nutcracker, Clark's

Clark's Nutcracker (*Nucifraga columbiana*), a member of the crow and jay family, is a western species that feeds mostly on the seeds of conifers. This nutcracker spends its nesting season in the high mountains, but can wander widely in the West at other times of the year according to this page from the Birds of North America site, which covers primarily its eating habits—including its close relationship with various pine species that it may help to spread.

http://www.birdsofna.org/excerpts/nutcracker.html

MEET THE MASTERS

It's Greek to Her

Names fascinate Julia Pahountis, Webmaster of the Nutty Birdwatcher <http://www.birdnature.com>. Her website has a section on the origin of bird family names and plans a section on bird names themselves (which may be online when you read this). "What's interesting about this little project is that I really didn't know that some of the bird family names came from Greek mythology!" she says. "My family and ancestors are from an island off Greece called Karpathos (which lies between the Islands of Crete and Rhodes) and every year or every other year I go back and spend three or four weeks with family." Of course, she birds while there. "I have been maintaining a list of birds that I have seen on the island between the months of April and October, and that list is approaching 100 birds," she reports.

Nuthatch, Brown-headed

The Brown-headed Nuthatch (*Sitta pusilla*) of the American Southeast is a small bird that searches the

Bid for Those Binocs

Although most of us look to merchants of new equipment when we're buying a pair of binoculars, a scope, or other gear, most of us also appreciate a bargain. For many shoppers, online auctions are the hot new way to buy merchandise—usually used.

The biggest auction site is eBay (*first address*), which at any given time lists more than a million items for sale. eBay isn't selling the stuff—people like you and me create their own miniature auction sites. eBay organizes them into an easy-to-use format and provides a search engine, which scans all the offerings in more than 1,000 categories to find what you're looking for. One day, we searched for "binoculars" and back came a list of 267, many including pictures. Some were antiques, some used, some new, and some toys (Mickey Mouse binoculars would probably not do well on your next field trip). Prices ranged between $5 and $650.

We found 50 bird feeders, 285 birdhouses (many probably more decorative than practical), and countless books about birds and birding. Bird-oriented collectibles—plates, trivets, decoys, carvings, etc.—were there. When we typed "bird" into the search field, back came 4,575 items! Plenty of help is available online. Once you're familiar with how the site works, you can spend hours wandering eBay looking for goodies. And some 80,000 new items are added each day, eBay says.

To use eBay, you need to register. There is no cost, and instructions are easy to follow.

Newcomers to the auction scene include Amazon. com (*second address*) and Yahoo! (*third address*). .

http://www.ebay.com
http://auctions.amazon.com
http://auctions.yahoo.com

outsides of trees and branches—often pines—for insects. These nuthatches often travel in small flocks, sometimes with other species such as woodpeckers, kingbirds, Pine Warblers, and titmice, notes the Nutty Birdwatcher (*first address*). To see what John James Audubon had to say about the Brown-headed Nuthatch, visit Audubon's Multimedia Birds of America (*second address*).

http://nuthatch.birdnature.com/brownnut.html
http://employeeweb.myxa.com/rrb/Audubon/VolIV/00411.html

Nuthatch, Pygmy

As its name suggests, the Pygmy Nuthatch (*Sitta pygmaea*) is the smallest of the North American nuthatches and can be less than four inches long. A southwestern bird, it spends most of its life in Ponderosa Pines (at elevations up to 10,000 feet in the Rockies) and in other pines along the Pacific coast, notes the Nutty Birdwatcher. You can both see and hear the Pygmy Nuthatch, thanks to the Biology Department at Loyola Marymount University (*second address*).

http://nuthatch.birdnature.com/pignut.html
http://eco.bio.lmu.edu/socal_nat_hist/birds/orders/pass/nuth_py.htm

Nuthatch, Red-breasted

The Red-Breasted Nuthatch (*Sitta canadensis*) is found mostly in the mountains in the eastern United States, across Canada, and up and down the western states. Some years, particularly when winters are harsh, they may dip down farther into the United States, showing up at many feeders where they haven't been seen before. The Nutty Birdwatcher notes that this species tends to move very quickly around tree trunks in its search for food, more quickly than the White-breasted cousin. They favor coniferous trees over the deciduous liked by the White-breasted. For close-up pictures of literally a bird in hand, see the second address.

http://nuthatch.birdnature.com/rednut.html
http://www.wbu.com/chipperwoods/photos/rbnhatch.htm

Nuthatch, White-breasted

The easily identified White-breasted Nuthatch (*Sitta carolinensis*) is found around the world, nearly always in forests. The White-breasted, the most widely distributed of North American nuthatches, is found wherever there are forests. They prefer deciduous trees in the wild and are regulars at backyard feeders where they enjoys seeds, suet, and peanut butter; its numbers have been increasing probably because of the many backyard feeding stations. Being so widespread, the bird has many common names. The Nutty Birdwatcher, which has a fine profile of the White-breasted Nuthatch, lists 11 names: Carolina Nuthatch, Common Nuthatch, Devil-Down-Head, Florida Nuthatch, Inyo Nuthatch, Rocky Mountain Nuthatch, Sapsucker, Slender-billed Nuthatch, Topsy-Turvy-Bird, Tree Mouse, and Yank.

http://nuthatch.birdnature.com/whitenut.html

White-breasted Nuthatch (*Sitta carolinensis*) (JJA)

Nuthatches

Nuthatches nest in cavities, such as old woodpecker holes, and may use mud to reduce the opening. They will also use nest boxes if natural cavities are unavailable. All of these active, little birds can easily be identified by their penchant for walking down trees as they search for insects. They are short-tailed with gray backs, dark caps, and straight, fairly long bills. Size varies from less than four inches for the Pygmy to five inches for the White-breasted. For a wealth of scientific information about the world's nuthatches, visit the Electronic Nuthatch (*first address*). Chipper Woods offers excellent, close-up photos of this Nuthatch with a good profile (*second address*).

http://alt-www.uia.ac.be/u/matthys/nuthatch.html

http://www.wbu.com/chipperwoods/photos/wbnut.htm

Oriole, Baltimore

The Baltimore Oriole (*Icterus galbula*), which went through a period of being called a Northern Oriole, is a flash of black and orange, a very attractive bird who tends to return to the same nesting site year after year. This is mostly an eastern and midwestern species; in the West, the similar Bullock's Oriole (*Icterus bullockii*) was once considered a form of the same species, and the Baltimore will sometimes hybridize with Bullock's in western regions. The male and female create a woven, hanging nest remarkable in its construction and usually visible only after the leaves have fallen. Good photographs of several types of orioles and information about their feeding habits and migratory patterns are on Paul Slichter's Northwestern Birds site (*first address*). The John Heinz Wildlife Refuge (*second address*), a stop for migrating orioles, offers explanations of why orioles are turning up more frequently at refuges while their general numbers are in decline. For people who'd like to offer orioles a boost on their way north, Journey North's Oriole site, Unpave the Way for Orioles (*third address*), suggests putting out nectar feeders with the orioles' favorite treat—grape jelly. There's a source for an oriole feeder and a jelly recipe, although it's noted that the birds will enjoy commercial jelly placed in a shallow dish. Oranges are another of their favorite foods; cut them in half and set them outside. "Each spring the oriole's clear rounded whistle first attracts my attention," writes Gerry Rising about the bird he is pleased to call "Baltimore" again after the many years it was called "Northern" (*fourth address*). Hear one at Tony Phillips's site (*fifth address*).

http://district.gresham.k12.or.us/ghs/nature/animal/bird/black/noriole.htm

http://www.learner.org/jnorth/fall1997/97september29.html

http://www.learner.org/jnorth/unpave/oriole.html

http://www.acsu.buffalo.edu/~insrisg/nature/nw97/oriole.html

http://math.math.sunysb.edu/~tony/birds/icterids.html

A B C D E F G H I J K L M N O P Q R S T U V W X Y Z

A
B
C
D
E
F
G
H
I
J
K
L
M
N
O
P
Q
R
S
T
U
V
W
X
Y
Z

Oriole, Orchard

The male Orchard Oriole (*Icterus spurius*), another handsome bird, is quite distinctive, whereas the female is similar to the Baltimore and Bullock's females. The Orchard Oriole favors the central United States and southeastern Canada; its distinguishing characteristics and a lot more are spelled out at the Patuxent Wildlife Research Center site (*first address*). Tony Phillips has recorded its strong, distinctive song on his New York Bird Songs site (*second address*).

http://www.mbr-pwrc.usgs.gov/id/framlst/
  i5060id.html
http://math.math.sunysb.edu/~tony/birds/icterids.html

Ovenbird

The Ovenbird (*Seiurus aurocapillus*) is a warbler much more often heard than seen. Its famous song, *teacher-teacher-teacher-teacher*, can be heard long distances in the forest. Unlike most warblers, the Ovenbird lives and nests on the ground where it hunts insects like a thrush—in fact, the bird, larger than most warblers, has been called a Golden-crowned Thrush, notes the Nutty Birdwatcher (*first address*). The bird is not named for the fact that it's good to roast but because the nest is shaped like an old-fashioned Dutch oven. To hear the Ovenbird's famous song, visit the New York Bird Songs page of warblers (*second address*).

http://nuthatch.birdnature.com/ovenbird.html
http://math.math.sunysb.edu/~tony/birds/
  warblers.html

Raven, Common

Common Ravens (*Corvus corax*), the largest members of the crow or Corvid family, are found around the world—not only in nature but also in folklore, art, song, and history. Yelth: The Raven (*first address*), a Czech-based website, is full of information about ravens and includes a children's corner. A bibliography of books about the Raven, both biological and mytho-logical, is offered by the Raven Archive (*second address*). The Canadian Museum of Nature has a nice, concise page devoted to the raven (*third address*), noting that the birds are "aggressive, clever, and inquisitive." Also provided on this site are tips on how to tell them apart from crows (*see Crows & Corvids earlier in this section*).

http://www.terminal.cz/raven/
http://www.rinzai.com/raven/bibliography.html
http://www.nature.ca/notebooks/english/raven.htm

Ravenlist

Ravenlist is a mailing list for a "serious community of Raven enthusiasts who are sincere in their desire to learn more about this fascinating bird and the mythol-ogy behind it." This page tells about the list. Signing up is as simple as entering your e-mail address and clicking Subscribe.

http://www.rinzai.com/raven/ravenlist.html

Redstart, American

The American Redstart (*Setophaga ruticilla*) spends most of its year in the West Indies or Central America but heads north each summer to breed through much of the United States and Canada. Pete Marra, who has spent a lot of time studying redstarts year-round, notes on this Smithsonian Migratory Bird Center page that the American Redstart is both *polygynous* and polyterritorial. In other words, one male "can some-times be paired with two females, but rather than hav-ing both females on the same territory they maintain two separate and disjunct territories," he says. Marra adds that the male isn't really handling two families at once, but waits till the first female starts incubating before advertising for a second. This technique enables him to fledge more young each season, which presumably helps with the survival of the species. Other fascinating facts about the American Redstart are found in Marra's well-written profile.

http://web2.si.edu/smbc/bom/amre.htm

American Redstart (*Setophaga ruticilla*) (JJA)

FEATHERED FACTS

Latrine Bird

The American Redstart winters in the West Indies where it is often known as the Latrine Bird because of its habit of hanging around outhouses and dumps looking for the flies they draw. It's sometimes called the Christmas Bird because it appears during the Christmas season.

—adapted from Pete Marra, Smithsonian Migratory Bird Center

http://web2.si.edu/smbc/bom/amre.htm

Robin, American

Robins are among the best-known and best-loved birds. American Robin—First Signal of Spring is an essay about the American Robin (*Turdus migratorius*) by Christine Tarski, as carried on the birding guide on About.com (*first address*). It includes links to sites with more information. If you're interested in making sure your spring robins hang around, visit the University of Nebraska's site (*second address*). "By offering them a little encouragement, you might be able to convince a pair that your garden is just the place to settle down and raise a family," says Mary Jane McReynolds, an extension assistant with the University of Nebraska Cooperative Extension in Lancaster County. She offers her suggestions for keeping robins around.

http://birding.about.com/library/weekly/aa032997.htm
http://ianrwww.unl.edu/ianr/lanco/enviro/pest/
   nebline/robins.htm

Sapsucker, Yellow-bellied

If ever a bird had a name that could star in a Monty Python comedy, it's the Yellow-bellied Sapsucker (*Sphyrapicus varius*). The name accurately describes a color and a habit of this migratory North American

woodpecker. The bird drills little holes in lines that spiral around a trunk, usually of a fruit tree, and sips the sap that appears. It also eats insects on the trunks, notes the Canadian Museum of Nature. Incidentally, some orchard owners dislike too many visits by sapsuckers, feeling their drilling weakens and threatens their trees.

http://www.nature.ca/notebooks/english/sapsuck.htm

Shrike, Loggerhead

The Loggerhead Shrike (*Lanius ludovicianus*) is an innocent-appearing bird, only nine inches long. If you look closely, you'll see a hooked beak, similar to a raptor's. Although it's a songbird, the Loggerhead Shrike is in many ways more like a hawk. It hunts down and kills other birds, but not quite in the same way as a hawk. Shrikes of all species catch birds and then impale them on a spine or broken branch of a small tree or jam them into a fork of two branches. Then they kill the victim. This seeming gruesome technique earned shrikes a lot of disfavor early in the 20th century, and many were shot, reports the Birds of North America site, which provides this excerpt about the species. It includes information about its conservation and management. The Loggerhead Shrike is found in most of North America, except the Northeast.

http://www.birdsofna.org/excerpts/lshrike.html

Shrike, Northern

Unlike the Loggerhead Shrike (*see above*), the Northern Shrike (*Lanius excubitor*) is found in northern North America, Eurasia, and even northern Africa. These birds share the same feeding habit of impaling its prey—birds, mice, or large insects—on thorns or broken twigs. The bird is also a singer and is capable of mimicking the songs of other birds, reports the Canadian Museum of Nature.

http://www.nature.ca/notebooks/english/nshrike.htm

A B C D E F G H I J K L M N O P Q R S T U V W X Y Z

A B C D E F G H I J K L M N O P Q R S T U V W X Y Z

MEET THE MASTERS

Capturing the Songs

Tony Phillips, Webmaster of the New York Bird Songs website <http://math.math.sunysb.edu/~tony/birds/index.html>, carries his recording equipment whenever he goes for walks in the spring and summer. "When I hear something new, I try to capture it for my site. I have let some great ones get away, but I keep trying. Last July I came across some exceptional Wood Thrushes just a couple of miles away from my home. They are now on the page." All of Tony's recordings are of birds found in New York State, but not all were necessarily recorded in New York. "When I hear a New York State bird out-of-state, it's fair game," he says.

Siskin, Pine

The Pine Siskin (*Carduelis pinus*) might be considered a magical bird—now you see it, now you don't. These finches normally live in northern North America but periodically irrupt in large numbers into the United States as far south as the Gulf of Mexico. According to the Cornell University Laboratory of Ornithology, scientists believe these incursions are due to a lack of food in their native territory. This Cornell page tells you how to identify the Pine Siskin, both by sight and by sound.

http://birdsource2.ornith.cornell.edu/pfw/birdid/pisi/index.html

Songbird Identification Charts

Opus, a manufacturer of bird feeders, has a beautiful, online Songbird Identifier to help the beginner identify the two dozen most common species of birds to frequent backyard feeders (*first address*). The illustrations are excellent and the thumbnail descriptions interesting. Pennington, a producer of wild birdseed, also has a wild bird identification chart with good illustrations and concise notes (*second address*). More than two dozen species are illustrated, and the site indicates what kinds of food each species eats.

http://www.opususa.com/songid.html

http://www.penningtonseed.com/Bird_feeding_main/feedcht/body_feedcht.html

Sparrow, American Tree

Backyard Birding has an online video of the American Tree Sparrow (*Spizella arborea*), a bird found widely in North America. An excellent photo is available at Aves.net (*second address*).

http://www.slivoski.com/birding/atspar.htm

http://www.aves.net/birds-of-ohio/birdtrsp.htm

Sparrow, Chipping

A Chipping Sparrow (*Spizella passerina*) doesn't hack away at things, much less play golf. It makes a series of short calls that sound—to the person who named it, at least—like chipping. Along with its breeding habits, these sounds are described in many words and some graphs on this page from the Birds of North America. However, to hear a Chipping Sparrow, visit Patuxent Wildlife Research Center's page about the species (*second address*), and select Song. Backyard Birding has both photos and the sounds of the Chipping Sparrow, plus a bit of observation (*third address*).

http://www.birdsofna.org/excerpts/chip_sp.html

http://www.mbr-pwrc.usgs.gov/id/framlst/i5600id.html

http://www.slivoski.com/birding/chipspar.htm

Sparrow, Grasshopper

Grasshopper Sparrows (*Ammodramus savannarum*) don't look like grasshoppers or specialize in eating them. Instead, this species *sounds* like a grasshopper. To hear its extremely high-pitched song and learn something of its ways, visit the Patuxent Wildlife Research Center (*first address*). To learn a lot more about its distribution and management—a problem since it is a ground nester—visit the Birds of North America page concerning Grasshopper Sparrows (*second address*).

http://www.mbr-pwrc.usgs.gov/id/framlst/
i5460id.html

http://www.birdsofna.org/excerpts/grsparrow.html

Sparrow, House

The House Sparrow (*Passer domesticus*) is an introduced species, covered in another section (*see North American Birds, Exotics*).

Sparrow, Lincoln's

See Sparrow, Song, later in this section.

Sparrow, Savannah

See next entry.

Sparrow, Song

The Song Sparrow (*Melospiza melodia*) is one of our easiest birds to identify by song, but one of the trickier to tell by looks. It's easily confused with the Savannah (*Passerculus sandwichensis*) and the Lincoln's (*Melospiza lincolnii*) Sparrows. This article, reprinted from *A Bird's-Eye View*—a youth publication of the American Birding Association—offers tips on telling them apart, as well as information about where and how they live (*first address*). To hear two examples of the delightful spring song of the Song Sparrow, stop by the site of the New York State Bird Songs (*second address*).

http://www.americanbirding.org/bevfea2.htm

http://math.math.sunysb.edu/~tony/birds/
sparrows.html

Sparrow, White-throated

The White-throated Sparrow (*Zonotrichia albicollis*) is a fairly common ground-feeding species that summers in the East and Southeast and winters across Canada and the northern states, notes the Nutty Birdwatcher's profile (*first address*). They often show up in yards and snoop on the ground under feeders. They are easily identified by either the distinctive, namesake patch below their beaks or by their distinctive song, first heard in late winter or early spring. For several different samples, visit the site of the New York Bird Sounds (*second address*) where Webmaster Tony Phillips observes that their song is like the "opening chorus in *Judas Maccabeus*." What's more, he gives you a sound bite of the Handel oratorio, so you can compare it with the sparrow songs also available.

http://nuthatch.birdnature.com/whtthrt.html

http://math.math.sunysb.edu/~tony/birds/
sparrows.html

White-throated Sparrow (*Zonotrichia albicollis*) (JJA)

A B C D E F G H I J K L M N O P Q R S T U V W X Y Z

A
B
C
D
E
F
G
H
I
J
K
L
M
N
O
P
Q
R
S
T
U
V
W
X
Y
Z

Sparrows

Betty Anderson of the Alaskan Department of Fish & Game has written a concise but excellent summary of eight species of sparrows found in Alaska. Most of these range far beyond the state and can be found coast-to-coast in the United States and Canada. The species covered are Fox, White-crowned, Golden-crowned, Song, American tree, Chipping, Lincoln's, and Savannah Sparrows.

http://www.state.ak.us/local/akpages/FISH.GAME/
notebook/bird/sparrows.htm

Starling, European

The European starling is a nonnative species that's covered in another section (*see North American Birds, Exotics*).

Swallow, Barn

The common Barn Swallow (*Hirundo rustica*) is so called for its fondness for living in barns and other old buildings, which it enters through holes or broken windows, reports the Canadian Museum of Nature. When not in the barn, they spend most of their time airborne, catching insects on the wing. This site has a good illustration to accompany its Barn Swallow facts.

http://www.nature.ca/notebooks/english/bswallow.htm

Barn Swallow (*Hirundo erythrogaster*) [*Hirundo rustica*] (JJA)

Swallow, Violet-Green

The Violet-Green Swallow (*Tachycineta thalassina*) "is truly a stunningly beautiful bird, when viewed under appropriate lighting conditions," reports Nest-Cam, a website where, in season, you can view the raising of a family of these birds. Using an inside-the-nest camera, Erick and Jerry Woods of Sebastopol, California, show how these swallows care for their young. Violet-Green Swallows breed from Alaska and central Canada, south to the mountains of Mexico. This site has some natural history, as well as photos of the species—and an explanation of how you could create your own nest-watching camera setup.

http://www.sonic.net/~erickw/nestcam/
wwwnestcam.html

Swift, Black

The Black Swift (*Cypseloides niger*) is a mysterious bird that winters in Central America and the Caribbean, and summers in northwestern North America, particularly the cliffs of British Columbia and in western mountains. Not an awful lot is known about it, and much of what is known has been discovered in the 20th century. Unlike other North American swifts, it likes to nest near water—lively water, in fact, sometimes building behind mountain waterfalls and more commonly on steep cliffs over a seashore of surf, notes John Sterling of the Smithsonian Migratory Bird Center. Black Swifts feed on aerial insects and hunt in the rising air currents that sweep large numbers of insects into the sky, he says. "No one really knows how far these birds venture from their nests in search of food, but legend has it that it is hundreds of miles each day."

http://web2.si.edu/smbc/bom/blsw.htm

FEATHERED FACTS

Biblical Migrants

"Recorded observations of migration date back 3,000 years. In the Bible in Job (39:26), 'Doth the hawk fly by thy wisdom and stretch her wings toward the south?' And in Jeremiah (8:7), 'The stork in the heavens knoweth her appointed time; and the turtledove, and the crane, and the swallow, observe the time of their coming.'"

—Don Richardson, Birds and Migration, Why and How Do They Do It, About.com

http://birding.about.com/library/weekly/aa011599.htm

Tanager, Scarlet

Look! High up in the trees, a flash of scarlet and black—it can only be the Scarlet Tanager (*Piranga olivacea*), which has been called the "flame of spring." That's the male tanager, of course, putting on his seasonal show; in nonbreeding and immature birds, the coloration is far less eye-catching, very similar to the female's, with yellow underneath an olive back, gray wings and tail with greenish feather edges. The male's wings and tail tend to be darker on the 6¼-inch bird. The bill is pointed but strong. Tanagers are neotropical migrants and produce one clutch of eggs in a season, nesting high in the trees. They live in woodlands in the eastern United States, and their diet is mainly insects, with occasional fruit (mulberry, blackberry, or try orange halves). According to one observer, the tanager may eat as many as 2,100 gypsy moth caterpillars in an hour. A Canadian postage stamp website (*first address*) has not only a description of the Scarlet Tanager (which is pictured on a beautiful stamp from Canada), but also offers a collection of links to more tanager sites. Birds of Nova Scotia (*second address*) provides more information, observations, and a close-up photo. The Illinois Department of Natural

Resources (*third address*) gives a concise profile of the bird, and the Patuxent site (*fourth address*) has identification and range information, as well as a sample of its song.

http://206.47.102.70/usagers/marcelg/tanga_an.htm

http://www.ednet.ns.ca/educ/museum/mnh/nature/nsbirds/bns0349.htm

http://www.inhs.uiuc.edu/chf/pub/virtualbird/species/scarlet-tanager.html

http://www.mbr-pwrc.usgs.gov/id/framlst/i6080id.html

Tanager, Summer

Normally, everyone would cheer a bird whose diet is solely insects. And most of us will love the Summer Tanager—except beekeepers. For this tanager, also called the "beebird," loves to hang out around hives, eating the beekeeper's stock. But the Summer Tanager (*Piranga rubra*) also consumes a wide variety of other insects, including wasps, grasshoppers, weevils, and grubs, reports Tina Bentz of the Smithsonian Migratory Bird Center in the site's detailed profile. The bird will also eat many kinds of berries. Because this species builds its nests very high in tall trees, little is known of its family life. The Summer Tanager is widespread in the southeastern United States and is found rarely in New England and in southeastern Canada.

http://web2.si.edu/smbc/bom/suta.htm

Thrasher, Brown

The Brown Thrasher (*Toxostoma rufum*) is widespread across the northern United States and southern Canada in summer, and across the southern United States in winter. Closely related to the Catbird, the Brown Thrasher has varied melodies, reports the Nova Scotia Museum of Natural History. In fact, this page notes that "Thoreau heard its song coming from a perch nearby while he was planting his garden and remarked that it could be interpreted as *drop-it drop-it cover-it-up cover-it-up pull-it-up pull-it-up pull-it-up*."

http://www.ednet.ns.ca/educ/museum/mnh/nature/nsbirds/bns0295.htm

A B C D E F G H I J K L M **N** O P Q R S T U V W X Y Z

A
B
C
D
E
F
G
H
I
J
K
L
M
N
O
P
Q
R
S
T
U
V
W
X
Y
Z

Thrasher, California

The California Thrasher (*Toxostoma redivivum*) is aptly named, living as it does only along the California coast and in Baja California, and using a thrashing technique to forage for food in leaf litter. This is our largest thrasher and a song-filled one, reports the Birds of North America site, which devotes a sample page to its habits and habitat.

http://www.birdsofna.org/excerpts/cathrasher.html

Thrush, Hermit

Among the first of the spring migrants to arrive in our woodlands is the Hermit Thrush (*Catharus guttatus*). Kenn Kaufman of *Birder's World* (*first address*) uses text and his own excellent illustrations to demonstrate how to tell the Hermit Thrush from its cousins, the Wood Thrush, Swainson's Thrush, Veery, and Gray-cheeked Thrush. The song of the Hermit Thrush is one of the most beloved—and distinctive—of the spring woods. In fact, F. Schuyer Mathews, a naturalist at the turn of the 20th century, claimed that "The song of the Hermit Thrush is the grand climax of all bird music; it is unquestionably so far removed from all the rest of the wildwood singers' accomplishments that vaunted comparisons are invidious and wholly out of place." To enable you to hear what Matthews meant, Tony Phillips's New York Bird Songs website has three sound bites of the Hermit Thrush song and one of its "chipping."

http://www2.birdersworld.com/birders/fieldguide/
 hermitthrush/HermitThrush.html

http://math.math.sunysb.edu/~tony/birds/thrushes.html

Thrush, Swainson's

Swainson's Thrush (*Catharus ustulatus*), found in southern Canada and parts of the northern United States in summer, is almost as good a singer as its cousin, the Hermit Thrush. However, says this page on the Nova Scotia Museum of Natural History's site, "its song lacks that bird's clear, pure tones and might be described as being 'throaty' and hurried." There's a good profile of Swainson's Thrush here, including a picture (click it to enlarge it).

http://nature.ednet.ns.ca/nature/nsbirds/bns0288.htm

Thrush, Wood

"And where the shadows deepest fell, the Wood Thrush rang his silver bell," wrote Henry Wadsworth Longfellow. Indeed, many have said that the Wood Thrush's song is the most beautiful sound in the forests of North America. Lang Elliott's NatureSound Studio (*first address*) has a fine recording of the song, along with a spectacular close-up photo of a singing Wood Thrush (*Hylocichla mustelina*). Bravo on two counts! How does the bird do its song thing? Trust the Smithsonian Institution to provide the answer. "The legendary *ee-o-lay* song of the Wood Thrush is actually a one-bird duet," writes Mary Deinlein in this top-notch essay offered by the Smithsonian Migratory Bird Center's site (*second address*). "Because the Wood Thrush has the equivalent of two sets of 'vocal cords,' it is able to sing two overlapping songs at once." This site provides a great deal of natural history on the Wood Thrush. Many findings of ornithological research regarding the vocalizations of Wood Thrushes can be found on an excerpt from the Birds of North America, which also includes information about its feeding habits (*third address*).

http://www.naturesound.com/birds/pages/woody.html

http://web2.si.edu/smbc/bom/woth.htm

http://www.birdsofna.org/excerpts/wthrush.html

Wood Thrush (*Hylocichla mustelina*) (JJA)

Thrushes

The Birds in Forested Landscapes survey at Cornell Laboratory of Ornithology has comprehensive, well-illustrated profiles of seven thrushes: Gray-cheeked, Bicknell's, Swainson's, Hermit, Wood, and Varied Thrush, plus the Veery.

http://birds.cornell.edu/bfl/

Titmouse, Tufted

One of the most familiar and popular bird feeder birds in the East is the Tufted Titmouse (*Parus bicolor*), which feeds on both seeds and suet and, according to Peterson Online (*first site*), is expanding its range in the north. The bird is among the friendliest and can also be taught to eat seeds from the human hand. They are

Tufted Titmouse (*Baeolophus bicolor*) [*Parus bicolor*] (JJA)

related to chickadees, with whom they are often seen. Many bird-watchers are surprised at the wide range of songs that titmice have; just when you think you've heard them all, a mysterious new one is heard, and you wonder what bird that might be. To hear a sampling of some of the more common songs, visit the New York Bird Songs site (*second address*). BirdSource at Cornell University's Laboratory of Ornithology has a page on the Tufted Titmouse that includes an animated map that shows in decade increments how the bird has expanded its range, beginning in 1901, through 1969 (*third address; be patient while the animated map downloads*).

**http://www.petersononline.com/birds/month/titu/
index.html**

http://math.math.sunysb.edu/~tony/birds/titmice.html

**http://birdsource2.ornith.cornell.edu/pfw/birdid/tuti/
index.html**

Towhee, Spotted

Some birds seem to be very variable. Take the Spotted Towhee (*Pipilo maculatus*), for instance. Ornithologists have identified at least nine subspecies of this handsome bird of the American West. This page from the Birds of North America site describes the geographic variations in this species. It's a lesson in how ornithologists study the differences in a single species of a bird.

http://www.birdsofna.org/excerpts/stowhee.html

MEET THE MASTERS

She Mines the Web

About.com is one of the world's top websites for information about almost any kind of activity and interest, including birds. In early 1999, *Yahoo! Internet Life* magazine ranked About.com (then called the Mining Co.) as one of the top five most visited news/information/entertainment sites on the World Wide Web. Its key to success is that it hires people with expertise in each area to run the many sites. These guides "mine" the Web for links to top quality information. A very successful case in point is Christine Tarski, who lives outside Dallas, Texas, with her husband and daughter, and who has been the guide for About.com's birding site <http://birding.about.com> since April 1997. "I have been birding for over 15 years and have never stopped learning about the birds of the world," says Christine, who lives in an area rich in species. "I am fortunate to be in one of the migration flyways," she says. "I also have relatives on the Texas coast where so many birds winter."

A
B
C
D
E
F
G
H
I
J
K
L
M
N
O
P
Q
R
S
T
U
V
W
X
Y
Z

Sidebar vertical alphabet: A B C D E F G H I J K L M N O P Q R S T U V W X Y Z

Veery

The Veery (*Catharus fuscescens*) has one of the most unusual, almost haunting songs, a set of descending notes that sound as if they were coming from the far end of a big, long culvert pipe. Tony Phillips has a fine recording of a Veery on his Bird Songs website (*first address*). He notes that in 1901, Bradford Torrey wrote a book called *Footing It in Franconia*, in which Torrey says: "The surpassing glory of the veery's song . . . lies in its harmonic, double-stopping effect—an effect, or quality, as beautiful as it is peculiar. One day, while I stood listening to it under the best of conditions, admiring the wonderful arpeggio (I know no less technical word for it), my pencil suddenly grew poetic. 'The veery's fingers are quick on the harp-strings,' it wrote." The Nova Scotia Museum of Natural History website (*second address*) calls the Veery "one of our best woodland songsters" and adds that this thrush is one of the last birds to stop singing in the evening. The bird winters in South America and breeds coast-to-coast in North America in a band that roughly follows the United States–Canada border. For another good recording, visit Greg Kunkel's Bird Songs site (*third address*).

http://math.math.sunysb.edu/~tony/birds/thrushes.html

http://nature.ednet.ns.ca/nature/nsbirds/bns0286.htm

http://ourworld.compuserve.com/homepages/G_Kunkel/
    veery.wav

Vireo, White-eyed

"A secretive and modest bird, the White-eyed Vireo (*Vireo griseus*) has many fascinating aspects of its behavior," reports Russ Greenberg of the Smithsonian Migratory Bird Center. For instance, the bird is an excellent mimic of other bird calls and songs. "Exactly why it does this remains a controversial topic and an ornithological mystery," Greenberg says. Found from the eastern United States down to and into Mexico, they migrate south from northern parts of the summer territory and are year-round in many southern portions. It is a bird of dry forests, even in Central America, Greenberg says in this excellent profile, and it has a close connection with the Gumbo Limbo tree whose fruits it eats and, through regurgitation, whose seeds it plants.

http://web2.si.edu/smbc/bom/wevi.htm

White-eyed Vireo (*Vireo griseus*) (JJA)

FEATHERED FACTS

Three Kinds of Flight

There are three types of flight among wild creatures: active, soaring, and passive. Birds use two of the three. Active flight consists of sustained powered flight, gained by actively flapping wings constantly or almost constantly. Soaring is a form of active flight, with sustained flight gained by riding rising columns of air called thermals. Passive flight is not sustained flight, but could be referred to as controlled falling or gliding. Modern examples of active flight would include backyard birds like Blue Jays or chickadees; soaring would include Turkey Vultures; and passive would include flying squirrels and flying lizards.

—adapted from Hooper Virtual Museum of Natural History

http://www.wf.carleton.ca/Museum/ptero/flight1.htm

Warbler, Bay-breasted

The Bay-breasted Warbler (*Dendroica castanea*) is one of our larger warblers and appears as early as April in the eastern United States, reports the Nutty Bird-watcher.

http://nuthatch.birdnature.com/baywar.html

Warbler, Blackburnian

The Blackburnian Warbler (*Dendroica fusca*), which breeds in the north spruce woods of Canada and the northeastern United States, can also be found in the higher elevations of the Appalachians all the way to Georgia. Because it nests so high in the treetops, little is known of its breeding ecology, notes Lisa Petit of the Smithsonian Migratory Bird Center. The best time to see them is while they are migrating and sometimes foraging lower in the trees. Petit notes that although populations have been stable for the last 30 years, rapid deforestation in their Andean wintering grounds may threaten future numbers.

http://web2.si.edu/smbc/bom/blwa.htm

FEATHERED FACTS

Year-Round Feeding

"If you enjoy feeding birds, there is no reason to stop (in summer). You can do it year-round. Feeding the birds throughout the summer will not make them 'lazy' or 'dependent.' If you keep your feeding station clean, there's no reason for you to stop feeding suet, sunflower, millet, fruit and nectar."

—Baltimore Bird Club

http://www.bcpl.net/~tross/by/feed.html#3

Warbler, Blackpoll

The Blackpoll Warbler (*Dendroica striata*), a black-and-white-striped species, migrates from the jungles of South America as far north as Alaska and across Arctic Canada to the North Atlantic. The Nutty Birdwatcher observes that it covers 30 to 35 miles a day—quite a journey for little fellows only five inches long. They provide plenty of opportunities for sighting in spring as they pass through the States and lower provinces.

http://nuthatch.birdnature.com/blackpoll.html

Warbler, Cape May

The Cape May Warbler (*Dendroica tigrina*), so-called because it was first identified at Cape May, New Jersey, in 1811, is a handsome yellow, chestnut, and black species that winters in the West Indies and the very southern tip of Florida, and breeds in southeastern Canada and the very northern parts of the United States west to Minnesota. The Birds of North America site has detailed information about its migratory and breeding habits, including a nice photo of the bird and an excellent illustration of how it locates its nests near the tops of evergreen trees (*first address*). Although these warblers are primarily insect eaters when they are in our neck of the woods, they are nectar-drinkers when in their winter ranges and can be commonly found in shade-coffee plantations and gardens, using their narrow bills and long, tubular tongues to sneak sips of the sweet liquid, reports Russ Greenberg of the Smithsonian Migratory Bird Center in his interesting profile (*second address*). The Nutty Birdwatcher relates a visit by many Cape May Warblers in mid-May in her backyard and offers some excellent photographs of these birds in her evergreens, as well as a good summary of information about the species (*third address*).

http://www.birdsofna.org/excerpts/capemay.html
http://web2.si.edu/smbc/bom/cmwa.htm
http://nuthatch.birdnature.com/capemay.html

A
B
C
D
E
F
G
H
I
J
K
L
M
N
O
P
Q
R
S
T
U
V
W
X
Y
Z

FEATHERED FACTS

Where There's Food, There's Family

When there's an outbreak of budworms in southern Canada, the Cape May Warbler may lay up to nine eggs in its nests. In normal seasons, these warblers lay an average of five or six eggs.

—adapted from *Birds of North America*

http://www.birdsofna.org/excerpts/capemay.html

Warbler, Connecticut

The only time the Connecticut Warbler (*Oporornis agilis*) is actually in Connecticut is on brief fall stop-overs along its migration route, notes the Nutty Bird-watcher. In its spring migration from South America, these birds head up the Mississippi Valley to their nesting areas in the north-central states and Canada, whereas on their return run, the Connecticut Warblers take a more easterly route. Also called a Swamp War-bler, it prefers to forage for insects on the ground and in relatively low vegetation, unlike many of the loftier warblers.

http://nuthatch.birdnature.com/conwarbler.html

Warbler, Golden-cheeked

The Golden-cheeked Warbler (*Dendroica chrysoparia*) is one of the North American summer songbirds being threatened by habitat destruction and fragmentation in its wintering grounds in Central American rainforests, reports Bagheera, a natural history education website. The bird breeds in Texas, but its numbers have declined from as many as 17,000 birds in 1974 to as low as 2,200 birds in 1990. It is officially listed as endangered.

http://www.bagheera.com/inthewild/
van_anim_warbler.htm

Warbler, Kirtland's

The Kirtland's Warbler (*Dendroica kirtlandii*), one of North America's rarest nesting birds, is making a come-back. The bird, which winters in the Bahamas, nests on the ground in northern Michigan in stands of jack pines, which is a low pine with branches that extend to the ground. "Historically, these stands of young jack pine were maintained by naturally occurring wildfires that frequently swept through northern Michigan," says the Michigan Department of Natural Resources. "Fire suppression programs altered this natural process, reducing Kirtland's Warbler habitat." In addi-tion, the expansion of the range of the brown-headed cowbird has resulted in the loss of some nests—cow-birds plant their own eggs in the nests of others. Only the Kirtland's males sing, and since they can be heard a long way, their song is often used as a counting method to avoid humans' coming too close to the nests. In 1974 and again in 1987, censuses found only 167 singing males in northern Michigan. Efforts were made to plant more jack pines and otherwise help the Kirtland's War-bler, and as a result, 766 were counted in 1995 and 805 in 1998, the highest recorded number since the censuses started in 1951. To learn more about the Kirtland's War-bler, and about a festival that celebrates the species, visit this page on the Kirtland Community College website (*first address*). The Canadian Museum of Nature (*second address*) says "the nesting conditions required by the Kirtland's Warbler appear about ten years after a forest fire and remain for only a few years, until the new trees shade out the undergrowth."

http://www.kirtland.cc.mi.us/~warbler/warb.html
http://www.nature.ca/notebooks/english/kirtwarb.htm

Warbler, Myrtle

The Myrtle Warbler (*Dendroica coronata coronata*) is actually the eastern race of the Yellow-rumped Warbler, report Garrett Lowe and Russ Greenberg of the Smithsonian Migratory Bird Center. Many remain in North America year-round and are found wherever the wax myrtles and bayberries of the genus *Myrica* live; it's the fatty berries of these shrubs that provide the food that keeps them going, even in the cold. They are not particularly shy warblers, either, and are among the easiest to spot. This page will tell you a great deal about this "different" warbler.

http://web2.si.edu/smbc/bom/yrwa.htm

Warbler, Nashville

How many naturalists have joked about the Nashville Warbler's country music? The fact is that *Vermivora ruficapilla* is so called because it was first identified near Nashville, Tennessee. What's more, it must have been just passing through because its breeding range is far to the north, and it winters in Mexico. But Nashville it is. And you can learn about its migratory and breeding habits in this excerpt from the Birds of North America site.

http://www.birdsofna.org/excerpts/nashwarb.html

Nashville Warbler (*Vermivora ruficapilla*) (JJA)

Warbler, Prothonotary

If ever a bird had a name that has confused and tongue-tied its admirers, it's the Prothonotary Warbler (*Protonotaria citrea*). Lisa Petit of the Smithsonian Migratory Bird Center explains the name origin, as well as the life history of this popular warbler of the southeastern and central United States. It seems, she says, the name was devised by Louisiana Creoles who thought its yellow and black plumage looked like the vestments of a *protonotarius*, a Catholic Church official who advised the Pope. Petit offers a thorough profile of this offbeat warbler, the only eastern species that nests in cavities, and one that may have helped create a President of the United States. How? Read her fascinating essay.

http://web2.si.edu/smbc/bom/ptwa.htm

Warbler, Red-faced

Many's the serious birder who has traveled to Arizona to spot the Red-faced Warbler (*Cardellina rubrifrons*), which can be found in the mountains of the Southwest. "This bird and the Painted Redstart, both Mexican border specialties, are our only warblers that wear bright red," notes Peterson Online, which provides a Roger Tory Peterson illustration that shows you why this beautiful bird is so sought-after. (Perhaps all that attention has embarrassed it into being red-faced?)

http://www.petersononline.com/birds/month/rfwa/ index.html

FEATHERED FACTS

Poor Singer

Though it can only croak, the Common Raven is considered North America's largest songbird—that is, member of the passerine family. Ravens can be up to 27 inches long.

—adapted from Peterson Online Fun Facts

http://www.petersononline.com

A
B
C
D
E
F
G
H
I
J
K
L
M
N
O
P
Q
R
S
T
U
V
W
X
Y
Z

FEATHERED FACTS

Non-Worm-Eating Warbler

The Worm-eating Warbler is so called three times: There's its English name, plus its scientific name, *Helmitheros vermivorus*, which are Greek and Latin words, both meaning *worm-eating*. Oddly enough, however, this warbler doesn't eat worms, and why the bird is so named is unclear. Perhaps it's because the Wormer— like most other warblers—likes caterpillars, which are colloquially called *worms*.

> —adapted from Russell Greenberg, Smithsonian Migratory Bird Center

http://web2.si.edu/smbc/bom/wewa.htm

Warbler, Worm-eating

Russell Greenberg studies Worm-eating Warblers (*Helmitheros vermivorus*) on two continents. In the winter, he wanders the tropical forests of Belize, observing this shy bird. In the summer, he may watch the chestnut oak foliage in New Jersey and other parts of the Northeast. What he's found from his years of study of this bird is described on the Smithsonian Migratory Bird Center site. One of the most fascinating aspects of the Worm-eating Warbler—which doesn't, by the way, eat worms—is its specialized source of food, especially in the tropics: it forages in aerial leaf litter. This "consists of leaves that are caught in the vegetation as they fall from the canopy, sewn to branches by fungal mycelium, and become home to large tropical spiders and insects," Greenberg explains. "These arthropods are protected from most birds. But a few, including our hero—by hanging on the leaf, inserting their bill into the leaf tube, and slowly opening their mandibles— can capture many of the juicy items within." One of the centers for North American research of the Worm-eating Warbler is Devil's Den, a 1,700-acre refuge in

central Fairfield County, Connecticut, operated by the Nature Conservancy (*second address*).

http://web2.si.edu/smbc/bom/wewa.htm
http://www.tnc.org/infield/preserve/devil/devil.htm

Warblers

Warbler Watch at the Cornell University Laboratory of Ornithology combines the observations of ordinary bird-watchers across North America with the state-of-the-art technology of BirdSource to track the migratory movements and breeding distribution of North America's warblers. "Some of these colorful songbirds are experiencing population declines," notes Warbler Watch. Your reports help scientists at Cornell determine just how much populations may be changing— and where. Online maps connected to the Warbler Watch database show you where different species are being reported and in what numbers. To participate in Warbler Watch, fill out an on-site survey. Complete instructions accompany the form.

http://birdsource.cornell.edu/warblers/

Swainson's Warbler (*Lymnothlypsis swainsoni*) (JJA)

Waxwing, Cedar

The arrival of a flock of Cedar Waxwings (*Bombycilla cedrorum*) is always an exciting event. These wanderers—some call them vagabonds or gypsies—will descend on a fruit tree in season and merrily consume the goodies till none is left. One interesting habit they have is passing food along a line of waxwings to the birds at the end, a very unusual phenomenon to witness. The Nutty Birdwatcher has a nice page about Cedar Waxwings (*first address*). These wanderers are such voracious eaters of small fruits that farmers once got the Vermont House to pass a bill allowing the birds to be shot, reports Robert Rice of the Smithsonian Migratory Bird Center (*second address*). However, the Vermont Senate rejected the bill and waxwings are still safe in Vermont. Rice describes the bird as looking a bit like a military officer. "Like a centurion standing guard, the cedar waxwing strikes a commanding pose with its natty garb and erect profile," he says. His excellent profile of the Cedar Waxwing includes the latest scientific thinking about the source of the bird's unusual name. *Bombycilla* comes from *Bombux* or *bombukos*, the Greek root for *silk*. The *cilla* is from Latin, and mistakenly was used to mean *tail*. "So the cedar

waxwing is the 'silky tail of the cedar,'" he says. But why is it a *waxwing*? Read his profile to find out.

http://nuthatch.birdnature.com/waxwing.html
http://web2.si.edu/smbc/bom/cewa.htm

Wood-Pewee, Eastern

A member of the flycatcher family, the Eastern Wood-Pewee (*Contopus virens*) is one of the last Central and South American migrants to arrive in the North American woods, reports Tina Bentz of the Smithsonian Migratory Bird Center. From then well into August—long after most birds have stopped singing—this wood-peewee will sing its namesake song, a *pee-ah-wee*. Bentz describes the techniques this bird uses to catch insects and how it raises a family. She points out that although the bird is still considered common, its numbers have dropped about 35 percent between 1966 and 1991, according to the Breeding Bird Survey.

http://web2.si.edu/smbc/bom/ewpe.htm

Woodpecker, Downy

"The Downy Woodpecker (*Picoides pubescens*) may be the most familiar woodpecker in North America," says the Chipper Woods Bird Observatory, which provides very close-up photos of the Downy, along with information about its habits and habitats.

http://www.wbu.com/chipperwoods/photos/downy.htm

Woodpecker, Hairy or Downy?

Telling a Hairy Woodpecker from a Downy is one of the chief challenges of many a beginning—and not so beginning—bird-watcher. They have virtually the same design. But Eirik A. T. Blom, one of the contributing editors to *Bird Watcher's Digest*, passes on the tricks for telling the two apart in this article from the magazine. Julie Zickefoose, whose art often enlivens the pages of *Bird Watcher's Digest*, provides the illustration.

http://birdwatchersdigest.com/bbn/articles/bbn98/
earlywinter98/earlywinter98.html

MEET THE MASTERS

The Beauty of Birds

Julia Pahountis started the Nutty Birdwatcher **<http://www.birdnature.com>** because she felt that the Web needed a site that covered some of the aspects of birds and birding that veteran ones didn't. "My goal for the website is educational," she reports. "I want people—especially the younger generations—to have an appreciation of the beauty and importance of birds. I wanted a website that would help children and adults alike to identify and learn about birds and give them an idea of when they can find migrating birds in their area (*see Bird Migration Tables, page 142*) and to also provide a birding site that is nice to look at, with pictures and graphics for the children."

A B C D E F G H I J K L M N O P Q R S T U V W X Y Z

Woodpecker, Ivory-billed

See North American Birds, Extinct, section.

Woodpecker, Pileated

The Pileated Woodpecker (*Dryocopus pileatus*) is, by far, North America's largest woodpecker and is always an eye-stopper when spotted. Many details about its habitat and breeding range are found in a selection from the Birds of North America site (*first address*). Marcel Granger's Canadian birds website has a concise description of the Pileated, plus links to other sources that focus on the species (*second address*). The Wild Birds Unlimited headquarters website has a video camera that monitors its feeders. Unlike most of us with suet feeders, WBU has managed to attract a Pileated Woodpecker to its feeder and has many pictures to prove it (*third address*). Ecologists consider the Pileated Woodpecker an important indicator species in determining the health of a forest, reports Walter McKee Shriner, an assistant professor of biology at Denison University, who offers a fine profile of the bird (*fourth address*). Incidentally, there are two schools of thought on the pronunciation of *pileated*: In the East, it's usually *pill-e-ated*, whereas in the West, it's often *pile-ated*. Take your pick.

http://www.birdsofna.org/excerpts/pileated.html

http://206.47.102.70/Usagers/marcelg/granp_an.htm

http://www.wbu.com/pics/pileatedwbu.htm

http://www.denison.edu/~shriner/Bio355/
Pileatedwp.html

Pileated Woodpecker (*Ceophiloes pileatus*) [*Dryocopus pileatus*] (JJA)

Woodpecker, Red-cockaded

The Red-cockaded Woodpecker (*Picoides borealis*), a bird that's on the endangered species list, is resident of open pine woodlands in the South and is found only in local pockets today. According to the U.S. Fish & Wildlife Service (*first address*), "it is estimated that there are about 4,500 family units (groups) of Red-cockaded woodpeckers, or 10,000 to 14,000 birds, living in clusters (groups of cavity trees) from Florida to Virginia and west to southeast Oklahoma and eastern Texas, representing about one percent of the woodpecker's original range." The important role this bird performs in the life of southern pine forests is described in considerable detail on this excellent page. One of the centers of research into the protection of the bird is the Noxubee National Wildlife Refuge in northeastern Mississippi (*second address*), where researchers are using various techniques to help the species survive. Among them are *snets*, specialized nets to keep Gray Rat Snakes from attacking the nests and artificial inserts in pine trees that imitate a hole that might be found in a rotting dead tree (in many places, not enough old, holey trees are available for the birds). You can also find out why the bird is endangered (*third address*).

http://www.fws.gov/r9extaff/biologues/bio_rcw.html

http://www2.msstate.edu/~goodman/noxubee.html

http://www2.msstate.edu/~goodman/rcw.html

Woodpecker, Red-headed

The numbers of Red-headed Woodpeckers (*Melanerpes erythrocephalus*) have, according to Peterson Online, been decreasing for years. The reason is not certain, though some believe it's because too many dead trees—which make excellent homes for cavity nesters like woodpeckers—are being felled in the woods. Others suspect that the European Starling (*see also North American Birds, Exotics*) are stealing their nesting sites. Widespread east of the Rockies in the United States, the Red-headed Woodpecker is, oddly enough, a rarity in New England, though it ranges both to colder and warmer locales.

http://www.petersononline.com/birds/month/rhwo/
index.html

Woodpeckers

Anthony Galván III shows his collection of photos of different species of woodpeckers from across the United States. Included are the Acorn, Downy, and Pileated Woodpeckers, and the Red-shafted Flicker.

http://www.dosgatos.com/birds/woodpeckers/
woodpeckers.html

Wren, Carolina

For a small bird, the Carolina Wren (*Thryothorus ludovicianus*) packs a loud voice, especially when singing the *tea kettle, tea kettle* familiar in the eastern part of the United States and Canada. Like other wrens, these birds are cavity nesters, although they will occasionally move into a garage and set up house behind some paint cans. A reddish-brown bird with a long, down-curved billed and white eye stripe, the Carolina Wren carries its tail in the jaunty manner of many other wrens, which is to say, turned up. The Chipper Woods site (*first address*) has excellent photos and natural history information about this bird, which seems to have a more socially acceptable lifestyle than the House Wren—it mates for life and eats mostly insects and seeds and is not as aggressive as the House Wren (*see next entry*). "Infamous for nesting in mason jars, dryer vents, and sometimes clothing left too long on an outside line, the Carolina Wren also shares a place beside the chickadees as a bird busybody," writes Jeff Crooke in the charming Birds of the Blue Ridge site (*second address*). To hear the song of the Carolina Wren, visit the New York Bird Songs page on wrens (*third address*).

http://www.wbu.com/chipperwoods/photos/
carowren.htm#top
http://rtonline1.roanoke.com/wingingit/cwren.html
http://math.math.sunysb.edu/~tony/birds/wrens.html

Wren, House

The House Wren is a dainty little brown bird whose Latin name, *Troglodytes aedon*, refers to its nesting habits in hollow trees or walls, usually low to the ground. This wren can be distinguished from the Winter Wren by its longer tail and heavier beak. Its wings and long tail are banded, its underparts are buff-brown, and there's a very thin yellowish-gray line from the upper beak to over the eye. Good close-ups of a House Wren at its house can be seen at the Nutty Birdwatcher site (*first address*) along with details about habitat and nesting. A fascinating account of one birder's study of the house wren, and her surprising conclusions about a bird she had nurtured, is found at the second address. Althea R. Sherman wrote a paper presented to the Iowa Ornithological Union in 1924, causing an uproar as defenders of the little birds were distressed by her conclusions. She observed that the house wren is responsible for destroying many nests of other species, damaging eggs, and driving out other birds. Wrote Sherman in 1925, "There is only one sin that causes constant mourning in sackcloth and ashes, that causes me to lie awake nights visioning the future condition of our country with its bird population consisting mainly of those undesirable aliens, the Starling, the English [House] Sparrow, together with the Grackles and the House Wrens: that sin was the putting up of bird houses and allowing them to be occupied by House Wrens." The Great Wren Debate was posted by Barbara Boyle of the Johnson County (Iowa) Songbird Project.

http://nuthatch.birdnature.com/housewren.html
http://users.aol.com/jimmcl/bbbox/wren.htm

Wren, Marsh

"Sputtering and stuttering from the cattails, Marsh Wrens play hide-and-seek with birders in marshes from coast to coast," observes Kenn Kaufman, artist and writer. In this profile for *Birder's World*, Kaufman explains how to tell the Marsh Wren (*Cistothorus palustris*) from its less common neighbor, the Sedge Wren (*Cistothorus platensis*).

http://www2.birdersworld.com/birders/fieldguide/
marshwren/MarshWren.html

Long-billed Marsh Wren (JJA)

WEB WORDS

The War on Puss

"The antipathy which the House Wren shows to cats is extreme. Although it does not attack puss, it follows and scolds her until she is out of sight. In the same manner, it makes war on the Martin, the Blue Bird and the House Swallow, the nest of any of which it does not scruple to appropriate to itself, whenever occasion offers."

—John J. Audubon, *Birds of America*

http://employeeweb.myxa.com/rrb/Audubon/VolII/00208.html

Wren, Winter

"Few sounds bring as much joy to my heart as the song of the Winter Wren, with its exuberant, cascading warble ringing out in the springtime forest," writes Christopher Majka in this essay originally published in the *New Brunswick Naturalist* in 1992 (*first address*). The Winter Wren (*Troglodytes troglodytes*) is among the nearly 60 species of wrens found worldwide, but this one is unusual in that it circumnavigates the Northern Hemisphere, singing its joyful song across North America, Siberia, northern Europe, and even into northern Africa. Majka describes studies of variations in the Winter Wren's beautiful songs throughout these regions, sounds that one researcher called "the pinnacle of singing complexity." Professor Gerry Rising, a columnist for the *Buffalo* (New York) *News*, says "The song is impossible to describe. To say that it is a long series of unexpectedly loud warbles and tinkles and trills, its notes higher than the highest on a piano, is like describing the painting of an old master by naming its colors." He devotes a whole column to the lusty song of this tiny bird (*second address*). If you want to hear it yourself, visit the New York Bird Songs website (*third address*) where Tony Phillips offers two splendid recordings of the Winter Wren

and passes on the 1901 observation of Bradford Torrey: "A jolly songster he is, with the clearest and finest of tones—a true fife—and an irresistible accent and rhythm." *Birder's World* magazine offers an excellent feature on the Winter Wren, written and illustrated by Kenn Kaufman (*fourth address*).

http://www.chebucto.ns.ca/Environment/NHR/wren.html

http://www.acsu.buffalo.edu/~insrisg/nature/nw98/winter_wren.html

http://math.math.sunysb.edu/~tony/birds/wrens.html

http://www2.birdersworld.com/birders/fieldguide/winterwren/winterwren.html

EXOTICS

This subsection covers some of the more unusual and some of the most common birds that appear in North America. You might call it a collection of birds who are where they weren't. They may be *escapes*—like the Monk Parakeet—that are settling in, or escapes that are very local, such as geese or ducks that hobbyists collect for their ponds and that show up in your yard. They may have been deliberately imported and "planted" in the wild as a bird to hunt; this is especially true of fowl-like species. They may also have found their way here on their own, such as the Cattle Egret, a native of Africa.

Canadian Ratite Home Page

Ratite?, you ask. Not your everyday word in North America. That's probably because ratites are not your everyday bird in North America—as natives, at least. Ratites are flightless birds that include ostriches, cassowaries, rheas, and emus. Most are found in Australia or Africa. But members of some species—particularly Ostriches—are becoming livestock. Ostrich steaks, Ostrich sausage, and Ostrich leather are increasingly common products on the North American market. This website is full of bibliographic information about ratites, as well as ratite information sources. So just in case one escapes from an area farm and comes trotting down your road, here's a source of information.

http://duke.usask.ca/~ladd/ratalt.htm

FEATHERED FACTS

Seasonal Birding Malady

Searching for arriving warblers high in the trees is an annual spring treat for many birders. But sighting these quick, little birds in the treetops is a challenge that often results in a malady birders called *warbler neck*.

—adapted from Lisa Petit, Smithsonian Migratory Bird Center

http://web2.si.edu/smbc/bom/blwa.htm

Dove, Rock (Pigeon)

The Rock Dove (*Columba livia*), another European import, is one of the most widely known and least loved birds in North America. In fact, many people out-and-out hate them for the messes they make. But they have a fascinating history, told on the Birds of the Rocky Mountains site (*first address*). But even more interesting, to scientists at least, is why pigeons come in so many colors. And you can help study this phenomenon by joining Project Pigeon Watch at the Cornell Laboratory of Ornithology (*second address*). You get a special kit and quarterly newsletters to help you contribute valuable data.

http://www.lonepinepublishing.com/birdsite/brdpgs/
   3131.htm
http://birdsource.cornell.edu/ppw/

Wood Duck (Dover)

Ducks of the World

The University of Tennessee at Martin has a nice collection of pictures of different species of ducks. Many may appear in North America because of importation as pets or pond decorations. If you run across a species that doesn't seem to match anything in your field guides, check here.

http://www.utm.edu/departments/ed/cece/ducks.shtml

Egret, Cattle

The elegant Cattle Egret (*Bubulcus ibis*) is rather unusual among the exotic birds that have arrived in North America: It was not introduced but apparently traveled on its own from its native Africa. In fact, the bird is spreading around the world on its own, according to Jan H. Ribot's Birds of Suriname site (*first address*). The first sighting in the New World occurred in 1880 in West Suriname in northern South America. "They must have flown from Africa over the Atlantic," says Ribot. "From 1930 on they began with a fast advance over South and North America, from the tropics to Argentina and Canada. On some places they outnumber the native herons." According to a Common Birds of Louisiana page (*second address, following the description of Brown Pelican*), the Cattle Egret first showed up in North America in 1922 when it was spotted in Florida. Today the handsome birds are widespread along coastlines and are becoming more established in inland locations. They are often seen in fields with cattle, feeding on the insects the livestock stir up. On Eldon R. Caldwell's Birds of the Imperial Valley page about the Cattle Egret in California (*third address*), you'll learn about an unusual—and beneficial—effect the species may have had on the environment of the Imperial Valley. All these pages provide pictures of the bird.

http://www.tem.nhl.nl/~ribot/english/egib_ng.htm
http://www.lapage.com/birds/birds1.htm
http://www.imperial.cc.ca.us/birds/c-egret.htm

A B C D E F G H I J K L M N O P Q R S T U V W X Y Z

FEATHERED FACTS

Feather Slaughter

In one year alone in the late 1800s, more than 130,000 Snowy Egrets were killed, mostly in Florida, to supply feathers for women's hats.

—adapted from Florida Audubon

http://www.audubon.usf.edu/whoweare.htm

Finch, House

Whereas most North American human settlers moved from east to west, the House Finch (*Carpodacus mexicanus*) moved west to east—with human help. Also called a *Linnet*, this bird from the western states and Mexico was being illegally sold in New York City pet shops until 1940, when dealers, fearing they might be prosecuted for selling native wild birds, set many free, explains the Chipper Woods Bird Observatory (*first address*). By 1943, the birds were breeding around New York and by 1971, were found from New England to North Carolina and were working their way westward, where they'd presumably meet their ancestors. To see where they are today, visit the Patuxent's page (*second address*), which has distribution maps, as well as the bird's life history, photos, songs, and links. One man's close relationship with a House Finch is described by Jim Cook in his account Beakmin's Story (*third address*). In 1994, Cook noticed a sick House Finch. "I first spotted her through the window, the swelling of both her eyes was clearly visible even from 15 feet away, just one of dozens of finches so afflicted I had seen by then. She had been sitting at the bird bath for some time, unwilling or unable to move." Jim captured the bird, which he named Beakmin and discovered that it had not only conjunctivitis that strikes House Finches but also a broken beak. This is the story of the bird's treatment and recovery—and of

much more that followed. Finally, a fine profile of the House Finch is at Bull's Birds of New York State site (*fourth address*).

http://www.wbu.com/chipperwoods/photos/ housefinch.htm

http://www.mbr.nbs.gov/id/mlist/h5190.html

http://members.aol.com/FinchMG/Beakmin.htm

http://birds.cornell.edu/fnysbc/bullhofi.htm

Florida Exotics

"Exotic: for many the word evokes images of rare beauty, perhaps mysterious and from yet unseen places," says Debbie Schwartz on this page on the Debzone, her Florida birding website. "When applied to conservation issues, it paints quite a different picture, describing species which compete for food, water and habitat to the detriment of native flora and fauna." Florida, and especially the southern part of the state, is particularly susceptible to the arrival of exotic species. Some are released by owners, a few have flown in from elsewhere (*see Egret, Cattle, earlier in this section*), and some even escape from zoos (for instance, during Hurricane Andrew of August 1992). This page has links to much information about exotics—not only birds, but also plants and other forms of wildlife.

http://host.fptoday.com/debzone/exotics/exotics.htm

FOR THE BIRDS

Has that Site Flown the Coop?

If you come across an address in the book that no longer works, please tell us about it. We'll investigate to see if the site has moved or a page name has changed. If we find a new address, we'll post it at <http://www. acorn-online.com/hedge/birdup.htm>. But we'll also e-mail you directly with the new information as our way of saying thanks for letting us know about a dead link.

Parakeet, Monk

During the last half of the 20th century, the noisy but beautiful Monk Parakeet (*Myiopsitta monachus*) has settled into pockets of North America, far from its native Argentina. Probably all escaped in one way or another. The Birds of North America site (*first address*) says that from 1968 to 1972, 64,225 Monk Parakeets were imported to the United States. Some owners, perhaps tiring of the loud and, frankly, unattractive noise they make, let them loose. Other parakeets reportedly escaped from damaged shipping crates—parakeets in Connecticut, it's believed, got free after a truck carrying them was in an accident near Bridge-port. Some zoos deliberately set them free. These siz-able green birds build huge, *colonial nests* of sticks. In colder areas, such as Connecticut and Rhode Island, these colonies invariably live near the sea, where the weather is more moderate than inland. An in-depth look at the phenomenon of the Monk Parakeet in coastal Connecticut was written in the mid-1990s by Linda Pearson and Alison Olivieri and appeared in *Bird Watcher's Digest*. The Connecticut Audubon Soci-ety republishes it here (*second address*). The Travis Audubon Society in Austin, Texas (*third address, under the heading Observations*), has a series of articles on the Monk Parakeet and the techniques it uses to survive in Texas.

http://www.birdsofna.org/excerpts/monk.html

http://www.ctaudubon.org/Nature/parowl.htm

http://www.onr.com/user/audubon/Backyard/
bkydintr.htm

Partridge, Chukar

The Chukar Patridge, or just plain Chukar (*Alectoris chukar*), is "one of the most commonly kept and bred of all game birds," reports Dan Cowell (*first address*). "There are some game bird farms in North America that produce thousands of Chukars each year for hunting reserves and release." A native of Europe and Asia, this species has been successfully introduced for hunting in the West and can be found widely in the wild. However, attempts to introduce it in the East have not been successful. Nonetheless, a lot of people who raise game birds as a hobby in all parts of North America have Chukars, and they escape frequently enough so that you might find one walking across your front lawn. Cowell's Game Bird & Waterfowl pages will provide you with two good photos of Chukars, as well as information about their lifestyles. And, the site notes, "Chukars are great birds for beginners as they are so easy to keep and breed." The U.S. Forest Service has a collection of pages on the Chukar with a lot of data about where it lives and what it likes to eat in the wild (*second address*).

http://home.att.net/~DanCowell/chukar.html

http://www.fs.fed.us/database/feis/animals/bird/
alch/

Partridge, Gray

The Gray Partridge (*Perdix perdix*) was so popular a hunting species in Europe that it was introduced into North America years ago. It has now developed strong populations coast-to-coast in areas of the north-ern United States and southern Canada that have prairies or many cultivated fields, where it eats seeds, leaves, and insects. According to Peterson Online (*first address*), it is common in many areas. Peterson has pic-tures, a range map, and natural history about the bird. Oddly enough, although it's doing well here, the Gray Partridge is an endangered species in England, where its numbers declined by 50 percent between 1969 and 1990, according to the British Department of the Envi-ronment Transport and the Regions (*second address*). The species is almost extinct in Northern Ireland. This site describes the causes of lost numbers and tells what the British plan to do to maintain and increase their populations of the Gray Partridge.

http://www.petersononline.com/birds/month/grpa/
index.html

http://www.jncc.gov.uk/ukbg/bap/species/perper.htm

A B C D E F G H I J K L M N O P Q R S T U V W X Y Z

Pheasant, Ring-necked

The Ring-necked Pheasant (*Phasianus colchicus*) is a native of Eurasia that was introduced into North America, both because of its beauty and because it's a popular object of hunters. The bird has been so successful here that it's now established virtually coast-to-coast, wherever it can find fields, brush, and marshes. According to the GeoZoo on Geobop (*first address; select Ring-necked Pheasant*), although they are good and silent fliers, Ring-necked Pheasants are also fast runners, making them a challenge for hunters—and for birders trying to confirm a sighting. Besides natural history, this site offers a quiz about Ring-necked Pheasants and lists books for more study. The Backyard Bird News (*second address*) describes the nesting habits of Ring-necked Pheasants, noting that the chicks are *precocial*—which means they're ready for action very soon after they are born. In fact, they're on the move within 24 hours, and the parents abandon the nest within one day of their birth. That's not surprising, since pheasants are ground nesters, which makes them susceptible to attack. Within a week of their birth, the chicks can even fly.

http://www.geobop.com/Birds/Galliformes/index.htm
http://www.wildlifehabitat.com/BBNOctober1998.html

Sparrow, House

The House Sparrow (*Passer domesticus*), also called the English Sparrow, is one of a handful of introduced species that have become so common, we almost think of them as natives. The bird was brought to North America from Europe around 1850 and, thanks to farmers and horses, found plenty of the grain it liked. The House Sparrow spread rapidly and has been considered a pest. "This bird's general unpopularity has been brought about by some of the undesirable traits it exhibits," said Robie Tufts, who wrote *The Birds of Nova Scotia*. For instance, it will take over the nesting places of native species, such as swallows. "Despite this," Tufts says, "the House Sparrow is a beneficial bird because its food in summer is largely insects that plague the farmer." This page has information about the House Sparrow's natural history, plus much information about its status in Nova Scotia.

http://museum.ednet.ns.ca/mnh/nature/nsbirds/
     bns0411.htm

FEATHERED FACTS

Tough Dad

The male Ring-necked Pheasant is very protective of the female while she is on the nest. A man in Ohio observed a male drive off a Red Fox that had been stalking a nesting female.

—adapted from *Backyard Bird News*

http://www.wildlifehabitat.com/BBNOctober1998.html

Starling, European

"The European starling, a nonnative species, has flourished over the past century in the United States," says William J. Kern Jr. of the University of Florida, who provides suggestions for "the ways of dealing with the nuisances they can cause." The site (*first address*) describes the natural history of *Sturnus vulgaris*, as well as some of the problems—including damaging the paint of your shiny new car. A variety of ways of controlling them are suggested. More on starlings can be found at the second address in Slovenia, including an example of one of its not-so-pleasant calls. (A relative of the Myna Bird, starlings can imitate many beautiful bird calls and songs.)

http://hammock.ifas.ufl.edu/txt/fairs/uw118
http://www.mobitel.si/old/eng/be74_e.html

Swan, Mute

The Mute Swan (*Cygnus olor*), seen in many inlets and on ponds in the Northeast and locally elsewhere, is a native of Europe. Though some state agencies and conservation groups want the alien eliminated from its newfound land, lest it take over natives' nesting places, others argue that Mute Swans do no harm and add much beauty to our waters. The Wetlands & Waterfowl's Guide to North American Waterfowl (*first address*) describes the history and habits of this bird. The Happy Hollow Park and Zoo in San Jose, California (*second address*), has more and a map of its native range. The Patuxent site (*third address*) offers facts, photos, ranges, and sounds. Chandler S. Robbins of the National Biological Service discusses the Mute Swan and other nonnative birds on the U.S. Geological Survey's Our Living Resources site (*fourth address*).

http://digitalsportsman.com/wetlands/MuteS1.htm

http://www.sjliving.com/happyhollow/website/
  Muteswan.html

http://www.mbr-pwrc.usgs.gov/id/framlst/
  i1782id.html

http://biology.usgs.gov/s+t/noframe/x177.htm

FEATHERED FACTS

First Penguin

The first penguin is no longer with us—and wasn't a penguin by today's standards. Early explorers called the Great Auk a penguin, a word whose roots may have meant pen-winged. This flightless bird of northern Arctic regions is now extinct, but when explorers came across similar flightless birds of the Southern Hemisphere, they called them penguins after the auks they saw up north. So the name lives on, even though the Great Auk doesn't.

—adapted from *Birds of North America*

http://www.birdsofna.org/excerpts/auk.html

EXTINCT

This is a sad section, for it tells tales of birds no longer with us. Some were birds once so numerous they literally darkened the skies whereas others were always limited in numbers and hunted down for their rarity or handsome plumage. We have already learned our lessons about overhunting of species, and today the concern is more about educating people about humanity's potential impact on bird habitat. One of the most recent extinctions, which occurred in the late 1980s, was due to thoughtless changes in the environment that played host to the species. More extinct species may be on their way—some of these rarities, like the Eskimo Curlew, are detailed in other chapters. These lost species are lessons for us all in the need for care and conservation of not just the creatures themselves but in the use of the land they need to live on. (*See also Conservation.*)

Auk, Great

The Great Auk (*Pinguinus impennis*) was the last flightless seabird found anywhere in the Northern Hemisphere. The Great Auk dove into the sea for its food, and to go deeper and deeper, the species evolved into a bigger and bigger bird, using its wings to propel itself underwater, reports the Birds of North America site. Because they were large and flightless, Great Auks were easy to kill for food, fat, bait, and their feathers. Colonies of Great Auks around the Arctic Circle, including those in Canada, were eventually wiped out. The last two known birds were killed in 1844 on an island off Iceland for a collector who stuffed them. This page shows how modern-day ornithologists try to piece together the life history of a bird that disappeared more than 150 years ago.

http://www.birdsofna.org/excerpts/auk.html

Birds Designated Officially Extinct in Canada

The Committee on the Status of Endangered Wildlife in Canada (COSEWIC) has officially designated at least three bird species extinct in Canada. This page tells what they were, where they lived, and why they disappeared.

http://infoweb.magi.com/~ehaber/extinct.html

A B C D E F G H I J K L M N O P Q R S T U V W X Y Z

A
B
C
D
E
F
G
H
I
J
K
L
M
N
O
P
Q
R
S
T
U
V
W
X
Y
Z

FEATHERED FACTS

Dumb as a Dodo?

Portuguese sailors discovered the Dodo on the island of Mauritius in 1598. The bird showed no fear at all, having no natural enemies, but the sailors mistook the "gentle spirit of the Dodo, and its lack of fear of the new predators, as stupidity." Consequently, the bird's name has come to mean someone who is stupid.

—adapted from Dave Reilly, *Tragedy of the Dodo*

http://www.davidreilly.com/dodo/

Dodo FAQ

Okay, the Dodo wasn't ever a North American species. But it's probably the most famous extinct bird species in the world, and its name is almost synonymous with extinction. That may be because of its odd name, its odd appearance, or perhaps because it was among the first bird species to be recognized as extinct. The last Dodo died around 1681, according to the official Dodo Frequently Asked Questions, a page anyone interested in extinct birds should visit (*first address*). That was less than a century after the first Dodo was discovered on the island of Mauritius, off the east coast of Africa. There are no complete specimens of dead Dodos, only paintings and word of mouth. Little is known about the bird. However, much of what *is* known, along with a good deal of speculation, is offered by Dave Reilly on his Tragedy of the Dodo site (*second address*). Here you'll find some of the few images known of the Dodo and even a picture of a few remains of the bird—mostly claws and skulls—at the Oxford Museum in England. You'll also learn that its lack of fear of humans, plus the introduction of domestic animals, such as dogs, that became feral, spelled the end for this odd bird.

http://www.davidreilly.com/dodo/dodo-faq.txt
http://www.davidreilly.com/dodo/

Duck, Labrador

The last known Labrador Duck (*Camptorhynchus labradorius*) was shot by a hunter on Long Island, New York, in 1875, according to the Committee on the Status of Endangered Wildlife in Canada (*first address*). Birds of Nova Scotia (*second address*) says the last one was shot by a boy in Elmira, New York, in 1878. Either way, the Labrador Duck is truly a dead duck. Once found along the North Atlantic seaboard from the Maryland north to Labrador, it was never a common duck, says both the Birds of Nova Scotia and the Internet Duck Memorial (*third address*), which is "dedicated to the memory of those ducks that have since ceased to grace our planet." The memorial says that the Labrador Duck "was neither distinctive nor striking in its appearance or habits, both sexes closely resembling each other, being a grayish-brown all over with a small reddish crest on the back of the head." The page also lists three other duck species that have disappeared in other parts of the world.

http://infoweb.magi.com/~ehaber/extinct.html
http://museum.ednet.ns.ca/mnh/nature/nsbirds/bns0069.htm
http://www.geocities.com/SunsetStrip/5283/Memorial.html

Extinct American Birds

John James Audubon saw and painted North American birds before the continent's population—and killing habits—became so great that any species had been "extincted," as this site puts it. Since Audubon's time, five birds have disappeared: the Ivory-billed Woodpecker, the Carolina Parakeet, the Passenger Pigeon, the Labrador Duck, and the Great Auk. You'll also find Audubon paintings and descriptions of each at this website

http://employeeweb.myxa.com/rrb/Audubon/extinct.html

Extinct U.S. Birds

The Nutty Hatch, also known as the Nutty Bird-watcher, provides a list of birds that once existed in the United States and its territories, and are now considered extinct. The list indicates where they lived and the year they were last seen.

http://nuthatch.birdnature.com/extinct.html

Heath Hen

The really sad thing about the Heath Hen (*Tympa-nuchus cupido cupido*) is that conservationists knew it was threatened a long time ago and thought they were doing the right thing to save it. Even though there seemed little chance of its ever reestablishing its lost numbers in much of its territory, a 1,000-acre preserve was set up in 1907 on Martha's Vineyard, Massachusetts, where, conservationists believed, the bird could survive and perhaps thrive. But it didn't, and the last one ever seen on this earth was a Martha's Vineyard male Heath Hen calling for a female who never responded—because she didn't exist. What happened to kill off the last of the Heath Hens is a lesson in intelligent conservation, provided here by the Massachusetts Chapter of the Nature Conservancy (*first address*). Bagheera's In the Wild page (*second address*) notes that the Heath Hen was considered very tasty and was easy to kill. Originally found from Maine to Virginia, the only birds left by the 1870s were on Martha's Vineyard. This website describes their decline on the island with even more detail—including the arrival of the raptors, which loved to eat Heath Hens. The page also has questions, designed to make you, and students of nature, think about what happened to kill off the Heath Hen.

http://www.tnc.org/infield/State/Massachusetts/
   article6.htm
http://www.bagheera.com/inthewild/ext_heathhen.htm

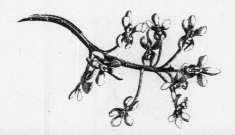

Parakeet, Carolina

The Carolina Parakeet (*Conuropsis carolinensis*) was done in by farming and the birds' taste for the things farmers grow. Before Europeans arrived to till the soils, the Carolina Parakeet was widespread east of the Great Plains. But, notes the Canadian Museum of Natural History site (*first address*), great flocks of them would descend on farmers' fields, much to the farmers' chagrin. As a result, many were shot and killed. Many others disappeared simply because the swamp forests they needed for nesting were being felled. The last wild Carolina Parakeets may have been seen in Florida around 1915. The last known bird in captivity died in 1918, reports Dr. Charles J. Brabec of North Carolina State University, who is not an ornithologist but a systems programmer who likes birds (*second address*). For a fascinating photo of two dead specimens of this parakeet, showing what a beautiful bird it was, see the Cornell University page (third *address*).

http://www.nature.ca/notebooks/english/caropara.htm
http://www4.ncsu.edu/eos/users/b/brabec/WWW/
   CP-story.html
http://muse.bio.cornell.edu/museums/images/carol.jpg

FEATHERED FACTS

Scene from the Past

"The richness of their plumage, their beautiful mode of flight, and even their screams lend charm to our darkest forests and most sequestered swamps," wrote John James Audubon. He was describing the Carolina Parakeet, once plentiful in the Southeast. The last one died in a zoo in 1918.

http://www4.ncsu.edu/eos/users/b/brabec/WWW/
   CP-story.html

A B C D E F G H I J K L M N O P Q R S T U V W X Y Z

A
B
C
D
E
F
G
H
I
J
K
L
M
N
O
P
Q
R
S
T
U
V
W
X
Y
Z

Passenger Pigeon (*Ectopistes migratorius*) (JJA)

Pigeon, Passenger

Perhaps the most outrageous example of man's exter-
mination of a harmless species is the Passenger Pigeon
(*Ectopistes migratorius*). "It has been estimated that
four out of every 10 birds in North America at the
time of its discovery was a passenger pigeon—that's
40% of the entire bird population on the continent!"
notes Steve Warmack, creator of the Typewritten Book
of the Not-So-Grateful Dead, a website devoted to
extinct species (*first address*). Audubon reported seeing
one flock so big that it took hours to pass by. And
Bagheera, a natural history education site (*second
address*), reports that the Passenger Pigeon was once
the "most abundant bird species on Earth." What happened? The Passenger Pigeon was systematically
hunted down for food and feathers with such vigor
that thousands of men were employed full-time just to
kill them. In 1900, a boy in Pike County, Ohio, shot the
last passenger pigeon ever reported seen in the wild,
and 14 years later, Martha, the last passenger pigeon
living in captivity, died at the Cincinnati Zoo. For a
remembrance of Martha's passing, read Joseph W.
Quinn's poem, "The Passenger Pigeon" (*third address*).

http://www.aristotle.net/~swarmack/pigeon.html
http://www.bagheera.com/inthewild/ext_pigeon.htm
http://angelfire.com/oh/raraavis/quinn.html

Sparrow, Dusky Seaside

The Dusky Seaside Sparrow (*Ammodramus maritimus
mirabilis*) may be the most recent bird to fall into the
unhappy category of extinct. It may also be the best
documented extinction. The bird lived on the east
coast of Florida, particularly around Merritt Island.
"The Dusky Seaside Sparrow depended on moist
cordgrass (*Spartina bakerii*) habitat for nesting sites,"
Bagheera, an educational website, notes. "Problems
with mosquitoes breeding in the marsh area adjacent
to the Kennedy Space Center led to a mosquito control
program in 1963 in which the marsh was flooded. No
attempt was made to reduce the harmful effects of the
flooding on wildlife that depended on that habitat,
such as the Dusky Seaside Sparrow." Another population of the birds was eradicated when the state of
Florida built a highway through its marsh and what
marsh was left was drained for real estate development. The last Dusky Seaside Sparrow died in 1987.
This site details the extinction of the bird and asks
questions to promote further thought.

http://www.bagheera.com/inthewild/ext_sparrow.htm

Warbler, Bachman's

Bachman's Warbler (*Vermivora bachmanii*) was always
rare, and if it still exists anywhere, it is probably the
rarest bird in North America, according to the University of Georgia Forestry Department page. One of the
last ones spotted was in Georgia in 1975. The exact
reason for its disappearance is not clear, but it is
known that its wintering habitat in Cuba had been
severely reduced in size. The bird's breeding grounds
were the southeastern United States, but the U.S. Fish
& Wildlife Service says in a detailed report on the
Bachman's Warbler that no confirmed breeding
records have been reported from the United States
since the mid-1960s (*second address*).

http://www.forestry.uga.edu/docs/for94-37.html
http://www.fws.gov/r9endspp/i/b/sab0z.html

Woodpecker, Ivory-billed

Cuba may also figure into the demise of the Ivory-billed Woodpecker (*Campephilus principalis*), the last examples of which were spotted in a hilly pine forest in eastern Cuba in 1986. The birds were "in dire circumstances," reports Martjan Lammertink in an essay for the Neotropical Bird Club (*first address*), and since no more were sighted in subsequent expeditions, experts believe they were all gone by 1990. Though never common, these majestic woodpeckers once roamed the pine forests of the southeastern United States. As the forests disappeared—mostly for logging, so did the birds. The last sightings in the United States were in the 1950s, though some observers claimed to have seen them in the late 1970s. The Ivory-billed looked somewhat like a Pileated Woodpecker with a white bill and required a huge territory to find enough food. The Typewritten Book of the Not-So-Grateful Dead site, devoted to extinct species, has more on the Ivory-billed Woodpecker's life when it lived (*second address*).

http://www.neotropicalbirdclub.org/feature/ivory.html
http://www.aristotle.net/~swarmack/ivory.html

Ivory-billed Woodpecker (*Campephilus principalis*) (JJA)

FOWL-LIKE

The woods, but more often the fields and prairies, of North America are home to a small number of birds that are sometimes classified as "fowl-like." They include wild turkeys, grouse, pheasants, ptarmigans, roadrunners, and quail. Since many of these are hunted species, some of the sites in this section were designed for hunters. But because these sites offer such useful information for anyone interested in the natural history of the species, they are included here. Note that many of our wildfowl are species that have been introduced from Europe or Eurasia. (*See also North American Birds, Exotics.*)

Bobwhite, Northern

The Northern Bobwhite, Bobwhite Quail, Common Bobwhite, or just plain Bobwhite (*Colinus virginianus*) is an example of a wild, native North American bird that is also widely raised in captivity. "The popular Bobwhite Quail is a favorite of game bird breeders, hunters and bird lovers alike," says Dan Cowell (*first address*). Despite the bird's scientific name, the native range of the Bobwhite is from Canada to the Gulf of Mexico east of the Rockies, and it has been introduced for hunting purposes on the West Coast. About 20 subspecies exist, but the most common, says Cowell, is the Eastern Bobwhite. Cowell's page has natural history and breeding information, as well as photos and a sound bite of the famous Bobwhite namesake call. To learn what the different subspecies are, where they live, what kinds of habitats they like, what their predators are, and a lot more, visit this U.S. Forest Service page (*second address*), written to provide information about the effects of wildfires on animals and plants! Geobop's GeoZoo has a nice set of pages about the life and lore of the Bobwhite (*third address*), including the interesting technique this quail uses to protect itself when accosted in the wild. The Nebraska Game & Parks Commission has a fine and long page of information about Bobwhites (*fourth address*).

http://home.att.net/~DanCowell/bobwhite.html
http://www.fs.fed.us/database/feis/animals/bird/covi/
http://www.geobop.com/Birds/Galliformes/Odontophoridae/Colinus_virginianus/index.htm
http://ngp.ngpc.state.ne.us/wildlife/quail.html

Grouse, Ruffed

No, it's not a "Ruffled Grouse," a name that turns up all too often. The Ruffed Grouse (*Bonasa umbellus*) gets its name from the tuffs on the back of its neck, called *ruffs*, which the bird raises when it's excited, notes this GeoZoo page on Geobop (*first address, then select Ruffed Grouse*). They are among the most fearless of wild birds, and there are many stories about Ruffed Grouse that walk right up to people and make themselves at home. However, when they are frightened in the wild, they often "explode" into the air, a technique apparently designed to frighten or distract the approaching critter—or person—long enough for the birds to escape. The U.S. Forest Service has a site full of this kind of information about the Ruffed Grouse (*second address*). To not only see a Ruffed Grouse but also hear its famous courtship drumming sound, visit Nature North Zine (*third address*). This site also has a lot of natural history about the species.

http://www.geobop.com/Birds/Galliformes/index.htm

http://www.fs.fed.us/database/feis/animals/bird/boum/

http://www.naturenorth.com/winter/grouse/Frgrse.html

Grouse, Spruce

The Spruce Grouse is a chicken-like bird that lives in the evergreen forests of the north country. Diane Porter relates a story about her first meeting with a Spruce Grouse on a birding expedition in Minnesota —a meeting that turned out to be somewhat more exciting than she expected. In the process, she tells us something about this uncommon bird.

http://www.birdwatching.com/stories/sprucegrouse.html

AVIAN ADVICE

Right Name

Some bird names are frequently written or spoken incorrectly, either because they are misunderstood or they are out of date. Common examples include "Canadian" Goose (instead of the correct Canada Goose), "Ruffled" Grouse (instead of Ruffed Grouse), and "Northern" Oriole (instead of the reinstated Baltimore Oriole). And, technically speaking, there's no such bird as a "seagull" (they're just plain gulls of various species, none "sea"). For a complete list of currently official North American bird names, both English and Latin, visit this page.

http://www.audubon.org/bird/na-bird.html

Pheasant, Ring-necked

See North American Birds, Exotics.

Prairie Chicken, Attwater's

Attwater's Prairie Chicken (*Tympanuchus cupido attwateri*), a subspecies of the Greater Prairie Chicken (*see next entry*), once numbered in the millions along the Gulf of Mexico coast, notes the Texas Audubon Society. According to a recent count, fewer than 60 birds were left in the wild. The bird lives in the Gulf Coastal prairies, a habitat that has been extensively developed, but efforts are under way to save the bird. Learn about them here.

http://www.audubon.org/chapter/tx/tx/attwater.html

Prairie Chicken, Greater

The Greater Prairie Chicken (*Tympanuchus cupido*) was once plentiful in midwestern North America, but as farms spread across the prairies, the habitat of this wildfowl all but disappeared, and so did the Greater Prairie Chicken—almost. It survives in a few pockets of Canada and the United States, and efforts are under way to protect its habitats in both countries, reports the Canadian Museum of Nature. The Heath Hen (*Tympanuchus cupido cupido*), a subspecies of the Greater Prairie Chicken, once roamed the eastern United States, including New England (*see also North American Birds, Extinct*).

http://www.nature.ca/notebooks/english/grtchick.htm

Prairie Chicken (*Tympanuchus cupido*) [Greater Prairie Chicken] (JJA)

Prairie Chicken, Lesser

The Lesser Prairie Chicken (*Tympanuchus pallidicinctus*) is, like its Greater cousin (*see previous entry*), a rare bird suffering from loss of habitat throughout its range on the Great Plains. Dick and Jean Hoffman (*first address*) describe some of the places in Colorado, Kansas, New Mexico, Oklahoma, and Texas where you can still see the Lesser Prairie Chicken. They also tell about their own journeys to see them and offer links to other observations. An excellent photo and natural history of the Lesser Prairie Chicken is offered by the Springfield, Colorado, Chamber of Commerce. It includes a description of the elaborate mating rituals of this bird.

http://www.geocities.com/Yosemite/4413/lepc.html
http://www.ruralnet.net/~spgfld/prchick.htm

Roadrunner

If it weren't for the Warner Brothers cartoons involving a coyote, the Roadrunner (*Geococcyx californianus*), sometimes called the Greater Roadrunner, might be a fairly obscure bird to all but those who know them from living in or visiting the Southwest. This snake-eating member of the cuckoo family can fly short distances, but its favored method of escape is running, and Roadrunners have been clocked footing it at up to 15 miles per hour. Desert USA provides a profile of the bird, along with information on the deserts in which it lives (*first address*). Students at the Ephesus Road Elementary School in Chapel Hill, North Carolina, have collected links and photos of Roadrunners (*second address*). Although he lives in Sweden (where Roadrunners are not native), Jan-Erik Malmstigen offers a half dozen links to Roadrunner photos and paintings, along with some facts (*third address*). Finally, *Arizona Highways* magazine offers a portrait of the Roadrunner, noting that "they are fun to watch. They are agile and quick, and not very shy" (*fourth address*).

http://www.desertusa.com/road.html
http://metalab.unc.edu/~ephesus/roadrun.htm
http://home.swipnet.se/~w-33148/vyk10_1.htm
http://www.arizhwys.com/Wildlife/roadrunner.html

Roadrunner (Dover)

Turkey, Wild

The Wild Turkey (*Meleagris gallopavo*) is an unusual example of an American bird success story. These large, woods-loving fowl were almost annihilated in much of their eastern range, both through over-hunting and from loss of their habitat as forests were felled to create fields for farmers (or for lumber, firewood, or charcoal). In Connecticut, for instance, the once plentiful Wild Turkey was extinct by the early 20th century. In the 1970s, however, a few were reintroduced by the state into parts of Connecticut that were becoming forested areas again. The result is that there are now tens of thousands of Wild Turkeys in Connecticut. Many other states are having the same successes. The Pennsylvania Chapter of the National Wild Turkey Federation (*first address*) has an excellent profile of the wild turkey, covering its natural history, populations, habitats, and habits. Although the site is written for hunters, naturalists can find a wealth of information about wild turkeys here. To learn why Benjamin Franklin thought that the Wild Turkey, not the Bald Eagle, should be used as a symbol of America, read

Professor Gerry Rising's column from the *Buffalo* (New York) *News* (*second address*). The Wild Turkey Hunting Network (*third address*) has perhaps the most comprehensive collection of features and information about hunting wild turkeys. However, if you are just interested in the birds, check out the writings of turkey expert Stu Keck, who provides detailed descriptions of the biology and habits of turkeys on this site. You can even download turkey sounds.

http://www.go2pa.com/panwtf/turkeyprofile.html

http://www.acsu.buffalo.edu/~insrisg/nature/nw98/franklinturkey.html

http://www.bowhunting.net/wildturkey.net/default.htm

MEET THE MASTERS

A Death Gives Life

A dead bird discovered nearly a decade ago has led to one of the Internet's most informative and interesting birding websites. Jack Paul's Chickadee Web <http://home.jtan.com/~jack/ckd.html> is a shining example of how in sharing their personal interests, amateur Webmasters can create online libraries that help countless others. Though it's "the most complete source of information about chickadees on the Internet," there's nothing glitzy about Jack's site. It's a straightforward, well-organized collection of pages and links that provide more information than you could imagine about these endearing birds. "I guess my fascination with them started when I found a chickadee that somehow got caught in an old fence around my house and died," says Jack, who lives in Hereford Township, Berks County, Pennsylvania. "The fence is now gone. I had never paid much attention to them before that accident and as I removed the tiny body, I felt a sadness that such a beautiful creature died such a tragic death. I guess I'm an old softie." After that, he began noticing the Black-capped Chickadees that are so common in the Northeast. "I started watching them visit my feeder and their acrobatics, vocalizations, and friendliness got me hooked," he reports.

Wild Turkey (*Meleagris gallopavo*) (JJA)

RAPTORS

No class of animal has become so connected with power than the raptors. The symbol of America is the Bald Eagle, and countless fighting units around the world have used hawks in their emblems. Oddly enough, the owls, also grouped with the raptors, have become known as the "wise" and cogitative birds. Yet they, too, are hunters and killers. But since they usually hunt by night, they seem to have escaped the fierce image that the eagle, hawk, and falcon have acquired. Because of the considerable interest in birds of prey, many websites are available, and so are photos of the species. This group also includes the vultures, which aren't really hunters but more like nature's clean-up crews, eating what other creatures, cars, or old age have killed. *(See also Photography.)*

Audubon Adopt-a-Bird

The Audubon Center for Birds of Prey in Maitland, Florida, receives more than 600 injured or orphaned raptors a year. "Nearly 85 percent of all injuries to the birds admitted are related to human interaction, including gunshot wounds, collisions with cars and power lines, poisonings and loss of habitat," the center says. "With prompt care, many birds can be returned to the wild." Those that can't be released are permanently cared for at the center's aviary. Since 1979, the Audubon Center says, it's treated more than 7,000 birds of prey and returned to the wild 3,200, including more than 200 bald eagles. Many of the non-releasable birds become "teachers"—they are used by Audubon staff in programs that instruct the public about birds of prey. The public can help by "adopting" individual birds. For a minimum donation (about $25), you receive an adoption packet that includes a photo and biography of your chosen bird, a personalized adoption certificate and gift card, a species information sheet, and an annual subscription to *Florida Raptor News,* the center's quarterly newsletter. "Our education-oriented Bird Buddy adoption kits also include activity sheets for the kids—great for classrooms and youth groups!" says the website, which has pictures and biographies of birds available for adoption. *(See also Audubon Societies & Sanctuaries and Aviaries; see the California, Carolina, and Rocky Mountain Raptor Centers later in this section.)*

http://members.aol.com/randystack/raptors.html

Bird Predators

At first, it seems odd, but in fact, it's reasonable: In nature, a bird's worst enemy is a bird. A lot of birds, actually. This site provides lists of what owls and hawks eat, and in many cases, most of their breakfasts, lunches, and dinners are birds. It stands to reason that birds are their own worst enemy: In the wild, what else could catch them? House and feral cats, of course, are big killers of birds, but they are unnatural. *(See also Quandaries, Cats & Wildlife and Cats Indoors.)*

http://nuthatch.birdnature.com/predators.html

Birds of Prey

John Battalio at Boise State University, Idaho, has been interested in raptors for more than 15 years and has conducted many hawk watches for the Hawk Migration Association of North America. On this site he offers many links to sites and sources about raptors and other birds of prey. This is one of the better raptor information directories on the Web.

http://www.boisestate.edu/english/jbattali/jaybat/birds/hawks.htm

FEATHERED FACTS

Pollution Detector

Because they are at the top of the food chain, birds of prey are sensitive to many forms of environmental change, such as chemical pollution, and they can provide an early warning for humans. In a sense, they are like the caged canary that coal miners once used to detect poisonous gases.

—adapted from Peregrine Fund

http://www.peregrinefund.org/BofPSong.html

California Raptor Center at UC Davis

Raptors have their own hospitals. Among them is the California Raptor Center at the University of California in Davis, which rehabilitates injured or orphan raptors. Of the 250 or so received each year, around 60 percent are released back into the wild. The center also undertakes raptor-related research, and some of its work is explained here. The site offers an adopt-a-raptor program.

http://www.vetnet.ucdavis.edu/ars/raptor.htm

Carolina Raptor Center

The Carolina Raptor Center near Charlotte was started in 1980 in a basement of a building at the University of North Carolina. Today, located at the Latta Plantation Nature Preserve, the center has 20 different species of nonreleasable birds of prey living in cages in its 47 acres of woodland. Some 90,000 people each year, including 55,000 school children, visit the center. The website has information about the center and its work, as well as bird biographies, photos, and statistics. It also describes an adopt-a-bird program that you can enroll in online.

http://www.birdsofprey.org

Condor, California

As few as nine California condors (*Gymnogyps californianus*) were living in North America in 1985. Thanks to the efforts of the San Diego Zoo and others, at least 121 were known only 11 years later. In a time-line format, this site explains the zoo's many programs and projects to save the California condor, the largest bird in North America.

http://www.sandiegozoo.org/cres/milestone.html

Eagle, American Bald

The American Bald Eagle (*Haliaeetus leucocephalus*) is a magnificent sight, with a bright white head and tail, accenting its dark brown body. A mature eagle (three years and older) measures about 36 inches from head to tail with a 6½-foot wingspan in males and a wing-span up to 8 feet in the larger, heavier females. The bird's feet are bright yellow. Not too many years ago, chances of seeing one in the wild were extremely limited. BaldEagleInfo.com (*first address*) notes that by 1967 Bald Eagles were declared endangered in all areas of the United States south of the 40th parallel, and only 417 breeding pairs were left in the contiguous states. Besides loss of habitat, a major cause of the eagles' decline was the pesticide DDT, which the eagles ingested through their favorite food, fish. By 1994 the eagles had rallied from endangered to threatened, and it's now possible to find eagles nesting along many of the same rivers whose pollution nearly caused their demise. Just about everything anyone could ask about the Bald Eagle is covered at this site, which also features free Bald Eagle postcards and links to other eagle and raptor sites. The Santa Cruz Predatory Bird Research Group (*second address*) is doing a high-tech study of West Coast eagles' migratory patterns, tracking birds who were banded with transmitters that permit researchers to receive "E-mail from eagles." See this site for up-to-the-moment updates of the tagged birds' travels, as well as much information about these birds and other raptors.

http://www.baldeagleinfo.com
http://www2.ucsc.edu/scpbrg/

FEATHERED FACTS

Hail to the Turkey

Benjamin Franklin once proposed the Wild Turkey as the official symbol of the United States, much favoring it over the Bald Eagle, which he considered a bird of "bad moral character."

—adapted from Gerry Rising

http://www.acsu.buffalo.edu/~insrisg/nature/nw98/franklinturkey.html

FEATHERED FACTS

High-Speed Dive

When diving for prey, the Golden Eagle can reach speeds of between 150 and 200 miles per hour.

http://www.nature.ca/notebooks/english/gldeagle.htm

Eagle, Golden

The Golden Eagle (*Aquila chrysaetos*) is found coast-to-coast, but much more commonly in the West. The wing span of 6½ to 7½ feet is similar to the Bald Eagle's. Immature Bald Eagles in flight may be hard to tell from Goldens, although the touches of white on the wings of the immature Golden Eagles are a clue. Golden Eagles are feathered to their feet, unlike Bald Eagles whose bright yellow legs are prominent. When mature, Golden Eagles are seen as brown from below with prominent beaks and a touch of gold (yellow-brown) at the back of the neck. They nest in trees or on cliffs. Some good photos of the bird and a canyon nest are at the first address. One of the greatest concentrations of golden eagles is found in the Diablo Mountains near San Francisco. The Santa Cruz Predatory Bird Research Group has a good deal of information about this eagle (*second address*).

http://www.lakepowell.net/~gnealon/golden.htm
http://www2.ucsc.edu/scpbrg/eagles.htm

Eagle Track

Space technology meets nature at Eagle Track, the University of Minnesota's Raptor Center, which has some fascinating case histories online of injured Bald Eagles and where they went after they recuperated and were released. For instance, you can learn about the Eagle with the Strange Growth—Case X-260, complete with pictures of the unknown "rocklike chunk of 'mineralized ingesta'" found inside the injured bird. The Bald Eagle survived and was released with a satellite radio tracking device on his back. You can see where X-260 went, and you can track other eagles who've been outfitted with these transmitters (designed to eventually fall off the bird, once the transmitter wears out). When we stopped by, we were able to track an eagle that the then-new governor, wrestler Jesse Ventura, released—ironically, the dazed bird, suffering from lead poisoning, had been discovered on Election Day. There are pictures of the governor releasing the bird, and then tracking information about where it went. Maps often help viewers follow the track of a released bird. When you first visit the page, you'll be asked to register so the university can learn who is interested in eagle migration. However, if you don't care to participate in the survey, you can skip the registration and click the Eagle Track box at the bottom of the page to proceed to the rehabilitation and tracking pages.

http://www.raptor.cvm.umn.edu/newwebdev/meeen/register1.html

Golden Eagle (Dover)

A B C D E F G H I J K L M N O P Q R S T U V W X Y Z

A
B
C
D
E
F
G
H
I
J
K
L
M
N
O
P
Q
R
S
T
U
V
W
X
Y
Z

Falcon, Peregrine

The Peregrine Falcon (*Falco peregrinus*) is an unusual raptor. Once seriously threatened by the pesticide DDT, the bird has made a strong comeback. One of the seeming ironies of this uncommon bird is that it loves cities. Peregrine Falcons are often reported living atop skyscrapers or communications antenna platforms. Their food? Why, the ultimate urban bird: the pigeon. Diane Porter of Birdwatching.com describes an encounter with a Peregrine Falcon and tells many interesting facts about its lifestyle (*first address*). In season, you can view many "live camera" shots of nesting falcons on the website of the Canadian Peregrine Foundation (*second address*). The foundation notes that the Peregrine Falcon is still on the endangered species list in Canada but is slowly recovering. The site offers news, links to other falcon sites, and even falcon-related products.

http://www.birdwatching.com/stories/hawks.html
http://www.peregrine-foundation.ca

Falconry & Raptor Education Foundation

Falconry is the ancient practice of flying trained birds of prey after wild game. The Falconry & Raptor Education Foundation provides information about the sport and beginners courses in falconry. If you're curious about the subject, this is a good place to start. Links to other falconry sites are provided.

http://www.falconryacademy.com/intro.htm

Florida Eagle Watch

Florida Eagle Watch provides videos of nesting eagles, in season, along with narratives explaining what is going on. The site has many eagle images, plus natural history, in a diary-style format, describing in words and pictures what is happening at the nest at different periods of the season. The camera was set up before the eagles arrived at the nest. The site, with links to places where you can see Bald Eagles in the wild, is a nice cooperative effort of the Florida Audubon Society, the *Orlando Sentinel*, and the Florida Game & Fresh Water Fish Commission.

http://www.orlandosentinel.com/projects/eagle/

Golden Gate Raptor Observatory

The Golden Gate Raptor Observatory at Fort Mason in San Francisco, California, was created to study migrating birds of prey along the Pacific Coast and to increase public awareness of the state of raptor populations. The website includes a Raptor Quiz that tests your ability to identify a few species, annual statistics about species sighted from the center and how they relate to previous years, a FAQ on raptors and the observatory, and links to other raptor sites.

http://www.ggro.org

Goshawk, Northern

The Northern Goshawk (*Accipiter gentilis*) is a bird-eating hawk found in northern North America, as well as Europe and Asia. Although there can be threats to its numbers through timber cutting, populations are considered strong. Why that's the case is among the information found on this excerpt from the Birds of North America site.

http://www.birdsofna.org/excerpts/goshawk.html

MEET THE MASTERS

Nutty Birdwatcher

A bird walking headfirst down a tree helped inspire one of the newer—and nicer —birding sites on the Web. "I thought about the name when I was participating in the Cornell Lab 'Project FeederWatch' and saw a white-breasted nuthatch going down (of course, headfirst) a tree trunk and thought 'those guys are nuts' and that's how I came up with 'nutty,'" says Julia Pahountis, Webmaster of the Nutty Birdwatcher <http://www.birdnature.com>.

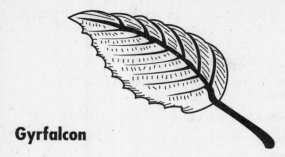

Gyrfalcon

The Gyrfalcon (*Falco rusticolus*), a large Arctic falcon, lives primarily in Canada and Alaska, but sometimes makes appearances in the northernmost of the lower 48 states. They are popular with falconers, notes this page about conservation and management, excerpted from the Birds of North America website.

http://www.birdsofna.org/excerpts/gyrfalcon.html

Harrier, Northern

The Northern Harrier (*Circus cyaneus*) is a widespread North American bird—also called a Marsh Hawk. An excerpt from the Birds of North America site explains in detail many aspects of its behavior, including the male's sky dancing display, used to attract a mate (*first address*).

http://www.birdsofna.org/excerpts/harrier.html

Hawk, Broad-winged

Although they are very common in spring and summer in North American woods and forests, few people notice the Broad-winged Hawk (*Buteo platypterus*) because it perches quietly in the woods, waiting to pounce on unsuspecting voles, chipmunks, or frogs, reports Lisa Petit of the Smithsonian Migratory Bird Center. (The first Broad-winged Hawk I saw, however, was one who was not so quiet. It stood over a branch of a woodland road, calling its high-pitched, musical *p-weeeeeeee*. Were it not for its call, I probably would not have noticed, though.) These are migratory hawks, and rather than flap their way to South America each fall, they use their broad wings to ride the thermals, soaring most of the way in huge flocks that number many thousands.

http://web2.si.edu/smbc/bom/bwha.htm

Hawk, Cooper's

Somewhat larger than the Sharp-shinned Hawk, with similar coloration, a Cooper's Hawk (*Accipiter cooperii*) can also be distinguished by its rounder tail. It, too, like the Sharp-shinned Hawk feeds on songbirds, preferring the larger ones such as starlings, robins, meadowlarks, and flickers, and occasionally a bird as large as a Ruffed Grouse. Chipmunks and red squirrels are also taken, and occasionally lizards, amphibians, and large insects. For a detailed description of this bird's feeding and breeding habits, visit the Hawk Conservancy's page (*first address*). The Cooper's Hawk is partially migratory, with some of its number wintering as far north as central New York. Found in deciduous woodlands and occasionally in urban areas, the Cooper's Hawk nests high in deciduous trees. Although its population was thought to be in decline, there are some indications that this is changing (*second address*). Population numbers of the smallish accipiter—medium-size forest hawks with short, broad wings and long tails—were reduced by the effects of DDT insecticide use. Backyard Bird News (*third address*) has a feature on Cooper's Hawk by Weir Nelson, who has actually held this bird while banding it.

http://www.hawk-conservancy.org/priors/coopers.htm

http://www.raptor.cvm.umn.edu/newwebdev/raptor/rfacts/coopers.html

http://www.wildlifehabitat.com/BBNJanuary1999.html

Cooper's Hawk (*Accipiter cooperii*) (JJA)

A B C D E F G H I J K L M N O P Q R S T U V W X Y Z

A
B
C
D
E
F
G
H
I
J
K
L
M
N
O
P
Q
R
S
T
U
V
W
X
Y
Z

Red-shouldered Hawk (*Buteo lineatus*) (JJA)

Hawk, Red-Shouldered

The Red-shouldered Hawk (*Buteo lineatus*) is smaller than the Red-tailed Hawk and is also different from its larger relative in its taste for fish. Although the Red-tailed dives for rats and mice, the Red-shouldered bird fancies food that's wet, although it also eats small rodents and other birds, not to mention insects. Red-shouldered Hawks have been known to take up a position at a trout farm and snag the young trout that come too close to the surface at the sides of the tank, reports this California State University at Bakersfield website (*first address*). Handsome birds, with rusty chests and shoulders and black, barred, tails and wings, Red-shouldered Hawks are sometimes the prey of Red-tailed Hawks and Great Horned Owls. They live mostly in the eastern half of the United States and in California; their numbers have been in decline, particularly in the East. The Raptor Center page at the University of Minnesota (*second address*) notes that this hawk was once considered the most common hawk in the northeastern United States. This site provides good natural history information about this hawk and other raptors. The Red-shouldered Hawk is most likely to be seen in spring, when it may perform elaborate aerial courtship displays (*third and fourth addresses*). Falconers, especially apprentice falconers, have worked with the handsome Red-

shouldered Hawk, which is considered fairly trainable (*fifth address*).

http://www.csubak.edu/FACT/redshoulder.html

http://www.raptor.cvm.umn.edu/raptor/rfacts/
   rshould.html

http://www.bham.net/oakmtn/treetop/redshoul.html

http://www.werewolf.net/~nicole/eagle/Bop/
   hawk1.html

http://brill.acomp.usf.edu/~fshivel/assign2.html

Hawk, Red-tailed

Also known as the Chicken Hawk, the Red-tailed Hawk (*Buteo jamaicensis*) probably should be known as the Rodent Hawk, since those species are a major part of its diet. An essay by Frederick M. and A. Marguerite Baumgartner from *Oklahoma Bird Life* takes a bird's-eye view of the hawk's life (*first address*). The Red-tailed Hawk is distinguished by its white chest and rusty tail, but general coloration is quite variable. In the West, there are much darker examples that still retain the rusty tail. The Henson Robinson Zoo in Lake Springfield, Illinois, has created species cards to teach about various species and has detailed descriptions and comparisons of the Red-tailed Hawks (*second address*). The Red-tail has a 4-foot wingspan and ranges in length from 18 to 25 inches; males are smaller, weighing up to two pounds; females may weigh as much as four. With its Latinate reference to Jamaica, it's not surprising to learn that the Red-tailed Hawk, known there as the Chicken Hawk, is a protected species on that island (*third address*). Red-tailed Hawks are marvelous hunters because they can soar for hours and their vision is sharp enough to spot moving prey as small as a mouse, from hundreds of feet up. One of the secrets to their visual success is their lack of color vision. To see one of them, its red tail unfurled on a dive, visit the fourth site.

http://www.tulsawalk.com/birding/redtail.html

http://www.hensonrobinsonzoo.org/
   home_i.html#introduction

http://www.jatoday.com.jm/environment/animals.html

http://nesc.org/wildlife/aotm/archive/aotm_8.html

Hawk, Sharp-shinned

In a flash, this small hawk (jay-sized) appears and snatches up his prey. *Accipiter striatus* is a raptor and lives by eating small birds; unlike the Broad-winged Hawks, the Sharp-shinned will sit quietly and wait for a likely meal to wander near (*first address*), or it may take the opposite approach to flush out its prey and rely on speed to catch it. The mature Sharp-shinned Hawk has rusty horizontal streaks on its chest, a gray back and head. A good photo of this bird, with prey pinned to the ground, can be found at the second address. An essay about the natural selection performed by these occasional bird-feeder visitors (at which sites they feed on the birds attracted to bird feeders) is at the third address. The Hawk Conservancy page on the Sharp-shinned Hawk goes into some detail about this raptor's feeding habits (*fourth address*): for example, a female of this species is capable of eating three small birds in a row, which she mostly plucks before devouring, though she eats the feet and beaks whole. Some birds are more likely to be prey than others: the chickadee for one is not commonly eaten.

http://www.chias.org/www/col/QTVR/sharp.html

http://eco.bio.lmu.edu/socal_nat_hist/birds/orders/falc/hawk_sh.htm

http://www.baldeagle.com/eagle/Bop/hawk2.html#B

http://www.hawk-conservancy.org/priors/sharpshin.htm

Hawk, Swainson's

Alexandre Gavashelshvili, a visiting biologist from the Republic of Georgia, studied Swainson's Hawk (*Buteo swainsoni*) at the Smithsonian Migratory Bird Center and reports many of his findings on this long-distance migrant (*first address*). Swainson's Hawk summers in western North America and winters on the pampas of southern South America. In South America and on its long journey, the hawk faces many threats, some being indirect. For example, when Argentina alfalfa and sunflower farmers used an *organophosphate* insecticide in 1995 and 1996 to bring a grasshopper outbreak under control, nearly 6,000 Swainson's Hawks were killed within a few days of feasting on the dead grass-hoppers. Other hawks died almost instantly from being directly sprayed with the insecticide while foraging the alfalfa and sunflower fields for insects. The irony was that the hawks were helping the farmers. The Swainson's Hawk nests in the American West and Canada and as far north as Alaska. It's apt to be found following farmers' mowing equipment, rounding up the rodents and insects disturbed by the activity (*second address*). The Hawk Conservancy page on the Swainson's Hawk (*third address*) describes this raptor as less impressive than some of its buteo relatives: "lank and long-winged; a little sluggish in its habits and, although well able to soar with the rest of the genus, more likely to be found perched on a post, low mound, or even on the ground." The Missouri Department of Conservation's excellent site—devoted to hawks, eagles, falcons, and vultures—includes comparisons and flight silhouettes for this and other species of hawks (*fourth address*).

http://web2.si.edu/smbc/bom/swha.htm

http://www.werewolf.net/~nicole/eagle/Bop/hawk2.html#B

http://www.hawk-conservancy.org/priors/swainson.htm

http://conservation.state.mo.us/nathis/birds/eagles/eagles.html

FEATHERED FACTS

Long-Haul Hawk

Many hawks migrate, but few nearly so far as Swainson's Hawk. This buteo summers in western North America and winters on the pampas of southern South America. Its annual round-trip totals more than 12,000 miles, placing it among the world's longest-distance migrating raptors.

—adapted from Alexandre Gavashelshvili, Smithsonian Migratory Bird Center

http://web2.si.edu/smbc/bom/swha.htm

A
B
C
D
E
F
G
H
I
J
K
L
M
N
O
P
Q
R
S
T
U
V
W
X
Y
Z

Help Us Help You!

Websites come and go. Addresses change. When it comes to birds and birding, we want to know about the comings, goings, and changings. Please report your observations to us at <http://www.acorn-online.com/hedge/birdup.htm>. And while you're there, check out the latest updates and additions.

Hawk Conservancy Website

The Hawk Conservancy is the premier Bird of Prey park in the United Kingdom, a member of the Federation of Zoological Gardens of Great Britain and Ireland, and the Southern Tourist Board's Top Attraction in the up-to-50,000-visitors class for 1998. It's located in Weyhill, Andover, Hants, and is open daily from the middle of February to the end of October. The website includes very detailed and entertainingly written information about a number of North American raptors and is well worth a visit.

http://www.hawk-conservancy.org

Hawk Mountain

Hawk Mountain, Pennsylvania, the world's first sanctuary for raptors, was established in 1934 to help bring a halt to the shooting of migrating hawks in the eastern Appalachians. The 2,400-acre refuge is staffed by 15 employees and receives more than 80,000 visitors a year. Its website brings you much information about Hawk Mountain, including regularly updated statistics on what species are being seen there. Also using statistics, there's a page telling the best times to see raptors there, by species. The center is currently preparing a book to be titled *101 Questions about Raptors* and is posting examples of the questions and answers online. The site also has three photo galleries: pictures of the sanctuary, raptors, and nonbird "critters" that are found on the mountain. Hawk Mountain sponsors an adopt-a-kestrel program for Pennsylvania school children and has free materials available about kestrels.

http://www.hawkmountain.org

Hawks

If you live in the Southwest, the work of Hawks Aloft Inc. will be of interest. "Hawks Aloft conducts a variety of avian research and survey projects in New Mexico," the website says. "Each is designed to increase our knowledge of raptors, passerines, and the habitats they occupy. This information provides land managers with the necessary tools to make informed decisions about land use in their areas." Studies include how the changing condition of the area's grasslands is affecting the endangered Aplomado Falcon, which requires the right environment to find the prey it needs. The group is also studying the ecology of Burrowing Owls at Kirtland Air Force Base. The site includes plenty of information about the society and its needs for help and has a neat Kids Corner, in which children offer their raptor-related stories.

http://www.rt66.com/~hawksnm/

Kite, Mississippi

Though it's a raptor, the Mississippi Kite (*Ictinia mississippiensis*) pretty much sticks to small stuff when it comes to prey, says Alexandre Gavashelshvili, a visiting researcher at the Smithsonian Migratory Bird Center. These kites are experts at catching insects on the wing—not with their mouths, as most insect-eaters do, but with their talons. And when the insects go, so do the kites, gathering in large flocks to migrate to South America as far south as Argentina. Its summering range in the United States is expanding, particularly in the Great Plains, but it's most common in the southeastern and south central states.

http://web2.si.edu/smbc/bom/miki.htm

Osprey

Known as the Fish Hawk, or the Fish Eagle, or Kalakotkas if you're Estonian, the Osprey (*Pandion haliaetus*) is found throughout the world. For all you'd ever need to know about this bird, visit the Kalakotkas, Site of the Osprey website (*first address*), created by a fellow who calls the Osprey his favorite bird and has devoted considerable time and space to sharing information about it. Ospreys are brown-backed with white heads (but with a black eye stripe), chests, and bellies, and they have a wingspan of about six feet. Females are larger than males, weighing up to five pounds; they also have a black ring across their chests. Look for Ospreys near water and, in many coastal locations, keep an eye out for human-made platforms supporting Osprey nests. These may be seen in fairly busy locations, alongside roads, for example. The nest is made of sticks and debris and may be in a tree, on a telephone pole, or even on the ground. Ospreys are sometimes mistaken for eagles; one way of identifying an Osprey is by its wings, which look like an "M" in flight, reports the Macbride Raptor Project in Iowa website (*second address*). Despite a drastic decline in their numbers due to pesticide use in the 1950s and 1960s, the Ospreys have been making a comeback. Their diet of fish makes them vulnerable to pollutants in rivers and other bodies of water, says the British Columbia Outdoors website (*third address*). The cleaning up of rivers has made fish not only safe to eat for humans but also safe for Ospreys. Ospreys have the advantage, as do owls, of a reversible outer toe, which enables them to grasp their prey more firmly. They also have nostrils that close when they plunge into the water to grab a fish, notes the Missouri Conservation Commission site (*fourth address*).

http://member.aol.com/kalakot2/1/osprey.html

http://www.ai-design.com/stargig/raptor/global/content/report/OspreyLarge.html

http://bcadventure.com/adventure/wilderness/birds/osprey.htm

http://conservation.state.mo.us/nathis/birds/eagles/eagles.html

Osprey (*Pandion haliaetus*) (JJA)

MEET THE MASTERS

Birth of an Idea

Jack Paul, Webmaster of Chickadee Web **<http://home.jtan.com/~jack/ckd.html>**, is a computer networking engineer who decided to combine that talent with his affection for chickadees. "I tell people I work on computers all day, but play on computers at night," he says. Jack first went online in early 1995. "It started out with just a few links on my very first webpage attempt," he notes. Back then, little was available, but as the Web grew, so did the sources of information about chickadees. "I decided they deserved their own special site." He scoured the Web for links. "There are a lot of them, more than most people think, which is a tribute to the popularity of the species," he says. "I decided to put all those links together into what I hoped would become one of the best birding sites on the Internet dedicated to a single family. I wanted others to come to love the chickadee as I do and to be able to find out anything they wanted to know without having to wade through thousands of links using search engines. Essentially I do all that for them and present the links and information in a series of easy to navigate pages. Over time, I added more and more specialized pages about hand-feeding, galleries, a general store, stories, etc."

A
B
C
D
E
F
G
H
I
J
K
L
M
N
O
P
Q
R
S
T
U
V
W
X
Y
Z

Owl, Barn

Few birds are as widely distributed, yet so infrequently seen, as the Barn Owl (*Tyto alba*). The bird lives on all six continents and through much of North America, reports the site of the Theodore Roosevelt Sanctuary of the National Audubon Society (*first address*). The Barn Owl has a spooky face, an attribute easily seen in the photos on this page; that plus its weird noises led farmers to sometimes think it was some sort of ghost. For a long time, farmers killed these raptors until they discovered that Barn Owls eat mostly rodents that farmers consider pests. Barn Owls like open spaces for hunting. In fact, as their name suggests, they like farms. Because so many farmers' fields are being developed into housing subdivisions or allowed to revert to forests, the hunting grounds of the Barn Owl are declining. In Maryland, the state Department of Natural Resources and the Southern Maryland Audubon Society has undertaken the Barn Owl Project (*second address*) to increase the state's seriously dwindling population of Barn Owls. They are setting up Barn Owl nesting boxes in locations considered ideal for the birds and are teaching farmers about the importance of these raptors, which feed on voles, gophers, moles, rabbits, and other creatures that don't exactly endear themselves to farmers. Arlene Ripley, who operates the Nest Box website and is an excellent nature photographer, accompanied a team of Maryland state naturalists who were banding owlets raised in nesting boxes in Calvert County, Maryland. Her photos illustrate the process. The site also has

FEATHERED FACTS

The Early Owl

Owls are famous for their eyesight, but many are also good listeners. The hearing of the Barn Owl is so good that the bird can find and capture prey in total darkness.

—adapted from Theodore Roosevelt Sanctuary

http://www.audubon.org/affiliate/ny/trs/baow01.htm

general information about Barn Owls, as well as links to other barn owl sites.

http://www.audubon.org/affiliate/ny/trs/baow01.htm
http://www.nestbox.com/barnowls.htm

Owl, Barred

The Barred Owl (*Strix varia*) is so called for the pattern on its breast, easily seen in the photo on this page of the Theodore Roosevelt Sanctuary site (*first address*), which has an aviary for caring for injured and nonreleasable birds. The site notes that the call of this widely distributed woodland owl sounds like *Who cooks for you? Who cooks for you all?* A couple of variations of the Barred Owl call can be heard on Tony Phillips' New York State Bird Songs site (*second address*).

http://www.audubon.org/affiliate/ny/trs/barr01.htm
http://math.math.sunysb.edu/~tony/birds/owls.html

Owl, Burrowing

The Burrowing Owl (*Speotyto cunicularia*) nests in holes dug in the ground by other creatures. As a result, although not yet endangered or rare, the species could be threatened by either the development of wild, uncultivated shortgrass lands or the decline in the numbers of hole-digging creatures, such as prairie dogs, observes the Canadian Museum of Nature, which has a good page on Burrowing Owls.

http://www.nature.ca/notebooks/english/burrowl.htm

Owl, Great Gray

The Great Gray Owl (*Strix nebulosa*) is North America's largest owl and also among its rarest. The bird inhabits boreal forests, mostly in Canada, but sometimes appears in odd places, such as Rowley, Massachusetts, north of Boston, where Don Crockett got some spectacular shots in 1996. These show the bird's amazing "stare," as well as its camouflage and what it looks like in flight.

http://www.virtualbirder.com/greatblue/birding/BOTW/GreatGray.html

Great Horned Owl (Dover)

Owl, Great Horned

Professor Gerry Rising tells of a middle-of-the-night attempt to meet a female Great Horned Owl (*Bubo virginianus*). In the process you'll learn a great deal about this large owl that eats squirrels, muskrats, opossums, and even porcupines. "They will be delighted to dine on small dogs or domestic cats, so they represent another reason to keep your pets inside at night," Rising notes (*first address*). To learn more about this majestic owl, visit Peterson Online (*second address*), which offers pictures, a range map, and much information. The bird, notes Peterson, is found in most parts of North America, coast-to-coast, tropics to Arctic.

http://www.acsu.buffalo.edu/~insrisg/nature/nw99/hornedowl.html

http://www.petersononline.com/birds/month/ghow/index.html

Owl, Snowy

Perhaps no North American owl has the majestic, mysterious aura of the Snowy Owl (*Nyctea scandiaca*). Large and almost all white, this bird is not common and appears as far south as the northern half of the United States only in certain winters when food supplies in its native northern Canada are low. That food is primarily lemmings, reports the Canadian Museum of Nature.

http://www.nature.ca/notebooks/english/snowyowl.htm

Owl, Spotted

The Spotted Owl (*Strix occidentalis*) has in recent years become as well known as most members of the U.S. Congress. In fact, it has been the subject of more politicking than probably any bird in recent years. That's because it's an endangered species that lives in old-growth Pacific northwestern forests that are highly desired by the timber industry. "The bird's ecology and conservation are the topic of vigorous debate among foresters, wildlife ecologists, academics, politicians, social scientists, and economists," notes the Birds of North America site, which has an online page that briefly describes the debate and shows a map with the ranges of three Spotted Owl subspecies: Northern, California, and Mexican (*first address*). The World Wildlife Fund in Canada has an excellent fact sheet about the Spotted Owl, describing its life history and the threats to its survival (*second address; then look under Resources, then Fact Sheets*). The fund says that in British Columbia, the Spotted Owl is close to extinction, with only 25 to 100 birds known to exist. The fund offers suggestions as to what individuals can do to help this bird. The U. S. Fish & Wildlife Service has a rundown on the habitat of the Northern Spotted Owl (*Strix occidentalis caurina*), including how it analyzes data on the owls (*third address*). The Mexican Spotted Owl (*Strix occidentalis lucida*), also endangered, can be found in Texas, where the Texas Parks and Wildlife Department site offers a fact sheet (*fourth address*). Diane Porter has an excellent essay about Spotted Owls at her Birdwatching.com website (*fifth address*). The population problems of this endangered species are described in some detail on this Fish & Wildlife Service page—if you can type its lengthy address (*sixth address*).

http://www.birdsofna.org/excerpts/spottedowl.html

http://www.wwfcanada.org/

http://www.fws.gov/r9endspp/i/b6k.html

http://www.tpwd.state.tx.us/nature/endang/mexowl.htm

http://www.birdwatching.com/stories/spottedowl.html

http://bluegoose.arw.r9.fws.gov/NWRSFiles/WildlifeMgmt/SpeciesAccounts/Birds/SpottedOwl/SpottedOwlHabitat.html

A B C D E F G H I J K L M N O P Q R S T U V W X Y Z

Share Your Knowledge

This book is full of websites dealing with birds. Why not join them? You could be providing birders around the world with some valuable information.

How could you, the amateur bird-watcher from Middletown, help the cause of birding? Here are some ideas.

- Create a site that lists the species of birds that have been seen in your neighborhood—even your yard. You can base it on your own sightings or the sightings of several bird-watchers. A website like this can give newcomers to the area or prospective visitors an idea of what can be seen in and about your community. If you have a local expert on birds with a long local life list, ask him or her if you can put it online.

- Tell where the good birding spots are in your area. Include parks and refuges, explaining the types of birds one is apt to see in each season. And don't forget to include directions to each location—many birders will be entering unknown territory when they come to your town.

- Share your photos of birds by scanning the images and placing them online.

- Provide late-breaking news of sightings of interesting or unusual birds in your area including the arrival of spring migrants.

- Create a site that has two or more of the above!

Putting together a website can be simple—and cost-free. (See Net Notes on page 158).

Owl Research Center

Around 162 species of owls are found on earth, but little is known about them because most are hard to observe. The Owl Research Institute in Missoula, Montana, which conducts research relating to owls, describes its work and accomplishments on this website. Also, a North American Owl Identification Guide, under construction when we stopped by, will provide useful information about many species.

http://www.montana.com/owl/

Raptor Center

The Raptor Center at the University of Minnesota is an international medical facility for birds of prey. "Our mission," the site says, "is to preserve biological diversity among raptors and other avian species through medical treatment, scientific investigation, education, and management of wild populations." The center can even arrange free transportation of injured raptors via major airlines. Among the many features of the site are a guide for handling injured raptors, Raptor Facts, raptor census information, legislation concerning raptors, pictures, sounds, and forums.

http://www.raptor.cvm.umn.edu

Raptor Links

The Raptor Center at the University of Minnesota has a fine collection of links to other raptor sites, as well as sites that specialize in wildlife rehabilitation.

http://www.raptor.cvm.umn.edu/newwebdev/raptor/ websites.html

Raptor Quiz

How far can owls turn their heads? What's the smallest raptor found in the United States? What raptor has the largest wingspan? These are some of the questions asked in the Raptor Quiz, offered by Hawks Aloft. The quiz includes a dozen questions, some of them illustrated.

http://www.rt66.com/~hawksnm/Quiz.htm

Rocky Mountain Raptor Center

The Rocky Mountain Raptor Center at Colorado State University in Fort Collins, Colorado, rehabilitates injured or orphaned raptors. The site has natural history information, usually accompanied by photos, about the Red-tailed Hawk, Great Horned Owl, Swainson's Hawk, Bald Eagle, American Kestrel, Prairie Falcon, Golden Eagle, Northern Harrier, Barn Owl, Burrowing Owl, Western Screech Owl, Short-eared Owl, Turkey Vultures, and others. The site also explains its work and offers an adopt-a-raptor program. You can also learn how to become a volunteer.

http://holly.acns.colostate.edu/~sharonh/rmrp/

Vulture, Black

The current trend of milder winters in many parts of North America seems to be extending the range of the Black Vulture (*Coragyps atratus*), once a bird of the southern and western United States and now a species that is working its way into New England, New York, and other cooler states. In the West it may be the most numerous bird of prey, says the Hawk Conservancy (*first address*), which also notes that the species can be found through most of South America to Patagonia. Both the Black Vulture and the Turkey Vulture (*see next entry*) have bare, featherless heads. The reason for this is explained by the Western North Carolina Nature Center in Asheville, North Carolina (*second address*), which has a good profile of the species—and a Black Vulture of its own at the center.

http://www.hawk-conservancy.org/priors/blackvul.htm
http://www.wncnaturecenter.org/af/blackvulture.html

Vulture, Turkey

One of the most interesting and skilled soaring birds in the world is the Turkey Vulture (*Cathartes aura*), also one of our largest birds and a close relative of the condor. This bird is commonly seen gliding gracefully for hours in the skies over much of the United States, and its year-round range continues to move northward. One of the few North American birds that has a sense of smell, Turkey Vultures can detect carrion from high altitudes and are among the most important of nature's janitors. To them, a stinking carcass is a tasty

Turkey Vulture (*Cathartes aura*) (JJA)

meal. The Turkey Vulture Society, which is devoted to the study of this species, reports that "One of the more important studies we will be conducting is the ability of the vulture's digestive system to kill the bacteria and virus of infected meat the bird consumes. The [vulture's] ability to disinfect rodent carcasses carrying the Hantavirus will be studied. This work could possibly be of much significance to human medical research." This site will tell all about Turkey Vultures, including their natural history, nomenclatures, folklore, and biology. Of course, there are pictures, too, of these birds that are so graceful in the air and awkward on the ground. (*See also Events, Mountain & Pacific.*)

http://www.accutek.com/vulture/

World Center for Raptors

The World Center for Birds of Prey in Boise, Idaho, houses more than 200 birds of prey whose young are released into the wild in the United States and around the world. This site explains its work. (*See also Aviaries.*)

http://www.peregrinefund.org/WCVMIntr.html

SEA & SHORE

Although they are often called seabirds, many species in this group in fact live far from the sea, though they usually like water of some sort nearby. The group includes gulls, terns, pelicans, and cormorants. Some authors have called these the *aerialists* because they do most of their foraging from the air. We've also included in this section the pelagic species, that is, the petrels and storm-petrels, shearwaters, albatrosses, and jaegers that are often found far offshore. These may occasionally be spotted close to land, but the most popular way to view them is to take one of the many pelagic tours offered periodically along the coasts. Many of these species—especially gulls and terns—can be difficult to tell apart, and the Web offers some noble efforts to help identify many look-alike species. *(See also North American Birds, Waders.)*

Gannet, Northern

With a wingspan of some five feet, the Northern Gannet (*Morus bassanus*) is North America's largest seabird but is rarely seen by the average person since it spends most of the year far at sea. However, in summer, they nest on steep cliffs of the Canadian Atlantic shore, sometimes cementing their nests with guano, reports the Canadian Museum of Nature, which offers natural history about and an illustration of the Northern Gannet (*first address*). Peterson Online (*second site*) recommends "Bonaventure Island on the Gaspe Peninsula of Quebec [as] the place to go to see large numbers of this species." Excellent Roger Tory Peterson illustrations show what this great bird looks like.

http://www.nature.ca/notebooks/english/gannet.htm

http://www.petersononline.com/birds/month/noga/index.html

Northern Gannet (Dover)

Gull, Black-headed

The Black-headed Gull (*Larus ridibundus*) is a small species, about 13 inches, that sports a dark brown head and a short, thin red bill. Bonaparte's Gull is similar but has a black bill instead of the Black-headed Gull's maroon-red bill. The Black-headed is found in coastal New England and most often in Nova Scotia. According to Environment Canada's site (*second address*), the Black-headed Gull is more at home in Europe but has been making inroads into North America. "It is very abundant in Europe and has been expanding westward; after colonizing Iceland at the turn of the century, it was reported nesting in Greenland, then in Newfoundland, and recently at several sites along the Canadian and northeast U.S. coasts," the Environment Canada says.

http://www.mbr-pwrc.usgs.gov/id/framlst/i0551id.html

http://www.qc.ec.gc.ca/faune/oiseaux_de_mer/html/Epp551.html

Gull, Franklin's

Franklin's Gull (*Larus pipixcan*) is clearly not primarily a bird of the seashore, spending its life in the Midwest, breeding as far north as Canada and traveling down into Texas, coastal Louisiana, south Florida, and the Keys during the winter. For a photo of this black-billed, gray and white gull, and distribution maps visit the Patuxent Wildlife Research Center site (*first address*). Franklin, by the way, is not Benjamin, but Sir John (1786–1847), a British navigator and explorer who mysteriously died with his crew on an Arctic expedition (some conjecture from poisoning by lead, which had contaminated their tinned goods). John Sterling of the Smithsonian Migratory Bird Center (*second address*) notes that this bird was once called Franklin's Rosy Gull for its rose-colored breast and belly, but says many prefer the name, Prairie Dove, descriptive of its breeding range near the lakes and marshes of the northern prairies of the United States and Canada. Sterling has a fine profile of this migrant that winters as far south as Peru and northern Chile.

http://www.mbr-pwrc.usgs.gov/id/framlst/i0590id.html

http://web2.si.edu/smbc/bom/frgu.htm

Gull, Glaucous

The Glaucous Gull (*Larus hyperboreus*) is similar to the Iceland gull, but larger and is a bird found mostly in the northern tier of the United States and Canada.

http://www.mbr-pwrc.usgs.gov/id/framlst/
i0420id.html

Gull, Glaucous-winged

A western species, the Glaucous-winged Gull (*Larus glaucescens*) is described by the Patuxent Center's writers (*first address*) as winning the "mean"-looking title among gulls, with its large bill and flat forehead. Unlike the similar Herring Gull, it has dark eyes. Steve Hampton's gull identification guide can help you identify this species (*second address*).

http://www.mbr-pwrc.usgs.gov/id/framlst/i0440id.html
http://www.west.net/~dj/gl-w_d.htm

Gull, Great Black-backed

With a 65-inch wingspan, the Great Black-backed Gull (*Larus marinus*) is another gull tagged with a "mean" appearance for its flat forehead and large bill. North America's largest gull is found mostly along the East Coast, north to Canada, according to Patuxent's site (*first address*). To hear a couple samples of its call, visit Tony Phillips' New York Bird Songs site (*second address*). Erik Toorman in Belgium, where this bird is also found, offers a good photo of one with wings up (*third address*). This bird, incidentally, is often called Greater Black-backed Gull.

http://www.mbr-pwrc.usgs.gov/id/framlst/
i0470id.html
http://www.math.sunysb.edu/~tony/birds/
shorebirds.html
http://sun-hydr-01.bwk.kuleuven.ac.be/hydraulics/
EToorman/b426.jpg

Gull, Herring

Herring Gull (*Larus argentatus*) is the bird probably most often described as a "seagull." Although Her-ring Gulls are most populous along the seacoasts, they are also common inland. The Herring Gull is a major scavenger, familiar as a "dumpster diver" and frequenter of parking lots or anywhere there might be scraps of food to be found. These big, yellow-eyed birds have a wingspan of about 55 inches and sport large yellow bills and yellow legs. Their wings and backs are gray, and their tails are white. They're similar to California Gulls (*Larus californicus*) but a bit larger, notes Environment Canada's site (*first address*), which reports that the Herring Gull is quite adaptive at nesting; although it usually builds its nests on the ground, it will also build them in conifers and even on the roofs of buildings. The Patuxent website has much life history and range data (*second address*).

http://www.qc.ec.gc.ca/faune/oiseaux_de_mer/
html/Epp510.html
http://www.mbr-pwrc.usgs.gov/id/framlst/
i0510id.html

MEET THE MASTERS

Great Online Libraries?

As of early 1999, Tony Phillips, Webmaster of the New York Bird Songs website <http://math.math.sunysb.edu/~tony/birds/index.html>, had recorded 82 species and placed them online. However, he hopes other sources will put their collections online as well. One of the world's greatest centers of birding knowledge is in New York State: Cornell University's Laboratory of Ornithology. Tony hopes that one day, "Cornell will put their Library of Natural Sounds on the Web. Their records are superb." He also hopes "to get the American Museum of Natural History to have a birdsong gallery where you could hear birds from all over the world, as well as looking at their poor, stuffed bodies. I'm going to keep bugging them until they do it."

A B C D E F G H I J K L M N O P Q R S T U V W X Y Z

A
B
C
D
E
F
G
H
I
J
K
L
M
N
O
P
Q
R
S
T
U
V
W
X
Y
Z

Gull, Iceland

The Iceland Gull (*Larus glaucoides*), concentrated in the Canadian Maritimes and New England, is a lighter, slighter version of the Herring Gull.

http://www.mbr-pwrc.usgs.gov/id/framlst/
    i0430id.html

Gull, Laughing

The Laughing Gull (*Larus atricilla*), which breeds along the East Coast, has a handsome black head and quite a hearty laugh; this page at Patuxent's site (*first address*) has a sample of the laugh, along with much other information. The Laughing Gulls are among the more friendly species, and one can often walk within a few feet of a flock of them along a beach. North Carolina Audubon notes that the Laughing Gull loses its black hood in winter (*second address*). This gull is a wide-ranging species; it is common in Hawaii, for instance, and the Honolulu Zoo site has a good profile of the bird (*third address*).

http://www.mbr.nbs.gov/id/mlist/h0580.html
http://www.ncaudubon.org/wb_02.html
http://www.honoluluzoo.org/laughing_gull.htm

Gull, Little

The Little Gull (*Larus minutus*) when breeding has a handsome black head that trims his mostly white body and tail, with pale gray back and upper wings, and red legs. As the name suggests, it's a little bird, only about nine inches, more tern- than gull-size. Nonbreeding adults have black smudges over their ears and grayer heads.

http://www.mbr-pwrc.usgs.gov/id/framlst/
    i0601id.html

Gull, Ring-billed

The Ring-billed Gull (*Larus delawarensis*) is one of the most common and most widely distributed gulls of the United States, having been seen in nearly every

Ring-billed Gull (*Larus delawarensis*) (JJA)

state, although rarely in the Southwest. The Patuxent site (*first address*) has distribution and natural history data about the Ring-billed Gull, which, as it name implies, has a black ring around its yellow bill. And for those who like to call gulls "seagulls," the Northern Prairie Wildlife Research Center's website (*second address*) notes that the Ring-billed Gull is the most common gull found in North Dakota, about as far from the sea as you can get in the United States. Like other gulls, this one likes trash; around cities in Quebec, it's been found that 30 to 40 percent of the Ring-billed Gull's diet is household waste (*third address*).

http://www.mbr.nbs.gov/id/mlist/h0540.html
http://www.npwrc.usgs.gov/resource/othrdata/
    marshbrd/ringgull.htm
http://www.qc.ec.gc.ca/faune/oiseaux_de_mer/html/
    Epp540.html

Gull, Thayer's

Add the Thayer's Gull (*Larus thayeri*) to the collection of confusing gulls who resemble the Herring Gull and the Icelandic Gull. For identification tips, see this Patuxent Center page.

http://www.mbr-pwrc.usgs.gov/id/framlst/
    i0518id.html

Gull, Western

The Western Gull (*Larus occidentalis*) is built much like the Herring Gull but with a much darker back and wings. It's concentrated along the West Coast, from southern California to British Columbia (*first address*). Although generally considered useful birds along the coast, some ornithologists believe they are a nuisance on islands where they may be predators of other species of nesting birds. Details of its population trends and efforts at its conservation and management are found on an excerpt from the Birds of North America site (*second address*).

http://www.mbr-pwrc.usgs.gov/id/framlst/
i0490id.html

http://www.birdsofna.org/excerpts/wgull.html

Birds at Your Local Library

The explosion of interest in the Internet has led to a most handy development for book lovers: Many local library catalogs have gone online.

From the comfort of your home, any time of the day or night, any day of the week, you may be able to visit your local library's card catalog to see if it owns a copy of a birding book you're looking for—and whether the copy is available. In fact, you can browse most online libraries for books by topic, or even by shelf.

To see if your library is online, give it a phone call and ask for the Web address. If it's after hours, try a search engine—if you live in Blatsburg and have a Blatsburg Public Library, try searching for "Blatsburg Public Library." You can also look for online directories. For instance, the St. Joseph County Public Library in South Bend, Indiana, has an online list of more than 560 libraries around the world—but mostly in the United States—that are online. Go to the home page and select Public Libraries. You'll then be given the option of searching for a library by name or location, or reading the whole list.

http://www1.sjcpl.lib.in.us

Gulls

If there were a prize for the most challenging bird identification category, gulls and terns would be up near the top. They molt as many as 11 times before reaching mature coloration, and that may require two to four years. Meanwhile, their plumage can be highly variable during any period. Don't despair if you find an identification eludes you; you're not alone. Yet there are sites where it is possible to sort through a bird's description (take careful field notes) and arrive at an educated guess, or possibly a conclusive identification. To break into the world of gulls, visit Steve Hampton and Don DesJardin's Gull Identification Mainpage (*first address*) featuring images, links to images, and individual species/subspecies descriptions. Photos, quizzes, charts, and well-written descriptions all provide tools that help to put a gull in its place, taxonomically. A section that reviews the different shades of gray is especially helpful: due to variable lighting conditions, this is one of the more difficult, yet one of the least variable of the gull identifying tools. Gulls are often considered "sea" birds, but they travel widely and are common migratory visitors in the Midwest. Thus, one of the better sources of information is the Northern Prairie Wildlife Research Center's site (*second address*); no photos are provided but the written descriptions and dates of sightings are useful. The Northern Prairie Wildlife Research Center offers some generic information (*third address*). Paul Slichter has profiles of Pacific Northwest Gulls (*fourth address*). The Yukon Gullery (*fifth address*) has great photos, as well as brief profiles on many gull species found in the Yukon.

http://www.west.net/~dj/gulls.htm

http://www.npwrc.usgs.gov/resource/1998/stcroix/
laridae.htm

http://www.npwrc.usgs.gov/resource/othrdata/
marshbrd/gulls.htm

http://district.gresham.k12.or.us/ghs/nature/animal/
bird/gull/gull.htm

http://www.yukonweb.com/community/ybc/gullery.html

A
B
C
D
E
F
G
H
I
J
K
L
M
N
O
P
Q
R
S
T
U
V
W
X
Y
Z

A
B
C
D
E
F
G
H
I
J
K
L
M
N
O
P
Q
R
S
T
U
V
W
X
Y
Z

Murre, Common

The Common Murre (*Uria aalge*), also called the Thin-billed Murre, is a bird of cold oceans, and is found in the northern Atlantic and Pacific. It comes ashore only to nest, reports the Canadian Museum of Nature.

http://www.nature.ca/notebooks/english/murre.htm

Pelican, Brown

The Brown Pelican (*Pelecanus occidentalis*), common in places like Florida, is threatened in Texas, according to the Texas Parks & Wildlife Department. The reason? "Pelicans almost disappeared from Texas because they were poisoned by the pesticide DDT, which caused them to lay thin-shelled eggs which broke during incubation," the state site says.

http://www.tpwd.state.tx.us/nature/endang/
  bpelican.htm

Pelican, White

The American White Pelican (*Pelecanus erythrorhynchos*) is an odd and somewhat uncommon bird. You'd expect pelicans to live along ocean shores and, indeed, in winter, they can be found in southern Florida and along the Gulf Coast. But in summer, the breeding season, most are well inland, in places like Montana, Nebraska, Manitoba, and Saskatchewan. The Patuxent Wildlife Research Center offers maps of summer and winter ranges—including an animated range map—plus lots of other data about the White Pelican (*first address*). Clark College's biology department has a concise page—but not so concise an address—on the White Pelican, with two excellent photos (*second address*). The Canadian Museum of Nature, which has a nicely done report about the White Pelican, notes that it is considered a threatened species (*third address*).

http://www.mbr.nbs.gov/id/framlst/i1250id.html
http://www.clark.edu/Academics/Biology/Fieldstudy/
  Malheur/Birds/pelican.htm
http://www.nature.ca/notebooks/english/wpelican.htm

Pelican Watch Page

The Pelican Watch Page is an online forum, devoted solely to pelicans. "We really hope that people all over the world will post their sightings of pelicans on this page," say the sponsors of the Redberry Pelican Project site (*see Pelicans, People, & Protected Areas later in this section*). "Apart from the fun for our readers of personally keeping track of their favorite pelicans, the information gathered will provide valuable information for conservationists about the migration, nesting activities, and population trends of the various species." Posting a message is as easy as connecting to the website—no special logging in information is needed.

http://ecocanada.com/seepel/wwwboard.html

Pelicans & Other Creatures

Photographer Wieslaw Kalinowski offers his pictures and descriptions of pelicans found around Naples, Florida.

http://gator.naples.net/~nfn04208/galeria.html

Pelicans, People, & Protected Areas

For the Redberry Pelican Project at Redberry Lake, near Saskatoon, Saskatchewan, pelicans are special. In the summer the lake has a colony of White Pelicans. The organization was formed in 1989 to protect the habitat and to encourage "environmentally sound ecotourism of the area." The website has a good deal of information about White Pelicans, as well as seven other pelican species found around the world. Redberry Lake, incidentally, is home to nearly 190 species of birds. Environment Canada's site has an extensive description of Redberry Lake and its wildlife (*second address*).

http://www.redbay.com/redpel/pelicans.htm
http://www.mb.ec.gc.ca/english/LIFE/MIGBIRDS/
  SANCTUARIES/REDBERRY.htm

Penguin, Adelie

Oceanographer Vicki Johns recounts her encounters with Adelie Penguins in Antarctica in this nicely done piece, called Search for Antarctic Spring, on the University of Tennessee website. "I was never able to photograph them swimming, but believe me, it was a beautiful sight," she writes. "The most amazing part was watching them land. They shot straight out of the water and landed on their feet!" This species, incidentally, builds its nests from pebbles.

http://www.utenn.edu/uwa/vpps/ur/ut2kids/
  penguins/penguin.html

Penguins

This site gives a good rundown on the different kinds of penguins found round the world, including pictures of many. Make sure you check out the stories and legends about penguins found in the link Penguins in Art.

http://www.galactic.co.uk/iainf/penguin.html

Puffin, Atlantic

Maine is the only place on the East Coast of the United States where you can see puffins. In fact, the Atlantic Ocean has only one species of puffin, and Mainebirding.net's Puffin Page (*first address*) has extensive information about the Atlantic or Common Puffin (*Fratercula artica*). This species—sometimes called a "sea parrot" because of its big, colorful bill—spends most of its time at sea. Centuries ago, it nested on at least a half dozen islands off Maine, but the birds were hunted down for both food and feathers. A century ago, only one pair of puffins was known south of the Canadian border. Partly thanks to special efforts described on this page and on links from it, puffins are now nesting again on at least four islands off Maine. The page has much natural history and includes lists of guides who will take you out to see the puffins. Incidentally, Atlantic Puffins are far from an endangered species within their range, which runs from Maine north through Canada, Greenland, and to Norway. There are an estimated *20 million pairs* of

them! It's just that their favorite haunts aren't usually our favorites. The Canadian Museum of Nature site (*second address*) has a nice write-up about puffins, noting that one colony off Newfoundland has an estimated 300,000 birds.

http://www.mainebirding.net/puffin.shtml
http://www.nature.ca/notebooks/english/puffin.htm

Puffin, Horned & Tufted

The western version of the Atlantic Puffin is the Horned Puffin (*Fratercula corniculata*), which is found along the coast of the Pacific Northwest. The Alaska Department of Fish & Game Wildlife Notebook offers a profile of both the Horned Puffin and the Tufted Puffin (*Fratercula cirrhata*), another Pacific Northwest species. "Horned puffins are the species most often depicted on souvenirs," the agency says at its site. "In summer they have a black back and neck with white on the sides of the head and on their breast. The white breast is so distinctive that in one Eskimo language puffins are called *katukh-puk*, meaning 'big white breast.' "

http://www.state.ak.us/local/akpages/FISH.GAME/
  notebook/bird/puffins.htm

FEATHERED FACTS

Small Family

The Common Puffin of the North Atlantic lays only one egg each season.

—adapted from Canadian Museum of Nature

http://www.nature.ca/notebooks/english/puffin.htm

A B C D E F G H I J K L M N O P Q R S T U V W X Y Z

Shorebird Handbook

WetNet, a cooperative network of wetlands conservation organizations, has an extensive library of information about the 49 species of shorebirds that breed in North America. Of these, 40 migrate in winter to temperate and tropical regions in Central and South America and 31 fly annually between the Arctic and South America. This site's categories of information about these birds include age determination; conservation; energetics (energy-storing ability) and metabolism; foraging behavior and biology; habitat requirements, selection, and use; migration; molting and plumage; nesting; nonbreeding behavior; population; roosting behavior; and systematics (such as subspecies differences). Although the site is scholarly, the rich collection of information is very readable by the layman.

http://www.wetlands.ca/wi-a/whsrn/sbirdbook.html

Saving Pictures

In browsing the Web, you'll run across many beautiful photos and drawings of birds, or maps of their ranges. Just about any of them can be instantly saved to your hard drive for future enjoyment or even use in a book report or other school project. With a Windows browser, you just right-click on the image, and a menu will appear, offering you the option of saving the image as a file or even as desktop wallpaper.

When you Save As to your disk, opt for JPG format, if you want only to view the picture again. The file size is much smaller than other formats and uses less space. (However, if you use a .BMP or "bitmap" format, you can later edit the picture with the Paint program that comes with Windows.)

On my hard drive, I have created a folder called "graphics" where I save photos, maps, and other illustrations.

Remember that many bird-related pictures on the Web are copyrighted. If you use these for any commercial or other outside purpose—other than your own enjoyment—you risk getting sued and billed for the picture.

Skimmer, Black

The Black Skimmer (*Rynchops niger*) is an unusual tern that has become specially adapted to catch food in an unusual way. Its lower mandible, or jaw, is longer than the upper. The bird flies along the surface of the water, often near surf, with its lower mandible in the water, hoping to scoop up little surface fish. It's found coast-to-coast and on major river systems, reports the WetNet site (*first address*). The Wild Texas website has an excellent photo of the Black Skimmer, as well as a chick (*second address*). Kodak has an even better action photo (*third address*).

http://red.glo.state.tx.us/wetnet/species/skimmer.html

http://www.wildtexas.com/wildguides/skimmer.htm

http://www.kodak.com/digitalImages/samples/images/
    jpeg/birds/bird04.jpg

Tern, Black

What bird may nest on top of a muskrat home? The Black Tern (*Chlidonias niger*), which lives in inland marshes, sloughs, and small lakes, and feeds on insects. Although it usually makes a floating nest of dead plant materials, it sometimes chooses the roof of a muskrat house to raise a family. The bird is about 10 inches long with a black head and body and gray wings; it's described as "gregarious year round" by a writer for the Northern Prairie Wildlife Research Center site (*first address*). For more population surveys and another look at the Black Tern, visit the Patuxent site, as well (*second address*). The distribution and eating habits of the Black Tern, which winters in Central and South America and summers in North America, are described in considerable detail in the Birds of North America site (*third address*).

http://www.npwrc.usgs.gov/resource/othrdata/
    marshbrd/blktern.htm

http://www.mbr-pwrc.usgs.gov/bbs/htm96/trn626/
    tr0770.html

http://www.birdsofna.org/excerpts/blktern.html

MEET THE MASTERS

Getting Specific

Julia Pahountis has visited many birding web-sites. "Most of the time, it's difficult to find any specific information (i.e., What birds do owls eat? What prompted the Christmas Bird Count, etc.). This is the kind of information I feel that people would want to know." And it's the kind Julia puts on the Nutty Birdwatcher <http://www.birdnature.com>.

Tern, Common

Familiar to fishermen, the Common Tern (*Sterna hirundo*) is a fisher, too: it dives for its supper and can be seen flying over schools of fish as it targets a meal. These terns nest along the Atlantic Coast from Nova Scotia to Virginia on isolated beaches and sandbars, lining a small depression in the sand with seaweed and grasses. They're reported to be fiercely protective of their offspring and will dive at and defecate on intruders, according to the Northern Prairie Wildlife Research Center (*first address*). The black-capped gray and white birds are about 14 inches long and have relatively long wings and forked tails. Their orange-yellow bills have a black tip and their call will be familiar to anyone who's ever visited the seashore. They winter in Florida and further south. The Assateague Island site (*second address*) includes a page about this bird, complete with photo and call. Tony Phillips' New York Bird Songs site (*third address*) has two good recordings of the call, which Frank M. Chapman described in 1903 as "a vibrant, purring *tearrr*."

http://www.npwrc.usgs.gov/resource/othrdata/
    marshbrd/comtern.htm
http://www.assateague.com/tern.html
http://math.math.sunysb.edu/~tony/birds/
    shorebirds.html

Tern, Gull-billed

The Gull-billed Tern (*Sterna nilotica*) is considered an endangered species. Similar to its Common Tern cousin, but stocky and with a gull-like black bill, the bird is found along the Atlantic and Gulf of Mexico coasts and winters in South America. This page comes from the Institute of Marine Sciences at the University of Southern Mississippi as part of its Species at Risk in the Gulf of Mexico site.

http://www.ims.usm.edu/~musweb/sternilo.htm

Tern, Least

The smallest tern, appropriately known as the Least Tern (*Sterna antilarum*), is a lively little bird who nests in colonies. The bird resembles its larger relatives, in gray and white, with a black cap and yellow, black-tipped bill. According to the Otter Island, South Carolina, site (*first address*), the Least Tern "breeds most successfully on unvegetated *dredge-spoil islands* or on flat rooftops in urban areas." It's found on the East and Gulf Coasts and winters in South America, but habitat loss may pose a threat for the species, and they're listed as endangered or threatened in most of their range. The Birds of North America site (*second address*) offers a top-notch essay regarding the migration and breeding habits of the Least Tern. Tina Bentz at the Smithsonian Migratory Bird Center (*third address*) offers a fine profile of the Least Tern, explaining why even personal watercraft are endangering the bird.

http://www.csc.noaa.gov/otter/htmls/data/species/
    ltern.htm#top
http://www.birdsofna.org/excerpts/lsttern.html
http://web2.si.edu/smbc/bom/lete.htm

Tern, Roseate

Audubon called the Roseate Tern (*Sterna dougallii*) the "hummingbird of the sea, so light and graceful were their movements." His drawing reflects his observations (*first address*). With a pink breast, black cap, and tail accented by streamers, this beautiful bird nests in Atlantic Canada and south to Long Island on coastal islands and winters on sandbars off South America, reports Environment Canada (*second address*). Ted C. D'Eon has been watching Roseate Tern nesting areas on the Brothers Islands off Nova Scotia and has some interesting notes regarding their population changes and their egg numbers (*third address*).

http://www.historical-museum.org/collect/audubon/roseate.htm

http://www.ns.doe.ca/wildlife/roseate/index.html

http://fox.nstn.ca/~deonted/ternrep.html

Tern, Royal

The biggest tern has the appropriate name, *Sterna maxima*, and its common name also connotes its leading status among terns. A crow-sized species, the Royal Tern can be found on the Gulf and East Coasts where it feeds almost entirely on fish. It's a jaunty-looking bird with a striking crested black cap and a large orange bill accenting its gray and white body. The tail is fairly long and forked; the legs are black. The Royal Tern is similar to the Elegant Tern (*Sterna elegans*); it does not reach adult plumage until the third year. For pointers on identifying Royal Terns, visit the Patuxent Wildlife Research Center site (*first address*). For a nice photograph of an Elegant Tern feeding its young, stop by the Pepperdine site (*second address*).

http://www.mbr-pwrc.usgs.gov/id/framlst/i0650id.html

http://hale.pepperdine.edu/~jlrosso/Elegenttern.JPG

Terns

Like gulls, terns are part of the Laridae family. Smaller and daintier than their gull cousins, they also are a bit pickier about what they'll eat. Like the gulls the terns have webbed feet, but are not as strong swimmers. A site that limits itself to Pacific Northwest terns and gulls (*first address*) is helpful for West Coast identifications, and makes it clear how difficult it is to determine what specific gull is being observed. Ted C. D'Eon has been studying the several species of terns in his area of Nova Scotia for some years and has a site full of interesting observations and sources of information about them (*second address*). He offers a map of Lobster Bay, showing where different species of terns and other seabirds nest.

http://district.gresham.k12.or.us/ghs/nature/animal/bird/gull/gull.htm

http://fox.nstn.ca/~deonted/ternrep.html

SWIMMERS

Sooner or later, almost any body of water—even a large puddle—is visited by some member of the "swimming" birds. These include the ducks, geese, coots, loons, grebes, and swans. (Although birds like gulls and pelicans can swim, they are covered in the seabirds section.) Readers should note that many species in this category are considered game birds. Ducks and geese, especially, are often sought by hunters. But for obvious reasons, hunting organizations are active in the conservation of these birds: unless their habitats are protected and their numbers encouraged to grow, the hunters will have little to hunt. Thus, some of the best sites for information about ducks and geese are provided by hunting organizations, such as Ducks Unlimited, or by government agencies that regulate hunting. These are not exactly "birding" organizations, but in the end, they do much to aid the preservation of species. This chapter contains sources of information about species and about whole groups of birds. (*See also Aviaries.*)

Red-throated Loon (*Gavia stellata*) (JJA)

FEATHERED FACTS

Right Names!

One of the columnists for *Bird Watcher's Digest*, a popular birding magazine <http://www. birdwatchersdigest. com>, is Dr. David M. Bird—it's his real name. And the president and CEO of the National Audubon Society <http://www. audubon.org> is John Flicker. But if that's not enough, consider that the man who suggested creating the Audubon Society back in 1886 was George Bird Grinnell.

Canvasback

Roger Tory Peterson's illustrations will help you identify the Canvasback (*Aythya valisineria*), "a large, fastflying duck admired by birdwatchers and hunters alike," on this Peterson Online page (*first address*). You'll learn about this diving duck and the fact that, because of loss of nesting habitat, the Canvasback had been declining in numbers. The Ducks Unlimited website (*second address*) has statements that are more optimistic about the populations, saying the Canvasback has been rebounding in the 1990s. "The 1998 breeding population survey was 700,000 ducks, which is above the North American Waterfowl Management Plan target population of 540,000, and a healthy increase from the 1993 breeding population of 496,000 ducks," says the hunting-conservation organization. Ducks Unlimited lets you see and read about the Canvasback, as well as hear them.

http://www.petersononline.com/birds/month/canv/
   index.html
http://www.ducks.org/info/duckbase.asp

Coot, American

"Of nature's extraordinary clowns on two wings, perhaps the loudest, oddest, and most laughable is the American Coot," report Anna and Myron Sutton, on the Preposterous Coot page, found on the Utah Nature Study Society website (*first address*). Although not beautiful in a showy sense, they are lovable birds, the writers say and go on to explain why. Though it looks like a small, black duck with a bright, white bill (it's sometimes called a Pond Crow), the American Coot (*Fulica americana*) is a member of the rail family. It's also called a Mudhen because it loves marshes and tends to walk like a chicken when it's on land. These dabbling and diving birds are common throughout most of North America and are gregarious, reports this page at California State University at Bakersfield (*second address*). Although most rails are shy, hiding in marsh reeds, the coot is an exception, says the Birds of Nova Scotia site (*third address*). Coots swim out in the open and, from our own experience, will let you approach them quite closely before taking off. In fact, says Zipper (*fourth address*), "coots are about as tame as any birds get." Summer and winter range maps, life history information, identification tips, photos, and links are all features of this page on the Patuxent Wildlife Research Center site (*fifth address*). The Carmel Valley Creek, California, website (*sixth address*) has some more natural history about the coot. For more photos of the coot, see the University of Georgia's Museum of Natural History site (*seventh address*).

http://www.softcom.net/users/naturenotes/coot.htm
http://www.csubak.edu/FACT/coot.html
http://museum.ednet.ns.ca/mnh/nature/nsbirds/
   bns0116.htm
http://www.zenzero.com/birds00.html
http://www.mbr.nbs.gov/bbs/htm96/map617/
   ra2210.html
http://www.geocities.com/RainForest/9971/p3.htm
http://museum.nhm.uga.edu/birdphotos/birdphoto16.
   html

Duck, American Black

The American Black Duck (*Anas rubripes*) is on the National Audubon Society's WatchList site, indicating that it's "in trouble." This page will tell you where to find it.

http://www.audubon.org/bird/watch/amd/amd.html

A
B
C
D
E
F
G
H
I
J
K
L
M
N
O
P
Q
R
S
T
U
V
W
X
Y
Z

Duck, Black-bellied Whistling

So-called for its high-pitched call, the Black-bellied Whistling Duck (*Dendrocygna autumnalis*) is a handsome southern Texas species that is rare elsewhere on the Gulf Coast but can also occasionally be seen in California, reports the Wild Texas website.

http://www.wildtexas.com/wildguides/whistlingduck.htm

Duck, Mallard

The Mallard Duck (*Anas platyrhynchos*) is probably North America's most populous and popular duck. Certainly, it is a favorite of hunters, and if you look up "Mallard Duck" on a search engine, chances are more than half the sites deal with hunting Mallards, Mallard calls, or Mallard recipes. One theory is that the name comes from Old French words, meaning a "dullard" or "sluggard" man—possibly related to the lack of support it gives the female duck in the raising of the family. According to the Southern Duck Hunter (*first address*), however, it isn't lack of brainpower. "It is said the male Mallard is more intelligent than the female Mallard," says the website, which has excellent illustrations of the bird. Whatever his lifestyle, the male is among our more colorful and handsome birds, with its green head and yellow bill. The Philadelphia Zoo has a good rundown on the Mallard (*second address*). A sharp photograph of a flock of Mallards can be found at Rarebird.com (*third address*).

http://duckcentral.com/MALLARD.HTM

http://www.phillyzoo.org/pz0077.htm

http://www.rarebird.com/images/jpg/mald.jpg

Duck, Wood

You do a double take. You blink your eyes a few times. You peer into the tree with all your ocular might. "Am I seeing things?" That might describe the typical first-time sighting of a Wood Duck in the wood. Seeing a duck sitting in a tree is odd. However, the Wood Duck (*Aix sponsa*), the only perching duck in North America, is a cavity nester, often using old owl or woodpecker holes in trees. It's also among the most colorful of ducks. David L. Gorsline of Reston, Virginia, finds

Wood Duck (*Aix sponsa*) (JJA)

Wood Ducks fascinating enough to set up a site full of excellent natural history about the bird (*first address*). He has worked with a nest box project at Huntley Meadows Park in Fairfax, Virginia, and explains the program with both text and many photos (*second address*). To make your own Wood Duck nest boxes, visit the Northern Prairie Wildlife Research Center (*third address*), which has a site devoted to boxes for not only the Wood Duck but also the three other cavity-nesting ducks: Hooded Merganser, Common Goldeneye, and Bufflehead. This site also has life histories of all four duck species. The Wood Duck is a game bird whose populations were once seriously threatened by loss of habitat. That prompted Ducks Unlimited, a conservation group sponsored largely by hunters, to support efforts to increase their numbers. The Ducks Unlimited site has a section on Wood Ducks, including information about establishing nest boxes (*fourth address*). Patuxent Wildlife Research Center has distribution maps and other information about the species (*fifth address*). Five excellent photos of Wood Ducks can be found at Rarebird.com (*sixth address*).

http://www.geocities.com/SoHo/Studios/4753/duckHome.html

http://www.geocities.com/SoHo/Studios/4753/duckBoxes.html

http://www.npwrc.usgs.gov/resource/tools/nestbox/nestbox.htm

http://www.ducks.org/info/woodduck_box.asp

http://www.mbr.nbs.gov/bbs/htm96/map617/ra1440.html

http://www.rarebird.com/image.htm

Ducks at a Distance:
A Waterfowl Identification Guide

Although primarily written for hunters, this site helps birders identify waterfowl on the wing. The illustrated guide emphasizes the birds' fall and winter plumage patterns, as well as size, shape, and flight characteristics, including typical flock patterns. Written by Bob Hines of the U.S. Fish & Wildlife Service, the guide covers puddle ducks like Mallards, Black, Pintail, and Shovelers, as well as diving ducks, geese, and swans. A few sentences for each species describe its habits, but the guide is primarily valuable for its excellent illustrations of fowl in the air, and on water. A map defines the main waterfowl migration flyways in North America. The site also explains how to order an inexpensive printed copy of the guide—very handy when you're in the field. Or you can use your own color printer to print the illustrations along with the text.

http://www.npwrc.usgs.gov/resource/tools/duckdist/
duckdist.htm

Eider, Common

The Common Eider (*Somateria mollissima*) has a problem: not only its meat but its feathers are prized. Hunters love the taste of these ducks, and others harvest them for their down, an excellent insulator. Environment Canada's site offers a profile of the bird, with special emphasis on how it's doing in the Gulf of St. Lawrence, where the population has been fairly stable—though some colonies are experiencing declines.

http://www.qc.ec.gc.ca/faune/oiseaux_de_mer/html/
Epp1600.html

Gadwall

The Gadwall (*Anas strepera*), a species of duck found around the globe in the Northern Hemisphere, has a name so unusual that experts don't know its origin. One guess is that it's related to the Anglo-Saxon, *gad*, which means *point* and which may refer to little projections on the bird's mandible. An online excerpt from the Birds of North America site describes its distribution and eating habits.

http://www.birdsofna.org/excerpts/gadwall.html

Goldeneye, Common

If ever a photograph showed whence a bird got its name, this shot of the Common Goldeneye (*Bucephala clangula*) is it (*first address*). To learn more about this circumpolar bird of the Northern Hemisphere, visit Patuxent Wildlife Research Center (*second address*.)

http://www.rarebird.com/images/jpg/coge.jpg
http://www.mbr.nbs.gov/id/mlist/h1510.html

Goose, Canada

Canada Geese (*Branta canadensis*) are perhaps unusual among the native wildfowl—they have become *too* successful. In many parts of the country, they are growing in numbers to the point that many people consider them pests—mostly because they poop on their lawns. Efforts to destroy Canada Geese have prompted the formation of the Coalition to Prevent the Destruction of Canada Geese, based in Pearl River, New York (*first address*). The site is overflowing with information about Canada Geese, including some natural history, but a lot on the politics of the goose issue. Recognizing that some people are annoyed by the superabundance of geese, the group has an online guide on "non-lethal methods of goose control." Also available on the site are news releases about parks and other operations that have successfully and humanely resolved goose problems. There are plenty of links to other sources on Canada Geese. A second site deals with an unusual perspective regarding this goose. In North America, many authorities complain about European birds that have been imported—starlings, English Sparrows, and Mute Swans, for instance. But the opposite happens, too, and some North American species have caused concerns abroad, in this case, in England. "Canada Geese are being killed every year in London's most famous parks and across the UK—despite the wishes of the majority of the public," says the Canada Goose Conservation Society (*second address*), which is defending this alien species on British soil. For Canada Geese fans, it makes interesting, often sentimental reading.

http://www.icu.com/geese/coalition.html
http://www.cgcs.demon.co.uk

A Load of Feathers

The Western Grebe, a ducklike diving bird of ponds and streams, wears some 20,000 feathers to help keep it warm and dry.

—adapted from Laboratory for Environmental Biology

http://www.utep.edu/~leb/add_in/aoccide.htm

Grebe, Horned

The widespread Horned Grebe (*Podiceps auritus*), so called because of golden ear tufts in breeding season, is a common member of this family of duck-like diving birds.

http://www.mbr-pwrc.usgs.gov/id/framlst/
i0030id.html

Grebe, Pied-billed

The Pied-billed Grebe (*Podilymbus podiceps*) is a wetlands bird found in much of North America. The website sponsored by the Patuxent Wildlife Research Center (*first address*) has the basics, including animated range maps. The Illinois Natural History Survey site has detailed scientific information about this grebe (*second address*). To see a "movie" of what one looks like and get identification tips, visit the Chicago Academy of Science Nature Museum's page (*third address*).

http://www.mbr-pwrc.usgs.gov/id/framlst/
i0060id.html

http://www.inhs.uiuc.edu/chf/pub/ifwis/birds/
pied-billed-grebe.html

http://www.chias.org/www/col/QTVR/pied.html

Grebe, Western

The Western Grebe (*Aechmophorus occidentalis*) has been called the most beautiful of the grebes. It also has one of the most lively courtship displays. The website of the Laboratory of Environmental Biology of the University of Texas at El Paso (*first address*) will tell you about that, and a lot more—including why, when on land, Western Grebes often fall over. For photos and range data, see the Patuxent Wildlife Research Center site (*second address*).

http://www.utep.edu/~leb/add_in/aoccide.htm

http://www.mbr-pwrc.usgs.gov/id/framlst/
i0010id.html

Foster Parenting

The Brown-headed Cowbird and the Yellow-billed Cuckoo are famous for being nest parasitizers—that is, they lay their eggs in the nests of other birds so that those birds will raise their kids for them. However, many other species will build nests of their own and raise families, but still deposit some eggs in the nests of other birds. Among the better known North American species that do it are the Canada Goose, Snow Goose, Wood Duck, Mallard, Pintail, Blue-winged Teal, Shoveler, Redhead, Canvasback, Common and Barrow's Goldeneye, Bufflehead, Hooded Merganser, Common Merganser, Red-breasted Merganser, White-winged Scoter, and Common Eider.

—adapted from Christopher Majka, *Queer Birds: Marsupial Avians, Compost Heaters, and Obligate Parasites*

http://www.chebucto.ns.ca/Environment/NHR/
queer.html

Grebes

The Great Plains of the United States is home to at least a half dozen species of grebes, duck-like diving birds of ponds and streams. Professor Paul A. Johnsgard of the Department of Physics and Physical Science at the University of Nebraska at Kearney has an excellent collection of concise natural histories on the university's website. His profiles cover the Pied-billed Grebe, Horned Grebe, Red-necked Grebe, Eared Grebe, Western Grebe, and Clark's Grebe. For each, there is a Great Plains range map. Many of these species range beyond the Great Plains, so Johnsgard's work is useful for most of North America.

http://rip.physics.unk.edu/nou/Johnsgard/
Page01.html

International Goose Research Group

Interest in Arctic-nesting geese—the kinds we find throughout most of North America—has increased greatly in recent years, especially since some species, such as the Canada Goose and the Snow Goose, have grown in numbers. For some people, these geese have become almost pests. The International Goose Research Group website was established to increase communication on the subject (*first address*). The site offers a rundown, including photos, of all the species of native geese in the genera Branta and Anser. This information is useful for anyone trying to figure out what that odd-looking goose at the neighborhood pond might be. (Remember, though, that a number of exotic species of geese imported into North America as "pond pets" have quite often escaped.) The site lists links to many organizations involved in goose research and management, describes projects being undertaken involving various species, and provides a system for getting in touch with goose experts, including the ability to join a goose mailing list. The site also has a searchable bibliographic database (*second address*) of references to more than 1,700 articles about geese, in case you *really* want to research the subject!

http://www.goose.org
http://www.goose.org/gooseref/

Loon, Common

The Common Loon (*Gavia immer*) is one of our oddest and most interesting birds, one that rarely leaves the water that it fishes in by diving. Its huge wings and heavy body need up to 400 yards of open water in order to take off, notes this excellent page from the University of Massachusetts's Biology Department (*first address*). Here you will find much natural history, good photos and—who could resist Loon Links. "The loon is most closely related to primitive birds, and its soliloquy of cries can sound eerily prehistoric," observes the Rickert family of Owatonna, Minnesota, who operate the lively Rickert's Garden website (*second address*). The page has a bit of loon lore and nice photos and a breeding range map. Loons are famous for their haunting sounds, and the page (on the website of the North American Loon Fund (*third address*) provides a good deal of information about the Common Loon's wails, yodels, tremolos, and hoots. Mary Kirschenbaum at the University of Texas's Laboratory for Environmental Biology has a good write-up on the Common Loon, though no pictures (*fourth address*).

http://www.bio.umass.edu/biology/conn.river/loon.html
http://www.holoweb.com/cannon/commons.htm
http://facstaff.uww.edu/wentzl/nalf/aCOLO.HTML
http://www.utep.edu/~leb/add_in/loon.htm

FEATHERED FACTS

Crazy as a Loon

The term *crazy as a loon* may come from the tremolos—the eerie, trembling, laughing sounds—that the Common Loon emits when it feels threatened.

—adapted from North American Loon Fund

http://facstaff.uww.edu/wentzl/nalf/aCOLO.HTML

A B C D E F G H I J K L M N O P Q R S T U V W X Y Z

A
B
C
D
E
F
G
H
I
J
K
L
M
N
O
P
Q
R
S
T
U
V
W
X
Y
Z

FEATHERED FACTS

No Landlubbers, Loons

Loons rarely leave the water because they are vulnerable on land where they can only thrust their chests forward a few inches and drag the legs back underneath the body. Consequently, they leave the water only to nest–very close to the shoreline–and to defecate.

—adapted from University of Massachusetts Biology Department

http://www.bio.umass.edu/biology/conn.river/loon.html

Loon, Red-throated

The Red-throated Loon (*Gavia stellata*) spends its summers in arctic regions and its winters in the warmer reaches of both coasts, reports the Laboratory for Environmental Biology's page sponsored by the University of Texas, El Paso (*first address*). This loon is also found in Asia and Europe, making it a *circumpolar species*. Photos and range maps of the species are provided by the Patuxent Wildlife Research Center (*second address*).

http://www.utep.edu/~leb/add_in/red_loon.htm
http://www.mbr-pwrc.usgs.gov/id/framlst/
i0110id.html

Loons

Populations of the Common Loon have been declining in many parts of North America, prompting the creation of the North American Loon Fund (*first address*). The organization's aim is to "promote the preservation of loons and their lake habitats through research, public education, and the involvement of people who share their lakes with loons." As might be expected, this site is a rich source of information about the five species of loons that nest in North America: the Common Loon,

Pacific Loon, Arctic Loon, Red-throated Loon, and Yellow-billed Loon. There are pages devoted to each, complete with photos and range maps, plus life histories. The site also has considerable information about threats to loons, including loss of nesting habitats, problems caused by power boaters, the dangers from fishing paraphernalia—lines, hooks, sinkers, predators, and water pollution. To help, you can join the North American Loon Fund—full details are online. Folks in New Hampshire who have been alarmed by declining loon populations have formed the Loon Preservation Committee, a project of the Audubon Society of New Hampshire (*second address*). The site tells what this organization is doing to protect loons and how you can visit the Loon Center that the group has established in Moultonborough, New Hampshire. Mercury contamination of waterways has been one hazard the loon has faced, and the Atlantic Cooperative Wildlife Ecology Research Network at Acadia University in Nova Scotia has information about this environmental problem (*third address*). This site is also good for links to other loon sites. Patuxent Wildlife Research Center has information about summer and winter ranges (*fourth address*).

http://facstaff.uww.edu/wentzl/nalf/analfhomepage.html
http://newww.com/org/lpc/
http://dragon.acadiau.ca/~acwern/jnocera/
JNOCERA.HTM
http://www.mbr.nbs.gov/bbs/htm96/map617/
ra0070.html

FEATHERED FACTS

Really Deep Breath

The Common Loon dives for fish and other aquatic creatures and can stay underwater for up to three minutes at a time.

—adapted from Laboratory for Environmental Biology

http://www.utep.edu/~leb/add_in/loon.htm

Merganser, Hooded

The Hooded Merganser (*Lophodytes cucullatus*) is a spectacular-looking duck with a black head bearing a white, fan-like crest that stands out brilliantly in the spring, especially when fully extended. These birds are found in much of North America and are among the few cavity-nesting waterfowl. The USGS's Northern Prairie Wildlife Research Center has information about the Hooded Merganser and how to build a nesting box for it (*first address*). For a spectacular close-up of the male Hooded Merganser, visit Rarebird.com's page (*second address*).

http://www.npwrc.usgs.gov/resource/tools/nestbox/ hooded.htm

http://www.rarebird.com/images/jpg/hm.jpg

Museum of the Canada Goose

Yes, the ubiquitous Canada Goose is so well loved by many that there is an online "museum" in its honor. Called Branta's Place: The Museum of the Canada Goose, the site has natural history, real-life stories, and art done by children and seems to be written for youngsters, as well as for adults. In the spring a live GooseCam documents a pair of Canada Geese as they lay and hatch their eggs, and raise their family of goslings. The site has plenty of photos, information about migration and banding, goose rescue resources, humane ways of discouraging geese from settling where they are not wanted, and more.

http://www.canadagoose.com

Canada Goose (Dover)

Oldsquaw

Be forewarned: The Oldsquaw's name is not politically correct. This duck (*Clangula hyemalis*) is very noisy, which prompted folks of another era to create a name that refers to an "old woman." Peterson Online (*first address*) is more diplomatic, saying that while the Oldsquaw is "talkative," it is also "musical." This diving duck is widespread on both the Atlantic and Pacific Coasts in winter, and nests in the high Arctic in summer. Its range and its lifestyle are both detailed on this page that includes fine Roger Tory Peterson illustrations. For some interesting observations of Oldsquaws at Farmington Bay, Utah, which is not their typical range, check the Utah Nature Study Society page.

http://www.petersononline.com/birds/month/olds/ index.html

http://www.softcom.net/users/naturenotes/oldsquaw. htm

Pintail, Northern

The Northern Pintail (*Anas acuta*), sometimes referred to as the Common Pintail, is so called because of its long, pointy tail, most noticeable when it's swimming. This duck is widely distributed in North America, says the Laboratory for Environmental Biology site sponsored by the University of Texas at El Paso (*first address*). However, reports the Ducks Unlimited of Canada site (*second address*), their numbers are declining. "Biologists blame reduced and degraded habitat as humans continue to convert land to other uses," Ducks Unlimited says. "If pintail numbers are to recover in the future, it will take a massive human effort to rehabilitate and preserve habitats." This site has an excellent picture of this long-necked duck. For a close-up shot of a pair of pintails, see Rarebird.com (*third address*).

http://www.utep.edu/~leb/add_in/aacuta.htm

http://vm.ducks.ca/naturenotes/pintail.html

http://www.rarebird.com/images/jpg/npt.jpg

Scoter, Black

The Black Scoter is also called the "Butter-nose Coot," reports Birds of Nova Scotia (*first address*). An excellent photograph of the Black Scoter (*Melanitta nigra*), showing its unusual yellow-knobbed bill, can also be found (*second address*).

http://142.227.51.1/educ/museum/mnh/nature/
  nsbirds/bns0072.htm

http://www.rarebird.com/images/jpg/blksc2.jpg

Scoter, Surf

Surf Scoters (*Melanitta perspicillata*) are among the least studied of our waterfowl, observes this sample pair of pages from Frank S. Todd's 500-page book, *Natural History of the Waterfowl* carried by the Virtual Birder site. They are so-called because they hunt for food in one of the most difficult grounds imaginable: the breaking surf. The male is noted for his multicolored "Roman nose" beak—effectively pictured on the site—which has earned the species its specific name, *perspicillata*, which means conspicuous or spectacular. Many details of this strange bird's life are described here, including the sophisticated way in which these birds try to avoid having their catches stolen by gulls.

http://www.virtualbirder.com/vbirder/ibis/SUSC/
  SUSC401.html

Swan, Trumpeter

The Trumpeter Swan (*Cygnus buccinator*) was nearly extinct at the turn of the 20th century, but conservation efforts brought back populations of these large white birds. The Canadian Museum of Nature site has information about the swan and its status in Canada.

http://www.nature.ca/notebooks/english/
  trumswan.htm

Teal, Blue-winged

Like other teal, Blue-winged Teal (*Anas discors*) are among the smallest of the ducks. Since the 1950s, their numbers have been on the decline, primarily because of habitat loss but possibly also due to droughts, to which they are quite sensitive, reports Ducks Unlimited of Canada (*first address*). For a fine photo and notes regarding its status in Ohio, visit Aves.net (*second address*). Patuxent Wildlife Research Center has range maps and other data about the Blue-winged Teal (*third address*). Rarebird.com has an excellent close-up photograph of a pair of Blue-winged Teals (*fourth address*).

http://vm.ducks.ca/naturenotes/blueteal.html

http://aves.net/birds-of-ohio/birdbwte.htm

http://www.mbr-pwrc.usgs.gov/id/framlst/
  i1400id.html

http://www.rarebird.com/images/jpg/bwt.jpg

Teal, Green-winged

The Green-winged Teal (*Anas crecca*) is even smaller than the Blue-winged (see earlier in this section), but they share similar ranges in summer and winter. The website of the magnificent book series, *The Birds of North America*, uses the Green-winged Teal to show a sample of what an entry is like, and thus there's a wonderful, online page detailing the eating habits of this species (*first address*), including a huge bibliography. The Patuxent website has range information, plus the basics about the species (*second address*). Three sample pages carried by the Virtual Birder website from *Natural History of the Waterfowl*, a 500-page book on more than 160 species, provide a great deal of information about the Green-winged Teal, along with some splendid photographs (*third address*).

http://www.birdsofna.org/excerpts/grteal.html

http://www.mbr-pwrc.usgs.gov/id/framlst/
  i1390id.html

http://www.virtualbirder.com/vbirder/ibis/GWTE/
  GWTE339.html

Trumpeter Swan (Dover)

FEATHERED FACTS

V for More Than Victory

Ever wonder why flocks of Canada Geese and certain other species fly in V formations? The flapping of their wings creates an "uplift" that helps the birds that follow. Scientists estimate that a flock can fly 71 percent farther than a single bird, just because of this phenomenon. If you watch a V long enough, you'll see that the lead bird, who must work harder than the rest, changes periodically.

—adapted from Branta's Place

http://www.canadagoose.com

True Geese of the World

The University of Tennessee describes many of the common geese of the world, some of which may suddenly appear as exotics in a local pond. *Anser* species are at the first address; *Branta* species—including several varieties of Canada Geese—are at the second address.

http://www.utm.edu/departments/ed/cece/trugeese.
  shtml

http://www.utm.edu/departments/ed/cece/trugeese2.
  shtml

Waterfowl of Chenoa

Maurice and Carla Field have a family project: to collect at least one pair of each of the 15 species of true geese and the six species of shelducks. Maurice is director of the Center for Environmental and Conservation Education at the University of Tennessee at Martin. He and Carla have created a sort of environmental refuge at their home in Chenoa for these waterfowl in western Tennessee and use it to teach others about wildlife and waterfowl. Thousands of school children and others visit the facilities each year. The Fields' website is a wealth of information about geese and shelducks (none of the latter are native, but many of the geese are). Fine photos illustrate each species, and the Fields offer much information about the environment these birds live in at Chenoa. The site includes useful links for more information.

http://www.utm.edu/departments/ed/cece/
  waterfowl.shtml

Waterfowl Resource

Birders who are interested in waterfowl—ducks and geese—should inspect the Waterfowl Resource website. Although designed for hunters, the site nonetheless has a rich collection of information for bird-watchers. One of the interesting features of this site are sound files with the calls of many ducks, mergansers, teal, and geese species. Look far down its home page menu for Images and the site's most spectacular resource: wonderful, crisp, close-up photos of a dozen major waterfowl species—many of each species, both resting and in flight. This feature includes some of the most spectacular pictures of ducks, geese, mergansers, redheads, pintails, wigeons, and shovelers we've seen on the Web. Many different views of each species are in the collection, including close-ups, take-offs and in-flight shots. (As this book was being completed, the Waterfowl Resource site was undergoing "major changes." We assume the described features will remain.)

http://www.wildfowl.net

Mallard (Dover)

Wigeon, American

Widgeon is an odd word that comes from the French, *vigeon*, which means a "whistling duck," and may have found its roots in the Latin word for a small crane. The latter seems more appropriate, for the sound of the American Wigeon (*Anas americana*) seems hardly whistlelike. You can hear and see this widespread duck found through much of North America by visiting the Pagoda Vista website in Canada (*first address*). WetNet's site has a close-up photo and brief description of the bird (*second address*). Another very fine photo of an American Widgeon can be seen at Rarebird.com (*third address*).

http://www.kwic.com/~pagodavista/widgeon.htm

http://red.glo.state.tx.us/wetnet/species/wigeon.html

http://www.rarebird.com/images/jpg/aw.jpg

WADERS

One of the oldest and most elegant groups of birds are the waders. Be they long- or short-legged, they slowly and deliberately step their way through wetlands, swamps, brooks, shorelines, and anywhere there's shallow water that holds the promise of food. In North America, the waders include herons, bitterns, storks, cranes, flamingos, plovers, rails, sandpipers, avocets, phalaropes, oystercatchers, and others. This section includes many birds of the orders Ciconiiformes (but not vultures), Gruiformes, and Charadriiformes (except Gulls, Terns, and Skimmers, covered in the North American Birds, Sea & Shore, section).

Avocet, American

The American Avocet (*Recurvirostra americana*) looks as if it has really cold feet. Or at least, chilly gams. Its long legs have a bluish tint, unusual in birds and the inspiration for its colloquial name Blue Shanks. American Avocets are found on mudflats, in saline lakes, in fresh water and saltwater marshes, and on coastal bays in the western United States in summer and southward into Mexico and Central America in winter. The Texas Parks and Wildlife Department site has some good, basic information about the American Avocet (*first address*). For a concise description of the avocet's ways—including a striking photo of an avo-

cet standing on one leg—visit the page sponsored by the Nature Conservancy (*second address*).

http://www.tpwd.state.tx.us/nature/wild/birds/avocet.htm

http://www.tnc.org/infield/State/DAKOTAS/SPECIES/avocet.htm

Crane, Sandhill

Sandhill Cranes (*Grus canadensis*) spend the coldest part of the winter in northern Mexico and southern Texas, Arizona, and New Mexico. In February, they begin heading hundreds of miles north, stopping in the Platte River Valley to *stage* and gain strength for their journey to Arctic regions of Canada, Alaska, and Siberia, where they nest for the summer. One of the best places to see Sandhill Cranes is in the spring near Grand Island, Nebraska, on the Platte River. In fact, they get their names from the gently rolling sand hills on the north edge of the Platte River Valley where they once nested and were first identified. These three- to four-foot-tall, stately birds are the specialty of the Crane Meadows Nature Center at Grand Island, and this page (*first address*) on the center's site tells a lot about Sandhill Cranes. Dr. Joseph T. Springer of the Biology Department at the University of Nebraska at Kearney has a good page (*second address*) of Sandhill Crane information. Kearney is in the Big Bend area, where many cranes visit on their migratory journey. To find out the status of the crane migration in the Big Bend area, the University of Nebraska's site has an update page (*third address*). A very extensive rundown of the natural history of Sandhill Cranes is provided by the Nebraska Wildlife Service site (*fourth address*). The U.S. Fish & Wildlife Service site (*fifth address*) has information about the Mississippi Sandhill Crane (*Grus canadensis pulla*), which it says is one of six Sandhill Crane subspecies. It's considered an endangered one. The International Crane Foundation (*sixth address*) has a good profile about this and many other species of cranes.

http://www.cranemeadows.org/crane.htm

http://platteriver.unk.edu/viewing.html

http://platteriver.unk.edu/migration.html

http://www.ngpc.state.ne.us/wildlife/cranes.html

http://www.fws.gov/r9endspp/i/b/sab4n.html

http://www.savingcranes.org/sandhill.htm

Sandhill Crane (Dover)

Crane, Whooping

The huge Whooping Crane (*Grus americana*), the rarest of the world's 15 crane species, stands more than five feet tall with a wingspan of nearly eight feet. Its loud call, audible up to three miles away, is the source of its name. Fossil evidence indicates this bird once ranged throughout most of North America, but land development by European settlers gradually drove the shy Whoopers to limited territories. Hunting, too, took its toll. By the 1940s, only 15 Whooping Cranes were known, and their nesting place in the Canadian wilderness was unknown until the 1950s when an Audubon researcher discovered it in a park. The cranes have been making a slow comeback. As many as 49 nests have been counted at Canada's Wood Buffalo National Park, up from a low of 28. To learn about the bird and the many measures being taken to preserve it, visit the

FEATHERED FACTS

Tallest Bird

At more than four feet in height, the Whooping Crane is the tallest bird species in North America.

—adapted from Texas Audubon Society

http://www.audubon.org/chapter/tx/tx/whooping.html

International Crane Foundation website (*first address*). The U.S. Geological Survey's Northern Prairie Wildlife Research Center studies Whooping Cranes and their preservation. According to its website (*second address*), "The species' historic decline, near extinction, and gradual recovery is among the best known and documented cases in the annals of conservation," the center says. "Over the last 50 years, a combination of strict legal protection, habitat preservation, and continuous international cooperation between Canada and the United States has allowed the only remaining wild population to increase steadily." This site has much information about Whooping Cranes, including maps of their migration routes, wintering locations, and nesting grounds. For information about their wintering territory in Texas, visit the Aransas National Wildlife Refuge website (*third address*).

http://www.savingcranes.org/whooping.htm

http://www.npwrc.usgs.gov/resource/distr/birds/cranes/grusamer.htm

http://southwest.fws.gov/refuges/texas/aransas.html

Cranes

The Northern Prairie Wildlife Research Center has a magnificent site covering all 15 species of cranes found around the world and a conservation action plan for many of them. Here, you will see photos of all the species, census data on how many are believed to exist, and whether those populations are increasing or decreasing. Covered in considerable detail on this site are Black-crowned Crane (*Balearica pavonina*), Grey-crowned Crane (*Balearica regulorum*), Demoiselle Crane (*Anthropoides virgo*), Blue Crane (*Anthropoides paradisea*), Wattled Crane (*Bugeranus carunculatus*), Siberian Crane (*Grus leucogeranus*), Sandhill Crane (*Grus canadensis*), Sarus Crane (*Grus antigone*), Brolga (*Grus rubicundus*), White-naped Crane (*Grus vipio*), Hooded Crane (*Grus monachus*), Eurasian Crane (*Grus grus*), Whooping Crane (*Grus americana*), Black-necked Crane (*Grus nigricollis*), and Red-crowned Crane (*Grus japonensis*). The site includes maps detailing the ranges of each species in their native lands. (*See International Crane Foundation later in this section.*)

http://www.npwrc.usgs.gov/resource/distr/birds/cranes/cranes.htm

A B C D E F G H I J K L M N O P Q R S T U V W X Y Z

A
B
C
D
E
F
G
H
I
J
K
L
M
N
O
P
Q
R
S
T
U
V
W
X
Y
Z

Curlew, Bristle-thighed

In May 1998, the coast of the Pacific Northwest was "invaded" by Bristle-thighed Curlews (*Numenius tahitiensis*), an extremely rare species that suddenly was migrating through that region. So many were sighted that local birders were calling it the Great Curlew Fallout. More than a dozen birds were identified along the California, Oregon, and Washington coast where virtually none had ever been seen before. "Not much is known about this species," reports Mike Patterson, who created this page called Knee Deep in Bristle-Thighed Curlews. "The size of the population is believed to be small," notes the site. "The breeding range is restricted to western Alaska. Record of its occurrence in North America outside its breeding range is documented by one unequivocally accepted report from Grant Bay, British Columbia, in May, 1969, and six other records that many find inconclusive." Why were these birds—and some other unusual ones—sighted that spring? This site attempts to answer the question and provides revealing information about how weather may affect migratory birds. The page includes Patterson's very good field sketches of the bird, as well as photos and much information.

http://www.pacifier.com/~mpatters/bird/btcu/btcu.html

Curlew, Eskimo

The Eskimo Curlew (*Numenius borealis*), a sandpiper that was once common in summers throughout most of Canada and in Alaska, has nearly suffered the fate of the Passenger Pigeon. It was hunted down to the point of near extinction because it was good to eat and easy to kill. Today, they are endangered. The bird winters in South America, but nests along the shores of Arctic Canada and Alaska. "Although its extinction has been treated as a foregone conclusion, this hasn't happened yet," says the USGS Northern Prairie Wildlife Research Center site (*first address*). Aside from Fred Bodsworth's best-selling 1954 novel *The Last of the Curlews* and a few sightings each year by active and expert birders, recorded in specialized journals of relatively small circulation, "little has been said about it or done on its behalf," the center says. "No habitat change or pesticide threat has been identified. The Eskimo curlew has failed to excite the interest of the general public." The website includes descriptions of where it can be still seen in North America, where it

Eskimo Curlew (*Phaelopus borealis*) [*Numenius borealis*] (JJA)

winters, what its life is like, many range, route, and breeding maps, how to identify it (other birds look like the Eskimo Curlew), and nearly two dozen pictures and drawings. This site, based on a publication by the Saskatchewan Natural History Society, is a book in itself. You can download the huge collection of pages, called "Eskimo Curlew: A Vanishing Species," as an 800,000-byte .ZIP file (*see page 46*) from the website. The Canadian Museum of Natural History site has a briefer look at the species (*second address*).

http://www.npwrc.usgs.gov/resource/othrdata/curlew/curlew.htm

http://www.nature.ca/notebooks/english/eskimo.htm

NET NOTES

Shockwave

Some of the more sophisticated websites use a Web browser plug-in called Shockwave or Flash to allow you to do things interactively. For instance, in some Shockwave websites, you can manipulate the actions of cartoonlike characters. Important for birding? Well, who knows what creative ideas ornithologically minded Webmasters may put Shockwave to? But the free browser plug-in is easy to obtain and install.

http://www.macromedia.com

Egret, Reddish

The destruction of wetlands along the southwestern coast of Florida, the Keys, and other wetlands along the Gulf of Mexico has drastically narrowed the breeding grounds of the Reddish Egret (*Egretta rufescens*), which was already having a tough time recovering from overhunting at the turn of the 20th century. These and other environmental factors have led the National Audubon Society to place the Reddish Egret on its WatchList of birds that may become threatened or endangered species (*first address*). Wetnet, an excellent website of the Texas Wetland Information Network, created by the State of Texas General Land Office, has a concise description of the Reddish Egret, along with natural history and range information (*second address*). The page has an outstanding photo of the species in its pinkish breeding plumage. Roy Jones of Tempe, Arizona, shares his experience spotting the Reddish Egret at the Gila River Indian Reservation in Arizona, a state where it's rarely seen, in August 1998 (*third address*).

http://www.audubon.org/bird/watch/ree/ree.html
http://red.glo.state.tx.us/wetnet/species/egret.html
http://www.primenet.com/~barbet/reddish.htm

Florida Wading Bird Group

Florida is home to many species of wading birds, some of which are seen nowhere else in North America north of Mexico. The Florida Wading Bird Group, a volunteer organization of scientists and birders, monitors the health of wading bird populations and their wetland habitats. The site, under construction when we stopped by, has information about two dozen species and about conservation areas where they are found, with population estimates for each. The site tells how you can help with the survey.

http://www.flmnh.ufl.edu/wadingbirds/default.htm

Heron, Great Blue

Anyone who has happened across a Great Blue Heron in a marsh, swamp, or along a lake or stream couldn't help but stand in awe as this majestic bird lifts into the air and takes off. These birds can stand four feet tall

Great Blue Heron (*Ardea herodias*) (JJA)

and have huge wingspans. Despite their size and seeming vulnerability, Great Blue Herons are found throughout most of North America, feeding on the fish of shallow waters. The Field Guide to the Birds of Kern County, California (*first address*), provides not only information and a photo but also the odd song of the Great Blue Heron. The Royal British Columbia Museum in Vancouver has a fine page devoted to the Great Blue Heron, with much information about habits, habitats, and nesting (*second address*). The Northern Prairie Wildlife Research Center site has a good illustration to help with identifying the Great Blue (*third address*). "Big Cranky" and "Long John" are other names for this heron, reports D. W. Crum of Jacksonville Beach, Florida, who has a profile of the bird and other birds found in Florida (*fourth address*). For a dramatic picture of a Great Blue Heron on a Washington beach, visit the home page of the Tahoma Audubon Society in Tacoma, Washington (*fifth address*).

http://frontpage.lightspeed.net/alison1/GBH.htm
http://rbcm1.rbcm.gov.bc.ca/nh_papers/gracebell/
   english/gb_heron.html
http://www.npwrc.usgs.gov/resource/tools/
   waterfwl/heron.htm
http://www.geocities.com/Heartland/5960/bheron.html
http://www.audubon.org/chapter/wa/tahoma/

A
B
C
D
E
F
G
H
I
J
K
L
M
N
O
P
Q
R
S
T
U
V
W
X
Y
Z

FEATHERED FACTS

Heron Heron

The Great Blue Heron's scientific name seems an example of redundancy. *Ardea herodias* means *heron heron*, *ardea* being Latin for heron and *herodias* being the Greek. It's probably a scientist's way of suggesting that this is the ultimate heron.

http://www.sosc.edu/library/jim/wildlife/gbluhern.htm

Heron, Green

The Green Heron (*Butorides virescens*), a species that hangs around wetlands, is a clever bird. According to the Western North Carolina Nature Center site, this heron uses a variety of techniques—even tools—when hunting food. A Green Heron has been observed employing a feather to attract small fish to the surface, whereupon it would grab them with its long beak. The heron will also use its feet to stir up creatures on the bottom in shallow water, may just stand still in the water waiting for food to pass by, or may even perch on a branch and dive for prey. This profile includes a description of the Green Heron's interesting courtship display.

http://www.wncnaturecenter.org/af/greenheron.html

Herons

Christine Tarski, the birding guide at About.com, has collected a set of pages on various heron species, many of which feature photos (*first address*). Michael Myers has many pictures of both herons and egrets from East Coast (*second address*).

http://birding.about.com/msub1-herons.htm
http://www.netaxs.com:8080/~mhmyers/egher.tn.html

Ibis, White

The coasts of the southeastern United States are the home of the White Ibis (*Eudocimus albus*), a tall, elegant bird of wetlands. Although populations in Florida are down from predevelopment levels, the White Ibis is still one of the most common, large, wading birds and, according to Peterson Online, is expanding its range, particularly northward along the Atlantic Coast. This page offers natural history, illustrations, and a range map.

http://www.petersononline.com/birds/month/whib/index.html

International Crane Foundation

Cranes inspire awe in people. Standing, they tower above almost all other birds. In flight, they are majestic and huge, with massive wingspans. "Cranes are a family of birds that have long been revered by people living near them," says the website of International Crane Foundation based in Baraboo, Wisconsin. "In Japan, the cranes are honored as symbols of long life and a happy marriage. In Vietnam, cranes are believed to carry the souls of the dead to heaven. In North America, Africa, and Australia, native inhabitants have incorporated the crane's graceful movements into their own dances and regard cranes as auspicious symbols." Cranes are also among the oldest group of birds, having existed on earth for between 34 and 50 million years. The foundation's aim is to conserve cranes and the habitats they live in, particularly wetlands and grasslands. The ICF website has a wealth of information about the 15 species of cranes found worldwide, plus special pages for children, an Adopt-a-Crane program, features from the *ICF Bugle* newsletter, and many other pages of information. An unusual and interesting feature is the sites travelogues of trips made by ICF officials to visit crane habitats around the world.

http://www.savingcranes.org

Killdeer

Even though it doesn't wade, we place the Killdeer (*Charadrius vociferus*) with the wading birds because it's a plover—ornithologists group plovers with waders because most plovers are shorebirds that wade! The Killdeer, however, is a plover of fields and even lawns, where it nests. (They'll also nest on the flat roofs of schools and shopping centers.) You can see and hear a Killdeer—so called for its voice, not its habits—on the Backyard Birding website (*first address*). The Killdeer is famous not only for its voice (hence its Latin name *vociferus*) but also for its pretense in certain circumstances of having a broken wing. Diane Porter provides an explanation of why it does this acting routine on Birdwatching.com (*second address*). You'll also learn a lot about the precocious babies of the Killdeer. For a map of its range, see Patuxent (*last address*).

http://www.slivoski.com/birding/killdeer.htm
http://www.birdwatching.com/stories/killdeer.html
http://www.mbr.nbs.gov/bbs/cbcra/h2730ra.html

Kildeer (Dover)

Limpkin

Only in Florida are you likely to find the Limpkin (*Aramus guarauna*), an odd wading bird that has no close relatives and looks like a cross between a rail and a crane, reports Peterson Online. These Caribbean and Central American birds have "piercing banshee wails, often heard at dawn or at night," Peterson says. The page notes that this bird was hunted almost to extinction in Florida, but is now making a decent comeback.

http://www.petersononline.com/birds/month/limp/index.html

Oystercatcher, American

The website WetNet in Texas has an excellent photo and brief profile on the American Oystercatcher (*Haematopus palliatus*), gull-like birds that, as their name suggests, eat bivalves such as oysters and clams.

http://red.glo.state.tx.us/wetnet/species/oyster.html

Oystercatcher (Dover)

Phalarope, Wilson's

Of the three phalaropes in the New World, only the Wilson's Phalarope (*Phalaropus tricolor*) lives solely in this hemisphere. The other two, the Northern and Red, are what is known as *circumboreal species* and are found in Arctic regions around the world. Wilson's Phalarope, reports John Sterling of the Smithsonian Migratory Bird Center, nests in shallow marshes of the West and the Great Lakes regions. After they raise a family, they gather on one of several sizable lakes in the West. There, they molt and eat and build up fat reserves, frequently doubling their weight, for what is truly an incredible feat: a nonstop, 54-hour flight to South America.

http://web2.si.edu/smbc/bom/wiph.htm

Phalarope (Dover)

A B C D E F G H I J K L M N O P Q R S T U V W X Y Z

A
B
C
D
E
F
G
H
I
J
K
L
M
N
O
P
Q
R
S
T
U
V
W
X
Y
Z

Piping Plover Guardian Program

The Piping Plover is an endangered species that nests on sandy beaches along the Atlantic shores from northern Virginia to Nova Scotia. "This small shore-bird is currently struggling for survival," notes the Piping Plover Guardian Program site in Nova Scotia. "In 1991, an International Piping Plover Census found only 239 pairs in Atlantic Canada, and that only 2,331 pairs existed in the world." Humans and their pets can be a major problem for Piping Plovers' breeding success. Sports activities, campfires, cars, beachcombing, and pets can be disruptive, resulting in the loss of nests and chicks. "It is mostly a matter of getting too close to the plovers too often," says the site, which describes how anyone can become a Piping Plover Guardian. The program includes posting nesting areas to warn people away; asking beach users to stay away from posted areas; publicizing the need to protect nesting areas; and working with enforcement officers. This page is oriented toward Canada but provides good information for U.S. residents as well.

http://www.chebucto.ns.ca/Recreation/
FieldNaturalists/guardian.html

Golden Plover (Dover)

Plover, American Golden

Imagine a bird that lives in the Arctic in the summer and in the pampas of southern South America in the winter! That's one heck of a spring and summer commute. In fact, the American Golden Plover (*Pluvialis dominica*) must fly more than 20,000 miles a year, an incredible feat for a bird weighing but six to nine ounces. Plovers can fly at speeds from 60 to 100 mph and in one portion of their southern journey, can traverse the Atlantic from eastern Canada to northern South America—some 3,000 miles nonstop. This Wilderness Society site, called Migratory Max, has information about the Golden Plover's nonmigratory life, too, and links to more information.

http://www.wilderness.org/migmax/index.htm

Plover, Mountain

The Mountain Plover (*Charadrius montanus*) is an insect eating species found in the West. The Birds of North America site describes both its eating habits and its habitat.

http://www.birdsofna.org/excerpts/mplover.html

FEATHERED FACTS

Double Whammy

The Piping Plover has suffered from two kinds of threats in two different eras. At the turn of the 20th century, the bird was hunted nearly to extinction. Laws protecting it as a migratory, nongame bird resulted in a recovery of its populations. But now, ever increasing use of beaches—where this bird builds its nests—has resulted in yet another threat to its future, especially in eastern states and provinces. It is listed as a threatened species.

—adapted from Canadian Museum of Nature

http://www.nature.ca/notebooks/english/piplover.htm

Plover, Piping

Piping Plovers (*Charadrius melodus*) are small, sand-piper-like birds that, in summer, live and nest on the beaches of the Atlantic north of Virginia and, to some degree, on the shores of the Great Lakes and in some prairie locations. They winter along the shores of the southeastern United States. Because nesting areas are so close to the same kinds of spots people enjoy at the shore, Piping Plovers are having a hard time raising their young. Dick and Jean Hoffman's Piping Plover page (*first address*) from their Shorebird Watcher web-site describes these plovers and offers an extensive collection of links to other Piping Plover sites. Lois Keeping and Trina Seaward of Port aux Basques, Newfoundland, provide a concise profile of the Piping Plover (*second address*). Sarah Dooling was a grad-uate research assistant at the University of Maine when she wrote a masterful essay "Promise for Plovers," which the USGS Northern Prairie Wildlife Research Center has online (*third address*). The report shows among other things how electronic mesh fenc-ing is being used to deter predators from invading nesting sites. Another USGS page at the Northern Prairie Wildlife Research Center describes "Plover Paradise," the desolate, almost ghost town of Appam, North Dakota, where U.S. Fish & Wildlife Service biologist Robert K. Murphy has studied the Piping Plover. "Appam may not be everyone's dream of a vacation at the beach, but to Piping Plovers—and lovers of the plovers—it's paradise!" says Murphy. This page (*fourth address*) will tell you why. The Delaware Audubon Society site has excerpts from a U.S. Fish & Wildlife pamphlet on this bird (*fifth address*). Last but not least is Lee Elliott's huge collec-tion of links, and other information on Piping Plovers (*sixth address*).

http://pw1.netcom.com/~djhoff/pipllink.html

http://cyberfair.gsn.org/stjamesel/plover.html

http://www.npwrc.usgs.gov/resource/othrdata/plover/
  plover.htm

http://www.npwrc.usgs.gov/resource/othrdata/plover/
  paradise.htm

http://pages.prodigy.com/delaud/pp.htm

http://www2.interconnect.net/lelliott/index.htm

Rail, Virginia

The Virginia Rail (*Rallus limicola*) is a bird more easily heard than seen, reports this excerpt from the Birds of North America site (*first address*). The bird hides among the reeds of freshwater wetlands. Despite its name, the Virginia Rail is found coast-to-coast. Its populations, once thought to be threatened, have now stabilized, this page notes as it discusses the habits and appearance of this rail. The song of the Virginia Rail can be heard at the site of the Patuxent Wildlife Research Center (*second address*).

http://www.birdsofna.org/excerpts/varail.html

http://www.mbr.nbs.gov/id/htmwav2/h2120so.wav

Red Knot

The Red Knot (*Calidris canutus*) loves the eggs of the horseshoe crab, especially when it's traveling. These ancient arthropods, more closely related to spiders than true crabs, were once found in great numbers in the Delaware Bay of eastern North America. Each spring Red Knots depart from their wintering grounds along the southeast coast of the United States and stop along the Delaware Bay to feed on these eggs to build up strength to continue their migration to the high arctic islands of Canada. However, reports the National Audubon Society (*first address*), overharvest-ing of horseshoe crabs for fertilizer and other uses has spelled problems for the Red Knot, which can no longer find enough of the food they need in the Delaware Bay area. On the West Coast, where the birds also winter, shoreside developments, oil spills, and other environmental changes have reduced the numbers of Red Knots, which are now on Audubon's WatchList of birds that may become endangered. The Red Knot is a circumpolar bird, meaning that it can also be found in Europe and Asia. The Arctic Bird Library (*second address*) has information about the esti-mated populations of Red Knot subspecies around the world. The Red Knot is a rare visitor to the Great Lakes, and Aves.net offers information about sightings in Ohio (*third address*).

http://www.audubon.org/bird/watch/red/red.html

http://www.wcmc.org.uk/arctic/data/birds/calcan.html

http://aves.net/birds-of-ohio/birdknot.htm

A B C D E F G H I J K L M N O P Q R S T U V W X Y Z

FEATHERED FACTS

Role Reversal

Phalaropes, wading shore birds, are among the few bird species in which the female is both the larger and more brightly colored. What's more, they often mate with more than one male, create more than one nest, and, after laying their eggs, feel perfectly free to move on, leaving their offspring in the care of the male. To complete the role reversal, flocks of females will often compete for a male.

—adapted from John Sterling, Smithsonian Migratory Bird Center

http://web2.si.edu/smbc/bom/wiph.htm

Sanderlings

Sanderlings, says Kenn Kaufman in *Birder's World*, "are so familiar in many areas that birders may take them for granted, identifying them by instinct rather than by field marks." Sanderlings (*Calidris alba*) are the tiny little birds that live at the edge of the surf, running along as if they were windup toys, looking for whatever the sea may wash up for them. They are found literally around the world. Using his own illustrations, Kaufman offers tips on how to identify four winter shorebirds including the sanderling.

http://www2.birdersworld.com/birders/fieldguide/ sanderlings/Sanderlings.html

Sandpiper, Buff-breasted

To attract a female, the male Buff-breasted Sandpiper (*Tryngites subruficollis*) dances for his date. He shakes and tips his bill upward. Other odd things happen in this mating show that ornithologists call *lekking*. John Sterling of the Smithsonian Migratory Bird Center explains the mating technique of the Buff-breasted Sandpiper in a profile of this threatened, long-range migratory bird that breeds in the Arctic, migrates through the Great Plains, and winters in the grasslands of Argentina, Uruguay, and southern Bolivia. "Their populations suffered tremendously from the settling of the Great Plains of North America and the Pampas of South America," Sterling notes. "Large numbers were shot by market hunters before legislation passed in 1918 [in the United States] (the Migratory Bird Treaty Act) and legislation in 1920 protecting them in Argentina."

http://web2.si.edu/smbc/bom/bbsa.htm

Sandpiper, Western

The Western Sandpiper (*Calidris mauri*) can put on quite a show in numbers in the Pacific Northwest. "The massing of Western Sandpipers at Grays Harbor, Washington, is truly an impressive sight," says Peterson Online. "In late April, as many as one-half million individuals have been seen there in one day, and seeing several hundred thousand is not uncommon." (*See also Events for information about the Grays Harbor Birding Festival.*) Despite its name, the Western Sandpiper can be found all along the coast of the American Southeast, as well as the three West Coast states during the winter months. It summers along the far western coast of Alaska on the Bering Sea.

http://www.petersononline.com/birds/month/wesa/ index.html

Sandpipers

Diane Porter offers some observations on techniques for identifying look-alike sandpipers. While she's at it, she discusses what makes a species a species in the world of nature and how in general to tell them apart.

http://www.birdwatching.com/stories/plato.html

Shorebird Watcher

Shorebirds, or waders, are not simply birds found at the shore, but include the plovers, sandpipers, and many other related families that are part of the order Charadriiformes, note Dick and Jean Hoffman of the Shorebird Watcher. "Most of these birds can be found along shorelines, especially in migration, but they are also found inland, upland, on Arctic tundra or at sea." The Hoffmans have created the Shorebird Watcher, a website full of information about plovers, curlews, sandpipers, godwits, whimbrels, rails, oystercatchers, snipes, and others of this group.

http://pw1.netcom.com/~djhoff/shorebrd.html

Spoonbill, Roseate

You may be hiking a trail through a Florida or Texas mangrove marsh when, out of the corner of your eye, you catch a glimpse of pink. A lot of pink on a large, otherwise white stork-like bird. It should take only a moment to realize you've spotted a Roseate Spoonbill (*Ajaia ajaja*), for no other North American bird has that long, namesake bill shaped like a spoon (except for the unmistakable, rarer and pinker American Flamingo, which has a short bill). In some parts of its range along the Gulf of Mexico and the Florida coasts, the Roseate Spoonbill was hunted almost to extinction by those seeking its pink, breeding-season feathers for Victorian women's hats. Destruction of its habitat hasn't helped. In Texas, reports the WetNet site (*first and second*

Roseate Spoonbilll (Dover)

addresses), they are now fairly common, and range southward all the way to northern Argentina. This site has a fine, close-up of a breeding male. For a good essay about the spoonbill, visit David Sarkozi's Birds of the Upper Texas Coast site (*third address*). Sarkozi notes that the Texas population of spoonbills was down to fewer than 200 birds in 1920. He also offers links for more information, as well as places to see them.

http://red.glo.state.tx.us/wetnet/species/spoonbill.html

http://www.glo.state.tx.us/wetnet/species/spoonbill.html

http://texasbirding.simplenet.com/birds/roseate.htm

Stork, Wood

The Wood Stork (*Mycteria americana*) is a large white, long-legged wader found in freshwater and coastal marshes in the southeastern United States. They can reach nearly four feet tall and have wingspans of more than five feet. A scientific study has been tracking four free-ranging Wood Storks from their summer breeding grounds at Harris Neck Wildlife Refuge in Georgia to their wintering locations in southern Georgia and Florida. This site, operated by the Wildlife Preservation Trust International, both tells you about Wood Storks and lets you follow the scientists as they track the birds. Also available are links to other wildlife tracking sites, not all of them birds.

http://allison.clark.net/pub/wcsweb/stork/

Turnstone, Ruddy

Quick little beach birds, Ruddy Turnstones (*Arenaria interpres*) are sandpipers that watch the edge of the surf for treats that may become available due to the turbulence of wave activity. They winter along the Gulf Coast and head for the high Arctic in the spring to raise their families, notes Wetnet. The turnstone has one of the more unusual names in the avian world, but as might be surmised, it comes from the bird's habit of turning over stones, shells, and other beach debris in search of food. Ruddy, of course, refers to its coloring.

http://red.glo.state.tx.us/wetnet/species/turnstone.html

A B C D E F G H I J K L M N O P Q R S T U V W X Y Z

Willet

The Willet (*Catoptrophorus semipalmatus*), a tall, long-legged and long-beaked bird, breeds in the prairie provinces of southwestern Canada, in the northwestern United States, as well as in eastern Canada, the East Coast, and on the Gulf Coast. In winter, it can be found along the Gulf Coast and much of the Atlantic and Pacific Coasts from Massachusetts and British Columbia south. Despite such a huge and varied range, the bird is on the list of species that are "in trouble," according to the National Audubon Society (*first address*). Possibly because of environmental threats, their overall numbers have been decreasing. Willets breed in Nova Scotia, and there they have become somewhat more common in summer in the past 20 years, reports the Nova Scotia Museum of Natural History (*second address*). The bird's name comes from its call. "These large, showy shorebirds are quite spectacular, especially when encountered on their nesting grounds," the museum says. "At first approach, an intruder is met by the excited and protesting members of the scattered colony which unite, often circling low overhead or alighting on treetops or other convenient perches, all scolding vehemently: *pill-will-willet pill-will-willet*, given in rapid succession."

http://www.audubon.org/bird/watch/wil/wil.html

http://museum.ednet.ns.ca/mnh/nature/nsbirds/
bns0132.htm

Woodcock, American

A relative of shorebirds, the American Woodcock (*Scolopax minor*, until recently known as *Philohela minor*) contents itself with the damp places of wooded areas and brushy thickets, wherever its favorite food, earthworms, can be found. It nests on the ground, depending on its protective coloration for cover, well illustrated by the Inver Hills (Minnesota) Community College's Tending the Nest Site (*first address*). Long-billed, with relatively large dark eyes, the woodcock's spring mating display is treasured by those who have seen it: A long spiraling ascent is followed by a high-speed descent, usually performed just at dusk. The dance of the woodcocks can apparently drive people mad, as evidenced by the account, titled Woodcocks and Brain Sucking Hyenas (*second address*), Charles Kennedy offers of his yearly attempts to lead a group to see the woodcocks in south Alabama. For identification tips, see the Patuxent site (*third address*), and for habitat and natural history, plus a description of an old-fashioned snipe hunt, see the Pennsylvania Parks Department site (*fourth address*). There is also a detailed description of the woodcock's courting display. Finally, to learn some of the unusual names for this bird—not the least of which is Timberdoodle—visit this River Bluffs Audubon Society page (*fifth address*).

http://www.ih.cc.mn.us/ihcc/Virtual%20Campus/Flora/
Other%20signs/flora_44.htm

http://www.alaweb.com/~kenwood/saba/articles/
hyena.htm

http://www.mbr-pwrc.usgs.gov/id/framlst/
i2280id.html

http://www.dcnr.state.pa.us/stateparks/spmag/
snpesp97.htm

http://www.audubon.org/chapter/mo/riverbluffs/
woodcock.htm

MEET THE MASTERS

A Youthful Helping Hand

One of the marvels of the World Wide Web is its agelessness—not in the sense of its history, but in the composition of its participants. And when you run across a website created by a 12-year-old boy that is not only entertaining but also useful to people of all ages, you can get a taste of the far-reaching possibilities of the Web as a communications tool. David Jordan was 11 years old when he began work on the David Jordan Bird Habitat website <http://members. aol.com/DJHabitat/>. David, who lives in Yorba Linda, California, was only eight when he began work with his dad on a backyard bird habitat that includes wildlife-attracting shrubs, a dozen feeders, and running water. The yard has since been certified by the National Wildlife Federation as "an official backyard wildlife habitat."

OPTICS

Probably no single tool is more valuable to the bird-watcher than a pair of good binoculars. But what *are* good binoculars? The World Wide Web is full of opinions, many of them provided by manufacturers of the optics themselves, but some are opinions offered by folks who've just tried different kinds and speak their minds. Many of the sites in this section belong to makers of binoculars or to retailers, and most offer at least some information to help you select among the many kinds and models. After all, you can pay anywhere from $50 to more than $1,000 for binoculars. And if you are really seriously into birding, you may want to consider a *spotting scope*, which is even more powerful. Birders often use other tools—everything from specialized packs to two-way radios and GPS gear. You can find it all on the Web—and more. (*See also Feeding & Watering and Retailers.*)

Adventure Camera

Adventure Camera specializes in outdoor and wildlife photography, and sponsors annual nationwide contests for nature photography; contest details can be found on the site. Adventure Camera sells new and used cameras and accessories—with a leaning toward equipment that's made for the wilds. Adventure Camera also sells optics, including Bausch & Lomb, Leica, and Swarovski binoculars. The site has a guide to the parts and functions of binoculars and what various terms mean. And so that you'll have somewhere to take your camera and binoculars, Adventure Camera offers tours to Central America.

http://www.adventurecamera.com

Better View Desired

How do you know which is the best binoculars or scope for the money you want to spend? Steve Ingraham's website Better View Desired is devoted to optics and provides reviews, features, and other useful information—such as how to test your optics. Bird Worthy Binoculars is an especially good discussion of what to look for in a good pair of birding binoculars. Another feature is How Much Scope Does a Birder Need. There are directories to both manufacturers and retailers of optics. Steve, incidentally, is Tools of the Trade editor for *Birding* magazine, and this site is cited by many bird-watching websites as *the* Web source for good optics information. The site is supported by donations.

http://www.lightshedder.com/sing/BVD

Binocular Tips

Mike Mencotti of the Macomb Audubon Society in Michigan offers a concise set of useful tips for selecting, setting up, and using binoculars for birding.

http://www.audubon.org/chapter/mi/macomb/ 4birds.htm#binocs

Portable Documents

In wandering around the Web, you'll find many birding sites that offer articles, charts, newsletters, and statistics in .PDF or "portable document format" files that you download to your computer. These files produce handsome documents that can contain photos, graphics, and several different text fonts—on matter what fonts you have installed on your computer and no matter whether you're using a Windows computer, a Mac, or even a Unix work station. But to view them or to print them, you need Adobe's Acrobat Reader. Some computers—specially new Macintoshes—come with Acrobat. If yours doesn't recognize .PDF files, you can get Acrobat Reader without charge. The software easily configures itself with your browser to appear automatically when you download a .PDF file so that, once installed, you never have to think about Acrobat Reader again. However, you can load it without the browser if you want to read or print a document stored on your hard disk. You can download your free copy from this address.

http://www.adobe.com/prodindex/acrobat/readstep. html

A B C D E F G H I J K L M N O P Q R S T U V W X Y Z

Binoculars for Latin America

The Fairfax (Virginia) Audubon Society's "Binoculars for Latin America Project" is looking for donations of used binoculars and telescopes "so that we can continue vital aid to ornithological and conservation education projects throughout the Americas." According to the society's binoculars coordinator, Gary Filerman, "Donating a pair of binoculars is one of the most consequential contributions you can make at the least cost." The equipment is used by Latin American ornithologists and field researchers, for whom buying a pair of binoculars could cost as much as a month's salary. Even Latin American colleges and universities have trouble affording binoculars. "Imagine trying to study ornithology without any binoculars available to the class," says the society. "But the high equipment cost is beyond the means of many curious and enthusiastic student naturalists." The website gives examples of how the binoculars are used and explains how to donate them. "Your smallest gift can make a difference," Fairfax Audubon says. To learn about the program, visit the site's home page (*first address*) and look for a menu link for New Life for Old Binoculars. Or try entering the page address directly (*second address*).

http://www.fairfaxaudubon.org
http://www.fairfaxaudubon.org/CoverArticles/
    binoculars/body.htm

Birding Optics

Michael Porter on Birdwatching.com has written an extensive guide to birding optics that covers birding scopes and binoculars and tells how to compare different models. The feature includes a glossary.

http://www.birdwatching.com/optics.html

Bogen Photo Corp.

Bogen Photo Corp. in Ramsey, New Jersey, distributes lines of specialty photographic hardware, many of which can be useful to birders. For instance, the company carries tripods and monopods that can be used with scopes, as well as cameras—you'll find suggestions on which kind may be best for your sort of photography. Also available from Bogen Photo is a line of remote camera and strobe triggering devices, very useful in close-up wildlife photography. Bogen distributes to some 2,000 dealers, and the site enables you to contact the company for dealers nearest you.

http://www.bogenphoto.com

Bushnell/Bausch & Lomb

Bushnell and Bausch & Lomb, long-standing manufacturers of optics, offer a birding forum, called HyperNews, where you can post questions, offer opinions, and otherwise chat with other birders via messages. The site has a gallery of fine photographs from around North America; if you're a photographer, the site invites you to submit your work for display. A guide to refuges in the United States, with an index that's a clickable map, is online. And, of course, there is plenty of information about Bushnell's products, including their binoculars and spotting scopes, many of which now sport the Bausch & Lomb name.

http://www.bushnell.com/birding/birdhome.html

Christopher's, Ltd.

Christopher's, Ltd., in Norman, Oklahoma, which sells a variety of brands of binoculars, spotting scopes, and accessories, has useful guides on how to pick a pair of binoculars or a spotting scope—and what the advantages and disadvantages of each are for birders. Select How To from the home page menu.

http://www.birdbino.com

Eagle Optics

Eagle Optics in Middleton, Wisconsin, a retailer of binoculars and scopes, has an excellent, concise Birdwatching Guide, which offers many practical tips for how, when, and where to see a wide variety of birds. On the equipment side, the site has an excellent set of buying guides covering binoculars, scopes, and tripods, plus a useful chart comparing the specifications of many models and brands of binoculars. The site has an online catalog.

http://www.eagleoptics.com

Focus Camera & Video

Focus, a large camera store in Brooklyn, New York, has a large collection of binoculars and scopes. Its sophisticated site uses multiple frames on its pages, and you can search for products by price range. The site also offers a lot of data about each product, useful for making comparisons. The site includes links to manufacturers' websites.

http://www.focuscamera.com

Hunt's

Hunt's Photo and Video in Melrose, Massachusetts, carries a wide selection of binoculars manufactured for birders. To help you select which model is best for you, the site has symbols to indicate models that are good for birding and an illustrated guide called "Considerations in Choosing Binoculars" that describes such features as field of view, exit pupil, near focus, coatings, and collimation. The site also illustrates the differences in magnification of the different powers of binoculars.

http://www.wbhunt.com/Binoculars/index.html

Kowa Sporting Optics

Kowa's specialty is spotting scopes for birders and others. Kowa also manufactures several models of binoculars. The site has a valuable FAQ page that's more like a glossary; it defines almost any term you are apt to run across when reading about outdoor optics.

http://www.kowascope.com

Leica

Leica manufactures high-end binoculars. When you go to the site, select the Camera section, and then click the English language version. You'll find binoculars toward the bottom of the camera section.

http://www.leica.com

Hermit Thrush (*Hylocichla guttata*) [*Catharus guttatus*] (JJA)

Lens Cleaner

Here's something you may not have known existed: a pen-shaped cleaner for binoculars. Called a LensPen, the small device contains a brush with a nonliquid compound "that will not spill or dry out" and is designed to clean lenses of all fine optics. This website will tell you all about it.

http://www.lenspen.com

Leupold

Leupold is an American manufacturer of spotting scopes and binoculars. Aside from its online catalog, one of the interesting features of the site is a "product ideas" form in which you, the public, can suggest optical devices that Leupold could make. Neat!

http:// www.leupold.com

Meade Instruments

Meade is a major manufacturer of both astronomical telescopes and several lines of binoculars, including the Safari Pro and RainForest Pro series that are popular with birders. When you get to the section on binoculars, look for the How to Select the Right Binocular guide. Although it obviously promotes Meade's equipment, the guide is excellently illustrated and written, and demonstrates how different kinds of binoculars work.

http://www.meade.com

A B C D E F G H I J K L M N O P Q R S T U V W X Y Z

A
B
C
D
E
F
G
H
I
J
K
L
M
N
O
P
Q
R
S
T
U
V
W
X
Y
Z

Minolta

Minolta makes a variety of binoculars—from ultra-compact to pocket, standard, and autofocus units. The website takes an interesting approach in that, before it even shows you the equipment, it presents a Choosing the Right Binoculars guide. The guide covers binocular basics, magnification, angle of view, coatings, and long eye relief, and explains what the exit pupil and brightness indexes are.

http://www.minoltausa.com

Mirakel Optical Company

Mirakel Optical in West Coxsackie, New York, has been in the optical business since 1923 and not only sells binoculars and scopes for birders but also fixes broken equipment. The site explains the kinds of binocular repairs that are performed and provides a form for sending in your binoculars for a free evaluation. The site also offers monthly specials on new equipment. When you order a free print catalog online, Mirakel will also send a 12-page booklet, *Know Your Binoculars.*

http://www.mirakeloptical.com

National Camera Exchange

National Camera Exchange, based in Golden Valley, Minnesota, carries more than 100 models of binoculars and spotting scopes. The site has an excellent, high-tech guide to binoculars, covering such topics as power, magnification, optical quality, focus types, and brightness.

http://www.natcam.com

Nikon

Nikon makes a wide variety of binoculars, as well as field scopes and spotting scopes "for the serious observer." The site has a FAQ page that explains terms, as well as the meaning of the numbers, like "7 × 35, 8.6," that appear on binoculars.

http://www.nikonusa.com

Optics for Everyone

Author and naturalist Pete Dunne of New Jersey Audubon provides a handy description of many of the Bausch & Lomb, Nikon, Kowa, Swarovski, Swift, and Zeiss binoculars, starting from the least expensive (around $80) and running to the most (more than $1,000). "Every couple of years or so, the Optikmeisters at Cape May Bird Observatory run their hands through the river of glass and choose their favorites," Dunne says. "These are the ones that we feel offer the best performance for the money. These are the ones that nose out other optics in their price category on the basis of functional attributes." The page also offers several things to consider before making a purchase. New Jersey Audubon sells all of the binoculars listed in its online reviews, so the write-ups tend to highlight what's right about each—though there are some warnings, such as the recommended model that may be out of alignment when you buy it. However, the models sold are the ones the jury selected after trying close to 180 units.

http://www.nj.com/audubon/genlmenu/optics.html

Pentax

Pentax makes both binoculars and monoculars—the latter, says Pentax, for when weight and space are at a premium, but yet when high quality optics may be needed. The site has a useful guide called Which Is Best for Me, for the birder, the sports fan, the outdoor lover, the serious sailor, the star gazer, and even the theatergoer.

http://www.pentax.com

Rough-legged Hawk (*Buteo lagopus*) (JJA)

Saving the Words

Sometimes you'll run across a page of information about the World Wide Web that you'd really like to save to read later. Modern Web browsers allow you to save what you see. You can save webpages, complete with graphics and all the razzle-dazzle. But odds are, you are interested mostly in the words. So you'll want to save the page as plain, old text. With Microsoft Internet Explorer and other browsers, go up to the upper left-hand corner and select File, then Save As. A window comes up that lets you choose where you want to store the file, what you want to call it (a name will be suggested, but you'll probably want to invent one more to your own liking). Your browser should then let you select in what format you want to save the file. This option is important, for it enables you to select "text file" or ".txt." This will strip out all the weird HTML (hypertext markup language) codes that are used to configure the webpage and leave you with just the words. And, after all, words are what it's all about, even on the Web.

Russian Binoculars

Although no one doubts the Russians' achievements in science—just look at their space program, for instance—few of us are aware of their achievements in optics. Yet, according to the Internet Telescope Exchange in Wilmington, North Carolina, the Russians are building some of the finest binoculars in the world. Whereas some may have been designed to give tank commanders the best view of the enemy (presumably not us any more), they can now be used to give birders the best view of passing warblers. You can learn about—and buy—Russian binoculars here.

http://www.burnettweb.com/ite/binocs.htm

Scope City

Scope City in Simi Valley, California, calls itself the "largest, most complete optical supermarket in the world." The site has a beginner's guide that covers binoculars and spotting scopes.

http://www.scopecity.com

Simpson Optics

Simpson Optics is a mail-order dealer for Brunton, Nikon, Pentax, Swarovski, Swift, and Zeiss binoculars and spotting scopes. Simpson has an online "catalog" along with some interesting, candid comments about different kinds of binoculars that a shopper might find useful. "We are customer-oriented with the goal of providing the customer with the optics that fit their needs at competitive prices," Greg Simpson told us. "We are not just a mail-order company focusing on price."

http://www.simpsonoptics.com

Swarovski Optik

Swarovski, an Austrian company, is a leading maker of fine binoculars, as well as laser range finders and night-vision telescopes (imagine having one of those on an owl prowl!). More than a catalog, the site includes birding and hunting features, and some links to birding and outdoors sites.

http://www.swarovskioptik.com

Swift

Swift is a manufacturer of binoculars, spotting scopes, and other optics. In fact, Swift makes a series of binoculars designed especially for birders. This page gives the rundown about Swift's birding binoculars and links at the bottom of the page lead to other areas of the Swift site for information about such products as Nighthawk spotting scopes. On the home page (*second address*) you'll also find a link to FAQs about binoculars with much useful information.

http://www.swift-optics.com/birdwatching.htm

A B C D E F G H I J K L M N O P Q R S T U V W X Y Z

Mac .SIT Files

If you are a Macintosh user, you will run across some downloadable program files on the Web that end in .SIT. These are Stuff It! files, which are for a Mac what .ZIP is for Windows (*see page 46*). They are highly compacted collections of files that need a special program to "expand" or extract them to make them usable. Stuff It! comes from Aladdin Industries, which offers a free "expander" program for Macs—and for Windows—that decompresses .SIT files (and will also handle .ZIP files). Yes, that's right, it's freeware. (Aladdin, though, charges for the main Stuff It! program that *creates* the .SIT archives.)

http://www.aladdinsys.com/expander/index.html

Tasco Binoculars & Birdwatching Kits

Tasco makes binoculars and other optics (*first address*). The company offers plenty of binocular models—look under Recreational Optics, then Binoculars. However, especially for birders, Tasco produces the NatureWatch birding kits, which include a pair of compact binoculars, birding book, pad and pencil, and a fanny pack in which to hold them all. Tasco says it will contribute 2 to 3 percent of the sale of each NatureWatch Kit to the World Wildlife Fund. The Tasco website has a dealer locator to help you find where to buy the products. The site also offers birder information and interaction. From the home page, select Interest Groups and on the next page, Birdwatching. There you'll find Tasco's feature articles, discussion group, chat room, letters, and birding-related "fun and games." Tasco's recently introduced line of binoculars, the Rare Bird collection, is manufactured for birders and are "the only binoculars now approved by the National Audubon Society," Tasco reports. Tasco has set up a special website to focus on them (*second address*).

http://www.tascosales.com
http://www.rarebirdbytasco.com

ORGANIZATIONS & ASSOCIATIONS

One might say there are two basic kinds of wildlife organizations: those that help humans appreciate wildlife, and those that help wildlife by seeking human appreciation. Often, they have both missions. The World Wide Web is an excellent source of information about clubs, societies, associations, and other organizations connected with birding and with wildlife. Most mentioned in this section can provide a lot of useful information for the birder, be it online or via print publications. (*See also Audubon Societies & Sanctuaries; Conservation; North American Birds, Wading; and Ornithology.*)

Alaska Bird Observatory

Because Alaska is such a vast and pristine environment that attracts more than 200 kinds of birds, many of them migrants who use it as nesting grounds, the Alaska Bird Observatory in Fairbanks, Alaska, was established in 1991. The observatory studies both the migrant and resident birds of the arctic, subarctic, and temperate regions of northwestern North America to increase our understanding of these species and to aid in their conservation. The center runs many educational programs for schools and organizations, organizes an Alaska Bird Camp in summer, has banding demonstrations, offers internships, and sponsors other programs. Although the website contains mostly information about the observatory, it provides a good section about birding around Fairbanks, in case you live in the vicinity or are planning a visit. Check out its excellent bird quiz, too.

http://www.alakabird.org/

Arctic Three-toed Woodpecker (*Picoides arcticus*) [Black-backed Woodpecker] (JJA)

American Birding Association

Founded in 1968, the American Birding Association is North America's largest organization for active birders, with more than 20,000 members. "Concern for the welfare of birds lies at the core of ABA and touches everything we do," the organization says. The ABA "will help you to learn more about birds, develop your birding skills, and bring you together with other birders." The ABA's website brims with information about all aspects of the hobby. Particularly useful is its Birding Resources section, which lists birding events, chat groups, training courses, tours, and travel tips. Highlighting the economic value of birding—the ABA believes that as politicians understand that wildlife preserves and conservation lands generate tourism dollars, they will place more value on these refuges—there's even a guide to restaurants near good birding locations (*see also Retailers*). The site explains how birders can help the cause of birding, for instance, by contributing data to North American breeding bird atlas projects. A large portion of the site is devoted to the ABA's Young Birders program, described in the section on Children and Birding. Online catalogs and many other features are also available.

http://www.americanbirding.org

American Society of Crows & Ravens

"If men had wings and bore black feathers, few of them would be clever enough to be crows," wrote Henry Ward Beecher in the mid-1800s. One can assume, then, that crow fans are clever, too. To see just how clever, visit the site of the American Society of Crows and Ravens, a laid-back "disorganization" of people devoted to our smartest birds, members of the corvid family. The corvids include crows, ravens, jackdaws, magpies, and jays. Besides lots of information about crows and ravens, the website carries current and back issues of the *Corvi Chronicle*, the entertainingly written ASCAR newsletter. Membership in ASCAR, incidentally, is free and entitles the "corvi," or member, to the paper edition of the newsletter, which is "published irregularly by corvis who have an interest in or need for doing so." The site is also a good place to find links to other corvid sources.

http://www.azstarnet.com/~serres/index.html

Crow (*Corvus brachyrhynchos*) (JJA)

Association of Field Ornithologists

The Association of Field Ornithologists, which originated in 1922 as the New England Bird Banding Association, is "a society of professional and amateur ornithologists dedicated to the scientific study and dissemination of information about birds in their natural habitats." The site has information about the association, plus abstracts from its journal (*see also Magazines & Periodicals*). The site also has a collection of links to other ornithological organizations.

http://www.afonet.org

Baltimore Bird Club

The Baltimore (Maryland) Bird Club has a sizable online presence with a very useful website offering hundreds of pages of information about all aspects of birding. Aside from helpful features about feeding birds and landscaping to attract them (*see also Feeding & Watering*), the site offers links to Rare Bird Alerts, the club news letter, and many other birding sites, both in and outside Maryland.

http://www.bcpl.net/~tross/baltbird.html

A
B
C
D
E
F
G
H
I
J
K
L
M
N
O
P
Q
R
S
T
U
V
W
X
Y
Z

FEATHERED FACTS

Little Bug Eater

The Ruby-throated Hummingbird is famous for its nectar-eating tendencies, and, in fact, scientists believe various red, tubular flowers coevolved with hummingbirds. However, this species is also a big consumer of insects, and ornithologists estimate that as much as 50 to 60 percent of its diet is spiders, mosquitoes, gnats, aphids, small bees, and even insect eggs.

—adapted from Birds of North America

http://www.birdsofna.org/excerpts/rth.html

Colorado Birding Society

If you live in or about Colorado, you can learn a lot about the birds and bird sightings in the state from the Colorado Birding Society website. The site has many late-breaking reports of interesting sightings, arranged by regions, then by county. There are also useful local links, plus a gallery of photos of Colorado birds.

http://home.att.net/~birdertoo/

Cooper Ornithological Society

The Cooper Ornithological Society caters to those of a scientific bent who are interested in avian biology. Members receive the society's magazine, the *Condor*. The website has much information about the organization, its functions, and its publications.

http://www.cooper.org

Hummingbird Society

No bird seems to fascinate people quite the way hummingbirds do. It's probably because they are so small and so amazing in the things they can do—such as the Ruby-throated Hummingbird's migrating at 40 miles per hour across hundreds of miles of the Caribbean to get to its North American summering grounds. For those who enjoy hummingbirds, the Hummingbird Society site is well worth visiting, full of information and photos, plus links. H. Ross Hawkins, a hummingbird devotee who's traveled throughout the Western Hemisphere to observe and photograph hummers, founded the society.

http://www.hummingbird.org

Illinois Ornithological Society

The Illinois Ornithological Society's site has some useful information about the state's birds—especially rare and endangered species. The site includes many photos of some of the rarer birds of Illinois, and you can find out about the society's planned field trips; even if you can't make the scheduled trips, the description of destinations is useful as a source of good birding spots in the state.

http://www.chias.org/ios/

National Bird-Feeding Society

Backyard bird feeding is probably the most popular way humans get together with wildlife. To encourage effective and safe feeding, the National Bird-Feeding Society was formed. Its website is particularly valuable for its collection of frequently asked questions about bird feeding, and its links. Information is also available as to how to join the society and about the benefits of membership.

http://www.birdfeeding.org

National Park Maps

Planning to go birding in a national park and want a free map of the park? The National Park Service offers, at no charge, highly detailed maps of most of its parks. They come in several formats: Adobe Illustrator, written for Macintosh computer users; Adobe Acrobat PDF files, usable on either Macs or PCs if you have the free Acrobat Reader program installed (*see page 237*); or JPEG files, which are common Internet image files, also readable on either kind of computer. The Acrobat files are generally the smallest; JPEGs, the largest—and most detailed. A shaded relief map of Acadia National Park in Maine runs 2.7 megabytes in JPEG, so make sure you have a decent connection to your Internet service. Of course, it helps to have a color printer if you want a hard copy of the map, but black-and-white works, too.

http://www.nps.gov/carto/

National Park Foundation

The National Park Foundation is like a PTA for the National Park Service. Created by Congress in 1967 as an official, nonprofit partner of the National Park Service, the NPF helps "conserve, preserve and enhance our national parks for the benefit of the American people." The organization supports programs primarily for education and outreach, visitor information and interpretive facilities, volunteer activities and National Park Service employees, and raises money for grants and assistance programs. For the family in search of parks information, the NPF website is in many ways more complete than the National Park Service's site. You can search for parks by name or state, or you can locate parks by special interest. The site also describes scenic and historic trails, and offers excellent regional tours of the parks available in different parts of the country. For each park, the NPF site gives descriptions, addresses and contact information, travel directions, activities, fees, and other information.

http://www.nationalparks.org

New York State Bluebird Society

Despite its name, the New York State Bluebird Society has information for anyone, anywhere, interested in setting up bluebird nest boxes. The site provides plans and help, natural history, information about an adopt-a-box program, and even information about how New Yorkers can get bluebird license plates for their cars. Information is provided about the society, its goals, and its meetings.

http://www.geocities.com/RainForest/2414/nysbs.htm

North American Bluebird Society

Few birds have built up fan clubs quite like bluebirds. After all, they have many magical qualities: they have beautiful color, they start appearing in late winter when signs of spring are psychologically important, they take well to human-made housing, and they perform a practical service. They also need our help. And that's why organizations like the North American Bluebird Society have sprung up. Bluebirds are great insect eaters and, as such, help keep pests under control, as well as make our lives a little more comfortable. But bluebirds have been declining in many areas as fields, their natural habitat, are being transformed into subdivisions or allowed to revert to forest. In addition, alien birds have been pushing them out of their traditional nesting places. The society helps bring back the bluebirds by offering information and advice on how to attract them to your property. Its site has not only the basics of bluebird culture but also detailed plans for building nest boxes for both the Eastern Bluebird and the Mountain Bluebird of the West—a great project for the whole family.

http://www.nabluebirdsociety.org/

Eastern Bluebird (*Sialia sialis*) (JJA)

Purple Martin Conservation Association

"Purple Martins are the only bird species totally dependent on humans for supplying them with nesting sites," notes the Purple Martin Conservation Association, which is affiliated with Edinboro University of Pennsylvania. "And they have been managed by man longer than any other North American species. If humans were to stop supplying martins with homes, they would likely disappear as a breeding bird in eastern North America." One aim of the association is to make sure they don't disappear, and the PMCA provides all sorts of assistance to those who would have Purple Martin houses in their yards—including a colorful, quarterly magazine *Purple Martin Update*, advice hot lines (telephone or e-mail), product discounts, and other support. Incidentally, if you become a Purple Martin landlord, you'll be in good company. The Smithsonian Migratory Bird Center estimates that more than a million Americans have Purple Martin houses.

http://www.purplemartin.org

Raptor Research Foundation

The Raptor Research Foundation describes itself as "a professional society concerned with the study and conservation of hawks, falcons, eagles, and owls." The international organization, founded in Wisconsin in 1966 by 13 people concerned about the decline in raptor populations, today consists of about 1,200 professional raptor biologists and scientists from more than 55 countries. The website describes the organization and its work and has a good collection of links to other raptor sites. (*See also North American Birds, Raptors.*)

http://catsis.weber.edu/rrf/

Purple Martin (*Progne subis*) (JJA)

FEATHERED FACTS

Likely Albinos

Some bird species are more likely than others to produce albinos. They include American Robins, American Crows, House Sparrows, and Red-winged Blackbirds among the songbirds, and Red-tailed Hawks among the raptors.

—adapted from *A Bird's Eye View*, American Birding Association

http://www.americanbirding.org/bevfea.htm

Roger Tory Peterson Institute of Natural History

Dr. Roger Tory Peterson was an artist and naturalist who virtually invented the modern birding guide with his *Field Guide to the Birds*, first published in 1934. Peterson, who died in 1996, went on to write many books and paint many birds, all with the aim of bringing people closer to nature. The mission of the Roger Tory Peterson Institute is "to create passion for and knowledge of the natural world, with children in particular, by inspiring and guiding the study of nature in our schools and communities." The institute offers workshops for teachers and other special programs. The Selborne Project, for instance, "connects children to a place in the real world, far beyond the counterfeit world of TV and video games. It enables teachers to structure a learning environment that takes advantage of their students' innate curiosity about nature and helps those students understand their role in it." The institute is in Jamestown, New York, Peterson's birthplace.

http://www.rtpi.org

Turkey Vulture Society

The Turkey Vulture (*Cathartes aura*) is described by its fans as "one of the most interesting and skilled soaring birds in the world." It's just when people get a closer look at a vulture working on a tasty rack of carrion that they may be put off by the bald-headed bird, which is somewhat ungainly on the ground. The Turkey Vulture Society is devoted to promoting the welfare and study of this widely found bird that is responsible for carcass removal. This species is usually so unobtrusive that people are often unaware of its presence except as a high-soaring shape in the sky. Besides illustrations and photos of vultures, the site provides membership information for those who would like to help contribute to the somewhat sketchy knowledge of the Turkey Vulture's habits and habitats.

http://www.accutek.com/vulture/

Turkey Vulture (*Cathartes aura*) (JJA)

Waterbird Society

The Waterbird Society is a scientific group "formed in 1976 to establish better communication and coordination between the growing number of people studying and monitoring colonially nesting aquatic birds, and to contribute to the protection and management of stressed populations or habitats of such species," the site says. There's information about the society's goals and its journal, *Colonial Waterbirds*, including recent tables of contents.

http://www.nmnh.si.edu/BIRDNET/CWS/

ORNITHOLOGY

Ornithology, the scientific study of birds, is not limited to scientists. Thanks in part of the Internet, there is a growing cooperation between citizen and scientist, and even the ordinary backyard bird-watcher can help ornithologists with their work. This section describes websites that can introduce the layperson to the science of birds, that can explain how non-scientists—even children—can assist with research in such areas as migration, population densities, and breeding ranges. Sites here also describe some of the projects that ornithologists in North America are involved in. (*See also Conservation and Organizations & Associations.*)

American Ornithologists' Union

If you begin to become serious about birding, you may want to consider membership in a serious birders' organization. Founded in 1883, the American Ornithologists' Union is the oldest and largest North American organization devoted to the scientific study of birds. "Although the AOU primarily is a professional organization, its membership of about 4,000 includes many amateurs dedicated to the advancement of ornithological science," says the AOU site. Although the pages here are mostly devoted to the union and its activities, the site carries useful abstracts of the current and recent issues of the *Auk*, one of the top journals of ornithology and one of the oldest. The AOU's *Ornithological Newsletter*, also online, carries reports of local news, activities, and studies, plus reviews and ads. A handy feature is the fact that e-mail addresses are attached to most entries so you can easily contact an expert if you see a topic that especially interests you.

http://pica.wru.umt.edu/AOU/AOU.HTML

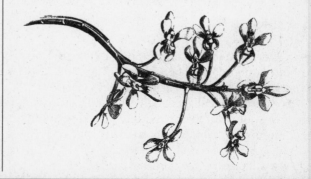

A B C D E F G H I J K L M N O P Q R S T U V W X Y Z

FEATHERED FACTS

Common as Gold

American Goldfinches are the most frequently reported finch by Project FeederWatch participants, appearing at 69 percent of all feeders in 1997.

—adapted from Cornell Laboratory of Ornithology.

http://birdsource2.ornith.cornell.edu/pfw/birdid/amgo/index.html

Be an Ornithologist

For some people watching birds is much more than a hobby: it's their job. This page, created by the Children's Museum of Indianapolis, Indiana, is designed to give kids an idea of what an ornithologist does by giving them some simple ornithological projects to do. The museum also has an online flight exhibit worth visiting (*second address*). The Children's Museum, incidentally, is considered one of the pioneer—and still premiere—museums designed for children,. A majority of its exhibits overturn the typical adult "Don't Touch" approach by encouraging just the opposite, offering sturdy exhibits that anticipate and encourage children to interact with them.

http://www.childrensmuseum.org/sornitho.htm

http://www.childrensmuseum.org/fly.htm

Bird Anatomy

Here's a short-and-sweet description of the parts of a typical bird, offered by Robert Hole Jr. The site includes an illustration of a bird that you can click on to learn about its external parts, especially useful if you are trying to figure out what the field guide is talking about when it refers to *primaries*, *secondaries*, or *wing coverts*.

http://www.interaktv.com/birdanat/anat.html

Bird Biodiversity

The Slater Museum of Natural History at the University of Puget Sound in Washington State has data and photos for birds of the Northwest, plus information for serious naturalists.

http://www.ups.edu/biology/museum/UPSbirds.html

BirdNet

BirdNet, a cooperative effort of a group of professional amateur birding organizations, is probably the biggest clearinghouse of ornithological and birding sources on the World Wide Web. Many features that a nonscientist would find useful can be located under the heading Birds & Birding Information and include: a well-indexed collection of bird images; checklists of birds; information about wildlife rehabilitation centers; reviews of recently published books; and links for scores of birding resources. The game Feather Quest challenges you to identify species of birds by their feathers. The site's home page offers links to ten of the leading ornithological organizations found online: the American Ornithologists' Union, Association of Field Ornithologists, CIPAMEX in Mexico, Cooper Ornithological Society, Pacific Seabird Group, Raptor Research Foundation, Society of Canadian Ornithologists, Society of Caribbean Ornithology, the Waterbird Society, and the Wilson Ornithological Society.

http://www.nmnh.si.edu/BIRDNET/index.html

Birds in Forested Landscapes

Scientists at Cornell University are enlisting the help of birders to study the habitat requirements of certain woodland birds. Called Birds in Forested Landscapes, the project involves periodically observing any of seven species of thrushes and two species of hawks to help biologists determine why their numbers are declining in some areas. Observers also look for cowbirds, which lay their eggs in other species' nests and may affect local populations (*Quandaries, Pesky Birds*). The website tells how to participate, what to look for, and gives profiles of all the species involved.

http://birds.cornell.edu/bfl/

BirdSource

Want to "bird with a purpose"? BirdSource is an unusual but now famous partnership between citizens and scientists, designed and managed by the National Audubon Society and the Cornell Laboratory of Ornithology (*see later in this section*). "Together, we track birds and contribute our findings online to define bird ranges, populations, migration pathways, and habitat needs," the site says. "Thanks to citizen participation, BirdSource is a powerful new tool for bird conservation." BirdSource, a modern and easy-to-negotiate website, includes a dozen or so projects to which all members of the family can contribute, such as the Warbler Watch, the Winter Finch Survey, Project Feeder Watch, Christmas Bird Counts, and the North American Breeding Bird Survey. Many of the features of the site are covered in other sections of this book.

http://birdsource.cornell.edu

Classroom Bird Watch

Kids love birds. Mixing bird-watching and school can be a rewarding experience for children, who can learn a lot about nature, biology, and the environment from their feathered friends. The program helps teach observation skills, promotes creativity, and "lends itself to wonderful inquiry opportunities," the site says. Students can have their findings, ideas, and art-work published in the program's national newsletter, *Classroom Birdscope*, copies of which are available online for all to read. Anyone can read and benefit from the findings of the participating schools—just go to the Data from Participating Schools page and click on the map to view what the kids are seeing in your neck of the woods. Classroom Bird Watch is sponsored by the National Science Foundation, the Cornell Laboratory of Ornithology (*see next entry*), and the National Audubon Society.

http://birdsource.cornell.edu/cfw/

Oriole (Dover)

FEATHERED FACTS

Big Spenders

The average member surveyed by the American Birding Association, the largest birding organization in the United States, spends around $3,000 a year on birding trips.

—adapted from American Birding Association

http://americanbirding.org/consecond2.htm

Cornell Laboratory of Ornithology

Cornell University's Laboratory of Ornithology is probably the premier research center on birds—its mission is "to interpret and help conserve the earth's biological diversity through research and education focused on birds." The home page is the jumping-off spot for learning about and participating in some of the lab's many projects. Although some of the website is meant to sell things like memberships or pictures of birds—all for the good cause of supporting the study of world birds—many features can be enjoyed without charge. These include the Bird of the Week, which gives an in-depth description of a species, along with many photos, range maps, and even sounds. Other features include the Sound of the Week; many of the articles from the current *Living Bird*, the lab's monthly magazine; and information about various ways you can help the work of ornithologists (*some of these, such as BirdSource, are noted earlier in this section; see also Events, Christmas Bird Count and Great Backyard Bird Count*). Every bird-watcher should visit, bookmark, and regularly keep in touch with this site.

http://birds.cornell.edu

A
B
C
D
E
F
G
H
I
J
K
L
M
N
O
P
Q
R
S
T
U
V
W
X
Y
Z

A B C D E F G H I J K L M N O P Q R S T U V W X Y Z

Electronic Resources on Ornithology

Natural history writer Christopher Majka has put together an excellent list of useful websites related to birds, broken down by bird types and regions of the world. Majka includes links to some of his own excellent natural history writings that have appeared in the New Brunswick Naturalist.

http://www.chebucto.ns.ca/Environment/NHR/bird.html

Father of Ornithology

Known as the "father of American ornithology," Alexander Wilson published the first natural history of American birds and was the first American citizen to publish any kind of work on birds. The nine-volume work, called *American Ornithology*, appeared between 1808 and 1814, two decades before Audubon, and contained illustrations of 268 species, including descriptions of 26 new species. This page (*first address*) from the Philadelphia Print Shop Ltd. website tells about Wilson and sells prints from the book; many of the prints are shown online. More on Wilson—who had come from Scotland where he was both a silk weaver and a well-published poet who once got in libel trouble—may be found at the website of the Kenyon Oppenheimer, Inc. gallery in Chicago (*second address*), which also sells prints from the book. A longer biography of Wilson, complete with his portrait, is available at the University of Michigan (*third address*). This site also has an old etching of his burial place at Old Swedes Church in Philadelphia. Incidentally, the venerable Wilson Ornithological Society (*see later in this section*) is named in his honor.

http://philaprintshop.com/wilson.html
http://www.audubonart.com/txtawil.htm
http://www.ummz.lsa.umich.edu/birds/AWilsoninfo.html

Glossary of Biological Terms

Serious birders occasionally encounter words too scientific for either their own vocabulary or for their household dictionary. The Museum of Paleontology at the University of California at Berkeley has a comprehensive glossary that explains biological terms in many natural history areas. For birders, the sections on ecol-

ogy, life history, zoology, and perhaps botany will be of interest. It's a good site to bookmark if you are curious about the science of birds—and biology in general.

http://www.ucmp.berkeley.edu/glossary/glossary.html

Guide to Graduate Studies in Ornithology in North America

Are you interested in a career in the science of bird study? The Wilson Ornithological Society has a huge guide to graduate studies in ornithology, arranged by North American regions. The guide describes each school, facilities, and what ornithological subjects faculty members are specializing in. Contact people for each school are also listed.

http://www.ummz.lsa.umich.edu/birds/studies.html

Tracking Down a Festival

You may have heard of a birding festival in a nearby town or state but can't find it in the section on Events or in one of the directories listed there. Don't give up! The Internet may still have the answer.

- Try using a search engine. First, search for the name of the festival, such as the Crowtown Crow Fest, making sure to use the search technique that will find that exact term (*see also the introduction, which explains how this is done*).

- If that doesn't work, check out the chamber of commerce in the town you suspect has the festival. For instance, do a search for "Crowtown Chamber of Commerce" or "Crowtown Visitors Bureau."

- If searches turn up nothing, try e-mail. Stop by rec.birds, the Usenet news group and post a query. Many special events, incidentally, are announced on rec.birds, so if you check the newsgroup regularly, you're apt to learn of festivals and other gatherings in your area.

Hudson Bay Project

More than 200 species of migratory birds use the coastal lowlands of the Hudson Bay region for breeding and for preparing for migration, notes Dr. Robert F. Rockwell, a population biologist with the American Museum of Natural History in New York City. However, he continues, changes in human activities in the southern part of these birds' ranges have led to an imbalance in the way animals and plants interact in the Arctic. "In particular, the Mid-continent population of Lesser Snow Geese, a keystone herbivore in coastal ecosystems of Hudson and James Bays, has tripled to nearly six million in the past 30 years," he reports. Because of the unusually large numbers of Snow Geese, large tracts of coastal wetlands are being stripped of their vegetation. And that's hurting all the species that inhabit this coastal region. The website describes the work of a team that includes Rockwell. An online slide show uses photos, tables, and maps to dramatically illustrate the effects of Snow Geese overpopulation. Other portions of the site describe the many-faceted and often complex research of the Hudson Bay Project team in its efforts to understand what is happening in this fragile environment. The aim is to learn how to slow or stop the degradation of this environment. It's an interdisciplinary effort, notes Rockwell. "The scope of the problem requires the integration of numerous areas of biological and physical sciences." The site is well illustrated and clearly written, offering birders a chance to look at and understand how ornithologists work.

http://research.amnh.org/~rfr/hbp/main.html

Snow Goose (Dover)

FEATHERED FACTS

Fortunate Flycatcher

Although many of our migratory birds are threatened by loss of forests in Central and South America, the Gray Flycatcher may be an exception. The reason is that it does not seem to require a habitat with commercially important timber and can live in semi-forested regions.

—adapted from John Sterling, Smithsonian Migratory Bird Center

http://web2.si.edu/smbc/bom/grfl.htm

Introduction to the Aves

"Although descended from the dinosaurs," Ben Waggoner notes on the Introduction to the Aves page, "birds have evolved remarkable specializations for flight: a unique 'one-way' breathing system, light yet strong hollow bones, a skeleton in which many bones are fused or lost, powerful flight muscles, and—most importantly—feathers." Waggoner, who teaches at the University of Central Arkansas, created these finely illustrated pages at the University of California at Berkeley to offer a scientific but understandable look at the creatures we call birds. Accompanied by pictures and links to explain concepts and terms, the site offers an excellent look at the fossil record of prehistoric birds, the life history and ecology of birds, their systematics (how they are classified), and their morphology (form and structure).

http://www.ucmp.berkeley.edu/diapsids/birds/birdintro.html

A B C D E F G H I J K L M N O P Q R S T U V W X Y Z

NET NOTES

Credit Carding on the Web

Many people remain afraid to buy a bird book or a new feeder on the World Wide Web because they fear hundreds of "hackers" will have access to their credit accounts if they use a credit card. Obviously, we should always be careful about using credit cards. Here are a few points to keep in mind.

- A reputable Web business will use a method of encryption—scrambling your card information—that only it can read when the information is sent over the Internet. Use only ordering pages or forms that say they have encryption or a "secure site." If your Web browser is so configured, it will even notify you if you are entering a secure site.

- Never send your credit card information in a standard e-mail message.

- Do business with outfits you trust. Many companies on the Web have been long established as conventional retailers. Others have become well established in e-commerce. If you've never heard of the company, and know of no one who has, don't use your credit card until you've done more investigating.

- Keep in mind that, riskwise, the Web is little different from most other situations in which you use a card. When you give your number over the phone to a mail order house, you are trusting that the unknown person at the other end won't make a copy for his own use. When you charge something at a store, that clerk you've never seen before has a copy of all your numbers. So do many other people who process your order or account.

Credit card companies and banks are developing new methods of further guaranteeing the safety of credit card information sent over the Internet. The Net is a vast new realm for retailing, and those involved in it want to make sure you are comfortable—and secure—using it.

Museum of Zoology

Ever wonder about the inner workings of a bird—such as the skeleton or how the feathers are constructed? Stop by the website of the Bird Division of the Museum of Zoology of the University of Michigan at Ann Arbor. Move down the home page menu to the section called Information on Bird Biology and check out the pages on Basic Anatomy & Topography. Here you'll find examples of different kinds of bird beaks and explanations of why each is shaped the way it is. The names of wing feathers, as well as the different parts of a feather, are illustrated on a nicely drawn picture. You can learn how wing feathers are attached to the skeleton. Other links on the site provide much more ornithological information. And if you like your data on paper, the site describes many of the bird-oriented publications of the museum, including a checklist of Michigan birds, and *The Birds of Michigan*, a 384-page book by a group of Michigan ornithologists and lavishly illustrated by people described as "five of Michigan's best-known wildlife artists."

http://www.ummz.lsa.umich.edu/birds/

Ornithological Web Library

The Ornithological Web Library—OWL for short—is Victor W. Fazio's massive collection of more than 1,100 websites that may be of interest to birders around the world. The library is arranged by 16 categories that include *general information hubs*, geographical birding in the United States, world birding, checklists, migration, research, sound and image collections, birding travel services, scientific sites, and more. Fazio lists how many sites can be found under each category.

http://aves.net/the-owl/

American Robin (Dover)

MEET THE MASTERS

Dead Wildlife

Steve Warmack has created a small website covering a surprisingly hard to find subject on the Web: extinct wildlife. The Typewritten Book of the Not-So-Grateful Dead <http://www.aristotle.net/~swarmack/deadbook.html> describes some of the better known species that have disappeared from the Earth, including several birds. "'Anything! You can find *anything* on the Web!' At least that's what everybody told me, and for the most part they were right," says Steve. But when he looked for information about extinct animals, he kept coming up empty-handed or with kid-created sites with essays like "The Passenger pigin; By Brandy, Age seven." So he set about researching the subject and ferreting out information which he is posting on his growing site. It's attracting more and more attention, and sure to be a source of information for students and birders who are interested in the history side of natural history.

Ornithological Jobs

If birds are more than a hobby for you, the Ornithological Societies of North America have an online listing of jobs open in the field of ornithology or related natural history fields. If nothing else, the ads make interesting reading, showing the kinds of work there is in the field—useful for anyone thinking to making a career in ornithology or field biology. A number of posts are temporary, and in the winter and spring, students may find many listings for summer jobs, such as field biologists. Some of the positions are volunteer, but at least all expenses are paid, plus the experience can be added to the student's job portfolio.

http://www.ornith.cornell.edu/OSNA/ornjobs.htm

Website Ornithology

The Ornithology Website is, according to its home page, "dedicated to the education of bird ecology and conservation. Our intent is to have the best library of information and best line of supportive products available." The site has feature articles about such subjects as attracting hummingbirds, building and cleaning birdhouses, feeding birds, hawk watches, creating backyard habitats, and employment and volunteer opportunities in the field of ornithology. A section is set aside on the site where avian researchers describe their projects; when we stopped by studies included Neotropical bird use of an urban riparian area and a couple of raptor research efforts. The site also has dozens of photographs taken by natural history photographers from around North America. Also available are a chat room, pen pals, conservation alerts, an events calendar, and links.

http://birdwebsite.com

Sightings at the Feeder

Project FeederWatch, the Cornell Laboratory of Ornithology–based effort to get backyard birdfeeding fans to tell what they see at their feeders, has maps that show the top 100 species sighted by participants and in what densities. These maps are great for telling you if you might see a given species in your area and they may just encourage you to join Project Feeder-Watch and report your own sightings. *(See also Events.)*

http://birdsource.cornell.edu/pfw/

Recent Ornithological Literature

The Recent Ornithological Literature page, sponsored by BirdNet and the Ornithological Council, is a compilation of citations and abstracts from worldwide scientific literature that pertain to birds and the science of ornithology. These huge documents are easy to search for a keyword (type CONTROL F or use APPLE F on your browser) and are valuable for anyone seriously researching a species or an ornithological topic.

http://www.nmnh.si.edu/BIRDNET/ROL/

A
B
C
D
E
F
G
H
I
J
K
L
M
N
O
P
Q
R
S
T
U
V
W
X
Y
Z

FEATHERED FACTS

Music Box Bird

Ravens are mimics. Besides their natural calls, they can also imitate other birds, the sound of falling water, and even the melody from a music box or the tinkling of an ice cream truck.

—adapted from Yelth, The Raven

http://www.terminal.cz/raven/

Wilson Ornithological Society

The Wilson Ornithological Society is an association of scientists and serious amateurs that calls itself "a world-wide organization of nearly 2,500 people who share a curiosity about birds." Founded in 1888, the society is one of the world's oldest organizations for the scientific study of birds. Its members, though not all ornithologists, tend to be professionals; as the site notes, "perhaps more than any other biological science, ornithology has been advanced by the contributions of persons in other chosen professions. The Wilson Society recognizes the unique role of the serious amateur in ornithology." The society publishes the *Wilson Bulletin*, a quarterly with some 800 pages per issue written for both professional and amateur ornithologists, and with articles covering the study of living birds, their behavior, ecology, adaptive physiology, and conservation. Lists of articles from recent issues are online, but not the articles themselves.

http://www.ummz.lsa.umich.edu/birds/wos.html

PHOTOGRAPHY

The World Wide Web allows a wonderful opportunity for the sharing of images. Modern computer monitors and sophisticated software that transform a full-color picture into relatively compact files of digital information permit us to transfer crisp and beautiful pictures quickly to anywhere in the world. This is of tremendous help to birders who are looking for photos or drawings to show what a species looks like— often, to help confirm a sighting. Most of the sites discussed in the sections on North American Birds include photographs or other art that illustrates their descriptions. The difference between those sites and the sites listed here is that these are primarily image-oriented, libraries of photographs provided by educational institutions, government agencies, professional photographers, or just amateurs who are good at using a camera and want to share the fun. Remember, however, that most of these images are copyrighted— even those on some of the government sites; before you employ any for more than personal use, check with the source and get permission. This section also describes several sites where the budding bird photographer can get tips on techniques and equipment. *(See also Artful Birds.)*

Adventure Camera Sights & Sounds

The website of Adventure Camera, which sells cameras, optics, and Central American tours, also has a nice collection of photos by Kevin C. Loughlin of birds of North and Central America. Many are accompanied by sounds recorded by Marty Michener.

http://www.adventurecamera.com/birdpage/birds.htm

Art of Bird Photography

If you are interested in taking bird photos, Arthur Morris, a noted lecturer, photographer, and author, has written two books on how to photograph birds: the 160-page *The Art of Bird Photography: The Complete Guide to Professional Field Techniques* and the 64-page *Bird Photography Pure and Simple*. The site describes the books and how to order them.

http://www.birdsasart.com

Birds as Art

Arthur Morris of Deltona, Florida, is a bit of a Renaissance person when it comes to bird photography. He's a photographer whose work has illustrated books, as well as many articles for such magazines as *National Geographic*, *Birder's World*, and *Bird Watcher's Digest*. He's an author who has written two books on bird photography: *The Art of Bird Photography: The Complete Guide to Professional Field Techniques* and the smaller, more concise *Bird Photography Pure and Simple*. He's a teacher who gives seminars around the country on how to photograph birds "artistically." He's a guide who gives photo tours of great birding locations. And he's a photo-artist who has prints for sale. This site touches on his many talents and tells how you can learn from his experience (*first address*). A particularly useful feature is the site's frequently asked questions section (*second address*), covering such subjects as What is the best focal length for bird photographs? What film speed and type do professionals use? How should one pack gear for air travel? Morris also has a small catalog of specialized and hard-to-find accessories that bird photographers will appreciate. Check out his suggested links, too; most deal with wildlife photography or birding.

http://www.birdsasart.com
http://www.birdsasart.com/faq.html

FEATHERED FACTS

Up & Down Owls

In the summer, Spotted Owls live in the lower, shaded parts of the forest trees. In winter, they roost high in the trees, staying away from the cold of the ground and taking advantage of the sun's warming energy.

—adapted from World Wildlife Fund, Canada

—http://www.wwfcanada.org/facts/spotdowl.html

Birds in Books

Brian K. Wheeler, the artist for the *Peterson Field Guide to Hawks*, is the photographer for *A Photographic Guide to North American Raptors*. When we visited his site, he was at work on still more books. His books are described here—and you can order autographed copies of the books from the site.

http://www.virtualbirder.com/bkwheeler/index.html

Birds of Canada

The Canadian Wildlife Service's Quebec Division has a website full of high-resolution photos—and sometimes sounds—of common eastern Canada birds. As is the case with many Canadian websites, pages are available in both English and French.

http://www.qc.ec.gc.ca/faune/imagier/html/oiseaux.html

Birds of North Brevard

Bob Paty is an outdoor photographer who lives in north Brevard County, Florida. He is a regular contributor to *Florida Wildlife Magazine*, a publication of the Florida Game & Fresh Water Fish Commission, and does most of his picture-taking at the Merritt Island Wildlife Refuge and Canaveral National Seashore, both on the east coast of Florida between Jacksonville and Miami (*see Destinations*). The site also offers fine photos by Brad Martin, another Brevard County wildlife photographer. These pages offer dozens of extremely crisp close-up photos of Florida birds. Click on any picture to get a larger version. Each shot is accompanied by a bit of natural history about the species. The site includes a special section of photos of the Florida Scrub Jay, an endangered species still surviving fairly well at the Merritt Island Wildlife Refuge.

http://www.nbbd.com/fly/birds1/index.html

A B C D E F G H I J K L M N O P Q R S T U V W X Y Z

A
B
C
D
E
F
G
H
I
J
K
L
M
N
O
P
Q
R
S
T
U
V
W
X
Y
Z

Bald Eagle (Dover)

Birds of Prey in the West

Greg Gothard and Barbara Samuelson travel through the West, photographing wildlife. This site displays their specialty—birds of prey, be they hawks, owls, vultures, falcons, or other raptors. With each shot they include a bit of natural history.

http://www.buteo.com

Birds of Rocky Mountain National Park

Wildlife photographer Rich Stevens has excellent shots of some of the more interesting birds at Rocky Mountain National Park in Colorado. The pictures are on the site of the Colorado Birding Society.

http://home.att.net/borealowl/rmnpbirds.htm

Bluebird Photographs

Arlene Ripley has a wonderful set of photos of a clutch of bluebirds, which includes some excellent bluebird close-ups. One of the birds is an albino.

http://www.nestbox.com/photos.htm

Cornell Slide Collection

Cornell University's Laboratory of Ornithology is one of the top centers of bird studies in the United States—and probably the world. The lab has a huge collection of color slides that you can use for your own enjoyment or to fill gaps in birding slide shows. Also available are sets of slides, some of which come with written scripts or recorded narrations—including natural sounds. For instance, there's a 73-slide set called "Silent Hunters of the Night: The Owls of North America" that includes the photos, a cassette narration, a printed script, and an information pamphlet. Other sets cover such subjects as feeder birds, warblers, shorebirds, colorful birds, grassland and prairie birds, and much more. Some 1,400 individual slides of North American species are available, each slide costing about $3. All are listed in pages in ornithological order; a handful of sample images are shown, but this site does not give you previews of each image.

http://birds.cornell.edu/closlides/index.html

Don DesJardin's Birds

Don DesJardin, a wildlife photographer from Ventura, California, offers at this site a collection of striking photos of western birds categorized under Shorebirds, Marsh Birds, Waterfowl, Gulls & Terns, Perching Birds, and Miscellaneous. Be sure to click on the pictures on the main page in order to reach the larger selection of photos in each category. Brief notes sometimes accompany pictures.

http://www.camacdonald.com/birding/DesJardin/ index.htm

Ducks & Geese

Rarebird.com is a small site that has one of the best collections of wildfowl photos we've run across. These images include many ducks, geese, and swans. Although no text accompanies them, the pictures alone are worth the visit. Most are little short of spectacular—close up, crisp, and excellent for helping confirm identifications.

http://www.rarebird.com/image.htm

Eagle Photographs

The place to see bald eagles in great numbers is during the salmon run in Alaska's Chilkat River outside the town of Haines, Alaska. Photographers Barbara Samuelson and Greg Gothard, who are major eagle enthusiasts, have numerous eagle portraits from the Haines area on display at this site.

http://www.wco.com/~bds/alaska.htm

Florida Birds

The Florida Museum of Natural History—referred to on its site as FLMNH—has a magnificent online collection of photographs of birds of the southeastern United States. Most of these species can be seen far beyond the Southeast, so don't let the site's geographical label put you off if you are from elsewhere east of the Rockies. I live in Connecticut, and most birds that I looked for were listed here (so were flamingos, not too common in New England!). For many species, more than one photograph is provided, which is helpful if you are trying to distinguish between two similar species (such as the House Finch and Purple Finch). These are crisp close-up shots, not junk scanned from some old guidebook. If you have a color printer, you can produce some great shots for school reports—or for hanging on the wall.

http://www.flmnh.ufl.edu/natsci/ornithology/
   sephotos/birdinde.htm

Harold Wilion's Photography Page

Harold Wilion, a photographer from eastern Massachusetts, has an attractive, online gallery of bird photos—many of them fine action shots. He also has useful information about his camera equipment, in case you'd like to try to take some high-powered nature photography. The site also carries photos of insects, animals, and landscapes, and offers links to sites of photographers specializing in nature shots.

http://home.earthlink.net/~h111/

NET NOTES

Quicktime

Some of the more advanced birding websites may use a program called Quicktime to show movies or panoramic views that you can manipulate. If you don't have Quicktime installed with your browser, you can download a copy of Quicktime Player for free.

http://www.quicktime.com

Live Pictures

The DebZone in Florida provides live webcam pictures of birds and an archive of past pictures, candid shots of various species at feeders—including escaped cage birds! If you use Windows Internet Explorer, you must click on a special link to get a home page with webcam software that works with your browser.

http://host.fptoday.com/debzone/

Michael's Photo Gallery

Not everyone has a 4,000-mm telephoto lens. Michael Myers enjoys his, and among the subjects he likes to shoot are birds. The Michael's Photo Gallery site offers close-up views of cardinals, Blue Jays, robins, eagles, hawks, gulls, egrets, herons, woodpeckers, and sundry backyard birds.

http://www.netaxs.com/~mhmyers/image.html

Blue Jay (Dover)

A
B
C
D
E
F
G
H
I
J
K
L
M
N
O
P
Q
R
S
T
U
V
W
X
Y
Z

A
B
C
D
E
F
G
H
I
J
K
L
M
N
O
P
Q
R
S
T
U
V
W
X
Y
Z

National Museum of Natural History

Just how good are the bird experts at taking photos of birds? Here's a photo collection of a few dozen species from around the world, shot by the staff of the Division of Birds of the National Museum of Natural History at the Smithsonian Institution. There are some neat pictures here but be prepared to see many birds you've never heard of. Click on the thumbnail images to see larger-size versions.

http://www.nmnh.si.edu/vert/birds/brdphoto.html

North American Nature Photography Association

The North American Nature Photography Association is the only organization created for the express purpose of helping nature photographers with information, support, and education. The website describes the organization and what it offers members, and has an excellent, well-written online guide, Information Resources for Nature Photography, that lists, describes, and evaluates the usefulness of various websites that might be valuable for background information concerning all aspects of natural history. These resources are broken down under the headings of general directories; nature subject guides; environmental organizations; government agencies; and parks, refuges, and preserves. The site also has a large catalog of books for photographers, news and alerts, and classified ads. This is all information that should be of interest to birders, naturalists, environmentalists, eco-travelers, or just about anyone interested in nature.

http://www.nanpa.org
http://www.nanpa.org/nature/

On Silent Wings

Many birders keep life lists, lists of species they've spotted over the years. Peter S. Weber is a bit different. His life list is not only online but also includes—where possible—a photograph that he has taken. A wildlife photographer specializing in birds, Weber has fine pictures of more than 100 species online (click on the thumbnail image to see a larger version). Any photo is available for purchase. This attractive site includes birding links and a photo quiz about birds.

http://www2.famvid.com/wings/

Ornithology WebSite Gallery

The Ornithology WebSite has a gallery of bird photos by many wildlife photographers, including Jan A. Allinder, Paul Bartholomew, Terry Ann Braaten, Christian Chaisson, Don Costanza, Terry Danks, Bernie Delgado, Don DesJardin, Toby Flathers, Kristen Garcia, Anthony Grady, Mark and Andrea Kaufman, Jack E. Monsuwe, Bill Morgenstern, Michael Myers, Gregg M. Pasterick, Narve Henry Pederson, Glenda Poulter, Jamie Ruggles, Pieter Slim, Bryan Stevens, Tamara Treine, and Gareth Watkins. Among them, they cover more than 100 species of birds.

http://mgfx.com/bird/gallery/index.htm

FEATHERED FACTS

The Beat Goes On

How fast a bird beats its wings varies greatly with the size of the bird and how big the wings are in relation to the body. The White Pelican, which is a big bird with huge wings, often glides and flaps its wings only 1.3 times per second, on average. The Ruby-throated Hummingbird, on the other hand, beats its wings 50 to 70 times a second.

—adapted from Canadian Museum of Nature

http://www.nature.ca/notebooks/english/wpelican.htm

Patuxent Wildlife Research Center

The Patuxent Wildlife Research Center in Laurel, Maryland, operated by the U.S. Geological Survey, has a large collection of photos of North American birds, arranged by families, genera, and species (*first address*). Not all are the sharpest of pictures, but all are close up and useful for helping to identify what you saw. You can also find more information about each bird, along with the picture (*second address*).

http://www.mbr.nbs.gov/id/pictlist.html
http://www.mbr.nbs.gov/id/framlst/framlst.html

Photography Blinds

Serious outdoor photographers often use blinds to hide themselves as they attempt to shoot birds and other wildlife. The Northern Prairie Wildlife Research Center has plans for duplicating two types of blinds: the low-profile A-frame blind and the modified portable fishhouse-type blind.

http://www.npwrc.usgs.gov/resource/tools/ndblinds/ndblinds.htm

Portraits of Birds

M. C. and Amanda Morgan have been photographing birds in the St. Augustine, Florida, area ever since they retired. "Their bird photos have been pleasing their friends and neighbors, and the members of St. Johns Audubon, for several years now," reports the Audubon chapter's website, which displays a gallery of Morgan photos. "This sampling of their Portraits of Birds will give you an idea of the patience and skill of these wonderful artists." Some of the photos are large-size graphics, so downloading all the images may take a couple minutes.

http://members.aol.com/SJAudubon/gallery.html

AVIAN ADVICE

Banded Birds

If you should find a wild bird wearing a band or a tag, the place to call is the Bird Banding Laboratory at Patuxent Wildlife Center in Maryland (800-327-BAND/800-327-2269). Patuxent will notify the bander, and eventually you'll receive mail that tells you when and where the bird you found was banded.

—adapted from *Bird Watcher's Digest*

http://www.birdwatchersdigest.com/faq/faq.html

Refuge Photography

Jim Clark of Virginia publishes the *Refuge Reporter*, a quarterly magazine about the National Wildlife Refuge system. In researching articles, he visited scores of refuges around the country and photographed the wildlife in them. Most of their work is bird related, and two dozen samples of their work—mostly wetland species—appear on this site.

http://www.gorp.com/refrep/photogal/photogal.htm

Southeastern Birds

The Museum of Natural History at the University of Georgia has a large collection of photographs of birds of the Southeast (which, of course, are also often birds of the East, the Northeast, the Great Plains, and other regions). You can look for species by image or, if you know the name, a keyword search. And you can even take a quiz to see how good you are at identifying birds of the Southeast. The site notes that the copyrighted pictures are for your personal use only.

http://museum.nhm.uga.edu/birdphotos/

A B C D E F G H I J K L M N O P Q R S T U V W X Y Z

A B C D E F G H I J K L M N O P Q R S T U V W X Y Z

Waterfowl Photos

The Waterfowl Resource, a site written for hunters, contains some of the most spectacular pictures of ducks, geese, mergansers, redheads, pintails, wigeons, and shovelers we've seen on the Web. Many different views of each species are in the collection, including close-ups, take-offs, and in-flight shots.

http://www.wildfowl.net/pictures.html

Wildlife Research Photography

Moose Peterson's Wildlife Research Photography website has been called the best place on the Web to find information about photographing wildlife. The site's more than 300 pages include Photo How-Tos that cover such subjects as exposure and using TTL flash systems. There are answers to reader questions, the Moose's Camera Bag that tells what Peterson himself uses, equipment reviews, and a large section about the Nikon F5. A large library of feature articles is offered about photography that Peterson has written for major magazines—ese are in Adobe Portable Document Format (*PDF*) files that can include pictures (*see page 237*). And, of course, the site has plenty of fine photos, including shots that appear in the *BT Journal*, "the biological and technical journal for wildlife photographers," written quarterly by Peterson. Many features from the journal are available online. The site also describes photo safaris and seminars offered by Peterson.

http://www.moose395.net

King Rail (*Rallus elegans*) (JJA)

Wisconsin Breeding Bird Atlas

The Wisconsin Breeding Bird Atlas, maintained by the University of Wisconsin at Green Bay, has pictures of more than 100 species of birds found in the central United States and southern Canada (and usually beyond). This picture encyclopedia is much better than many because it offers a variety of different kinds of photos (not all available for all species), including: adult, adult on nest, adult at nest with young, adult with young, immature, nest, nest with eggs, nest with young, and young.

http://wso.uwgb.edu/images.htm

MEET THE MASTERS

Living with the Dead

"I have always been interested in extinct animals—and surviving ones too, for that matter," says Steve Warmack, Webmaster of the Typewritten Book of the Not-So-Grateful Dead <http://www.aristotle.net/~swarmack/deadbook.html>. "When I first got on the Internet a few years ago, I immediately began looking for information or pictures of extinct animals, but was soon frustrated by the lack of pages dealing with whatever extinct animal I was looking for." So he took it upon himself to create a site that provides details about extinct species in an informal, often entertaining way that doesn't lecture (much), but still succeeds in letting us know how we failed these creatures. "I'm no scientist, and not much of a writer, but I try to check my info out, as well as I can for a guy sitting in his apartment," he says. Steve Warmack may not be a scientist or a writer, but his profession fits in well with his website. "I am, by trade, a forensic photographer at the State Crime Laboratory here," he reports. "I do take pictures of dead people for a living, but that is merely a coincidence. . . . I think—I mean—I hope." It's a line of work in which you need a sense of humor.

PREHISTORIC BIRDS

Especially in view of all the scary dinosaur movies and the textbook pictures of gigantic creatures that once roamed the earth, it's hard to think of our birds today as being the direct descendants of giant reptiles. But that's what scientists believe. Of the Web's many sites where you can explore the world of dinosaurs, we've included some sites that specialize in prehistoric birds, from the Archaeopteryx that everyone nowadays seems to know, to the Holy Confucius Bird that some scientists believe is closer to the true ancestor of the birds. You can even learn how birds may have figured into the demise of the dinosaurs from which they sprang. Many of these sites will interest both youngsters and adults.

Web Window Woes

Web surfers often run into a bit of confusion when more than one copy of their browser appears on their desktop.

What usually happens is that you'll visit a links page, click on a link to a new website, and view the resulting page. When you go to click the Back button to return to the original links collection page, the button is grayed out and doesn't work. Why is that? Because the webpage with the links sent instructions to your browser to open a new browser window to hold the new page. The original page is sitting underneath the new page on your computer screen. To get back to the original page, just close the new window. Websites, mostly commercial ones, do this to keep you "on" their site while allowing you to visit others. This can be not only confusing but also annoying as numerous windows open up on your desktop. It can also be useful if, in fact, you want to keep that original page handy. If it bothers you, try a software add-on that controls such problems. The *New York Times* suggests a free program called Pop Off, available on various freeware and shareware sites (*see page 40*).

Archaeopteryx, Ancient Birds, & Dinosaur-Bird Relationships

Jeff Poling's excellent Dinosauria, a huge site devoted to those ancient critters, has a couple dozen articles and other items about ancient birds, and the links between dinosaurs and birds. You will find essays with such titles as Earliest Beaked Bird Discovered, Feathers, Scutes and the Origin of Birds, and How *Archaeopteryx* May Have Used Its Wings. Some of the latest findings in the study of ancient birds are posted here, and often you will find sources for more information.

http://www.dinosauria.com/jdp/jdp.htm#archie

Archaeopteryx: Is This Bird a Fraud?

In 1985, in the *British Journal of Photography*, a noted English scientist and his associates published an article in which they maintained that Archaeopteryx, the famed prototype dinosaur-bird discovered a century earlier, was a fraud and a forgery. "From examining the specimen in the British Museum and from photographs which they took of it, they argue that the impressions of feathers in the stone were faked," writes Christopher Majka in an article originally published in the *New Brunswick Naturalist* in 1992. In this well-written and lively piece, Majka looks at the history of Archaeopteryx and the reactions to the 1985 article of the scientific community. It makes for a fascinating *paleobiological* mystery.

http://www.chebucto.ns.ca/Environment/NHR/archaeopteryx.html

Avialae

Avialae includes birds both ancient and modern, plus their very close relatives, and this easy-to-negotiate database describes various ancient avialans. The database tells where specimens were found, when, and what the remains were like, and then gives notes regarding each species or genus. The text is hyperlinked to definitions of terms—and these paleontologists have plenty of tongue-twisting terms that need defining.

http://dinosaur.umbc.edu/taxa/avialae.htm

A B C D E F G H I J K L M N O P Q R S T U V W X Y Z

A B C D E F G H I J K L M N O P Q R S T U V W X Y Z

Bird Fossils & Evolution

EnchantedLearning.com, a site written for youngsters, has an interesting, informative section devoted to Bird Fossils and Evolution that could teach adults, as well as children about the basics of prehistoric birds. The site shows examples of bird fossils, describes many prehistoric species, especially Archaeopteryx, tells us about Thomas Henry Huxley who argued that birds and reptiles descended from common ancestors, and explains why, though they have survived far longer than the dinosaurs, birds as a group are declining in numbers from a peak seen more than a quarter million years ago.

http://www.enchantedlearning.com/subjects/birds/
Birdfossils.html

Diatryma, Bird of Terror

Here is a bird among birds: Diatryma, a seven-foot-tall, parrot-beaked, flightless wonder of a carnivore. For a rendition of what it might have looked like (it lived during the Eocene period), visit the first address. For more illustrations of this huge bird, see the second address, part of the site for Prehistoric Lives interactive touring holographic exhibition.

http://library.advanced.org/20886/diatryma.html

http://www.mcm.com.au/p.lives/P.Lives.Scenes/Scene24
.html

Dino Express: The Word from China

The Dino Express site reports that a Chinese researcher has found what he believes is a much more credible ancestor of modern birds. Lianhai Hou and his team from the Institute of Vertebrate Paleontology and *Paleoanthropology* in Beijing believe Archaeopteryx was an evolutionary dead end, whereas the Holy Confucious Bird, *Confuciusornis sanctis*, had developed more closely in the direction of today's avian population. The fossil is dated as late Jurassic; all examples were found in the province of Liaoning, China. Hou suggests that early birds may have appeared as much as 60 million years before Archaeopteryx. There are great sound effects on this site, and for youngsters enamored of dinosaurs, many pages to explore. For a further

report of the discussion of this bird ancestor, see the second address.

http://www.dkonline.com/dino2/private/express/
issue02/ world.html

http://www.eurekalert.org/E-lert/current/
public_releases/deposit/ fossilbirds.html

Hesperornis: It Had Teeth & Swam

Evidence that the Hesperornis was a swimmer is found in the fossils of late Cretaceous seas. An illustration of its skeleton can be found at the first address; it's an adaptation of plates from the University Survey of Kansas, volume 4, Paleontology, part 1, Upper Cretaceous. About the size of a loon, Hesperornis appears to have been totally devoted to swimming, since its small wing bones couldn't have lifted it off the ground. Its contemporary, Icthyornis, also had teeth, but was smaller, gull-sized, and built for flight (*second address*). The fossil records of both birds are found in an inland sea from the age of the dinosaurs where the present-day state of Kansas is now.

http://www.oceansofkansas.com/hesper.html

http://www.keystonegallery.com/fossils.html#Hesp

FEATHERED FACTS

Fragile Fossils

There aren't a lot of prehistoric records of birds because most of their light, hollow bones did not survive long enough to become fossils. Nonetheless, scientists have been uncovering a growing number of well-preserved fossil birds, which are contributing a great deal to our understanding of bird evolution.

—adapted from Ben Waggoner, Introduction to Aves

http://www.ucmp.berkeley.edu/diapsids/birds/
birdfr.html

Hooper Virtual Natural History Museum

Not all museum websites are put together by professional Web designers and scholars. Sometimes students do the work and do it really well. The Hooper Virtual Natural History Museum, run by Carleton University and the University of Ottawa, has an excellent visual explanation of how flight evolved in birds (on the main page, select Flight). Using either still pictures or animations, depending on your connection speed, the museum describes the "flying dragons"— pterosaurs. As a nice touch, the site has a pronunciation guide that downloads a human voice telling you how to say *Anurognathus*, *Dsungaripterus*, *pterodactyloid*, or other tongue twisters. Here, among many other things, you'll learn how birds may have figured in the demise of the giant flying reptiles. The Evolution of Birds is covered in an effective set of pages that use fine illustrations to explain just what a bird is, modern bird anatomy, the basics of flight, and the latest theories about the origins of birds. Another section on flight delves into Archaeopteryx, the famous "first bird" of some theories. Since much of the site was prepared by undergraduate students of evolutionary paleoecology, you may notice a few typos or spelling mistakes—don't let them bother you. The award-winning site is supervised by paleontology professionals and is rich with useful scientific information clearly and graphically presented for the general public.

http://www.wf.carleton.ca/Museum/lobby.html

Museum of Paleontology, University of California

The Museum of Paleontology at the University of California at Berkeley was one of the earliest sites on the World Wide Web. Since 1993, the museum has been dispensing information about ancient life. The neat thing about the site is that it avoids the kinds of electronic "frills" that can make downloading pages a slow process. Only useful graphics are provided here. To learn about ancient birds, click the home page option under Online Exhibits for Animals and Plants, then pick Archosauria, the classification that includes dinosaurs, crocodiles, and birds. Then under Aves, you can learn about such ancient creatures as *Archaeopteryx lithographica*, and the *Neognathae*, which includes the vast majority of living birds. Or you might want to check out *Palaeognathae*, a group that includes the flightless birds. Other portions of the site provide information about fossils, natural history, books, online journals, and much more.

http://www.ucmp.berkeley.edu

FEATHERED FACTS

The Importance of Feathers

Feathers, believed to be really modified scales evolved from dinosaur ancestors, help birds in several ways. Soft down feathers insulate a bird by trapping air close to the skin (which is why we humans like down jackets and comforters). In flight, contour feathers streamline the body, reducing the friction between bird and air. Flight feathers create the aerodynamic surfaces of the wings and tail. Flycatchers and some other species have yet another kind of feather: they are like bristles located around the mouth to help trap insects in flight.

—adapted from Ben Waggoner, University of California Museum of Paleontology

http://www.ucmp.berkeley.edu/diapsids/birds/birdmm.html

Passenger Pigeon (*Ectopistes migratorius*) (JJA)

A B C D E F G H I J K L M N O P Q R S T U V W X Y Z

A B C D E F G H I J K L M N O P Q R S T U V W X Y Z

FEATHERED FACTS

Cocklebur Consumer

Few people have use for the cocklebur, a spiny wildflower of southern fields. But for the Carolina Parakeet, a species once widespread in the eastern United States but extinct since the 1910s, it was like filet mignon. At dinner time, huge flocks of these colorful birds would head for the nearest patches of cockleburs and eat their seeds.

http://www4.ncsu.edu/eos/users/b/brabec/WWW/CP-story.html

QUANDARIES

Birds can present quandaries, and they can find themselves in quandaries (sort of). Whatever the problem, the World Wide Web is a good place to find answers. One of the most common dilemmas bird watchers or their neighbors run across is injured or baby birds found in the yard. What do you do? Where can you go for help? Fortunately, the Web has plenty of sources of expert information about dealing with orphaned or injured birds, and on rehabilitators, the people who can help in many cases. Other sites will describe how to cope with pest birds—pigeons and starlings, for example. Quite a few will offer tips for dealing with the archenemy of anyone with a backyard feeder—the squirrel. But there are other problems: Cats kill untold millions of birds each year. So do the windows of skyscrapers and of ordinary houses. Woodpeckers will attack clapboards on houses. Cowbirds may parasitize nests of rare species. Diseases can fell feeder birds, such as House Finches. Each of these problematic areas is covered in this section. *(See also Feeding & Watering and North American Birds, Raptors.)*

PESKY BIRDS

Advice on Problem Birds

If woodpeckers are drilling holes in your clapboards, if sparrows are nesting in your air conditioner, or if a bird manages to get trapped inside your house, there's a place to turn for help. This page offers advice from a wildlife rehabilitator about these and other fairly typical bird-related problems.

http://www.applink.net/cpollard/problemsbirds.htm

Backyard Bird Problems

Have birds been hitting your picture windows? Are hawks eating your chickadees? Did the wrong kind of bird set up house in the box you put out? These are just a few of the many Backyard Bird Problems that are addressed in this excellent page put together by Terry Ross of the Baltimore Bird Club and based on a U.S. Fish & Wildlife Service pamphlet, *Homes for Birds*.

http://www.bcpl.lib.md.us/~tross/by/byprob.html

Bird-X

"Who's smarter—you or the birds?" asks Bird-X, a company that calls itself the "bird control x-perts" and that suggests you can be the smarter. Bird-X, based in Chicago, Illinois, offers a line of products designed to humanely keep away pigeons, gulls, geese, and other "pest" birds, and it's interesting to look at the gadgets and how they work. A number of products use ultrasonic technology, which the company calls "harsh, but harmless UHF waves" that are used to repel birds. The company also has Terror-Eyes, an inflatable scare device; BirdProof, a sticky liquid or gel that discourages birds from roosting; BirdNet, plastic netting to seal openings; and Irri-Tape, "holographic diffraction foil" that creates a "discomfort zone" to keep birds away.

http://www.bird-x.com

Cowbird Parasitism

Cowbirds have become a problem in some parts of North America, but that wasn't always the case. The Brown-headed Cowbird (*Molothrus ater*) was a species of the plains, following the herds of bison and feeding on the many insects they stirred up. Because they were always moving with the bison, they didn't have time to settle down and nest, and instead stuck their eggs in the nests of probably a relatively small number of other species. But as the buffalo were killed off and the plains became developed, the cowbird adapted and spread across the continent. It still likes open spaces, and suburbia provides enough of that. And it still lays its eggs in the nests of at least 220 other species. Although some of these species will toss the foreign eggs, as many as 150 other species may raise them, often at the expense of their own chicks. However, new research indicates that the population of cowbirds, though more widespread now than long ago, is again declining. What's more, the latest studies indicate that, with a few exceptions of rare, localized species, declines in songbird populations in North America are not affected by cowbird parasitism. To learn more about the cowbird and the latest research on the species, and on the value of trying to control it, visit this National Audubon Society page.

http://www.audubon.org/bird/research/

Cowbird (*Molothrus ater*) [Brown-headed Cowbird] (JJA)

PREDATORS & OTHER DANGERS

Bald Birds

One of the more alarming sights for a fan of backyard bird feeding is the appearance of a bald-headed bird—usually a cardinal. Looking like some spooky, ghostly creature, the bird seems otherwise all right, eating away at the sunflower seeds you've put out. But isn't he or she diseased? Yes, maybe, and no. It could be all of those. Gerry Rising, a columnist for the *Buffalo (New York) News*, explored reports of bald-headed cardinals (which are about as ugly-looking as a wild bird can get) and came up with an answer. But not everyone agrees it's the right answer in all cases. To learn about the mystery of bald-headed birds, read Professor Rising's column—and all the notes that follow it.

http://www.acsu.buffalo.edu/~insrisg/nature/nw98/baldbirds.html

Bang, Bonk, What Was That?

"Birds cannot perceive the glass as a barrier," notes Judi Manning in this article about the Owashtanong Islands Audubon Society website in Michigan. "It is most dangerous when the birds can see through a house from front to back—it looks like a passageway to them." She offers eight suggestions for helping to prevent such often-deadly crashes.

http://www.macatawa.org/~oias/bang.html

Cat Bib

An Oregon company has invented a device that it says can stop your pet from killing birds. "The CatStop has proven to be a reliable method of preventing domestic cats from catching and killing wild birds," the site says. "Yet, while wearing the CatStop, your cat will be able to run, jump, climb trees, and even catch mice!" The CatStop is a patented, biblike device that Cat Goods Inc. maintains is comfortable for the cat. The site has compete details on the product, as well as much information on the problem of cats killing birds.

http://www.catgoods.com

A B C D E F G H I J K L M N O P Q R S T U V W X Y Z

Cats & Wildlife

Few people can imagine the effect that outdoor cats—be they pet or feral—have on the bird population in North America. Some estimates say more than a billion birds are killed each year by cats. Another says *three million a day* die in the claws of cats. "The effect of out-of-doors cats on the natural world is disastrous," writes Gerry Rising in a column that appeared in the *Buffalo* (New York) *News* (*first address*). Professor Rising discusses the problem and strongly advises cat owners to keep their animals indoors. Bells and declawing do little good, he observes. The Golden Gate Audubon Society (*second address*) in California describes some of the programs for dealing with feral cats and explains its opposition to the increasingly popular TTVAR effort (Trap, Test, Vaccinate, Alter, Release) that is supposed to be reducing the wild cat population. According to this Audubon group, there's no data to support that claim, and meanwhile, the released cats continue to kill huge numbers of birds.

http://www.acsu.buffalo.edu/~insrisg/nature/nw98/cats.html

http://www.audubon.org/chapter/ca/goldengate/ggasferalcats.htm

Cats Indoors!

Are you tired of your neighbor's cats killing birds and other wildlife on your property? Are you concerned about the health and well-being of your outdoor cat? If you are interested in these topics or in turning your outdoor cat into a "contented indoor pet," check out the Cats Indoors! project of the American Bird Conservancy. "Cats Indoors! encourages cat owners to keep their cats indoors and advocates laws, regulations, and policies to protect cats and birds, including the humane removal of free-roaming cats from areas important to wildlife," the conservancy says. "The campaign promotes grassroots efforts to address the issue at state and local levels." The site has a large library of information about the subject of cats and nature. Among the topics covered in the download-able reports are What You Can Do about Your Neighbor's Cats in Your Yard, Cat Predation on Birds and Other Wildlife: Recent Studies, Why Allowing Cats Outdoors Is Hazardous to Cats, Wildlife and Humans, Cat Licensing, and How to Make Your Outdoor Cat a

AVIAN ADVICE

Harass Those Cats

One way to discourage neighborhood cats from attacking and killing your birds is to harass them "without mercy" until they're trained to understand that they are *Cattus non gratis* in your yard.

—adapted from *Bird Watcher's Digest*

http://www.birdwatchersdigest.com/faq/faq.html

Happy Indoor Cat. There's even a downloadable poster or newspaper advertisement that can be used to promote the cause. And there are also public service announcements you can pass on to local media outlets. The downloadable files are in WordPerfect format; however, most recent versions of Microsoft Word recognize the format and can open the files.

http://www.abcbirds.org/catindoo.htm

Climate Changes & Birds

The United Nations Intergovernmental Panel on Climate Change projects that there will be an increase in global mean temperature of between 1° and 3.5°C (2 to 6° F) by the year 2100. "How will these changes impact North American birds?" asks the American Bird Conservancy. Under a grant from the Environmental Protection Agency, the ABC, the University of Michigan, Goddard Institute for Space Studies, Boston University, and Stratus Consulting are studying this question. "ABC's role in this study will be to develop models examining how the summer distributions of North American birds might change under various climate change scenarios." This page outlines the studies and provides a link to more information about global warming.

http://www.abcbirds.org/climchg.htm

Conjunctivitis

In the early 1990s, many birders on the East Coast began to notice that House Finches and Purple Finches visiting their feeders had strange-looking eyes. One or both might be closed or almost closed; crusty looking material surrounded the eye opening; the bird was reluctant to move off the feeder or a branch. The cause was conjunctivitis (*Mycoplasma gallisepticum*), a disease that jumped from poultry to certain finch species and began to spread rapidly. The ailment can nearly blind a bird in one or both eyes, making it difficult or impossible for them to find food or avoid predators. Birds in more than 35 states have been found to have the disease. Its spread was helped by the fact that the disease is transmitted by close contact—just what happens at bird feeders. To explain this life-threatening disease that affects the eyes of House Finches and some related species in eastern North America, Jim Cook has created a comprehensive, well-illustrated site devoted solely to House Finch Conjunctivitis. Most important, he tells you how to prevent the spread of the disease. Go to the bottom of the home page and click the arrow to see the full index of site features.

http://members.aol.com/FinchMG/Home.htm

AVIAN ADVICE

Suet Thieves

Squirrels are mostly vegetarians but will sometimes go after suet, especially if the suet is a mixture that includes seeds or peanut butter. If your mixed suet is under attack from squirrels, try switching to the pure suet product.

—adapted from Connecticut Audubon Society

http://www.ctaudubon.org/q&a.htm

Dealing with Squirrels

A couple of useful ideas for discouraging squirrels are offered on this page from the extension service at the University of Nebraska. The designs are both illustrated. The page also describes how to keep "less desirable" birds such as starlings, pigeons, and grackles off your feeders; one technique is the Magic Halo, invented by the university. The page also describes how to deal with "nuisance wildlife," such as snakes.

http://www.ianr.unl.edu/pubs/wildlife/g1332.htm#bfs

Guide to Assisting Wildlife Babies

One of the hazards that bird parents face each spring is falling babies. The nest may be getting crowded, or the chick may be getting rambunctious—whatever the cause, a baby bird is found on the ground. What do you do? "In most cases," says Ronda DeVold, a licensed wildlife rehabilitator in North Dakota, "wild animal babies should be left alone." Her website offers suggestions on what to do if you find fledgling or nesting birds—including babies being threatened by cats or dogs. (*See also Wildlife Rehabilitation Information Directory later in this section.*)

http://wildliferehab.virtualave.net/guideto.htm

How to Locate a Wildlife Rehabilitator

Where can you get help when you come across an injured bird? The Web. Here's an extensive list of rehabilitators, especially in the United States, but also in Canada and other nations around the world. For each there's a phone number plus, when available, an e-mail address.

http://wildliferehab.virtualave.net/contact.htm

Injured Birds of Prey

What should you do if you find an injured hawk, owl, or other bird of prey? The Raptor Center at the University of Minnesota has a special site that offers tips for handling injured raptors. In fact, the center can often arrange free transportation via major airlines for injured birds. The details are here.

http://www.raptor.cvm.umn.edu/newwebdev/raptor/injured.html

Killer Buildings

Crashing into tall buildings and other lofty, human-made objects is one of the hazards faced by birds that migrate at night. One estimate puts the death rate at some 80 million birds a year in North America. "Over 150 species have met this fate," says columnist Gerry Rising, who describes the problem. Professor Rising has some suggestions about what persons living in or working in high-rises can do to help curb the number of bird deaths from buildings.

http://www.acsu.buffalo.edu/~insrisg/nature/nw93/birdsvbuild

WEB WORDS

Fighter Planes

"Cooper's Hawks, which prefer to eat quail-size birds, are patient observers of their territory, and will sometimes sit above a cowering quail in the brush until the prey just can't stand it any longer and bolts—so much for that quail! This powerful hawk's short wings are built for rapid acceleration and optimum maneuverability in tight quarters—they'll often follow prey in hot pursuit right into the thick brush. He's the fighter plane of the bird world!"

—Doug Von Gausig

http://Naturesongs.com

FEATHERED FACTS

Century of Counting

Hunting inspired the original Audubon Christmas Bird Count. Frank Chapman, an official of the then-fledgling National Audubon Society, was upset at the annual Christmas Day tradition of the "Side Hunt," in which hunters tried to shoot as many birds as possible in one outing. He suggested counting birds instead, and on December 25, 1900, the first Christmas Bird Count took place among 27 people who saw 18,500 birds and 90 species. A century later, nearly 50,000 people count more than 600 species and literally millions of birds each Christmas season.

http://birdsource.cornell.edu/cbc/

Killer Towers

Radio and television antenna towers, some of which are more than 1,000 feet tall and stand atop hills equally as high, can be unexpected hazards for birds migrating at night. Countless thousands are killed in crashes with towers each year. Professor Gerry Rising goes on a trip with Arthur Clark, curator of vertebrate zoology for the Buffalo Museum of Science, who has kept track of the number of birds killed by antennas near Buffalo, New York, for 30 years. At one site, "we found about 50 more birds at the three towers, including many other warblers and vireos, a few thrushes and sparrows, and a catbird," he notes. "Almost all of the bodies had been ravaged by local Horned Owls, for whom these fields serve as autumnal smorgasbords." The killing is unfortunate and not fully understood. However, in this case, it's not wasted death. The records Clark keeps of what he's found over the years are useful in learning about nighttime migration patterns.

http://www.acsu.buffalo.edu/~insrisg/nature/nw96/tower_kills.html

Killer Windows

Houses are using more and more glass to let in the sunlight. But, under the wrong conditions, glass becomes a mirror to a bird, and countless songbirds and wildfowl are killed each year in collisions with windows. "Small, quick, ground birds (mainly songbirds and thrushes) are the most susceptible to our windows," says Kevin Slagboom (*first address*). "Lighter birds have a better chance of bouncing off the glass and surviving the impact but larger birds like the robin are more likely to incur severe injury." Slagboom is owner of the Birding in British Columbia website and author of an essay called "Song Birds and Killer Windows." In it, he not only recommends a solution but also gives you the device to do it with. Birds are afraid of merlins, a hawklike predator. Slagboom provides a printable silhouette of a merlin, with instructions for taping it on your problem windows to keep crashers away. The National Audubon Society offers a page full of tips and techniques for decreasing the reflectivity of windows, creating barriers, and other ideas (*second address*). The U.S. Fish & Wildlife Service reports that, according to one professor's estimate, between 100 and 900 million migrating birds are killed each year in collisions with windows. The wide gap in the estimate shows that no one is certain how many die, but it's a lot. Although most migrators run into large office buildings, many hit windows in houses. The Fish & Wildlife Service offers its own suggestions to prevent fatal collisions between birds and your windows (*third address*).

http://birding.bc.ca/articles/birds-windows.htm

http://www.audubon.org/educate/expert/window.html

http://www.fws.gov/r9mbmo/pamphlet/songbrd.
  html#Collision

FOR THE BIRDS

New Websites

If we discover new websites of value to birders, we'll post them on our *Internet Guide to Birds and Birding* updates page, <http://www.acorn-online.com/hedge/ birdup.htm>. We welcome your discoveries, too.

National Wildlife Rehabilitators Association

Rehabilitators are the people who nurse injured creatures back to life. It takes a special skill, as well as a special license. Many of those who are rehabilitators belong to the National Wildlife Rehabilitators Association, a "nonprofit, international membership organization committed to promoting and improving the integrity and professionalism of wildlife rehabilitation and contributing to the preservation of natural ecosystems." The site describes what the association does and has a good collection of links to other wildlife websites.

http://www.nwrawildlife.org/default.asp

Squirrel War Room

"Squirrels," says Jeff Crooke. "You either hate them, or you . . . well, you tolerate them. If you feed birds, it had better be the latter, however, for you will be seeing quite a bit of them. Squirrels in mid-air, squirrels running, upside down squirrels." Crooke, the lively, entertaining Webmaster and an editor of *Winging It*, has put together the Squirrel War Room to provide advice and links to those who would rather fight than give in to these "tree rats." The site provides links with sources of advice—or just commiseration.

http://rtonline1.roanoke.com/wingingit/squirrels.html

What to Do When You Find a Baby Bird

Peggi Rodgers, a licensed wildlife rehabilitator in Oregon, tells what to do if you find a baby bird. Along the way she dispels some of the myths about bird babies—such as the parents' rejecting babies that have been touched by people because they smell of humans (most birds can't smell). The page also has tips for safely capturing a wild critter that needs to be transported to a rehabilitator.

http://wildliferehab.virtualave.net/advice4.htm

FEATHERED FACTS

Babes in the Water

It doesn't take long for baby Canvasback Ducks to learn how to swim. Only a few hours after they hatch, their mother leads them to water, and off they go. And mom doesn't have to worry about food. The newborn ducklings know how to feed themselves already.

—adapted from Peterson Online

http://www.petersononline.com/birds/month/canv/index.html

Wildlife Rehabilitation Information Directory

Ronda DeVold is a licensed wildlife rehabilitator, and her site at the University of North Dakota is like an information-central on the Web for wildlife rehabilitation (*first address*). You'll not only find out what to do if you discover a baby or injured bird but also learn about the career of a wildlife rehabilitator, how to find one in your neighborhood, the websites of wildlife agencies in many states, information about nuisance wildlife, professional organizations, statistics, and even poems and humor related to the field. A large collection of links to online rehabilitation centers around the world is provided by the site's Wildlife Rehabilitation Center Home Pages directory (*second address*), which includes listings for each state and for Canada.

http://wildliferehab.virtualave.net/
http://wildliferehab.virtualave.net/contact.htm

RETAILERS

One has only to read about the incredible growth of Internet stocks to realize that the World Wide Web is big business. There's virtually nothing today you can't buy "virtually." And that includes scores of items related to birds, be it binoculars, feeders, houses, seeds, or field guides. There are chains of franchised bird stores and there are local, independent stores. There are outlets specializing in feeders and outlets specializing in optics. There are even restaurants that cater to birders. The benefit of all this online merchandising is that the birder can check out a wide variety of products without having to drive around to a half dozen stores—if those stores even exist in the neighborhood. And even if stores do exist, you can comparison shop. You are able to see the many kinds of equipment and devices available before you make a buying choice—whether that purchase is on the Web or at a neighborhood shop. What's more, almost all the retailing sites have consumer information or birding information to help you make decisions, as well as enjoy the hobby. (*See also Gear, Feeding & Watering, and Software.*)

Backyard Bird Feeder

The Backyard Bird Feeder is a birders' supply store in Los Gatos, California, with a sizable inventory of products, such as feeders, houses, and books—many of which are described online. The site also offers some basic bird feeding tips and notes regarding bird walks that have taken place in the Los Gatos area.

http://www.backyardbirdfeeder.com

Bird Central

Based in Scotts Valley, California, Bird Central.com is an online store selling feeders, houses, and accessories for birds, bats, and butterflies. Products are well-illustrated and described. The site also offers birding tips, a picture gallery to which you can contribute, and a collection of bird, bat, butterfly, nature, and gardening website links.

http://www.birdcentral.com

A B C D E F G H I J K L M N O P Q R S T U V W X Y Z

Birdwatch America

Birdwatch America is a twin site of sorts—part is about the hobby of birding and part is about the business of birding. The recreational birding side of the site has news, features, and tips, whereas the trade side is, the site says, "America's most complete source of information about products and services for retailers in the wild birdfeeding and birdwatching industry." There, when you request and receive a free password, you'll find a "virtual trade show" of product and company information.

http://birdwatchamerica.com

BirdWatchers.com

BirdWatchers.com, located in Michigan, does a mail-order business in all sorts of bird-watching supplies, and can have some great sales (we saw $1,500 Bausch & Lomb binoculars clearance-priced at half price). The online store carries feeders, houses, birdbaths, binoculars, scopes, books, videos, and other supplies and equipment. The site also has tips for attracting birds.

http://www.birdwatchers.com

Campmor

Campmor, one of the nation's leading mail-order camping supply houses, offers a good collection of links to outdoors websites including parks and recreation sites, outdoor magazines on the Internet, outdoors organizations, and guides and instructions. Its online catalog carries clothing, footwear, packs, binoculars, and compasses that are useful for the hiking birder. The illustrated online catalog contains many items, but the famous newsprint paper catalog—which Campmor will send you if you fill out an online form—has more items.

http://www.campmor.com

Ecomall

The Ecomall is an online gathering of businesses that sell environmentally friendly products. The mall includes a section for birding businesses, in which a half dozen or more retailers are listed, with links to their websites. However, you can also find nearly 60 other categories of "eco-friendly" businesses. The website also offers "Green Shopping Magazine," which tells how to buy environmentally friendly products, offers news and views about such subjects as global warming, rain forests, and air pollution, and provides many links to resources. Scroll down the home page for tips on saving energy, Shopping with Consciousness, ten reasons to Go Organic, and more.

http://www.ecomall.com

Nature Store

The Nature Store, based in Doylestown, Pennsylvania, sells "products related to butterflies, birds, bats, insects, and the rest of our natural world." The site has many books, videos, educational materials, kits, supplies, and more. Its bird book collection seems particularly strong on hummingbirds and gardening for birds.

http://thenaturestore.com

P'lovers

P'lovers, an environmentally friendly store in Halifax, Nova Scotia, says it believes that "by modifying our lifestyles, using our purchasing power to reflect our values, and supporting activities which respect and protect the diversity of life, we can make a difference." Although the website carries many and varied products, if you go to Catalogue, and then For the Outdoors, you will find a number of bird-related products, including feeders, seeds, and calls.

http://www.novasight.com/plovers/

A
B
C
D
E
F
G
H
I
J
K
L
M
N
O
P
Q
R
S
T
U
V
W
X
Y
Z

Restaurants for Birders

Yes, you read the headline correctly. The American Birding Association with the help of participants of BirdChat e-mailing list has put together a guide to restaurants that cater to birders. Why? One of the ABA's missions is promoting the economic importance of birders to local communities. "We aim to encourage local birding groups to gather the necessary information that will convince business people and politicians of the economic value of their local wildlife habitats. Traveling birders can have an economic impact in small communities by spending money on local services including restaurants." The website provides tips for dining and restaurant finding and has a guide to Great Restaurants near America's Birding Hotspots from Maine to California. Each restaurant is described by a BirdChat or ABA member who has recommended it.

http://americanbirding.org/conseconeat.htm

Upstart Crow

Upstart Crow in Evanston, Illinois, operates a store for birders, carrying not only optics but also equipment cases and bags, map cases, portable chairs, and specialty outdoors clothing, including shirts, pants, and guide vests. The store also sells outdoor footwear. A special section is devoted to tips about buying such equipment as binoculars. If you live near Evanston, you might be interested in the site's Virtual Tour of the store to get an idea of what Upstart Crow carries in off-line products.

http://www.upstart-crow.com

Wild Bird Centers

Wild Bird Centers of America began in 1985 as a single store in Cabin John, Maryland, which, its website is proud to note, is "not far from a cottage once occupied by Roger Tory Peterson." Today, the company has grown to more than 100 franchised Wild Bird Center and Wild Bird Crossing stores in the United States and Canada. This site will fill you in on the products these stores sell, but you can't order online. Instead, check the online store directory for an outlet near you. Some have websites of their own or at least e-mail addresses. The site has information about—but not articles from—*Wild Bird News*, WBCA's feature-filled newsletter about birding that can be picked up at stores or mailed to you; there's an online form for receiving a sample copy. You can also learn the basics about starting your own Wild Bird Center franchise.

http://www.wildbirdcenter.com

Wild Bird Emporium

The Wild Bird Emporium in Auburn, New Hampshire, sells a wide array of birding supplies online, including bird feeders, houses, CD ROMs, software, and birding gifts. One of the interesting services the Emporium offers is bird seed subscriptions. You can order three-, six-, or twelve-month subscriptions to wild bird feed mix, niger, wild finch mix, gourmet mix, safflower seed, oil sunflower seed, or striped sunflower seed. The parcels are delivered monthly in the quantity you specify, or you can have them sent in any interval you find convenient. To learn about the subscription program, click Bird Seed on the main home page menu. The site offers a good selection of books, including a special section on children's books. You can find an unusual section of "do it yourself products" that includes birdhouses, pine cone feeder kits, and jewelry. The site also offers free coloring pages (*see also Children*), feeding tips, and even sample birdsongs online.

http:// www.wbird.com

Wild Bird House

The Wild Bird House in Rainbow City, Alabama, sells houses for birds (plus housing for butterflies, bats, bees, and ladybugs), as well as bird feeders. Besides standard-brand feeders, Wild Bird House carries unusual Woodlink Coppertop feeders, made of cedar, copper, and other long-lasting materials. There's also a Coppertop bluebird house. The store also sells Schrodt Designs etched or painted hummingbird feeders.

http://www.wildbirdhouse.com/products.htm

Find a Great Site We Don't List?

If you discover a new birding website or an old one that we overlooked, please pass on the address. E-mail us at *jacksanders@ridgefield-ct.com* or visit our updates page, <http://www.acorn-online.com/hedge/birdup.htm>.

Wild Bird Marketplace

Wild Bird Marketplace has stores in more than a dozen states in the eastern and central United States, and the website provides a store index. There's also information on backyard birding—mostly articles from *Around the Birdfeeder*, the newsletter of Wild Bird Marketplace. If you're interested in the business, the site also has information on franchising.

http://www.wbm-bird.com/menu.htm

True Grit

Providing some grit, such as sand or fine poultry or canary grit, can help wild birds who use it in the gizzard to help grind seeds. When snow covers the ground, birds may consume grit from old roofing shingles, which may be bad for their health. Ground up eggshells can serve as grit and may also provide needed calcium during the egg-laying season. Mix grit with seeds or place it in a tray or on the ground.

—adapted from Ron J. Johnson, University of Nebraska Cooperative Extension Service

http://www.ianr.unl.edu/pubs/Wildlife/g669.htm#gri

Wild Birds Unlimited

Wild Birds Unlimited, which has more than 250 franchised birding stores around North America, provides a lot of useful information for the birder at its headquarters website (*first address*). The site carries many bird-oriented essays, including a bird-watching series by noted naturalists Don and Lillian Stokes. The Educational Resources section consists of tips and techniques on topics including bluebirds, feeders, fruit-eating birds, using mealworms as food, dealing with squirrels, window strikes, and nesting birds. However, if you can't find an answer to a question, the site offers an Ask the Expert service (*second address*). Wild Birds Unlimited has a bird feeder webcam set up in Indianapolis, Indiana. The camera has captured some unusual sights and offers a library of shots of some of the best visitors (including Pileated Woodpeckers!) and even a webcam life list. Any of the photos can be downloaded and used as wallpaper on your computer. The site provides an online catalog of bird feeders, birdhouses, birdbaths, books, and other accessories, and a directory of Wild Birds Unlimited stores. A form is provided that you can fill out to receive a free, 20-page birding guide by snailmail. And if you are interested in setting up a Wild Birds Unlimited franchisee, there's information about starting your own store.

http://www.wbu.com
http://www.wbu.com/edu/askexpert1.htm

Wildlife Habitat

The Wildlife Habitat, established in 1977 in Cedar Rapids, Iowa, is a feeders and accessories retailer that stocks more than 750 bird feeding products from 46 manufacturers, "giving you one of the widest selections you'll find." The site also carries an excellent newsletter, *Backyard Bird News*, written by Weir Nelson and featuring profiles of interesting species.

http://www.wildlifehabitat.com

A B C D E F G H I J K L M N O P Q R S T U V W X Y Z

SOFTWARE

For decades publishers have produced field guides, handy-sized books that allow birdwatchers to identify on the spot what they are seeing. In the years since Roger Tory Peterson's landmark guide came out in the 1930s, publishers and authors have refined field guides to make them as useful as possible. Nonetheless, nearly a dozen electronic guides have appeared in the past decade. Few of us are able to lug a computer into the field, so why are these software programs proliferating? Because they can do at least one thing print guides can't: tell you exactly what a bird's song or call sounds like. Some programs provide more text, more pictures, even video clips. And most have interactive systems to help you identify the bird you've seen. Other software found on the Web includes birding databases, customizable systems that allow you to keep track of what you've seen. If you get the least bit serious about birding, you'll want to keep track of your sightings—which birders call "life lists." There are many ways to arrange your sightings—by location, species, or season, for instance. There are plenty of formats to produce them in, from lists to maps, and many kinds of information you may want to record—the date, place, environment, weather conditions, notes, and more. A few programs are free. Some can be downloaded online and used almost immediately. Others require you to order the software—some programs are so big they need a CD. Often, you'll be able to see on the website a sample of what the software looks like. *(See page 40 to learn about shareware programs that may be downloaded on the Web, and then used or tried out for free.)*

Audubon's World Screensaver

If the avian artwork of John J. Audubon enchants you, Cinegram Media can help enliven your computer desktop with the Audubon's World Screensaver. This program, which works on both PCs and Macs, randomly displays up to 30 different images from Audubon's Birds of America collection. The program, endorsed by the National Audubon Society, also has printable information about Audubon and the society named for him. The software has plenty of set-up bells and whistles, all detailed on this page.

http://www.cinegram.com/gift_shop/audubon.asp

Avian Notebook

Avian Notebook is a record-keeping program for Windows-based computers that is intended to be easy to use. For example, it includes a list of more than 900 known species in North America and enables you to drag-and-drop them into your personal database as you spot them. What's more, the software permits any number of people on your computer to keep separate life lists of their sightings—which the authors say will help get the family more involved in birding. Although designed to be simple, fun, and easy to use, the program has many sophisticated features and can keep track of all sorts of information, including location, begin and end times, temperatures, ground cover conditions, precipitation types and amounts, and notes. The creators, Chaos Management, also maintain the program is a lot less expensive than others with similar features.

http://www.chaosman.com/aviannotebook/

FEATHERED FACTS

Monks & Their Monasteries

The Monk Parakeet, an Argentine species that has escaped and set up colonies in various parts of the United States, builds huge nests of sticks. The nests are full of chambers—averaging fewer than 20 and as many as 200. The heat generated and retained by having a large number of birds together inside a nest allows this parakeet to survive in colder areas—such as southern New England—than it would find in its native Argentina.

—adapted from Birds of North America

http://www.birdsofna.org/excerpts/monk.html

AviSys

AviSys is a Windows birding database that calls itself "superior birding software: Fast as a falcon, powerful as an eagle, friendly as a chickadee." The program enables you to keep detailed track of your bird sightings and to produce sophisticated reports. "You enter sightings and run reports with just a few straightforward mouse clicks," the site says. "Fundamentally, AviSys works just like you think it should. And remember our philosophy: 'Software is a tool—it shouldn't be as difficult as your VCR.'" Reports include birds seen and birds not seen; checklists of state, national, and world birds; various bird censuses; and several summaries. All are customizable. Many examples of what the program looks like and does are online. The software comes with prepared lists of birds for North America and the world, including Clement's Birds of the World, the American Birding Association Checklist of the Birds of North America, United States checklists (50 states, 49 continental states, lower 48 states), a Canada checklist, all 50 state checklists, and all Canadian Province checklists. If you are a world-traveling birder, you can add on the optional Shawneen Finnegan World Wide Nation Checklist containing 254 checklists of the nations of the world. What's more, you can also get data sets for butterflies, dragonflies, snakes, frogs, and even skinks. AviSys also sells AviSys Song, a program that enables you to more easily listen to and manipulate several different commercially available CDs of birdsongs (such as Peterson's and National Geographic's).

http://www.avisys.net

Better Bird-Watching CD-ROMs

Better Birdwatching sells a set of CD-ROMs covering birds and bird-watching in Colorado. Needless to say, the contents could be valuable to birders in nearby states, as well as birders who visit Colorado. The set covers 275 species, includes nearly 1,000 photos, plus video clips, sounds, and range maps. There are also interactive quizzes. The website offers a sampling of the contents. Versions for both Windows and Macintosh computers are available.

http://members.aol.com/birdcdroms/

Bird Brain

Macintosh users sometimes get an inferiority complex when they see all the software that's available for Windows computers. When it comes to birding, however, there's no need to feel left out. Bird Brain is a birding database that's designed for Mac users, allowing them to record all kinds of information about their sightings. The birder can maintain many different types of lists—backyard, state, life, and more. The easy-to-use program includes a built-in database of all North American bird species; all the birds in the world can be added for a small fee. A detailed description of the Mac-based program (it's not available for Windows), including sample screens, is available at Birdwatching.com.

http://www.birdwatching.com/software/birdbrain/birdbrain.html

Bird Watcher

"If you love birds and bird watching, this is the birding experience for you!" says WizardWorks, the company that produces Bird Watcher, a simulation game for birders. These are the same folks who make the top-selling game, Deer Hunter, but in this case, you aim your binoculars, not a rifle. The game, designed to test your bird identification skills, simulates birding in the wild. More than 140 species of North American birds are apt to show up in the environments you can visit. Along the way, the online birding guide can offer you tips on becoming a "better birder." And in an unusual feature, Bird Watcher lets you turn into a raptor and go hunting like a bird of prey. The Windows-based game includes an introduction by noted naturalist Peter Dunne of the New Jersey Audubon Society. And it's one of the more modestly priced interactive games around, costing about $20 retail.

http://outdoors.wizworks.com/bird_watcher/birdw.htm

Wood Thrush (*Hylocichla mustelina*) (JJA)

White Vancouver Robins

Some areas of the continent seem more likely to have albino specimens of birds than others. For example, the area around Vancouver, British Columbia, is said to have a higher percentage of American Robins that are albino than other parts of North America. No one knows why.

—adapted from *A Bird's Eye View*, American Birding Association

http://www.americanbirding.org/bevfea.htm

BirdBase

Santa Barbara Software makes BirdBase, a Windows-based birding database, about which the company claims: "nearly all birders who declare life lists over 6,000 in the latest American Birding Association List Report, and who use computers, use this software. It is the birding software most widely used by all those over the 1,400 species reporting threshold." You can see a demonstration of BirdBase, as well as BirdArea, a sophisticated program for telling what birds can be found in which region. The website also has a users bulletin board with the latest tips and information about the software.

http://members.aol.com/sbsp/

Birding CD-ROM Reviews

The arrival of the home computer has brought with it a wide selection of CD-ROMs that are, in effect, electronic books. But unlike paper books, CDs can provide multimedia, that is, sound and motion pictures along with the words and stills. However, notes the Cape May Bird Observatory of New Jersey Audubon, "these vary greatly in quality, and are often more expensive than books. Some are worth the extra cost, while oth-

ers are not; and unlike books, you usually cannot preview them before you buy." To help you, this Audubon group provides reviews and ratings—the ratings range from a high of 8 to a low of ½. For each package, New Jersey Audubon also provides a recommendation: strongly recommended, generally recommended, limited recommendation, or not recommended. Detailed reviews of each CD are offered; however, some reviews seem to be old, so there may well be newer versions of the software packages available.

http://www.nj.com/audubon/genlmenu/cdrom.html

Birds of Europe

Springer, the huge German publishing house, has produced an interactive CD-ROM called *Birds of Europe* that contains information about 447 species, with photos, drawings, songs, distribution maps, video clips, and much more. The site, entirely in English, includes samples from the CD. This program works on Windows or Mac computers.

http://www.springer.de/newmedia/lifesci/eti/boe/birds.htm

Long Haul

The Northern Wheatear has one of the more unusual migrations of any bird that summers in North America. Populations of wheatears that nest in the Arctic regions of northeastern Canada winter in Africa. They travel to Canada via Greenland and Europe. Wheatears that nest in Alaska and northwestern Canada migrate across the Bering Strait through Siberia, China, and eastern Asia to reach Africa.

—adapted from Peterson Online

http://www.petersononline.com/birds/month/nowh/index.html

Birdstar

Birdstar is another great example of taking the abilities of the computer and compact disks, and turning them into effective and entertaining learning tools. *Birdstar*, produced by Larry James Bond of Ontario, Canada, is essentially a field guide to North American birds. However, instead of just presenting a lot of pictures for you to look through in your quest for a bird's identification, *Birdstar* is interactive and actually interviews you about what you saw. It asks when and where you saw the bird, and questions you about the shape, size, field marks, and behavior, and then, filtering more than 900 species in North America, the program suggests the likely species that you saw. Along with each picture, you can also play the song or call of the bird (the recordings are unusually crisp and clear from the demos we heard on the website). Birders can hone their listening or observing skills by using quizzes and games that are part of the CD-ROM. "Birdstar will assist beginners in learning how to make accurate identifications," said the jacket. "Experienced birders can test and sharpen their skills by identifying birds from memory." You can, of course, also locate birds the old-fashioned way— by name or pictures. The CD has distribution and abundance maps for each species. The website offers many demonstrations and descriptions of the different abilities of Birdstar, with many sample photos and sounds, and reviews by people who've tried the program. Birdstar also comes with a listing program to keep track of what birds you've sighted. *Birdstar* is available only for Windows 95/98 or NT computers.

http://www.birdstar.com

Lanius Software

Lanius Software produces a series of "professional-quality" Windows databases for a variety of birding or ornithological uses, according to its website. Excalibur, a database for keeping sophisticated track of your sightings, contains lists of birds of North America and other parts of the world, and can be customized in many ways to handle your record-keeping. Inflight is a CD-ROM-based reference of neotropical birds, a compilation of 129 species accounts from the U.S. Department of Agriculture. EZCBC is described as the "ultimate Christmas Bird Count database." These and other natural history database programs are described on Lanius's website.

http://www.glenalpine.com/lanius/

Map List by Flying Emu

If you like to travel and to go birding when you do, Map List by Flying Emu Software may be your program. Map List records sightings by using a point-and-click system on a zoomable map of the United States and Canada. Joel Herr, its creator, says this Windows-based program has an expandable taxonomic tree and a database of nearly 400 seasonal checklists, which are presented on the map with colored symbols to show abundance during each season. The software can easily generate a life list, state/province lists, county lists, year lists, state-in-year lists, and other lists from your sighting records. At this website you can download a demonstration version of the software that has all features except the ability to save sightings. You can also see a screen shot of what the program looks like.

http://www.flyingemu.com

AVIAN ADVICE

Don't Get Shot

If you're birding in the wild during hunting season, be extra careful. Don't make a point of hiding—you may be mistaken for a deer or some other critter. Wear brightly colored clothing. And if you hear or see hunters in the area, shout to them so they know you are about.

—adapted from Nutty Birdwatcher

http://nuthatch.birdnature.com/birdgear.html

A B C D E F G H I J K L M N O P Q R S T U V W X Y Z

A
B
C
D
E
F
G
H
I
J
K
L
M
N
O
P
Q
R
S
T
U
V
W
X
Y
Z

Merlin Species Watcher

Merlin Species Watcher is a multilanguage database for birders and other naturalists, written for Windows 3.x and 95, that enables you to record your birding observations "quickly, easily, and accurately." With this software you can view your records in different ways, and you can pop up your life list at any time. Free utilities available on the website allow you to convert your location data into maps, using various readily available mapping programs; sample maps are online. You can download a fully functional demonstration copy of the program on the site. The site also shows you some of the screens you'll see in Merlin, so you'll have a sense of what the program can do for your record-keeping.

http://www.hyperscribe.org/merlin/

NestBox for PCs

NestBox is a Windows-based program for those who maintain bluebird and other kinds of wild bird nest boxes, and want to keep track of how they are used by birds. NestBox "can be used to record bird nesting activities, as well as maintain lifelist(s)," author Jim Kunz tells us. "The program also supports multiple trails of nestboxes and can generate nesting summary reports. The nesting reports can be summarized by nestbox number, nestbox type, and/or trail. There is also fully integrated help available." You can download a free demo version of the software at the address that follows. If you want to buy it, the program costs about $20.

http://www.geocities.com/RainForest/2415/
senddemo.html

O'See

O'See is a Windows-based database that keeps track of your bird or any other kind of outdoor sightings. The program can maintain records for more than one observer and would be especially handy for recording family or group birding expeditions. The software keeps track of the species seen, weather, terrain, and names of observers, and includes unlimited space for field notes. You could use the flexible program not only for birds but also for butterflies, wildflowers, beetles, or just about anything else you find in nature (pre-compiled database lists of North American birds, world birds, and North American butterflies are currently available). The website shows snapshots of the different O'See screens and enables you to download an evaluation copy of the program, which is produced by Magnolia Software in Magnolia, Texas.

http://magnoliasoftware.com

Roger Peterson: Online

No one in the 20th century better epitomized birdwatching than Roger Tory Peterson, the artist who in 1934 created the first popular guide to birding, *A Field Guide to Birds*. Since then the book has gone through many editions, two dozen other Peterson field guides have been added to the series, and now guides are available on CD-ROM. Publisher Houghton Mifflin sponsors this website, about which as one reviewer quipped, "Warning! You could spend hours on this site." There are many features for the birding family, including bird identifications, a calendar of birding events around North America, and tips about bird identification. And, of course, you can learn about the Peterson Multimedia Guide: North American Birds. There are many samples of pages, plus reviews, descriptions of features, and more. You can order the guide online; oddly enough, the CD-ROM is less expensive than any print field guide to birds, including Peterson's. Only a Windows edition is available.

http://www.petersononline.com

Silhouette Spotter

If you own a Macintosh computer, Houghton Mifflin has a free program that lets you test and improve your ability to identify 24 species of shoreline birds by their silhouettes. Just download this file and follow the instructions. The site at one time had a Windows version of this program but did not when we last checked. However, one may eventually become available again.

http://www.petersononline.com/birds/skillbuilders/
index.html

WEB WORDS

Clever Crows

"If men had wings and bore black feathers, few of them would be clever enough to be crows."

—Henry Ward Beecher

http://www.corvus.org/quotes.phtml

Thayer Birding Software

Thayer Birding Software produces several popular programs for the birder. Its Birder's Diary is designed to provide easy point-and-click data entry. You can make your own checklists and even your own birding quizzes; the software comes with species lists for more than 225 countries. The program lets you generate many kinds of reports and life lists—such as by region or time of year. It comes with a free CD-ROM U.S. mapping program. Birds of North America is a multimedia field guide covering 925 species seen in the United States and Canada. There are more than 3,000 photos, 121 videos, 700 song recordings, hundreds of range maps, abundance maps, and identification tips. The program includes links to birding sites, quizzes, screen savers, and more. For Birder's Diary and Birds of North America, sample screens are provided online. Thayer also produces an electronic version of *Birds of the World* by Dr. Charles G. Sibley, an electronic database of more than 9,000 species (*see also Books*). Aside from describing its products, Thayer's lively website also has an online bookstore with more than 1,500 titles, plus birding checklists, information about the best places to go birding, bird jokes, links to other sites, and more.

http://www.birding.com

Windows Desktop Themes

Users of Windows software, either Windows 98, or Windows 95 with Plus! or a themes add-on, can set up desktop themes that include photos, sounds, and color schemes. John and Janet Slivoski's Backyard Birding website has several birding-oriented themes, including cardinals, birds in black, woodpeckers, Black-capped Chickadee, goldfinch, Mourning Dove, sparrows, House Finch, and Eastern Bluebird. And, most kind of the Slivoskis, all are free of charge.

http://slivoski.com/birding/themes/index.html

YardBirds

Some software field guides list all or most of the more than 900 species in North America. YardBirds doesn't come close to that, nor does it necessarily want to. This program is for the backyard birder, the person who wants to identify that bird at the feeder or in the bush. For the eastern United States, that means around 190 birds (though you can add more). The designers, Ramphastos LLC of Dover, New Hampshire, maintain that the program has "unique images, the clearest songs, a searchable birding journal, and detailed descriptions of each species. We spent five years developing our own search design so advanced that there is nothing like it in any other nature software. Every field mark in our database relates to every other in a way that lets YardBirds 'think' along with you." According to Kathy Varney, director of Ramphastos, Thomas Butler, the program's author, has been a birder for 50 years. "When I first met him, he wouldn't even touch a computer— now you can't keep him away from computers. He realized that we identify birds by mentally processing data that we have seen—red nape, white wingbars, in New Hampshire, in the summer. What better tool than a computer to help do this?" She adds that many of the songs in the program come from his recordings, as well as the Cornell Laboratory of Ornithology and the Borror Laboratory of Bioaoustics. The program includes excellent illustrations by Paul Bunning, sounds, range maps, natural history, spotting tips, habitats, and the ability to add your own notes about each species. Using screen shots, the website shows you the steps to follow to identify a bird by field marks and habits.

http://www.ramphastos.com

FEATHERED FACTS

Poor Singer

Though it can only croak, the Common Raven is considered North America's largest songbird—that is, member of the passerine family. Ravens can be up to 27 inches long.

—adapted from Peterson Online Fun Facts

http://www.petersononline.com

SONGS & SOUNDS

As far as birders are concerned, one of the most useful features of the World Wide Web is its ability to transfer sounds. Thus, a birder who wants to learn or confirm a bird song has only to sit down at the computer and listen in. A growing number of websites are supplying songs. Although some of the biggest collections are offered by government agencies, universities and even private citizens are putting collections online. Most are quite good, but keep in mind that many birds have more than one song or call. Some have so many, it would be almost impossible to have them all online. Most sites will have the most frequently heard songs, but they can still vary from site to site. For instance, the Veery song on Patuxent Wildlife Research Center's site is quite a bit different from that on Tony Phillips' New York Bird Songs site, but both are good examples for the species. Thus, if you are confirming an identification or just trying to learn a song, try to check out more than one site. We've provided quite a few good sources, and more are turning up all the time. Of course, the ability to hear sounds over the Web assumes you have speakers on your computer and that your software is set up properly. Sidebars in this book offer some tips on audio, but if you need basic help with your computer, try logging onto <http://www.microsoft.com> if you use Windows, and <http://www.apple.com> if you have a Macintosh. Some sites in this section also offer help.

Birding by Ear

Dick Walton is an expert at identifying birds by their songs and has joined Robert W. Lawson in creating a series of CDs and tapes, called *Birding by Ear*, produced by the Peterson Field Guides people. Using high-quality recordings, they provide birders with a "proven system to learn and recall birdsong as an aid to field identification," Walton says on his own website. Two different three-CD sets are available for eastern and central birds, and one set covers western birds. Walton's site also offers a good collection of nature links, including sources of information about digital video and video production.

http://www.concord.org/~dick/

Borror Laboratory of Bioacoustics

The Borror Laboratory of Bioacoustics at Ohio State University's Department of Zoology has one of the world's largest collections of recorded animal sounds, including nearly 20,000 recordings of almost 800 species of birds. The site has an extensive online catalog of the species whose recordings are available, but the sounds themselves are not online. Contact information about how to acquire recordings at the site.

http://iris.biosci.ohio-state.edu/borror/blbhome.html

Corvidae Calls

Crows, ravens, magpies, jays, and jackdaws make up most of the Corvid family of birds, and the Aviary has a fine collection of sounds of these birds, mostly North American species.

http://www.shades-of-night.com/aviary/sounds/sounds.html

Florida Bird Songs

Ever wonder what a Scrub Jay sounds like? Or maybe even the extinct Dusky Seaside Sparrow? You can find them here along with scores of others. Most Florida bird species are not limited to Florida, so it's a fine site for hearing bird calls in general. Most sound clips are offered in short and long versions—from a few seconds up to a minute or so long. Excellent photos or drawings accompany many of the species. What's more, there are visual representations of the sounds of most birds so that you can compare their "shapes." J. W. Hardy, curator emeritus in Ornithology and Bioacoustics at the Florida Museum of Natural History, made the recording and offers a brief recorded introduction to the site.

http://www.flmnh.ufl.edu/natsci/ornithology/ sounds.htm

Grace Bell Collection

Grace Bell (1900–1986), who lived in British Columbia, was a pioneer of bird song recording. She started out in 1952 when her brother-in-law returned from the Korean War and decided to correspond by tape instead of by letter. Grace could never warm up to taped correspondence, but she did use the recorder her brother-in-law sent to experiment with taping the birds in her yard. Then in her 50s, she began a project that would eventually lead her to sophisticated recording devices and the creation of a library of thousands of recordings of birds of British Columbia and the Pacific Northwest. The Royal British Columbia Museum has placed many of Grace Bell's recordings and notes online for all to enjoy.

http://rbcm1.rbcm.gov.bc.ca/nh_papers/gracebell/ english/index.html

Greg Kunkel's Bird Songs

Greg Kunkel's Bird Songs is a website "dedicated to the recording of bird vocalizations with simple, inexpensive equipment," says Kunkel, who provides a collection of bird songs he's recorded, as well as information about sonograms, the printed diagrams that show how the sound "looks" over a period of time—or, as Kunkel says, "It plots the sounds frequency against

time." There's quite a bit of information about sonograms and how to create and interpret them. You'll also learn how Kunkel inexpensively but effectively records his sounds and digitizes them so they can be saved on a computer or transmitted over the Web.

http://ourworld.compuserve.com/homepages/G_Kunkel/ homepage.htm

Guide to Animal Sounds on the Net

Although the page is called "animal sounds," by far the greatest number of sounds here is bird songs and calls. Herman Miller has put together a massive collection that's lots of fun to listen to. The collection includes general bird songs, accentors, albatrosses, ground antbirds, tropical antbirds, auks, boobies, buntings, bushtits, cardinals, chickadees, cormorants, cotingas, cranes and rails, creepers, crows and other corvids, cuckoos, currawongs and woodswallows, dippers, doves, drongos and monarches, ducks and geese, falcons, finches, flamingos, flycatchers, frigatebirds, gnatcatchers, grackles, grebes, grosbeaks, gulls, hawks and eagles, herons, honeyeaters, hummingbirds, jacanas, kingfishers and relatives, kinglets, kiwis, larks, loons, lyrebirds, mockingbirds, mudnesters, nightjars, nuthatches, orioles, ovenbirds, owls, parrots, penguins, pheasants and relatives, plovers, sandpipers, shrikes, sparrows, starlings, storks, swallows, swifts, tanagers, tapaculos, thrushes, tinamous, vireos, wagtails, Australian warblers and relatives, wattlebirds, waxbills, waxwings, whistlers, whiteeyes, woodpeckers, and wrens.

http://members.tripod.com/Thryomanes/ AnimalSounds.html

Lark in the Morning Bird Calls

Lark in the Morning is a Mendocino, California, musical instrument dealer, but in its huge collection of products are bird whistles. Among them are many Samba whistles for South American birds, Audubon bird calls, French bird calls, and others. A nice feature of the site is that you can listen to examples of many of the calls and whistles being used. From the home page, select Musical Instruments, and the list will include bird calls.

http://www.larkinam.com

A
B
C
D
E
F
G
H
I
J
K
L
M
N
O
P
Q
R
S
T
U
V
W
X
Y
Z

Library of Natural Sounds

The Library of Natural Sounds at Cornell University's Laboratory of Ornithology is the largest collection of its kind in the world. Housed within its walls are the calls and songs of, among other things, more than 6,000 of the world's 9,600 or so species of birds. Alas, these are not online (though there are many who would love to see them available on the Web). It explains how you can use the LNS collection, which is open to birders, as well as scientists and even commercial movie and TV producers who often use sounds for backgrounds. The LNS website is also useful to anyone interested in the art and science of recording and studying bird calls. If you want to try your hand at recording bird calls, the site provides one of the best guides on the Web, describing the different kinds of recorders, microphones, parabolic reflectors, shockmounts (to cut noise), playback speakers, and headphones. Often the library mentions specific brands and will tell you ranges of prices. There's a discussion of sound accuracy—aside from having a good microphone, the tape must be running at just the right speed, and a pitch pipe is used to confirm accuracy of recordings. The site lists suggested readings, where to find equipment, and information about the Cornell Lab's own workshops in sound recording. There's even an address by means of which you can e-mail the library with questions. The site is not totally without sound, either, and the home page features a Sound of the Week, plus an index of sounds from previous weeks.

http://www.ornith.cornell.edu/LNS/index.html

FEATHERED FACTS

Ancestral Duck

The Mallard is the ancestor of almost every breed of domestic duck.

—adapted from Texas Audubon Society

http://www.audubon.org/chapter/tx/tx/mallard.html

FEATHERED FACTS

Feeder Friend

The range of the Tufted Titmouse has been steadily extending northward and scientists suspect this may be because of the growing number of people who are feeding birds.

—adapted from BirdSource, Cornell University

http://birdsource2.ornith.cornell.edu/pfw/birdid/tuti/index.html

Nature Songs

Doug Von Gausig loves the sounds of nature and wants to share them. "I . . . want to promote nature recording and archiving, and I want to provide a library of sound that people can refer to when they hear an unidentified sound," says Von Gausig, whose Naturesongs.com is an excursion through the North American skies, woods, ponds, and shores. Literally hundreds of bird songs are online (including a collection from Central America), in clear, crisp recordings that Doug also makes available on CD. What's more, he *explains* the sound—for instance, what the bird was doing when the recording was made. He also tosses in some natural history and personal observations about the species. In addition, Von Gausig has a section of the site devoted to making your own recordings of bird and other nature sounds. He describes the equipment, offers tips about making the recordings, and then tells how to manipulate the digital recording files. The site also carries sounds of other animals, as well as insects, and has links to other sound sites.

http://www.naturesongs.com

FEATHERED FACTS

Risk of Being Albino

Albino birds—ones whose feathers are mostly or all white--occur occasionally in nature when the bird lacks the cells that produce melanin, the pigment that colors the feathers. Although these birds can be strikingly beautiful, many don't last long because they stand out to predators.

—adapted from *A Bird's Eye View*, American Birding Association

http://www.americanbirding.org/bevfea.htm

Nature Sound Studio

Lang Elliott, coauthor of *Common Birds and Their Songs*, is a professional at recording the sounds of birds and other wild creatures. His site offers many samples of his recordings—as well as his photos. Make sure you enjoy the six-minute "Sora Dawn" cut on the site's main page. Among Elliott's products are compact discs featuring excellent stereo recordings from habitats and regions across North America. "Each title presents a series of pristine field recordings, sequentially blended to tell a story with sound," he says, adding that no music or narration accompanies the sounds. Among the titles are Prairie Spring, Voices of the Swamp, Seabird Islands, and Wings over the Prairies. Coming titles include Forest Melodies, Frog Concertos, Northern Spring Everglades Soundscape, Mountain Thunderstorm, and Song of the North. A one-time photo specialist for the Cornell Laboratory of Ornithology, "I embarked on my own sound recording in 1987 and was doing it full-time by 1991," he told us. "I make my living recording wildlife and making products. My current focus is book design and production, still with emphasis on nature sounds (books with CDs). And I'm doing a lot of photography." Enjoy his many online samples.

http:// www.naturesound.com

New York Bird Songs

Don't let the name fool you. The New York Bird Songs collection of calls and songs works well across much of North America because most of the species are widespread. Often, more than one example of a call is given, and pictures accompany each. The calls and songs are arranged by major families of birds. The site's creator is mathematician Tony Phillips, who, after taking a course in website design in 1995, realized he could combine this skill with his interest in birds. Webmaster Phillips is featured in Meet the Masters sidebars.

http://math.math.sunysb.edu/~tony/birds/index.html

Panama Audubon Society

The jungles of Panama offer some of the world's most interesting birds, and the Panama Audubon Society is kind enough to let us all listen to them. Here you can hear the Slaty-backed Forest-Falcon, the Buff-throated Foliage-Gleaner, the Barred Antshrike, and many others. Be prepared for the site to take a few minutes to load—it offers you sounds automatically, and these can take a few moments to transfer.

http://www.pananet.com/audubon/sounds.htm

Patuxent Wildlife Research Center

The Patuxent Wildlife Research Center, operated by the U.S. Geological Survey, has a collection of songs of more than 175 species of North American birds. They are arranged in scientific order and are all .WAV sound files. The second address is also at Patuxent.

http://www.mbr.nbs.gov/id/songwav.html
http://www.mbr.nbs.gov/id/songlist.html

A B C D E F G H I J K L M N O P Q R S T U V W X Y Z

FEATHERED FACTS

Butter Birds

Bobolinks were often served as food in American restaurants early in the 20th century. They still are eaten in Jamaica where they are called Butter Birds, a name that reflects how fat they are as they stop by the island on their migrations between North and South America.

—adapted from Mary Deinlein, Smithsonian Migratory Bird Center

http://web2.si.edu/smbc/bom/bobo.htm

Song Post

The Song Post is a website "devoted to the academic study of bird song." Scott MacDougall-Shackleston offers concise answers to such questions as What is a bird song? What is a songbird? Why do birds sing? And, in the end, why study bird song? The site also has reviews of some books that might be read by those with a somewhat scholarly interest in bird songs and also offers links to websites with a focus on bird songs.

http://www.princeton.edu/~shackles/song.post.html

Upper Texas Coast Birds

Armed with a Sennheiser ME-80 shotgun microphone and a Marantz PMD-222 tape recorder, David Sarkozi has recorded some of the species found along the upper Texas Coast.

http://texasbirding.simplenet.com/sounds.htm

World's Best Singers

Tony Phillips of the Math Department of the State University of New York at Stony Brook has collected lots of bird songs (*see New York Bird Songs earlier in this section*). However, he has also put together a page of what he calls "Candidates for the World's Best Singers," including wrens from the Amazon and from Panama, and the good old Wood Thrush of North American forests—"arguably the best of the North American singers." My favorite is the Rufous-and-white Wren (*Thyrothorus rufalbus*) from Panama.

http://math.math.sunysb.edu/~tony/birds/
    best_singers.html

TIPS & TECHNIQUES

Anyone can be a bird-watcher. But to be a *good* bird-watcher, you should acquire some skills and use some techniques that can help you not only find birds but also identify them. This section offers some sites that can help you bone up on your birding skills and can teach you tips that may even bring the birds to you. You can find suggestions about where to go looking for birds and how to keep records about what you see, an activity that can be a lot more important than you think. (*See also Audubon Societies & Sanctuaries, Destinations, Gear, Optics, and Quandaries.*)

Alaskan Bird Quiz

The Alaska Bird Observatory offers an excellently executed Bird Quiz that questions you at three levels: Rookies, Intermediate, and Expert or "So you think you know *Empidonax*." There are pictures and sounds to go with each mystery bird, as well as clues to help you with the identifications. From the home page, select Bird Quiz.

http://www.alaskabird.org

Beginners Notebook

"So you're new to birding?" asks Ernest Stokely of the Birmingham (Alabama) Audubon Society. On this well-done page, Stokely provides advice for beginners about equipment, yard feeders (especially hummingbird feeders), learning about local birds, and tips for identifying new species.

http://bmewww.eng.uab.edu/BAS/beginner_birding.htm

Beginning Birding

One of the reasons the ranks of bird-watchers are swelling is that it's so easy to get started, says Milan Bull, director of the Connecticut Audubon Society's center at Fairfield. "Really, all you need is a relatively inexpensive (less than $100) pair of binoculars and a $17 field guide. . . . Immediately, an amazing new world begins to come into view." Bull, an expert birder, offers some simple but knowledgeable tips that you may not find elsewhere.

http://www.ctaudubon.org/Nature/Begin_Birding.htm

Birder's Gear Checklist

The Nutty Birdwatcher offers a list of items that could or should be taken on any serious birding expedition. The checklist is set up to be printed. Also available is advice about safety in the woods.

http://nuthatch.birdnature.com/birdgear.html

Birding Ethics

Yes, even in birding, there are right and wrong things to do. To help guide you down the proper path, the New Jersey Audubon Society offers a page on birding ethics, including notes on etiquette and the Ten Commandments of Birding.

http://www.nj.com/audubon/genlmenu/ethics.html

Bird-Watching Guide

Eagle Optics, a retailer of all sorts of binoculars and scopes, has a nice, concise Birdwatching Guide that is an excellent introduction to the basics of the pastime. "Besides offering relaxation and enjoyment, it is relatively inexpensive and an easy way to keep physically fit while gaining an understanding of our natural and wildlife resources," Eagle Optics says of bird-watching. "No matter what your age, anyone who picks up a pair of field glasses and a field guide can easily command the essential elements of the hobby." Though you might expect the website of a binoculars manufacturer to be heavy on binocular-use tips, this essay covers a much wider range of subjects, including when and where to go looking for birds and the effects of weather on bird-watching.

http://www.eagleoptics.com/eagle/birdwatching/birdwatching.html

Calling Birds

Here's a page for everyone who has ever wondered about those odd noises the expert birders make when they're out in the woods and fields. Pishing is the most popular, a sound that is supposed to draw curious birds to investigate the source. "The truth is, those silly noises do work, . . . most of the time," says Kevin Slagboom, Webmaster of Birding in British Columbia, who has put together this neat page on calling birds. He not only discusses the various sounds, how to make them, and why they may work, but also has online recordings of them that you can play (with Real Player). He even has a recording of the famous Audubon Bird Call in action. The site has tips for calling birds, such as "Stand in the bushes or under a low tree. Sometimes birds will come right up to you to investigate so provide them somewhere to land."

http://birding.bc.ca/articles/callingbirds.htm

FEATHERED FACTS

Seasonal Birding Malady

Searching for arriving warblers high in the trees is an annual spring treat for many birders. But sighting these quick, little birds in the treetops is a challenge that often results in a malady birders called *warbler neck*.

—adapted from Lisa Petit, Smithsonian Migratory Bird Center

http://web2.si.edu/smbc/bom/blwa.htm

A
B
C
D
E
F
G
H
I
J
K
L
M
N
O
P
Q
R
S
T
U
V
W
X
Y
Z

A
B
C
D
E
F
G
H
I
J
K
L
M
N
O
P
Q
R
S
T
U
V
W
X
Y
Z

Daily Tips

Daily Tips are tips about backyard birding, e-mailed to you each day. "Participate in the discussion, ask questions, or just sit back to read the tips and information," says the site, which also offers free subscriptions to daily tips on Amazing Animal Facts, Cats, Dogs, or Horses. The messages cover a wide variety of wildlife facts, tips, and discussions. Often, e-mail reaction to earlier tips is included with a dispatch.

http://www.dailytips.com

Finer Points of Identification

Ever wonder how you can tell a Fish Crow from the common American Crow? Or a Black-capped Chickadee from his southern cousin, the Carolina Chickadee? Don't feel alone—some birds are really tough to tell apart. Only small variations in color or markings, or in voice, may be the major distinguishing characteristics for the average observer. "The Finer Points of Identification" consists of nine articles by Dr. Paul McKenzie that have appeared in the *Bluebird*, the quarterly magazine of the Audubon Society of Missouri, whose site posts the series. In it, McKenzie tells about the differences among Semi-palmated, Snowy,

FEATHERED FACTS

Hungry Snowy Owls

Every four or five years, a shortage in the supply of lemmings, their favorite food, sends Snowy Owls southward from their Arctic habitats, and sightings of them in the northern United States become widely publicized.

—adapted from Canadian Museum of Nature

http://www.nature.ca/notebooks/english/snowyowl.
htm

and Piping Plovers, or the "Little vs. Bonaparte's vs. Common Black-headed Gull vs. Black-legged Kittiwake vs. Sabine's Gull." More than 100 commonly confused species are covered, and anyone who's stuck for an identification should check through these articles, which are well written and quite clear. Unfortunately, they are not indexed by species, but you could easily use the Find function (CONTROL F in Windows browsers) to search each of the nine pages for the species you're wondering about. The series concentrates on birds one could find in Missouri, but most of those species are wide-ranging, making the guide useful for birders in most of North America.

http://mobirds.mig.missouri.edu/audubon/asmhtmls/
mckenzie.html

Guide to Birding

The Unami Audubon Society in Pennsylvania has a clever Guide to Birding that tells you in seven steps how to get going with the hobby of bird-watching, starting with finding a good pair of binoculars and continuing through selecting a good field guide and places to go birding, and ending with general sources of more information about birds and birding.

http://www.audubon.org/chapter/pa/unami/
birding.html

Guide to Ultimate Wildlife Watching

Heading out into the woods or fields in search of birds would seem a simple thing. Grab your binoculars, field guide, and maybe a map and compass, and start trekking. Well, you can do it that way and scare half the birds into the next county, or you can be a subtle bird-watcher who blends in with the environment. A Guide to Ultimate Wildlife Watching, produced by the conservation-oriented National Watchable Wildlife Partners, is a concise set of tips for blending into the wild world around you. Suggestions include wearing natural colors, avoiding scented lotions, giving nests wide berth, and using your peripheral vision effectively. The page even includes tips for taking good pictures.

http://www.gorp.com/wwldlife/ultimate.htm

How to ID a Bird

Identifying a strange bird seems simple enough: You just look at the bird and then look at a book. Right? Well, it's often not that simple since many species look alike. This page, designed by a New York State school system, offers the basics on how to identify birds by noting their size, field marks, behavior, and song, and by knowing their habitat and range.

http://home.eznet.net/~arnesp/idbirds.html

How to Watch Birds

Two professors at Clark College in Washington offer a concise and very useful guide to watching birds. The page is part of a larger site devoted to their Field Studies in Biology program. Also, check out their bird species chart and bird lists found at the bottom of the page.

http://www.clark.edu/Academics/AppliedTech/EP/
BioWeb/wildlife/birds/birdwatc.htm

OnLocation

You're strolling along a beach. Up ahead, you see several long-legged birds in the water just off shore. You grab your binoculars for a closer look, and you hear one cry its call. "It's a Black-necked Stilt," you say. "Sorry," says your birding partner, "that answer is incorrect. Try again." If your birding partner sounds a little "stilted" himself, it's because he's your computer and you are on a virtual birding expedition to Cape Cod. And when you try again, this time guessing that it's an American Oystercatcher, your birding buddy replies, "That's right," and you earn 75 points. OnLocation on the Virtual Birder, a web magazine for birders, consists of interactive adventures that allow you to select the location you are in, direction of travel, whether to use binoculars, and so forth. In many cases you can hear what birds sound like. You get points and ratings for your identification abilities. "There are new or updated tours that come online every month or two and there are always two or three tours active at a time," reports Don Crockett, the editor and Webmaster of the Virtual Birder. "Which ones are active depends on the time of year since the tours are supposed to be an example snapshot of the site at a particular time of year and I try to release tours at about

that time of year." Each tour features articles related to the location, so you can get an in-depth look at a great birding neighborhood. OnLocation virtual tours include Springtime in Boston; Hawk Mountain, Pennsylvania; South West Florida; Sachuest Point, Rhode Island; Churchill, Manitoba; Chincoteague National Wildlife Refuge, Virginia; Washington County, Maine; and Illinois shrubland and grassland.

http://www.virtualbirder.com/vbirder/onLoc

Plato among the Sandpipers

Telling one species from another may not be easy. Using sandpipers as an example, Diane Porter of Birdwatching.com discusses what makes a species a species in the world of nature and how in general to tell them apart. How does Plato fit in? Stop by and see.

http://www.birdwatching.com/stories/plato.html

Silhouette Builder

If you have a Mac computer, Peterson Online has a free program that can help you build your skills at identifying birds by their silhouettes. *(See also Software.)*

http://www.petersononline.com/birds/skillbuilders
/index.html

FEATHERED FACTS

Butcher

The Northern Shrike has also been called the Butcher Bird because of its habit of impaling its prey on broken tree twigs, thorns, or even barbed wire. That's because it doesn't have strong, hawk-like talons to hold its prey.

—adapted from Canadian Museum of Nature

http://www.nature.ca/notebooks/english/nshrike.htm

A B C D E F G H I J K L M N O P Q R S T U V W X Y Z

A
B
C
D
E
F
G
H
I
J
K
L
M
N
O
P
Q
R
S
T
U
V
W
X
Y
Z

Southeastern Bird Quiz

If you're from the southeastern United States or if you visit there, you can test your identification skills on 10 of the more common land and shore birds at this site, sponsored by the Museum of Natural History at the University of Georgia.

http://museum.nhm.uga.edu/birdphotos/
birdquizpg1.html

Tips for Success

The Cooperative Extension Service at the University of Nebraska has published a series of NebGuides on backyard wildlife, one of which offers an excellent and varied collection of tips for backyard birding. Here you will find advice for dealing with squirrels, keeping out pest birds and other creatures, using water to attract birds, how to prevent birds from striking windows, how to discourage woodpeckers from making Swiss cheese of your clapboards, and using brush piles to draw birds. There's even a tip on keeping a backyard journal. From the main menu, look for the secetions under Urban Wildlife.

http://www.ianr.unl.edu/pubs/wildlife/

FEATHERED FACTS

Tree Duck

The Black-bellied Whistling Duck was once called the Black-bellied Tree Duck because it often nests in tree cavities.

http://www.wildtexas.com/wildguides/whistlingduck.
htm

Sandpiper (Dover)

Tools for Learning about Birds

Birds come alive—well, almost—on this website, operated by the Patuxent Wildlife Research Center in Laurel, Maryland, an arm of the U.S. Geological Survey (*first address*). Here you can find not only photographs of birds but also videos and sound tracks. There are also concise tips to help you identify most of the species you are apt to find in North America. Online quizzes (*second address*) let you test your knowledge of North American bird identification by photos, by distribution in winter and in summer, and by song. You can decide whether to take the beginner or advanced quizzes. If you do a winter distribution quiz, for instance, maps showing a bird's winter range will appear, and you'll get a multiple choice of answers. This quizzing aims to test and improve your identification skills, as well as your awareness of ranges. Try the song quiz; it's a good way to bone up on your knowledge of bird songs and calls which, sometimes, are the only signs of a species' presence that you'll get in the field.

http://www.mbr.nbs.gov/bbs/ident.html
http://www.mbr.nbs.gov/bbs/trend/birdquiz.html

Watching Birds

Don and Lillian Stokes are noted naturalists who've written many books about birds, birding, and other natural history subjects. On this page, sponsored by Wild Birds Unlimited, they offer a collection of useful bird-watching techniques and background information. Among the topics are Watching for Spring Migration, Fall Changes for Birds, Attracting Nesting Birds, Winter Finches, Chickadees and Titmice at Your Feeder, and Who's Singing in the Summer? The Stokeses are fine writers, and these are all well-done essays.

http://www.wbu.com/stokes/copy.htm

What Good Is a Life List?

Diane Porter of Birdwatching.com finds much practical and sentimental value in maintaining a life list of the birds she's seen. "The list becomes a chronicle not only of birds but also of one's life—travels, past homes, old friends," she writes in this excellent essay. She gives examples of experiences she's had related to seeking new birds for her life list, and then offers tips for keeping the list and suggests some software packages that make it easier. She points out that she began the old-fashioned way, using file cards, but "the project got complicated when I wanted to keep several life lists, for different states and countries. I also started to keep a year list, and it was hard to tell what was in each list." Computers made such listing a lot easier.

http://www.birdwatching.com/stories/lifelist.html

TOURS & EXPEDITIONS

Let's face it: it often helps to have an expert on hand, especially when you are in unfamiliar territory. Many birding tour operators, both commercial and non-profit, have websites describing adventures that would make any avid birder drool. This section includes everything from simple three-hour trips through parks or onto offshore islands to two-week journeys into the Amazon rain forest. Even if you're not planning to travel to many of the more distant destinations, you can learn a lot about the world of birds just reading some of the tour guides' sites. *(See also Audubon Societies & Sanctuaries, Destinations, and International.)*

GENERAL

Bird Treks

Bob Schutsky, a biologist and ornithologist for many years, is the owner and operator of Bird Treks, whose goal is "to provide you with a quality, enjoyable, professionally organized birding experience, to beautiful and exciting destinations, all at a reasonable and affordable price." Destinations include many beautiful locations, including Costa Rica, Belize, Jamaica, Trinidad and Tobago, the mountains of Mexico, south-

east Arizona and the Grand Canyon, Big Bend, Hill Country and the Lower Rio Grand Valley of Texas, New Mexico, the Colorado mountains and grasslands, the Pacific Northwest, Chincoteague National Wildlife Refuge, Virginia, the Dry Tortugas, South Florida and the Florida Keys, Coastal Maine, Gaspe Peninsula, Iceland, the Outer Banks of North Carolina, Montauk Point, and Niagara River Gorge of New York and Ontario. All the tours are fully described and include photographs, favorite species lists, and highlights from previous tours. Slide programs for presentation to bird clubs and Audubon societies are also described.

http://www.birdtreks.com

Borderland Tours

Borderland Tours in Tucson, Arizona, offers birding tours in the Southwest United States, and to Alaska, Mexico, Central and South America, the Galapagos Islands, Kenya, and Great Britain. Both journeys and leaders are fully described. A nice feature is that the site includes the company's newsletter, which has interesting essays about exotic birds, reports on past trips, and notes about the guides who lead trips.

http://www.borderland-tours.com

Cheeseman's Ecology Safaris

Cheeseman's Ecology Safaris in Saratoga, California, runs small-group birding trips to Costa Rica, Ecuador, Brazil, Kenya, Tanzania, Alaska, Botswana, Australia, Hawaii and Midway Islands, Mexico, and even Antarctica. "We offer only a very few trips, all with knowledgeable enthusiastic leadership, custom high quality itineraries, and we spend more time in the field," says the Cheeseman family. "Our safaris are for non-smokers who love nature." Full trip itineraries are described on the well-illustrated site.

http://www.cheesemans.com

C
D
E
F
G
H
I
J
K
L
M
N
O
P
Q
R
S
T
U
V
W
X
Y
Z

...s

...m history, and history is a unique
...gle-Eye Tours' website—which makes it
...lot of fun. Like most tour sites, there are tempting
descriptions of the trips planned in the coming year—
Eagle-Eye runs dozens of birding and nature expeditions in North, Central, and South America, as well as
a few to other parts of the world. However, Eagle-Eye
also offers rundowns on what happened on past
jaunts back to 1996. These give you a good sense of
what the trips are about and what birds you are apt to
see on the ones to come; they are also fun to read. The
site offers lists of resources, including books that
would be good to read before a trip and field guides
that would be handy once on it. The site has a nice
collection of some of the best birding links.

http://www.eagle-eye.com

EarthFoot

Looking for a birding or nature guide in a particular
region? Try EarthFoot, which describes itself as a
source of "small-scale, low-impact, info-rich, eco-
events hosted by earth-savvy folks near their own
homes." Here you might find an expert who can lead
you into the Everglades of Florida, around the San
Juan Islands of Washington or along Peter the Great
Bay on the Siberian coast. You can search by destination or trip themes, including birding. The site, operated by nature and ecotourism writer Jim Conrad, is
new and the listings are growing.

http://www.earthfoot.org

Field Guides

How's that for a great name of a birding tour company? Based in Austin, Texas, Field Guides Inc. has
professionally guided tours to hot birding locations
through North, Central, and South America, as well as
Africa, Australia, the Pacific, and Europe. You can
look up tours by time of year or by destination. The
site provides detailed information about the trips,
plus some photos of the birds and scenery you're apt
to see. There are also entertaining biographies and
photos of the company's birding guides. The "news"
page has up-to-date information about the latest tours,

AVIAN ADVICE

Best Time

The best time of day to see birds is in
the morning when they are feeding
after a long night's rest. Especially in
the spring, it's also the best time to
hear them singing, often a technique
they use for letting nearby birds know
the singer's territory.

—adapted from Environmental Education
Center, Miller School, Albermarle County,
Virginia

http://monticello.avenue.gen.va.us/Community/
Environ/EnvironEdCenter/Habitat/AnimalStudy/
Bird/Bird.HTML

whether trips have been fully booked or if trips need
more members. The site also has general travel information and links to useful websites.

http://www.fieldguides.com

Focus on Nature

Since 1990, Focus on Nature Tours has offered journeys to destinations in North, Central, and South
America, the Caribbean, Europe, and Asia. "All of the
tours relate to nature, and most have a particular
emphasis on birding," say Armas and Risë Hill, owners and founders. The site describes many tours, but
fans of raptors will especially appreciate the Raptours,
which seek out birds of prey in such far-flung locales
as Israel, northern India, and Mexico, as well as destinations closer to home in North America. In fact,
Focus on Nature also offers the sometimes hard-to-
find pelagic tours, looking for those birds you can see
almost only far out at sea. The site describes some of
the past journeys offshore and what was sighted.

http://www.focusonnature.com

Society Expeditions

Society Expeditions operates wildlife cruises to Alaska, Antarctica, and the South Pacific. Journeys are aboard the small ship, *World Discoverer*, which holds up to 137 passengers. "We focus on the wildlife, natural history and culture of each region," says Society. "Antarctica, Alaska and the South Pacific offer unparalleled opportunities for birding, photography and sightseeing."

http://www.societyexpeditions.com

Where the Wild Things Are

Audubon Magazine took a look at the ecotour business and suggested 25 of the most interesting ways to get close to nature. Most involve birding, and each is rated by how "bare-bones" or "luxurious" the tour is and the types of accommodations. At the bottom of the collection of trip descriptions is a useful directory of ecotour providers, including links to their websites where you can find many more tours of possible interest.

http://magazine.audubon.org/travel/

EASTERN

ACE Basin Tours

If you are interested in water birds and wildlife of coastal South Carolina, Captain Richard's ACE Basin Nature Tour covers the "low country where the salt and fresh waters of the Ashepoo, Combahee, and the Edisto Rivers join with the land to create a swampy Eden." The site provides basic descriptions and contact information.

http://www.theoffice.net/acebasin

Amazing Adventures

Amazing Adventures offers wildlife and nature tours of Newfoundland, on the east coast of Canada. Tours of up to 11 days include visits to places where you can see colonies of Atlantic Puffins, Black-legged Kittiwake, Common Murre, and the world's second largest colony of Storm Petrels. Among the stops are the Witless Bay Ecological Reserve, home to some two million seabirds.

http://www.gorp.com/amazadv/

Bold Coast Charter Company

Rich and elegant sections of shoreline are often called the Gold Coast. Maine, however, seems a place that's rougher and more down to earth—or sea. Perhaps that's why there's a Bold Coast and a Bold Coast Charter Company in Cutler, Maine, which offers birdwatching tours. "If you're a birder or a nature lover, I conduct half-day landing excursions to Machias Seal Island, summer home to spectacular nesting colonies of Atlantic Puffins, razorbills, and Arctic Terns, among many others," says Captain Andrew Patterson. "For close range puffin observation and photography, no other birding destination can compare!" Captain Patterson says that besides nesting seabirds, other oceanic species commonly spotted are shearwaters, gannets, and storm petrels. Machias Seal Island, incidentally, is home to the largest puffin colony on the coast of Maine, with several thousand of these nesting seabirds. Other nature-oriented trips are available.

http://www.boldcoast.com

Florida Jay (*Aphelocoma coerulescens*) [Florida Scrub-Jay] (JJA)

Nature Tours by Alan

Alan Knothe offers a wide range of birding tours in Florida—from three-hour walks in wildlife refuges and parks to full-day journeys. His service can also provide guides to many birding areas in the state as well as to hot spots in Louisiana and Texas. Descriptions of tours and possible destinations for custom-guided expeditions are provided, along with what seem to be reasonable prices for groups of up to 12 people. Knothe also offers a birding school that includes six full days of birding, two instructional evening programs, seven nights lodging, 20 meals, transportation to and from the birding hot spots, and more. The school is based at Fort Walton Beach, Florida.

http://www.birdtours.com/

South Florida Birding

Larry Manfredi is a Florida native who's been interested in birds since he was six years old and has had a life list since he was eight. Now in his 30s, Manfredi leads birding tours in south Florida and to Dry Tortu-

gas, the Bahamas, and the Caribbean. Trips are described in detail and usually include lists of some of the more interesting species you're apt to encounter. Even if you're not planning a trip, the site is worth visiting just to see the fine photographs of south Florida and Caribbean birds. The site also has a collection of useful links and a guide to affordable places to stay in the greater Miami area. Incidentally, Larry's wife Christine, a native of France, is no amateur at spotting birds. In their first year of birding together, she identified more than 300 species, most in south Florida.

http://www.southfloridabirding.com

Sunny Days Catamarans

The Dry Tortugas National Park is a group of islands 70 miles west of Key West, Florida. Sunny Days Catamarans in Key West (*first address*) runs high-speed trips to Dry Tortugas that allow travelers to see such sights as nesting Sooty Terns and Brown Noddies, Frigate birds, Masked and Brown Boobies, Roseate Terns, Brown Pelicans, and other Caribbean species at this famous, but difficult to access national park (which John James Audubon visited in 1832). For details on Dry Tortugas National Park, visit the Nation Park Services page about the park (*second address*).

http://www.drytortugas.com
http://www.nps.gov/drto/

MOUNTAIN & PACIFIC

Discovery Voyages

Discovery Voyages in Cordova, Alaska, provides small-group birding and wildlife tours of Alaska's fjord country aboard the motor vessel *Discovery*. "Designed as a stage for learning, exploring, photographing, or simply relaxed sightseeing, the *Discovery* voyage brings guests of all ages face-to-face with the diverse and prodigious wonders of Alaska's wild beauty," says the Discovery Voyages website. Among its trips are a nine-day spring birding and wildlife journey, described in considerable detail. So are the accommodations aboard the *Discovery*.

http://www.discoveryvoyages.com/index.html

FEATHERED FACTS

Lumpers and Splitters

In the field of taxonomy, a lumper is a scientist who tends to emphasize the similarities among species and group them together in the same genus wherever possible. A splitter tends to go the opposite way, emphasizing differences between species and increasing the number of genera. In modern taxonomy lumpers appear to outnumber splitters and many formerly separate genera are no longer considered separate.

—adapted from the Bird Dictionary

http://birdcare.com/birdon/birdindex/

FEATHERED FACTS

Bald Cardinals

Occasional bald-headed cardinals show up at feeders—red birds with no feathers on their heads. Their rather ugly aspect usually distresses those who see them, but chances are the cardinal is suffering from avian feather mites, and it's not life-threatening. Birds can use their beaks to preen these mites away from most parts of their bodies, except, of course, their heads. Fear not for the bird, however. New feathers will grow in.

—adapted from *Bird Watcher's Digest*

http://www.birdwatchersdigest.com/faq/faq.html

High Lonesome Ecotours

"We at High Lonesome Ecotours are committed to providing high quality, personalized trips for birders who don't enjoy squeezing into a van with ten other people or struggling to get a good look at a bird because the group is so large," says the company's website. High Lonesome Ecotours, which is in Sierra Vista, Arizona, runs birding trips in Arizona, and to Texas, Alaska, and Mexico, some in conjunction with the Arizona Chapter of the Nature Conservancy. "Accommodations are at the best B&Bs or hotels. We eat only at the best restaurants in each area with a focus on interesting/or regional cuisine," the website says.

http://www.hilonesome.com

Kenai Fjords Tours

Kenai Fjords National Park, about 125 miles south of Anchorage, Alaska, consists of some 580,000 acres of rugged coastal peninsula, and includes glaciers. It is rich in birdlife, including puffins, murres, and Bald Eagles, plus marine mammals including Sea Otters, Steller sea lions, Dall's porpoise, orcas, and humpback

Gyrfalcon (*Falco rusticolus*) (JJA)

whales. Kenai Fjord Tours runs trips that range from 3 to 10½ hours, sailing from Seward. The site describes the operations, including the vessel and other options for activities in the Seward and Kenai Fjords area.

http://www.kenaifjords.com

Paths in Paradise

If you're headed for Maui and would like an expert's-eye view of the birds and other beauties of nature on the island, check out Paths in Paradise, which offers half-day and full-day hikes in search of wildlife. All tours are guided by Dr. Renate Gassmann-Duvall, who holds a doctorate in veterinary medicine and has been active in saving Hawaii's vanishing wildlife for many years. In her online biography, you'll learn that Gassmann-Duvall and her husband came to the Big Island of Hawaii in 1984 to breed, raise, and release Hawaii's unique endangered birds for a federally funded breeding program. In 1986 the family moved with the program to the island of Maui. Look for the small type near the bottom of the page for the link to Gassmann-Duvall's birding tours.

http://www.maui.net/~corvusco

Sound Eco Adventures

Sound Eco Adventures in Whittier, Alaska, offers overnight birding tours in the Prince William Sound area. Marine birds seen here include several species of loons, grebes, tube-noses, cormorants, waterfowl, shorebirds, jaegers, gulls, terns, and alcids.

http://www.alaska.net/~sea/seasite.html

A B C D E F G H I J K L M N O P Q R S T U V W X Y Z

A
B
C
D
E
F
G
H
I
J
K
L
M
N
O
P
Q
R
S
T
U
V
W
X
Y
Z

St. Paul Island Tours

St. Paul Island is in the remote Pribilof Islands, located in the Bering Sea some 250 miles west of mainland Alaska and about the same distance north of the Aleutians. St. Paul Island Tours operates birding expeditions on this remote island rich with birds, as well as other forms of wildlife. The best months are May through August, and the site notes that "during these months Gray-tailed Tattlers, Sharp-tailed Sandpipers, ruffs, and often Mongolian Plovers are more frequently observed." However, plenty of other unusual species can be seen in the Pribilofs, and the website has detailed lists of them by time, indicating the best seasons and how common they are. The company, based in Anchorage, has three- to eight-day tours from May 21 through Sept 1.

http://www.alaskabirding.com

INTERNATIONAL

Aventuras Naturales

There are a lot of birds in Guatemala, and Aventuras Naturales specializes in small-group expeditions in the Central American nation. Its five different guided bird-watching trips are designed to cover most of the country and offer the opportunity to spot more than 660 species. Tours are led by experienced ornithologists.

http://www.centramerica.com/aventuras/

Belize Tours & Travel

Belize, in Central America, calls itself "Mother Nature's best kept secret." The Maya Mountain Lodge and Tours website is presumably intent on revealing this "secret," including the fact that some 500 species of birds can be found in Belize. Many tours are described.

http://www.belizetravel.org

FEATHERED FACTS

The Horse Bird

One reason for the rapid spread of the House Sparrow after its importation from Europe in the 1850s has all but disappeared in many places. These birds were fond of the grains that were fed to horses and would also eat the undigested grain in horse droppings. Thus, they survived in cities, as well as in the country on farms. With the rapid decline in the number of horses after the invention of the car, as well as the gradual decline in the number of farms in parts of the country, the numbers of House Sparrows have also dropped.

—adapted from Robie Tufts, *Birds of Nova Scotia*

http://museum.ednet.ns.ca/mnh/nature/nsbirds/bns0411.htm

BirdEcuador

BirdEcuador is a family-operated business that specializes in birding tours of Ecuador and the Galapagos Islands. "Owner and tour leader, Mitch Lysinger, resides in Ecuador and is generally regarded as one of the great birding talents in Ecuador today," says the BirdEcuador website. "Mitch is constantly crisscrossing the country as he explores for new birding hot spots and records the bird sounds of Ecuador." One of the company's tours, called the Deluxe Andean Birding Tour, recorded 472 species during its 13-day journey in 1998. That included 50 different hummingbird species! According to the site, Ecuador, which is the size of Colorado, boasts over 1,600 species of birds—650 more than are found in all of North America.

http://www.southfloridabirding.com/birdecuador/index.htm

FEATHERED FACTS

World's Formerly Rarest Bird

The Mauritius Kestrel was once the world's rarest bird. In the early 1970s the entire population of these kestrels had been reduced to but four known specimens. An intensive program of breeding them in captivity and releasing them has increased the wild population to more than 350 birds.

—adapted from Mauritius Island Online

http://www.maurinet.com/wildlife.html

Birding in China

China is a huge and mysterious nation, full of fascinating wildlife. Founded in 1988, Kingfisher Tours is the only birding-specialized company based in Hong Kong. Kingfisher offers private and scheduled birding tours of Hong Kong and mainland China lasting from three to 30 days. The site includes a huge checklist of birds of China.

http://kthk.com.hk/birdchina.html

Churchill Nature Tours

Churchill is in remote northeastern Manitoba, on the shores of Hudson Bay. Since 1985, Daniel and Thuraya Weedon's Churchill Nature Tours has been operating birding expeditions to this remote, bird-rich region, as well as to even more remote Baffin Island. The company also has birding tours of southern Manitoba, featuring Oak Hammock Marsh and Riding Mountain National Park. "This province is endowed with very diverse habitats and rich natural ecosystems," the Weedons report. "Manitoba is a vast wild province and remains a tourism frontier . . . offering quiet, qual-

ity encounters with nature." All these expeditions are in spring and summer months.

http://www.churchillnaturetours.com

Diversity Tours

If you are a birder with an adventurous side who doesn't mind camping in the jungle, Belize may be a good destination for you. Diversity Tours, based in New Mexico, offers birding and nature expeditions to Belize in Central America. Many of the trips involve canoeing and jungle camping.

http://www.newmex.com/diversitytours/

Emu Tours

If you're heading for Australia and looking for tours of great birding spots, Emu Tours in Jamberoo, New South Wales, may be your outfit. Most tours use a modern, 22-seat air-conditioned bus. "Some involve an element of camping, which gets us into those remote areas that are otherwise inaccessible," says Emu. All equipment is supplied. A dozen or so tours, ranging from seven to 31 days in length, are described.

http://www.ozemail.com.au/~emutours/

Atlantic Puffin (*Fratercula arctica*) (JJA)

A B C D E F G H I J K L M N O P Q R S **T** U V W X Y Z

Explorama Lodges

Explorama (*first address*) has been offering visits to the Amazon rain forest of Peru for some 35 years. "Professional, multilingual naturalist guides are assigned to each small group of visitors," Explorama says. Among its featured trips are eight-day Amazon birdwatching workshops. "The workshops, led by Dennis DeCourcey together with native Amazonian naturalist guides, feature birdwatching from the spectacular Amazon Canopy Walkway, the longest such walkway in the world [it's 120 feet up in the trees!]. Other habitats range from the Amazon River edge to interior black water lakes and from pastures and small open fields to environments deep within the primary rainforest." The site offers a gallery of photos of the regions covered in the journeys, as well as the accommodations at the Explorama Inn or Explorama Lodge. You can also find more details regarding the Amazon Rainforest Birdwatching Workshops (*second address*).

http://www.explorama.com
http://www.amazon-travel.com/workshops.htm

Fantastico Sur Birding & Nature Tours

The place names sound exotic enough: Patagonia, Tierra del Fuego, the High Andes, the Humboldt Current. The birds in these places sound just as exotic: Thom-tailed Rayadito, Gray-breasted Seedsnipe, Green-backed Firecrown. These are the kinds of places and creatures that Fantastico Sur (Fantastic South) Birding and Nature Tours in Punta Arenas, Chile, hopes to show you on its Birding the End of the World tours. The site provides many illustrations of the birds along the way.

http://www.chileaustral.com/birding/

Geo Expeditions

Geo Expeditions in Sonora, California, operates journeys to Latin America, Asia, and Africa, as well as polar voyages. All involve viewing wildlife, and many have an emphasis on birdlife.

http://www.geoexpeditions.com

Holbrook Travel

Holbrook Travel specializes in birding and natural history trips to Central and South America and to Africa. Its very graphical website includes travel diaries that describe past trips and both photos and some valuable tips (don't forget the repellant for the huge mosquitoes and sand fleas in Honduras). The site's trip search feature lets you select "birding" as a feature of your expedition, after which you can plan the details of the trip and make reservations online.

http://www.holbrooktravel.com

International Expeditions

International Expeditions in Helena, Alabama, calls itself a "world leader in nature travel." The company offers small-group and custom independent tours, using "exceptional" guides. The lavishly illustrated site describes journeys to every continent, and there is a search function so that you can find trips that would be of most birding interest.

http://www.ietravel.com

International Ventures

International Ventures offers scores of safaris in nearly a dozen African nations. Many are wildlife tours that include opportunities for birding. Trips are customizable, and both luxury and economy jaunts are available.

http://www.internationalventures.com

Marine Expeditions

Marine Expeditions, based in Toronto, Ontario, offers shipboard journeys to many Arctic locations, such as Baffin Island, Greenland, the Russian Far East, and the Bering Sea, as well as to the Amazon, the South Pacific, and the Falkland Islands. One of the nice features of the site is the reference section, which provides general interest wildlife and travel articles about destinations—interesting, whether or not you are planning a Marine Expeditions trip.

http://www.marineex.com

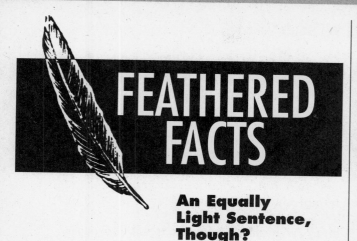

FEATHERED FACTS

An Equally Light Sentence, Though?

Under United States law, it is illegal to possess a migratory bird, its parts or nest; an endangered species; or to ship an animal part or product in international commerce. That means that literally, without a permit or a license, you are breaking the law by simply picking up a bird feather and keeping it.

—adapted from U.S. Fish & Wildlife Service

http://www.fws.gov/r4eao/wildlife/permits.html

Neblina Forest Tours

"Why Ecuador?" asks the menu item on the Neblina Forest Birding Tours website. "Biologically, South America is the richest of the earth's continents," the website says. "Its Amazon basin holds the largest and most diverse block of tropical rain forest in the world, while its major mountain range, the Andes, has crested special environments ranging from tundra-like Páramo and cloud forest to arid rain-shadow valleys to deciduous deserts. . . . Of these 3,100 species of South American birds, over half can be found in our tiny country of Ecuador." Neblina Forest offers birding tours throughout Ecuador, as well as to the Galapagos Islands, owned by Ecuador. Many tours cover parts of the Amazon rain forest whereas others, such as a stay at Sacha Lodge, seek birds in the cloud forests of the High Andes. Some tours combine both kinds of locales. The site is sprinkled with photos of exotic Ecuadorian birds, such as the Fiery-throated Fruiteater and the Rufous Antpitta.

http://www.ecuadorexplorer.com/neblina/

Rainbow Adventures

Rainbow Adventures offers a bird-watching ecotour of Playa Cativo Life Preserve in Costa Rica, which, the website notes, is home to more than 850 species of birds. "It is not unusual for visiting bird watchers to have first sightings of at least two dozen species at the preserve," Rainbow says. "Egrets, hummingbirds, Crested Guan, toucans, toucanets, Great Curassows, and many varieties of parrots can be seen." The site includes a list of a couple hundred species spotted at Playa Cativo. And while you're viewing the list and pictures, you can listen to the sounds of jungle birds. The site has plenty of information about other activities you can participate in.

http://www.rainbowcostarica.com/bird_watching.htm

Sawtelle Nature Tours

"Boasting more than 830 species of birds, Costa Rica ranks as one of the top birding destinations in the world," says Sawtelle Tours. The company offers tours to the Pacific and Caribbean slopes of Costa Rica that last from 9 to 15 nights. The website both describes the tours and provides comments from people who have taken them. Other parts of the site tell about some of the birds you'll see, as well as the rain forests, cloud forests, and dry forests that trips traverse.

http://www.birdcostarica.com

Sunny Land Tours

Sunny Land Tours, based in Hackensack, New Jersey, offers bird-watching tours to Argentina, Belize, Brazil, Chile, Ecuador, Galapagos, Guatemala, Honduras, Kenya, Mexico, Panama, Peru, and Venezuela. Each is described in a concise, day-by-day format, with some photos. (To reach the listings for trips that feature birding, click the Activities button at the top of the home page.)

http://www.sunnylandtours.com/activity.htm

A
B
C
D
E
F
G
H
I
J
K
L
M
N
O
P
Q
R
S
T
U
V
W
X
Y
Z

FEATHERED FACTS

Bountiful Bunting

The brilliant Indigo Bunting is actually more populous and widespread today than it was when the Pilgrims landed. That's because there's more of the habitat it likes: abandoned fields, forest clearings, and the woodland edges one finds along roads and power line clearings.

—adapted from Mary Deinlein, Smithsonian Migratory Bird Center

http://web2.si.edu/smbc/bom/inbu.htm

Victor Emanuel Nature Tours

Here's a testimonial that any tour service would be proud to display: "Some of the best birding experiences of my life have been on Victor Emanuel Nature Tours." Its author was Roger Tory Peterson, perhaps the world's most famous birder, and his words appear on the opening page of the Emanuel site, where you'll also find some pretty spectacular journeys. For example, the company offers cruises for birders, cruises in which everyone aboard ship is interested in birds. One is a 10-day cruise up the Amazon aboard the MS *Explorer*, which can comfortably house 88 birders plus the accompanying guides—including Emanuel. Other cruises go to Antarctica, the Falkland Islands, northern Europe, the West Indies, the Galapagos Islands, and other destinations. But that's only a small part of the Emanuel tour choices. The site describes nearly 140 tours to more than 100 destinations. A sophisticated search engine permits you to investigate the catalog by destination, by date, by tour leaders, or by a keyword, such as "cruise" or "France" or "puffins." An entertaining feature of the site is the collection of reports from past trips. The site also has a modest, but good collection of links to other sites—they call them Resources.

http://www.ventbird.com

Wildside Tours

Adventure Camera in Exton, Pennsylvania, which specializes in outdoor cameras and optics, runs tours to great birding areas of Central America: Belize and Honduras. "Hundreds of migrating bird species as well as incredible Central American species invite long looks through binocular and scope," Wildside says. Scheduled and custom itineraries are available. "The small group size and maximum client to guide ratio of only 4:1 for most of our tours makes for a friendly and fulfilling experience!"

http://www.adventurecamera.com/belize_pages/bzintro.htm

Wings

Wings, which has been operating international birding tours for more than a quarter of a century, now has trips to some 60 nations on seven continents. "Our trips are planned as ones that we ourselves would like to go on, so they are very strongly oriented toward birds," say Wings' owners, who include the appropriately named Davis Finch, and who with Will Russell founded the company in 1973. The home page enables you to quickly look for a tour by month of the year or by country. Each trip is described in considerable detail, and there's complete information about pricing and arrangements.

http://wingsbirds.com

Zegrahm Expeditions

Zegrahm Expeditions in Seattle, Washington, likes to note that its modes of travel include "by plane, yacht or elephant caravan." They should add rocket. Although it's hardly a birding destination, Zegrahm will begin adding space flights to its ecotours, beginning in 2002. The company already offers a broad range of trips to exotic birding locales—from Iceland and Greenland to Botswana and the Solomon Islands. The site's search engine enables you to look for tours that specialize in or include birding. On some trips ornithologists like Peter Harrison are among the leaders.

http://www.zeco.com

VIDEOS

Words and pictures, be they in books, magazines or Web pages, are our primary source of knowledge about birds. But in the birding world, it might be said that actions speak louder than words, and a good video can give us insights into the lives, the looks, the habits, and the habitats of birds in a way that words text and illustrations cannot. Here are some places to find information on bird and birding videos.

Ducks Unlimited Video Guide

Although aimed primarily at hunters, *Ducks Unlimited's VideoGuide to Waterfowl and Game Birds* is also advertised as being valuable for naturalists who want accurate identification and natural history. The video, also available on laser videodisc, covers 43 species of waterfowl and 21 upland game birds, with motion pictures, stills, and animated graphics and maps. Calls are provided by the Cornell Laboratory of Ornithology. This video, produced by Mastervision, appears at the bottom of the Audubon Society videos page.

http://www.masterv.com/mv-bird.html

Hewitts' Videos

The American Birding Association's online store carries the sizable collection of birding videos by Karis and Don Hewitt, including *Birds of Alaska, Birding Southeastern Arizona, Birds of Southern California, Rare Birds of Sanibel* (Island, Florida), *Spring Migration at the Dry Tortugas, Birding Hotspots in Texas, Birding Montana and the Big Sky Country*, and *Northern Gannets on Bonaventure Island & Birds of Gaspé*. These tapes run from 52 to 105 minutes and each is described on this page, which also includes regional videos by other producers.

http://americanbirding.org/abasales/catavmm1.htm

Large Gulls of North America

Gulls are among the trickiest kinds of birds to identify—to the casual observer, many species look the same. Jon L. Dunn, a leading birder, has helped put together *The Large Gulls of North America*, the first in

Ring-billed Gull (*Larus delawarensis*) (JJA)

the Advanced Birding Series to be issued by Peregrine Video Productions in Niwot, Colorado, to help birders identify and learn more about the larger gulls. (The species include California, Glaucous, Glaucous-winged, Great Black-backed, Herring, Iceland, Kelp, Lesser Black-backed, Slaty-backed, Thayer's, Vegae, Western, Yellow-footed, and Yellow-legged Gulls.) The videos use slow motion, stop action, and split screen effects to help you better see the birds and their identifying features and characteristics. Mr. Dunn, incidentally, is co-author of the Peterson field guide on warblers and was chief consultant on the National Geographic Society's *Field Guide to the Birds of North America*, which many people consider the leading birding field guide.

http://www.peregrinevideo.com

Life of Birds

The BBC's monumental series, *The Life of Birds*, is available in a set of five tapes totalling 600 minutes. The series, written by David Attenborough, consists of 10 episodes: To Fly . . . Or Not to Fly?, The Mastery of Flight, The Insatiable Appetite, Meat-Eaters, Fishing for a Living, Signals and Songs, Finding Partners, The Demands of the Egg, The Problems of Parenthood, and The Limits of Endurance. To learn details, visit this site and select the Home Video option, then Factual, for the menu that will bring you to *The Life of Birds* page.

http://www.bbchomevideo.com

A
B
C
D
E
F
G
H
I
J
K
L
M
N
O
P
Q
R
S
T
U
V
W
X
Y
Z

National Audubon Video Guides

Although the National Audubon Society doesn't create videos on its own, it has licensed Mastervision's production of the *Audubon Society's VideoGuide to the Birds of North America.* These five cassettes cover more than 500 species that breed in North America. "Moving pictures show each bird's markings, in its natural habitat, with bird calls and sounds that complement informative narration and stunning visuals," reports Mastervision. The first volume covers 116 species of loons, grebes, pelicans, swans, geese and ducks, hawks, vultures, and falcons and the chicken-like birds; volume 2 describes 112 species of water birds, including herons and egrets, cranes, shore birds, gulls, terns, and alcids; volume 3 covers 76 species of pigeons and doves, cuckoos, owls, nighthawks, hummingbirds, swifts, trogons, kingfishers, and woodpeckers; and volumes 4 and 5 describe more than 200 species of songbirds. Price and ordering information is available on the site.

http://www.masterv.com/mv-bird.html

Video Birding Page

Most people take film cameras on their birding expeditions. Canadian writer Ronald Orenstein takes a Canon ES1000 Hi-8 Video Camera—and not necessarily just for motion pictures. In fact, using a video camera is "easier by far than still photography, because the birds don't have to hold still and the light can be quite low," says Orenstein. His site, the Video Birding Page, describes his expeditions to Madagascar and to the Andes of Venezuela with many stills taken from his video camera's recordings (using a device called a Video Snappy). You can enjoy his journeys and his bird shots, as well as pick up tips on how to take effective bird videos yourself.

http://members.home.net/ornstn/videobirding.html

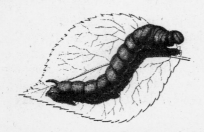

FEATHERED FACTS

Pushed Out?

Although Blackburnian Warblers love to feed on budworms, studies found that Maine populations of the species declined in years when there were great outbreaks of Spruce Budworms. One theory is that the Blackburnian avoids competition with species like the Cape May Warbler, which increase their numbers during good budworm years.

—adapted from Lisa Petit, Smithsonian Migratory Bird Center

http://web2.si.edu/smbc/bom/blwa.htm

Watching Warblers

Warblers represent one of the greatest—and most entertaining—challenges for many bird-watchers. In most places they are passing-through birds, showing up during the spring and fall migrations on their way north or south. In the spring many are decked out in their best feathers, full of color or at least fine design. Trouble is, most are high up in the trees where it's hard to spot them. Adding to the challenge is the fact that many are tiny and quick moving. However, most help us find them with their songs and calls. Warbler enthusiasts Michael Male and Judy Fieth spent six seasons over 10 years filming a video guide called *Watching Warblers.* It was "a labor-of-love made for birders" by two people "who have been making award-winning natural history programs for television since 1980," says the site of the Blue Earth Video Library in Ho-Ho-Kus, New Jersey. The video has also been well reviewed. In mid-1999, Male and Fieth completed *Watching Waders.* We spent "two years filming it, and the last six months editing," Male told us. It's "an intimate look at 20 species—herons, egrets, ibis, bitterns, cranes, limpkin, wood stork, and roseate spoonbill—feeding, courting, nesting and raising their young."

http://www.blueearthfilms.com

Index

Alaska
80–83, 93
289 293
242

Bird Songs
94
Feeders
97 99